John Drake
March 10th.
2005

Historic Airports

Proceedings of the
International 'L'Europe de l'Air' Conferences
on Aviation Architecture

Liverpool (1999) Berlin (2000) Paris (2001)

Historic Airports

Proceedings of the
International 'L'Europe de l'Air' Conferences
on Aviation Architecture

Liverpool (1999) Berlin (2000) Paris (2001)

Edited by Bob Hawkins,
Gabriele Lechner and Paul Smith

ENGLISH HERITAGE

Published by English Heritage, 23 Savile Row,
London W1S 2ET

Copyright © English Heritage 2005

First published 2005

ISBN 1 873592 83 3

Product code 50932

British Library Cataloguing in Publication Data
A CIP catalogue record for this book is available from the British Library.

Brought to publication by Adèle Campbell, English Heritage Publishing
Edited by Wendy Sherlock
Designed by Geoff Green
Printed by Butler & Tanner
Translation by Carys Evans and Paul Smith (Antwerp-Deurne airport by Bea Maes)

Front cover: 1939 Lufthansa timetable (courtesy of John King)
Back cover: Schiphol airport (Ruud Taal © Capital Photos)

This publication brings together the proceedings of three international workshops organised by the 'L'Europe de l'Air' cultural project, supported by the European Union's Raphael programme (1999–2001) which aimed to encourage the conservation, safeguarding and enhancement of the cultural heritage by means of European co-operation.

The texts presented here in English may be read in their original language – French, German or English – at the 'L'Europe de l'Air' website: www.culture.fr/europe-air/

Les textes présentés en anglais dans cette publication peuvent être consultés dans leur langue d'origine – français, allemand ou anglais – sur le site web du projet 'L'Europe de l'Air': www.culture.fr/europe-air/

Die hier in Englisch wiedergegebenen Texte können in ihrer Originalsprache – Französisch, Deutsch oder Englisch – auf der Webseite des Projektes 'L'Europe de l'Air' eingesehen werden: www.culture.fr/europe-air/

France
Ministère de la Culture et de la Communication
Direction de l'architecture et du patrimoine
Bureau des actions européennes et internationales

Germany
Landesdenkmalamt Berlin

Landesdenkmalamt

England
English Heritage

ENGLISH HERITAGE

With the help of:
Musée de l'Air et de l'Espace, Le Bourget
Aéroports de Paris
Speke-Garston Development Company, Liverpool

Contents

Speakers

Yves Abbas, Head of Airport Development, Air France, Paris
Paul Andreu, architect, engineer, Aéroports de Paris
Corinne Bélier, curator, Cité de l'Architecture et du Patrimoine, Paris
Roger Bowdler, Inspector, English Heritage
Jozef Braeken, architectural historian, Afdeling monumenten en Landschappen, Brussels
Günter Braun, President of the association Bayrische-Flugzeug-Historiker e. V. Oberschleißheim
Michael Cramer, Berlin Chamber of Deputies, transport spokesperson of Bündnis 90/Die Grünen Berlin
Christina Czymay, curator, Landesdenkmalamt Berlin
Gabi Dolff-Bonekämper, curator, Landesdenkmalamt Berlin
Axel Drieschner, architectural historian, Berlin
Didier Hamon, Head of Public Relations, Aéroports de Paris
Bob Hawkins, Inspector, English Heritage
Manfred Hecker, curator, Landesdenkmalamt Berlin
Almut Jirku, landscape designer, Berlin
Werner Jockeit, Cornelia Wendt, architects, Büro für Architektur und Stadtgeschichte, Berlin
John King, aviation historian, London
Marieke Kuipers, architectural historian, Rijkdienst voor de Monumentenzorg, Zeist, Netherlands
Jeremy Lake, Inspector, English Heritage
Bob Lane, Chief Executive, Speke-Garston Development Company, Liverpool
Jean-Luc Lesage, General Inspector, Direction générale de l'Aviation civile, Paris
Thomas Mellins, architectural historian, New York
Jean-Christophe Morisseau, architect, Paris
Jacques Repiquet, architect, Hyères, France
Bernard Rignault, Assistant Director, Musée de l'Air et de l'Espace, Le Bourget
Paul Smith, historian, Inventaire général, Paris
Bernard Toulier, curator, Inventaire général, Paris
Vogt Landschaftsarchitekten, landscape designers, Zurich
Wolfgang Voigt, Assistant Director, Deutsches Architektur Museum, Frankfurt am Main
Ola Wedebrunn, architectural historian, Royal Danish Academy of Fine Arts, Copenhagen

Preface

The Airbus consortium, founded in 1970, has recently opened one of the largest industrial structures ever built, at Blagnac near Toulouse: an assembly hall for what will be the largest commercial airliner ever constructed, the A380. Designed for hub-to-hub connections, this double-deck behemoth will be capable of carrying as many as 800 passengers. The new airliner, of which more than a hundred are already on order, will be assembled from components manufactured in France, Germany, Spain and the United Kingdom. The aircraft industry thus seems to offer one of the most striking and tangible illustrations of the way post-war Europe, starting out from a common market for coal and steel, has developed into an integrated economic community.

The European Union is not only an economic community, however, but also a cultural one with shared democratic values founded on its shared history. The present publication, which English Heritage is delighted to produce on behalf of our French and German partners, is a modest manifestation of this fact. Resulting from a project supported by the European Commission's Raphael programme for encouraging cooperation in the field of the cultural heritage, it is a collection of conference papers on the understanding and intelligent conservation of the built heritage of aviation in Europe. Alongside the motor-car and electrification, aviation was indisputably one of the major technical revolutions of the 20th century, and one that was markedly European from the early years, from Bleriot's first crossing of the Channel in 1909 to the first commercial air routes between Paris and London in the years immediately after the First World War.

The physical heritage that this revolution has left us is a difficult and vulnerable one, complex to understand and manage, and comprised essentially of open expanses of ground with a handful of structures – hangars, workshops, control towers, terminal buildings – at their periphery. Air raids during the Second World War, and the rapid development of mass air travel during the jet age that followed, has meant that sites surviving from aviation's early years, in the first half of the century, are rare indeed. Based on the comparative analysis of three of these rare survivors, in Berlin, Liverpool and Paris, this book examines some of the ways in which aviation heritage on the ground can be kept for future generations. What emerges from these papers – apart from the powerful lesson that the maintenance of original use is the best way to preserve both the heritage and its intrinsic character – is the vital need for a more informed approach to conservation and management. This means further research, supported by inventory and survey work, especially in the context of a European community now enlarged to embrace twenty-five member states.

I hope that this publication and the papers in it will inspire and inform future work in this important field.

SIR NEIL COSSONS
Chairman
English Heritage

Préface

À Blagnac, près de Toulouse, Airbus, le consortium européen fondé en 1970, vient d'inaugurer l'une des plus grandes structures industrielles jamais conçues, une usine d'assemblage pour ce qui sera le plus grand avion commercial jamais construit, le A380. Destiné à des liaisons de 'hub' à 'hub', ce mastodonte volant sera capable de transporter jusqu'à 800 passagers. Le nouveau gros porteur, dont plus d'une centaine a déjà été commandée, est assemblé à partir de composants fabriqués en France, en Allemagne, en Espagne et au Royaume-Uni. L'industrie aéronautique est ainsi l'une des manifestations les plus frappantes et les plus tangibles de la manière dont l'Europe de l'après-guerre, à partir d'un marché commun de l'acier et du charbon, s'est transformée en communauté économique intégrée.

Pourtant, l'Europe n'est pas seulement une communauté économique, elle est aussi une communauté culturelle avec des valeurs démocratiques partagées, enracinées dans une histoire commune. Cette présente publication, éditée par English Heritage au nom des ses partenaires français et allemand, est une modeste manifestation de ce fait. Fruit d'un projet soutenu par le programme Raphaël de la Commission européenne destiné à promouvoir la collaboration européenne en matière du patrimoine culturel, c'est une collection d'essais portant sur la conservation et la mise en valeur du patrimoine bâti de l'aviation. À coté de l'automobile et de l'électrification, l'aviation émerge sans conteste comme l'une des plus grandes révolutions techniques du vingtième siècle, européenne dès l'origine, dès la première traversée de la Manche par Blériot en 1909 et dès les premier vols commerciaux entre Paris et Londres au lendemain de la Première Guerre mondiale.

Le patrimoine que cette révolution nous a légué au sol est particulièrement difficile à appréhender, à conserver et à gérer. C'est un patrimoine vulnérable, consistant essentiellement en de vastes champs ouverts bordés de quelques structures : des hangars, des ateliers, des tours de contrôle et des aérogares. Les destructions de la Deuxième Guerre mondiale et la démocratisation du voyage aérien au cours du 'jet-age' qui la suivit a fait que les sites qui survivent des débuts de l'aviation pendant la première moitié du vingtième siècle sont fort rares. Articulée autour d'une analyse comparative des trois des rares survivants, à Berlin, Liverpool et Paris, cette publication examine quelques-unes des démarches élaborées pour pouvoir conserver ce patrimoine pour des générations futures. Ce qui ressort de ces textes – en dehors de la leçon habituelle que la meilleure manière de conserver le patrimoine et ses valeurs de témoignage est de conserver l'activité pour laquelle il était conçu – est notre besoin commun d'une approche mieux informée des problèmes de conservation et de mise en valeur, fondée surtout par des études et des inventaires à entreprendre dans le contexte d'une communauté comptant aujourd'hui vingt-cinq membres. En partageant plus largement les leçons apprises au cours du projet "L'Europe de l'Air", en plaçant le patrimoine de l'aéronautique dans le contexte européen qui est le sien, nous espérons que cette publication sera une contribution à cet effort commun.

MICHEL CLÉMENT
Directeur de l'Architecture et du Patrimoine
Ministère de la Culture et de la
Communication, Paris

Vorwort

Kürzlich eröffnete das 1970 gegründete Airbus-Konsortium in Blagnac bei Toulouse eine der größten je entworfenen Montagehallen, in der die Teile des größten je gebauten Passagierflugzeuges – des A 380 – zusammengesetzt werden sollen. Dieser Riesenflieger mit zwei Passagierdecks, der für "hub – to – hub" Verbindungen vorgesehen ist, wird insgesamt 800 Personen transportieren können. Das neue Großraumflugzeug, von dem bereits mehr als hundert geordert wurden, wird aus Teilen zusammengefügt, die in Frankreich, Deutschland, Spanien und England hergestellt wurden. So manifestiert sich in der Flugzeugindustrie auf schlagende und überaus greifbare Weise, wie das Nachkriegseuropa sich vom gemeinsamen Markt für Stahl und Kohle zu einer integrierten Wirtschaftsgemeinschaft gewandelt hat.

Indes ist Europa nicht nur eine Wirtschaftsgemeinschaft, sondern auch eine Kulturgemeinschaft, deren von allen geteilte demokratische Werte in ihrer gemeinsamen Geschichte wurzeln. Das vorliegende Buch, das English Heritage im Namen seiner französischen und englischen Partner produziert hat, ist ein bescheidener Ausdruck dieser Tatsache. Es enthält eine Zusammenstellung von Vorträgen und Texten zum Verständnis und zur Erhaltung von Bauten der Luftfahrtgeschichte – die Ergebnisse eines von der Europäischen Union im Rahmen des Programms Raphael geförderten Projektes – ein Programm, das eigens aufgelegt wurde, um die europäische Zusammenarbeit im Bereich des Kulturerbes anzuregen und zu unterstützen.

Neben dem Automobil und der Elektrifizierung war die Luftfahrt ohne Frage eine der bedeutendsten technischen Neuerungen des 20. Jahrhunderts und zwar eine, die von Anfang an ausdrücklich europäisch geprägt war, seit Blériots erster Kanalüberquerung im Jahre 1909 und den ersten kommerziellen Flügen zwischen Paris und London unmittelbar nach dem Ersten Weltkrieg.

Die Bauten, die uns diese revolutionäre Neuerung als Erbe hinterlassen hat, sind nicht leicht zu verstehen noch einfach zu erhalten. Es handelt sich um ein sehr empfindliches Erbe, das im Wesentlichen aus weit gedehnten Flächen besteht, gesäumt von einer handvoll Bauten – Hangars, Werkstätten, Kontrolltürmen, Empfangsgebäuden. Die Luftangriffe des zweiten Weltkriegs und die anschließende schnelle Entwicklung des Massenluftverkehrs im Jet-Zeitalter hatten zur Folge, dass erhaltene Stätten der Luftfahrtgeschichte aus der ersten Hälfte des 20. Jahrhunderts sehr rar geworden sind. Die Beiträge des Buches basieren auf der vergleichenden Analyse von dreien dieser seltenen Exemplare in Berlin, Liverpool und Paris und fragen nach Wegen, das Erbe der Luftfahrt für zukünftige Generationen zu erhalten.

Aus den Texten ergibt sich zum Einen wieder einmal, dass ein Denkmal und sein Zeugniswert am besten erhalten werden, wenn es für den Zweck genutzt wird, für den es entworfen wurde. Zum anderen erfahren wir, wie dringlich es ist, Erhaltungs- und Managementprobleme gemeinsam und besser informiert anzugehen, gestützt auf vertiefende Erfassungen und Studien, insbesondere mit Blick auf die Europäische Gemeinschaft, die nunmehr 25 Mitgliedstaaten umfasst. Dazu möchten wir mit den Ergebnissen aus unserem Projekt "Europa der Lüfte" beitragen – ein Projekt, in dem wir das Erbe der Luftfahrt in den ihm gebührenden europäischen Rahmen gestellt haben.

DR JÖRG HASPEL
Landeskonservator
Landesdenkmalamt Berlin

Introduction: 'L'Europe de l'Air'

Paul Smith

For better and for worse, the realisation of mankind's age-old dream of flight is probably one of the collective adventures that best characterises the century we have just left, its greatest novelty. In the space of only three or four generations since the first heavier-than-air hops during the opening decade of that century, aviation has conquered the entire planet, becoming one of its leading sectors of activity on the ground and marking the skies of both its hemispheres with evanescent vapour-trails. Since the dawn of the jet age in the mid-20th century, ushered in by the rapid technological progress of the war years, flying has developed into a transportation for the masses: is there a reader out there who has never passed through an airport?

The history of this short adventure has countless specialists, professionals and amateurs, their eyes for the most part on its flying machines, the military ones in particular. Collections of well-documented vintage aircraft, some of them kept lovingly air-worthy, draw large crowds to shows and to museums, the oldest of which, France's national air and space museum, dates back to 1919. But the open fields and ground structures without which this modern adventure would not have been possible have survived less well and have received far less attention. From the outset and up to the end of the First World War, these structures – the pylons, viewing stands, makeshift restaurants and clubhouses of the earliest display grounds, the mass-produced huts and tent-like hangars of the war – were not built to last, or rather were designed to be dismantled and to serve on another field. At the beginning of the 1920s the birth of commercial air services, the carrying of paying passengers, mail, newspapers and small items of freight in converted bombers, made aviation's settlements less nomadic but, even before the decade was out, had already demonstrated one of their defining characteristics: their extremely rapid obsolescence, their losing race to keep up with the technical advances and increasing size of new aeroplanes and with swelling numbers of air travellers. After a hesitant start, influenced simultaneously by the architectural traditions of the railway station and of the hippodrome, the modern airport passenger terminal developed in Europe during the 1930s as a specific and highly prestigious new building type, but precious few examples survive from that era. During the Second World War, any site used by aircraft or associated with aircraft manufacture was likely to be a prime strategic target for air raids. Those that survived the war were subsequently modernised, extended and rebuilt, or else abandoned, their empty fields offering valuable and well-situated building land. Among contemporary airports only the most recent are not also permanent and immensely complicated building sites: the planning of runway number three, the extension of terminal number two, the provision of new satellites, new people-movers, new rail links, car parks, hotels, business parks, shopping malls, conference centres...

International airports have developed into hubs, into multi-modal interchange nodes and sleepless airport 'cities'.[1] With immense working populations but few full-time residents, they can cover territories almost as large as the cities they have the names of, and even larger ones for the nuisances they generate. Their growing organisational complexity compounds their intrinsically paradoxical status as places of in-betweenness, always in change but held in stasis at the interface between earth and sky, an inner frontier between landside and airside, between departure and arrival, separation and reunion, hello and goodbye. Conceived for the most rapid means of transport available to the general public, they condense untold hours of dead time, anticipated or not, spent in departure lounges, transit halls, baggage-claim facilities, bars, restaurants and shops, queuing at check-in counters, security filters and gates. But the parts of the airport that this waiting and often fretful public frequents are only a small fraction of the whole: the fields and runways, the airport's core functional feature, are among the most inaccessible and carefully protected tracts of land anywhere, driven over by fleets of improbable motor vehicles and populated only by hearing-impaired rabbits. Over the last two decades of the 20th century, since Norman Foster's Standsted say, planned from 1981, airports have clearly become one of the favourite challenges for the most prestigious names on the international architectural market, coming to the fore in glossy anthologies of contemporary buildings and in sponsored exhibitions.[2] But as terminals and their architectural design thus come to play a crucial part in the commercial rivalry between airport companies, most of them now privatised, for many ordinary users they remain among the most characteristically anonymous 'non-places' of the post-modern world, along with supermarkets and motorways.

Looking at Heathrow, Reyner Banham, architectural critic and chronicler of the immediate future, was one of the first to consider airports historically, pinpointing their 'pastoral' origins, their perpetual obsolescence and the visual chaos, the 'hysteria', of their sprawling landscapes.[3] At the time he was writing, in the early 1960s, airports were about to lose one of their primary original functions as places of spectacle. During the 1920s and 1930s, airports attracted far more spectators than actual air travellers, still a glamorous and wealthy elite. All were designed to integrate viewing platforms for these massed spectators, for 'aeronautical propaganda' or for nurturing 'civic air-mindedness' as the speeches and competition briefs put it. Orly, south of Paris, one of the last major terminals to integrate such terraces for the non-flying public, opened in 1961 and attracted four million visitors in 1964, making it the most visited French monument of its day, well ahead of the Eiffel tower. But the new Orly-Ouest terminal, opened only ten years later, had no such facilities. The threat of terrorism in the early 1970s condemned the public terraces while the increasing ordinariness of air travel gradually put paid to the airport as an exciting destination for a family outing.

Here and there, however, from the late 1970s on, a handful of surviving airport buildings on both sides of the Channel (and both sides of the Atlantic) began to receive recognition and measures of statutory protection. At Croydon, south of London, one of Europe's first purpose-built air passenger terminals, designed in 1928 by the Air Ministry's Directorate of Buildings and Works

and a base for the state-owned Imperial Airways, was listed in 1978, though the airport itself, superseded by Heathrow, had closed down in 1959. Converted into office accommodation the building, incorporating a central control tower, now looks out over a rather nondescript industrial estate. Liverpool's 1935 municipal airport buildings at Speke, made redundant by a new terminal opened in 1986 (John Lennon airport today), were listed in 1985. In France, the 1937 terminal at Le Bourget, hastily constructed for the international exhibition in Paris that year and which survived the war (though not unscathed) to remain in commercial use up until 1977, was designated as a historic monument in 1994. Curiously though, the site's older and even more exceptional ranges of hangars, some of them of German origin and taken by France as war damages in 1919, were omitted from this protective measure. In the same year of 1994, the monumental building of Berlin's Third Reich airport at Tempelhof, another 'miraculous' survivor of wartime air raids, almost immediately becoming a key site of the Cold War, was given statutory protection, as was the celebrated Trans World Air Flight Center at New York, designed by Eero Saarinen in 1956, a 'landmark' in the form of a giant concrete bird in soaring flight.

Such measures of protection, however, variously inspired by considerations of architectural quality or historical significance and not informed by any broad-based appreciation of the surviving stocks of civil or military aviation sites, were all enacted within national terms of reference. Yet from the outset commercial aviation was very much an international affair. In 1921, the connection between Paris and London was the world's busiest with up to six departures a day. Throughout the inter-war period, as the air routes multiplied all over the continent, the comparisons made where the provision of new facilities on the ground was concerned were European ones. National and municipal delegations (and American observers as well) travelled throughout Europe and to Germany in particular – because of its size, but also because of the ban on military aviation imposed by the Treaty of Versailles, this country was a pioneer in civil aviation – in order to identify the most successful organisational and architectural solutions, models that were also widely circulated in the professional and architectural press.

For understanding aviation's architectural

heritage, its emergence, evolution and survival, the advantages of a similarly European-wide view are manifest. Croydon, for example, may be compared with Le Bourget; Bron, near Lyons, with Elmdon, near Birmingham; Liverpool's Speke with its model at Fuhlsbüttel, near Hamburg; Gatwick in 1936 with Budaörs, near Budapest, in 1937 or even with Roissy-1 in the early 1970s... Indeed, few other sectors of the built heritage are so clearly in need of a European perspective, not only for assessing significance but also for appreciating why the preservation of this heritage is important and for finding the best ways to achieve this.

'L'Europe de l'Air'

At the beginning of 1999, with the financial support of the European Commission's now defunct Raphael programme – 48 per cent of a total budget of €498,000 – an international project on aviation's architectural heritage was set up at the instigation of the architecture and heritage department of the French Ministry of Culture, associated with two other institutional partners: English Heritage and Landesdenkmalamt Berlin, the official heritage body of the *Land* of the German capital. The French title given to this project, which may be feebly translated as 'Under European Skies', insisted on the fact that this heritage is best seen as a shared one, marked of course by the national and nationalistic rivalries characteristic of its time and bearing witness to conflict as well as to more comfortable memories of taking off, landing or plane- and celebrity-spotting, but transcending Europe's national frontiers today. The project's primary aim was to contribute to the better understanding and conservation of this common heritage by bringing together experts already working in the field to form an informal cooperation network. Following the rules of the Raphael programme, 'pilot-sites' in three different countries were chosen on which to ground this network and articulate its exchanges. These three sites, all rare survivors from the late 1930s – Berlin-Tempelhof and Paris-Le Bourget, two national airports, and Liverpool-Speke, a major municipal one and the most ambitious and costly of its time in Britain – were not difficult to identify. They offered the additional interest of existing in the different states in which the built heritage is to be found today: a site still in activity and with the activity for which it was

originally designed (Tempelhof); a building that has lost its original use and found a new and rather appropriate cultural one (the terminal at Le Bourget, which now houses the French air and space museum); and finally, at Speke, a derelict site, practically in ruins in 1999 but on the point of undergoing a comprehensive regeneration programme to accommodate new and entirely unaeronautical uses.

The products of the 'L'Europe de l'Air' project comprised the creation of a web site[4], the publication, in May 2000, of an illustrated, trilingual book on the parallel histories and contemporary destinies of the three airport sites[5], and the mounting of temporary exhibitions at each of them, linking them together, underlining their common features and setting out succinctly the project's awareness-raising ambitions. But the establishment of an international network of expertise on aviation's architecture took place essentially by means of three international workshops: the first, organised at Liverpool in October 1999, on the question of how to identify and preserve the sites worth keeping; the second, at Berlin in June 2000, on the place of the airport in the 21st-century city; and the last, at Paris in June 2001, on the future of historic airports in general. These workshops brought together between sixty and a hundred participants each time, coming from a total of nine different countries: historians, architects, conservation and heritage professionals, museum curators, representatives of local authorities and development agencies, of local associations and of airport and airline companies. Most of the papers these participants gave or heard are published here, and their diffusion in this volume will hopefully give the cooperation network renewed reality.

Before briefly summarising how they have been edited for this publication, however, it is perhaps worth recalling another important aspect of the way in which the 'L'Europe de l'Air' network was consolidated, which cannot be read in these pages: the visits that accompanied each meeting. These visits concentrated primarily on the pilot-sites themselves, the airport buildings and their adjoining airfields at Tempelhof, Le Bourget and Speke. But at Liverpool the meeting also offered participants the chance to discover one of Britain's earliest and best-preserved civil airports at Barton (Manchester's airport up to 1938), its grass airfield still used for light aviation by one of the

United Kingdom's oldest aero clubs and its free-standing control tower of 1933 (listed in 1987) still in daily use. An additional excursion also took some participants to Duxford, one of Britain's best-preserved fighter bases of the period up to 1945 and now home to the Imperial War Museum. The workshop at Berlin was accompanied by visits to some extraordinary 1930s military aviation sites in Brandenburg: Rangsdorf, Jüterbog-Damm and Niedergörsdorf. These sobering remnants of the enormity of the Nazi war effort were occupied by Soviet forces in 1945 and abandoned by them in the early 1990s and, since then, have gradually been reclaimed by nature. The Paris workshop, held in the prestigious headquarters of the Aero-Club de France, one of the first such clubs in the world dating from 1898, comprised visits to the still-busy, early-1960s terminal at Orly and to Chalais-Meudon. This bucolic setting a few miles to the west of Paris, already home to a ballooning school during the French Revolution, conserves not only the oldest dirigible hangar in the world – the so-called 'Y' hangar erected in 1879 using metallic trusses from an exhibition building – but also a remarkable wind tunnel constructed in 1935 as part of France's pre-war rearmament programme. This stunning reinforced-concrete structure, designed for aerodynamic testing of full-size aircraft, their motors running, remained in use up to 1976. The recognition of its importance and its designation as a historic monument in September 2000 was facilitated by comparisons with other surviving wind tunnels in Europe: at Farnborough in England and at Johannisthal near Berlin. In February 2000 an intermediate meeting organised at Toulouse allowed members of the Raphael network to visit Montaudran airport, home of Latécoère's celebrated Aéropostale company during the 1920s, and even to stay a couple of nights at the Hôtel du Grand Balcon, which was frequented by that company's pilots (Antoine de Saint-Exupéry stayed in room 32). Finally, in March 2002, at the generous invitation of the Speke-Garston Development Company, members of the network stayed two nights in the Marriott hotel that had been opened inside Speke's former terminal building a year earlier; a chance to appreciate this remarkable example of new life being breathed into an old building and to take a last look, too, over the still empty airfield.

The handful of readers fortunate enough to have been present at these different meetings will perhaps appreciate these passing reminders of them; reminders that, without the possibilities for discussion offered not only by plenary sessions but also by coach journeys, site visits and shared meals, cooperation networks are little more than dormant lists of e-mail addresses. For other readers, and with three or four regrettable exceptions of contributions that failed to materialise as written papers, this volume offers the proceedings of the three 'L'Europe de l'Air' workshops held at the turn of the century. For reasons of coherence, the papers do not follow the original order of their presentation at these workshops but have been slightly rearranged, under four main headings.

The first, Europe's heritage of aviation architecture, groups together six contributions that offer general overviews of national and regional situations, with an introductory essay on the development of airport architecture in Europe by one of the leading experts in this field: Wolfgang Voigt, who the initiators of the project were fortunate enough to have on board from the outset. Jeremy Lake's contribution then gives an account of how military aviation sites have been surveyed, assessed and protected in England. Largely for historical reasons – aviation's heroic and decisive role in the Battle of Britain and the place subsequently occupied by Spitfires and Hurricanes in the nation's airfixed collective memory – the sites and buildings associated with aviation in Britain have had a longer history of survey and in-depth study than similar places elsewhere in Europe; first by scholars in anoraks then by teams at English Heritage. English Heritage's lead in this field has recently been re-affirmed by a pioneering study on the structures, buildings and landscapes left over by the Cold War.[6]

If France has any 'mythical' sites in its aviation history, these do not date from the Second World War but rather from the earlier, pioneering days of manned flight: the playing fields at Bagatelle where Santos-Dumont first flew in 1906; the military parade-ground at Issy-les-Moulineaux for Henry Farman's first 1-km circuit; Port-Aviation, also near Paris, the world's first planned aerodrome which opened in 1908; the school at Pont-Long near Pau set up by Wilbur Wright in 1909; Le Bourget in 1927, for Charles Lindbergh, flying in from New York to become the century's first international media hero... The notion of the anorak is not a familiar one in France, neither in its railway stations nor at its airfields and, as the two French contributions suggest here, preliminary – 'dry' – inventory work on aviation's built heritage has still to leave the libraries and documentation centres to tackle recording work in the field; such measures of protection as have been enacted are the piecemeal result of local or regional initiatives. In Germany most historic aviation sites are almost inevitably associated with troubled national memories either of the Nazi years or of the Cold War; sometimes both. At Rangsdorf, in Brandenburg for example, huts for slave labour working at the Bücker aircraft factory juxtapose kitsch commemorative monuments to Soviet fighter pilots. Under these circumstances, and also because of the sheer numbers of only recently accessible installations dating from 1934 to 1939, it is perhaps not surprising that research and fieldwork are still in their early days though, as Christina Czymay's piece describes, this work has now begun and some remarkable First-World-War hangar buildings surviving at Berlin-Karlshorst have been identified and documented. The last contribution in this section, by Marieke Kuipers, gives an account of the nationwide inventory work carried out in the densely-populated and space-conscious Netherlands, identifying but a handful of civil aviation structures surviving from the inter-war period and now coming to terms with the contradictory legacy of the German wartime occupation.

Historic airports, the second section of the book, offers a closer look at the individual histories and present-day uses of some exceptional airport buildings which date primarily from the 1920s and 1930s. It begins with the three sites on which the project was based. Berlin-Tempelhof here receives special attention in two articles, not only as the largest of the three but also as place of particular complexity that has accumulated several layers, not only of use but also of ideological identity. A relatively modest, centrally-situated city airport today, Tempelhof operates from what was originally the largest European airport complex of its day: the 'world' airport of the thousand-year Reich, remembered and valued by most Berliners for its associations with the airlift of 1948. At Oberschleißheim near Munich, Bavaria's oldest military aviation site dating from 1912, a First-World-War maintenance shop survived the air raids of the Second World War and the demolitions of the 1950s

and 60s and since 1992 has housed an aviation museum. The future of other buildings on the site, however, and the integrity of its flying field, are still uncertain. Two civil airports, Antwerp-Deurne and London-Gatwick, are also studied in this section, offering further examples of the ways passenger terminals were conceived during the 1930s and how they have fared since. Finally, Thomas Mellins's contribution on the preservation of New York's civil aviation heritage, and on Saarinen's TWA terminal in particular, provides a comparative view of the subject from across the Atlantic and a reminder too that where aviation is concerned, even the European perspective is a parochial one.

The next section, entitled 'Airports in Mutation', offers two examples of the kind of detailed studies that should underpin conservation strategies once the historic significance of a monument has been recognised. One of the stated objectives of the 'L'Europe de l'Air' project was to define common methodological approaches for the understanding and management of this heritage. The work carried out by the teams represented here by Jean-Christophe Morisseau and Werner Jockeit, on Le Bourget and Tempelhof respectively, are good examples of good practice in this respect, analysing the sites in terms of their recorded history and the present-day archaeological evidence of their buildings, and then setting out priorities, space by space, floor by floor, room by room even, for future repair or restoration work. Jacques Repiquet also gives an account of how the recent renovation of Orly-Sud by Aéroports de Paris was founded on a similarly painstaking accumulation of historical and archaeological understanding, the better to inform the necessary negotiations between contemporary requirements, in terms of security and operational efficiency, and the intelligent preservation of relatively recent but now fully recognised heritage values. Ola Wedebrunn describes a more radical approach to safekeeping aviation's 1930s heritage at Copenhagen where, in the summer of 1999, Lauritzen's 1939 passenger terminal was physically uprooted, turned round, and carried a mile to be set down on the other side of the airfield. For all the admiration this engineering prowess inspires, it begs the question of the building's new functional role and of its functional relation to the flying field. For practical and financial reasons too, it offers an act that will be difficult to follow elsewhere. The felicitous case of Shoreham on the south coast of England, which opened in 1936 as the municipal airport for Brighton, Hove and Worthing and was listed in 1984, is presented here by Jeremy Lake. The story demonstrates once again, as if it were necessary, that the best way of preserving this kind of architecture and its associated airfield landscapes is by maintaining the site's original aeronautical function.

Economically, however, this solution is not often an option, as the example of Speke shows. Bob Lane, chief executive of the Speke-Garston Development Company, sketches out the situation in the mid-1990s: a disused flying field with a trio of remarkable but derelict buildings, situated in an area badly hit by the decline of manufacturing industry and characterised by exceptionally high levels of long-term unemployment. The task of his company, formed in 1996 with considerable Objective 1 European funding, was to create new business premises to attract investors and new jobs to the area. The rehabilitation and new uses found for the airport buildings played a key part in this process, not least in terms of image. The leisure and fitness centre in one of the hangars and the four-star hotel in the former terminal building are now acknowledged and award-winning success stories. The contribution of the Raphael 'L'Europe de l'Air' project to this success is comparable to that of the mouse on the elephant's back (looking back and impressed by the amount of dust they're kicking up together). The new 160-bedroom Marriott hotel pays due homage to Speke's specific aviation history and its association with a golden age of air travel. Historical photographs of the airport abound and in the middle of the forecourt a full-size mock-up of a De Havilland DH 86 reasserts this association for visitors and passers-by. The problem is that, like the 1950s Heron mounted in front of Airport House at Croydon, this aeroplane is on the wrong side of the building. As Bob Hawkins's contribution on the lessons of Speke suggests here, on Speke's airside, economic and cultural priorities no longer coincide: the landscape of the open flying field, without which the peripheral airport buildings themselves, however well restored and interpreted, lose most of their meaning, has itself been lost.

In the final section of this book, on the place of the historic airport in the future, Didier Hamon, head of public relations at Aéroports de Paris, offers a personal flight of fancy on a possible future for the terminal at Le Bourget, if ever the French air and space museum were to be re-located. We then return to Berlin for another look at the future of Tempelhof, still in the air despite the decision taken in 1996 to close the site and to replace both Tempelhof and Berlin-Tegel by a new, single 'hub' for the German capital: Berlin-Brandenburg International, at Schönefeld. Michael Cramer offers some economic and ecological reflections on this prestige-driven project and Vogt Landschaftsarchitekten, landscape designers in Zurich, present their project for the future of the airfield if and when it is abandoned, a study commissioned by the Berlin Senate in 1998. The scenario seeks to preserve most of the open space, underlining its association with the Berlin Airlift, but it would irreversibly condemn the field for any aviation use. Almut Jirku broadens the horizons with a look at what has been done at some of Berlin's other historic transport sites: the former airfields at Adlershof and Gatow, but also several railway landscapes which have been transformed into urban parks.

The precedent of railway stations – seen today almost without exception as heritage assets, to be treasured and restored to their earlier splendour rather than destroyed and replaced by airport-inspired passenger terminals (London's Euston, for example) – crops up again in the last part of this section, an edited transcription of the round table held in Paris on 22 June 2001. The ambition of this round table was to open up the debate by confronting the views of the project's 'friends of old airports' with those of some of the other players in the contemporary airport world: an airport company (ADP), an airline company (Air France), a representative of France's official civil aviation service, and architect Paul Andreu, designer of Roissy-1 and subsequently of many other major airport terminals throughout the world. This discussion puts our heritage preoccupations into a broader perspective. In the age of the dominant hub and low-cost, easy-jetted flying, uncertainty prevails where the architectural design of the terminal is concerned. Architecture and architectural quality in any case never seem to be vital requirements for passengers and the niche markets that might be a way of keeping historic airports alive are of but little interest to the airline companies, who rarely entertain the idea of keeping the old alongside the new.

The reader will notice that the discussion is pre-11 September 2001. Time, as is its wont, has not stood still since the end of the three-year Raphael 'L'Europe de l'Air' project: Concorde has left the air for the museum while hypersonic flight becomes a reality; the plans for a third Paris airport have been put back into the drawers as the first twin-deck, four-aisle airliner, the A380 superjumbo (555 passengers at a go!), approaches the assembly-line stage. As with the airports themselves, obsolescence has already struck some of the papers published here. We apologise to our readers, and to the authors too, but then, after all, regrettable and unexpected delays are an intrinsic part of the airport experience…

Notes

1 Güller M and Güller M (Güller Güller architecture urbanism) *From airport to airport city*. Barcelona: ARC, Airport Regions Conference, 2001

2 Cuadra, M *World Airports/Weltflughäfen, Vision and reality/Culture and technique/Past and present*. Frankfurt: DAM & Junius Verlag GhbH, 2002 (catalogue of the exhibition organised by the Deutsches Architektur Museum at Frankfurt am Main)

3 Banham, R 'The Obsolescent Airport', *The Architectural Review*, no. 788, October 1962, pp 250–3

4 http://www.culture.gouv.fr/europe-air

5 Smith, P and Toulier, B (eds) *Berlin-Tempelhof, Liverpool-Speke, Paris-Le Bourget, Airport Architecture of the Thirties*. Paris: Editions du Patrimoine, 2000

6 Cocroft, W D and Thomas, R J C *Cold War, Building for Nuclear Confrontation 1946–1989*. Swindon: English Heritage, 2003

Europe's Heritage of Aviation Architecture

The birth of the terminal: some typological remarks on early airport architecture in Europe

Wolfgang Voigt

When civil air transport began after the end of the First World War, there were hundreds of airfields all over Europe, but there was no clear idea about the form or the architecture of the 'aerodrome', as aviation's ground stations were called in the early days. The aeroplane itself and the parameters of its movements on the ground were changing rapidly as its technology progressed. Until the end of the 1930s, further uncertainty was caused by the fact that different forms of air travel – by airship, aeroplane or seaplane – were still competing with each other.

This paper will look at the genesis and the typology of the ground stations for aviation but I will limit my remarks to the European history of the subject, to heavier-than-air aircraft and to airports primarily intended for commercial air travel. Fascinating though they are, I will not deal here with the buildings erected for airships, nor will I speak about military or factory airfields, which, of course, all deserve the same research investment. I will focus on the typological developments of airfields and on what was to emerge as the airport terminal, and I will conclude by giving a brief overview of the discussions taking place about 1930, crucial for the next generation of airports, built after the Second World War.[1]

San-Niccolo in Venice: a typical 1930s terminal

Before starting with aviation's prehistory, about 1900, let me begin by taking a look forward at an 'average' European terminal of the mid-1930s. In Venice, the first San-Niccolo airport, which opened on the Lido in 1935, has been preserved practically untouched since the 1950s, when Venice's airport relocated to the mainland. Its remarkably authentic buildings are still used by the local flying club which operates small aircraft and maintains the airfield according to its modest needs.[2] This so-called 'airway station' of San-Niccolo was designed by the

architect Mario Emmer in a dynamic version of Italian rationalism, using the steamship metaphors which, since Le Corbusier's 1923 publication, *Vers une Architecture* (*Towards an Architecture*), had so frequently inspired modern architecture. Apart from the furniture, nothing substantial has been lost from the original building:

- the dramatically-curved stairs leading to the observation terrace on the roof of the restaurant wing
- the control tower, in steel and glass, topped by a platform with rails; it was painted red and white later and equipped with an antenna, but apart from that it is unchanged
- the concourse which was laid out at a

Top: *Venice, airside of the terminal at San-Niccolo airport, 1935 (from Wood, 1940)*

Venice, the terminal at San-Niccolo airport (photo Wolfgang Voigt)

Venice, San-Niccolo airport, petrol station (photo Wolfgang Voigt)

slight angle to the building's axis, ending on the airside in three windows framed by brick pillars and still retaining their slender steel profiles

- the apron, with its original surface and an extension, ending some 30m in front of the building
- the ramp used for loading baggage and mail
- the original signal mast, once bearing flags and balls to indicate weather conditions and to give pilots their clearance for flight
- next to the building, the petrol station (belonging to Standard Oil), a standard element in smaller airports
- the forecourt, with a circular decorative basin and parking spaces
- the slightly curved gates, with the gate lodge to one side
- and finally – lest we forget that we are in Venice – a canal with a landing stage for the vaporetti going to the city.

San-Niccolo is not and will never be a key building in our history, but because of the striking completeness of the airfield, the building and all its period details, I consider it to be a document of prime importance in the understanding of how early airports and their architecture were conceived. Today, it is a sleeping beauty, with no apparent signs of organised preservation as a historic monument.

From the hippodrome to the aerodrome

The year 1909 was a crucial one for aviation in Europe. Louis Blériot's successful crossing of the English Channel in a home-made monoplane marked a major breakthrough in motor-driven, heavier-than-air flight, which finally passed its first testing phase. Immense enthusiasm for flight spread far beyond France and it inspired artists such as the painter Robert Delaunay, whose *Hommage à Blériot* celebrated the rotation of the propeller that had actually lifted the plane into the air. Air meetings, first organised in this same year, played a major role in the future of flying by providing an effective stage for the pioneers of flight.

Setting the style was the *Grande Semaine de Champagne*, organised by French businessmen in August 1909, at Bétheny, near Reims. A 10-km-long rectangular circuit was pegged out on open fields with pyramid-shaped wooden pylons marking the corners. On one of the shorter sides of the rectangle, a row of hangars was erected with workshops and three comfortable viewing stands, on which figures from Parisian high society gathered.[3] Similar air shows were held in the autumn of 1909 at Brescia in Italy, at Brooklands in England and at Johannisthal, near Berlin. This last was the German capital's first airfield, created and equipped by a private company specifically set up for this purpose.[4] The meetings resembled a travelling circus, since the prize money offered led the same aviation pioneers to make frequent appearances, their prizes financing improvements to their machines.

In terms of their design, the facilities were essentially the same at Reims or at Johannisthal. They were open grass spaces with simple, lightweight buildings erected at the periphery: wide viewing stands, along with hangars some distance away, all in unpretentious order and with no precise plan. Their architectural language was clearly rooted in the world of sports and horse-racing, with the hangars – modest wooden buildings – replacing the stables. The terms 'aerodrome' or 'air-drome', used early on in the history of airports, owe their inspiration to the 'hippodrome' and its more recent variant, 'autodrome', coined in about 1900. The verbal confusion, with words often borrowed from French, suggests the cultural and technical models that were the force behind the evolution of flight. Today, some of flight's vocabulary still comes from racing, some from agriculture and some from the world of railway transport.

Perhaps the earliest coherent vision of a municipal airfield was created by the French urban designer Donat-Alfred Agache. In

1912 Agache received third prize in the international competition for the new federal capital of Australia, present-day Canberra. An airfield – called an 'aerostatic station' here – features in his project, located in the green outskirts of the city, beyond the blocks comprising the capital's centre.[5] The airfield took the shape of a traditional architectural space with monumental Beaux-Arts forms, dominated by a symmetrical group of three domed administrative buildings, which could just as easily have been school buildings or courts of law. The other facilities followed the layout of the structures at the Reims meeting, with the addition of three airship hangars. The rectangular shape of the airfield, however, was reduced to the dimensions of a parade ground. Such a cramped space alone would have made the installation unusable, but this by no means diminishes Agache's achievement in presenting aviation as an essential and integral part of modern urban development.

Still belonging to aviation's prehistoric period is another vision created in 1914 by the Italian architect Antonio Sant'Elia, author of the *Manifesto of Futuristic Architecture*. His *Stazione Aeroplani Treni* was one of the illustrations of this famous pamphlet that pioneered the Modern Movement in architecture in Italy and Europe. Sant'Elia's transportation junction began with a metropolitan railway station as its foundation, thus linking the 19th-century form of transport with the aeroplane, one of the Futurists' favourite symbols of the new age. Rising from the railway platforms, elevators were to move passengers to the roof area of a symmetrical terraced structure with protruding twin towers; beneath it tracks and roads for motor cars disappeared into tunnels. A rooftop terrace with low hangars on both sides served as the take-off and landing platform for aircraft. Sant'Elia gave them a status they had not yet acquired in reality, for in this vision they have already become a normal means of transportation, such as the automobile and the train.[6]

Early air travel and its ground stations

Only after the First World War, following its immense development during the four years of conflict, did aviation reach a critical mass that enabled it to become a transport industry. The aircraft of 1918, with their powerful engines and large load capacities, had little in common with the fabric-covered flying

machines of the pre-war era. The first post-war machines used on commercial air routes were converted bombers, with windows cut into their fuselages for the small passenger cabins. On 6 February 1919, the first scheduled daily flight between Berlin-Johannisthal and Weimar took place, carrying two pilots, one passenger, mail and newspapers. This was to become the first civil air route operated to an established flight plan. The first international air route followed on 25 August 1919, with a flight from Hounslow airfield near London to Le Bourget near Paris, also with one passenger.[7]

The airports of this first generation were very modest, a far cry from the pre-war visions of Agache or Sant'Elia. The airline companies were tenants, tolerated by the military owners of the flying fields. Passenger processing and passport and customs formalities took place in light buildings and hangars left over from the war years. At Croydon, used as a military aerodrome during the war and officially transformed

Top: Reims-Bétheny, the viewing stands at the international air meeting Grande semaine de Champagne, August 1909; in the foreground, Curtiss's aeroplane, with a Zodiac III airship in the sky (Musée de l'Air et de l'Espace, Le Bourget)

Berlin-Johannisthal, the airfield in 1914 (Museum für Verkehr und Technik, Berlin)

Königsberg, East Prussia, the airport terminal in 1922 (Lufthansa Archive)

into the international 'air port' of London in March 1920, a row of barracks topped by the airlines' billboards suggest an atmosphere of a gold rush town.

At Le Bourget, near Paris, commercial aviation activities were permitted on the eastern side of the airfield, where barracks and hangars had been vacated by the military. Le Bourget's 'air port' (*port aérien*) was the birthplace of a new type of building, the terminal, which was called the 'air station' or 'airway station' because its function was comparable to that of the passenger buildings at a railway station. The word 'terminal' also came from the world of railways, first appearing in the mid-1930s alongside these earlier terms, and ultimately replacing them after 1945.

As the wartime buildings at Le Bourget appeared inappropriate for the new post-war era, the French Under-Secretary for Aerial Navigation started planning new buildings in 1921–2, though he made the mistake of transforming a temporary situation into a long-term one. Thus, an ensemble of neoclassical pavilions replaced the barracks, but retained the impractical division of administration, passport and customs control, weather services, telegraph services and airline offices, separated between various buildings. A neo-baroque garden *à la française* filled the free space between the buildings, preparing arriving passengers for the mood of the French capital.[8]

From Königsberg to Fuhlsbüttel: a building type is established

The airport terminal was being re-invented only some months later – and with more success – in the East Prussian city of Königsberg (present-day Kaliningrad). On a rectangular airfield situated at the periphery of the city, work started with the construction of two hangars, placed at right angles to each other in the corner of the field closest

to the nearby main road. The 'air station', completed in 1922 to the designs of the architect Hanns Hopp, was erected at an angle between the ends of the hangars. Hopp's terminal unified the splintered programme of Le Bourget into a single, symmetrical building, with symmetrically staged terraces on its flat roofs and an elevation with heavy, protruding pillars, greatly influenced by the verticalism of Peter Behrens.[9] Murals inside and cast-iron balustrades outside, both decorated with silhouettes of aircraft, show how images of the new technology were brought into the architecture by the applied arts. That the first modern airport in Europe was built in the most out-of-the-way corner of Germany can be explained politically. The Treaty of Versailles had separated East Prussia from the rest of Germany; the airport was intended to mitigate this isolation, making Königsberg the distribution point of air traffic from Berlin to the Baltic and to the Soviet Union.

The terminal was now beginning to evolve as a distinctive architectural ensemble, an important moment in the history of European airports. The buildings, almost always placed at the field's periphery, are not simply lined up, but rather arranged according to a recognisable plan. The airfields of the first period were omnidirectional grass fields, 800–1,000yd (732–914m) in diameter, and requiring expensive care and drainage. Paved surfaces – the so-called aprons – were affordable only in front of the terminal building and the hangars. By the end of the 1920s, the most important airports – London's Croydon, Amsterdam's Schiphol and Berlin's Tempelhof – had illuminated airfields, which permitted night flying. For ease of orientation from the air, it was common to demarcate the airfield with a white circle, 150ft (46m) in diameter, with the name of the airfield in giant letters.

Königsberg was the prelude to the building of Tempelhof I, Berlin's commercial airport. Opened in 1923 to replace Johannisthal, it was to be the model for many other airports.[10] The symmetrical succession of hangar-terminal-hangar reappears here on a substantially larger scale, although in a linear fashion with only a slight concave curve on the northern periphery of the airfield. This curve followed the irregular fence of a nearby cemetery, which at the time prevented a straight border. What was originally an unintentional form, then, was later adopted at many other airports, because it satisfied an organic ideal that the airfield should be circular, as though the arriving aircraft were received by the buildings with open arms.

At Tempelhof, work began on the hangars in 1924; a radio office followed, placed on the axis of the complex and leading directly onto the apron. This office represents an early form of the free-standing control tower, which was not further pursued at that time, and found successors only after the Second World War. A command platform, with a cylindrical glass house in the centre, topped this octagonal pavilion. The terminal, erected from 1926 to 1929 to the prize-winning design of the architects Paul and Klaus Engler, contained administrative offices, passenger-processing facilities and a large restaurant for spectators.[11] The street elevation of this long, slightly curved, flat-roofed building was divided quite simply from one end to the other with continuous horizontal bands of windows. The Englers' design was the first to make future expansion of the terminal possible, since it could easily be lengthened at either end. Of the four sections planned, however, only two were in fact built. Rapidly growing air traffic led to a new project on the same site, culminating, at the end of the 1930s, in the construction of the well-known buildings of Tempelhof II.

Soon after Tempelhof I, the city of Hamburg had erected what was possibly the most innovative terminal of the period at its Fuhlsbüttel airport.[12] This became a model for different European airports of the 1930s, notably the terminal at Speke, near Liverpool. The reinforced concrete structure with brick facings was completed in 1929 to a competition design by the architects Friedrich Dyrssen and Peter Averhoff. Their building imitated the concavely curved plan of Tempelhof and its location between two large hangars at the periphery of the airfield. The control tower, which was isolated from the building at Tempelhof, was now integrated into the middle of the terminal on the airfield front. The glazed shaft of this tower grew out of the façade and supported a gallery platform topped by a crystal-like cabin for the air-traffic controller.

The essential innovation, however, was concealed within the terminal. For the first time, the airport's various functions were strictly separated into different zones and levels, a feature without which every present-day terminal would immediately seize up. A sophisticated arrangement of ramps, stairways and lifts, both inside and outside,

Left: *Berlin-Tempelhof, the free-standing radio building and control tower in 1924 (Lufthansa Archive)*

Berlin-Tempelhof, the first terminal building in 1929 (Lufthansa Archive)

made it possible for travellers to be kept separate both from spectators and restaurant customers and from the flow of luggage and freight. The main entrance of the building received its characteristic profile from the stairs on either side, which had no other function than to separate the different groups before they entered the concourse. The view from the airfield side was unusual: here, the façade was broken into a series of terraces, reminiscent of an amphitheatre.

No other terminal showed the typological legacy of the hippodrome and of the stands at the earliest air meetings as clearly as Fuhlsbüttel did. It was hoped that the terraces and an adjacent spectator garden would accommodate up to 35,000 spectators during air shows. This number was never

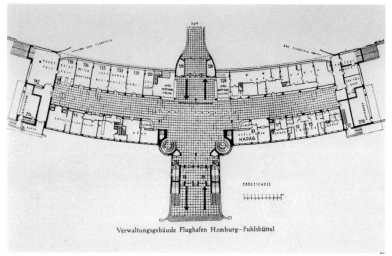

Verwaltungsgebäude Flughafen Hamburg–Fuhlsbüttel

Top: Hamburg-Fuhlsbüttel, airside view of the terminal building in 1931 (from Voigt, 1999)

Hamburg-Fuhlsbüttel, ground floor plan with staircase and concourse (from Voigt, 1999)

reached, although at times the numbers of non-flying visitors did reach the thousands. The architecture at Fuhlsbüttel demonstrated the financial dilemma of these municipal airports, which were as generously dimensioned as they were modern.

Air traffic was indeed growing at a steady pace, but, until after the Second World War, it remained too modest to cover the costs of these buildings, which were paid for then out of public funds. The number of passengers using Fuhlsbüttel airport was in a striking contrast with numbers of expected spectators. In 1928, when the building was under construction, the average number of passengers for scheduled flights was not more than 62 per day; ten years later, in 1938, after a remarkable upswing in commercial aviation all over Europe, there were still no more than 125 passengers a day.[13] Air travel remained the privilege of a small elite, which benefited indirectly from the large subsidies given to the airlines, as much as 80 per cent of their budgets at the beginning[14] and 35 per cent in the late 1930s. The principle that this burgeoning industry 'must fly by itself', as Winston Churchill put it in 1920, was not to be realised anywhere.

Probably the strongest public support for

flight was in Germany,[15] a country which played the role of draught horse in European civil air traffic right from the outset and kept this role until the late 1930s, when Great Britain and the United States in particular recovered lost ground with regards flight technology and airport provision. During the two first decades after the war, however, Germany had the densest air network, the largest number of commercial airports serviced by regular flight schedules and a modern, stylistically formative aeronautical architecture that was a major influence on that of other countries. It might come as something of a surprise that the principal loser of the war should have achieved this rank. A decisive factor, without which history would have taken an entirely different course, was article 1 of the Treaty of Versailles, which denied Germany a military air force. Involvement in civil air traffic offered the nation a way of developing its aeronautical infrastructure and gave the German public the chance to compensate for the shame of defeat through successes in civil aviation.

The airport as a system: the debate of the 1930s

At the end of the first decade of civil air travel, discussions began in several countries about the shortcomings of existing airports and the perspectives for the construction of new ones. The debate was especially lively in Britain, where the Royal Institute of British Architects (RIBA) had set up a committee to examine the weaknesses of existing facilities.[16] Members of this committee were sent to look at experiences in the United States and on the Continent. Partly as a result of this work, some of the most striking airport buildings of the 1930s were created in Britain: Gatwick, Birmingham, Liverpool, Jersey and several others.

The future of airports was also discussed about 1930 in Germany, France and the United States. Experts agreed that modern airports represented a planning problem and that the future of commercial air travel would be decided not in the air, but on the ground. The increase in flights and passengers and the growing weight and dimensions of commercial aircraft required new typological concepts both for the buildings and for the whole airfield, and it is with the latter that the next generation of airport construction concerned itself. The form and the surface of the airfield itself was analysed

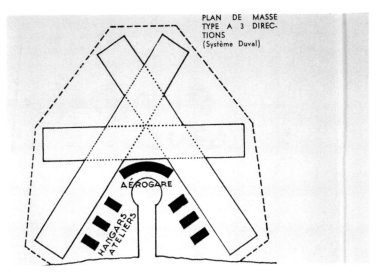

and it became clear that the airport needed a master plan.

Looking at the experts involved in planning, we can see a remarkable change taking place during the 1930s. The manifest complexity of the airport as a system encouraged the development of specialised architectural firms: Norman and Dawbarn in Britain, Ernst Sagebiel in Germany or Delano and Aldrich in the United States. If we look at the firms engaged in the same field at the end of the 20th century – Norman Foster in England, Helmut Jahn in the United States, Paul Andreu of Aéroports de Paris in France, von Gerkan, Marg und Partner in Germany – it is clear that the market for airport design has kept its centralised and specialist structure.

A serious problem in many airports, caused by the absence of forward-thinking planning at the outset, arose at the moment when the airport needed to expand. Many airports simply could not be enlarged because their edges had been cluttered up with hangars and other buildings. In 1929, the French engineer Duval developed a principle of a wedge-shaped building zone, which projected from the edge of the field towards its centre, so that 80 per cent of the periphery could remain unbuilt.[17] During the 1930s, this wedge scheme dominated many proposed developments. It was adopted, in 1931, at the airport of Bron, near Lyons, and in 1937 at Birmingham and Helsinki-Malmi, the last two of which are still in existence.

The heavier airliners of the 1930s, such as the Junkers 52 or the DC-3, were now causing damage to the grass flying fields, as their wheels and tail skids destroyed the turf. The days of the 'pastoral phase' of the airport, as Reyner Banham has called it,[18] were numbered. Paved aprons often small in size, which had been introduced to obtain a hard-surfaced area for loading and boarding the passengers, were enlarged. Take-off and landing strips with hard surfaces, as were already standard in the United States, now became inevitable in Europe. A compass shape, generally comprising four or more strips, was planned in order to exploit various wind directions, since the aircraft relied on wind strengths to a much greater degree than the jets of today. In 1935 the airport at Bromma near Stockholm was the first to be equipped in this way.

Various patterns of runways were studied in order to achieve a rational layout according to the different functions required of the airport. All kinds of geometrical figures were analysed in terms of their consumption of space, so as to minimise land use and expensive concrete surfacing. In Germany, the concept of the oval airfield was developed, a compromise between the grass field and the concrete airstrip, in order to reduce the cost of paving. Its axis was oriented in the direction of the predominating winds and its periphery was surrounded by a taxiway, on which the aircraft moved into the so-called 'start stumps' prior to take-off. In the 1930s, Tempelhof and the new airports at Munich and Frankfurt were equipped in this way.

The need to plan the airfield and its buildings as a coherent whole changed the attitudes of architects and planners. Public architectural competitions, intended to solicit a broad range of solutions for the next generation of airports, were held in Britain and the United States. The most spectacular of these initiatives was the Lehigh competition of 1928, organised by a cement company from Pennsylvania.[19] The prize-winning proposals were published all over the world and some of the ideas raised in the contributions left their mark on the airport buildings of the 1930s. The most

Top: A B Duval's design for a wedge-shaped airport, 1929 (L'Architecture d'Aujourd'hui, no. 9, 1936)

Stockholm-Bromma, paved airport runways, 1935 (Lufthansa Archive)

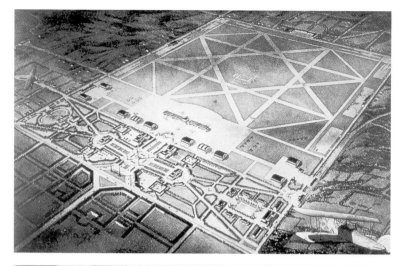

Top: *The Lehigh Airports Competition of 1929; Odd Nansen & Latham C Squire's entry, which won third prize (Lehigh Portland Cement Company 1930)*

Chicago O'Hare airport, proposed double-runway pattern, 1943 (from Froesch & Prokosch, 1946)

formal gardens are also obvious. The need to provide landing strips in different directions led the designers to produce formal solutions and ornamental conceptions in the shape of hexagons, stars, fans, blossoms, etc.

The Lehigh competition had an influential formal legacy. The ornamental airfield left its mark up to the 1950s, when the higher take-off thrust of the airliners, such as the Super-Constellation or the Douglas DC-7, reduced not only the dependence on wind directions, but also rendered obsolete the large number of runways at the airport. Some international airports, such as today's John F Kennedy Airport at New York or Chicago's O'Hare,[21] which were designed towards the end of the Second World War, still show fragments of their once ornamental layout, with numerous double runways for simultaneous take-offs and landings; Heathrow, similarly, still preserves its impressive hexagon, with the building zone located at the centre of the airfield.

Let us return now to the airport discussions of the early 1930s. By this time, at all the larger airports, the first-generation buildings could no longer meet functional requirements. The limits of the older type of terminal buildings rapidly became clear at the major airports. They now strongly resembled single-track railway stations, conceived for a plane to be prepared individually: it would come to a stop in front of the building, freight would be loaded and passengers would board and then the aircraft would taxi away for take-off. The distance the passengers had to cover to get to the aeroplane was short and safe at first, but, with the rise in traffic, this became less so, as more and more aircraft were parked simultaneously in front of the terminal. In 1936 there were already as many as ten take-offs and landings per hour at Tempelhof and Croydon at peak hours. To increase capacity and to save time, two options were available: either the airliners approached the terminal with their motors running, or they could be prepared next to each other in parallel positions.

For the first time the airport was conceived as a system with complex rules which became the subject of scientific research along Taylorist lines. According to the functionalist spirit of the age, it was subjected to the kinds of analysis that had been developed for industrial production and for housing. Diagrams of aircraft movements on the ground were drawn up, following the methods used for the study of kitchens and room

striking impression is the urbanistic view taken of the airport, with formal layouts which were still common in the United States, but out-dated in Europe, where the Modern Movement had not only fundamentally changed architecture, but also notions of town-planning. If we look, for example, at the winner of the third prize, we can see eight runways in four directions, two each for take-off and landing, all brought together in an octagonal figure, framed by the taxiways at the edges of the airfield. There is a building zone separated from this airfield, with a symmetrical system of streets and green areas, inspired by the Garden City Movement of the early 20th century.[20]

Ignoring here the functional quality of these schemes, we can see how the Lehigh designs opened up both artistic and urbanistic approaches quite unlike European designs, such as the merely functional airfield at Bromma. The aesthetic expressions are those of the Beaux-Arts school, which was still a leading influence in the United States at the time. The airport is seen as a sort of ideal city, with runways and taxiways representing a grid of streets. Analogies not only with the city, but also with

London-Croydon, a mobile
covered gallery in about
1930 (collection Wolfgang
Voigt)

systems in mass housing introduced in the 1920s by Alexander Klein. In 1930, the airport company at Berlin commissioned time and motion studies to determine how rationalisation could increase efficiency at Tempelhof.[22] And as early as 1928 various proposals, including the entries in the Lehigh and RIBA competitions, had made practical recommendations for more subtle systems for passenger movements. The aim was to untangle the confusion on the apron by creating two levels: passenger tunnels that led directly to the waiting airliners, or bridges leading down to aeroplanes waiting in parallel formation.

Some of these ideas feature in additions to existing buildings, such as the covered gallery at Los Angeles Airport in 1929, or at the new terminal building of Gatwick airport, near London, where in 1936 the idea was worked out into a rational system with flexible canopies, telescoping back and forth on rails. For the public, interestingly enough, all these solutions were propagated under the reassuring slogan of 'dry boarding'.[23] No mention was made of the fact that more was involved than shielding the flying elite from wind and rain: passengers also had to be protected from life-threatening contact with rotating propellers and moving aircraft.

Beehive and coat-hanger: Gatwick and Tempelhof, ancestors of the super-airport

The cantilevered designs of Birmingham airport (1939) and Tempelhof, sheltering the aircraft under a protective roof, derive from this debate, which also gave rise to the promising new concepts of piers, gates, and fingers, organising the 'Fordist' terminal, which now entered its industrialised phase. Terminals were becoming highly organised machines, laid out for mass air travel, and giving decentralised access to many airliners in parallel positions. Soon after the Second World War, Charles Froesch and Walther Prokosch published their manual *Airport Planning* based on these concepts. The conception of 'super-airports', with seventy-five to ninety aeroplane positions, took shape.[24]

Before the war, in 1936, an innovative and promising solution was demonstrated at the famous 'beehive' terminal at Gatwick airport near London. A pedestrian tunnel led from a specially created railway station to a circular building – designed by the architects Hoar, Marlow and Lovett – located in a corner of the airfield. The passengers left this terminal via gates and reached the aeroplane through the telescopic passageways that spread out like rays from the building. This system made it possible for six aircraft to load or unload simultaneously. Gatwick was criticised because its circular form made the future extension of the terminal impossible. Nonetheless, this unpretentious modern building, of exemplary functionality, was ahead of its time. Before airports had to deal with the problems of the new scales of the post-war period, Gatwick's form already provided a practical and economical answer to the organisational problems of large airports of the future. Critics of the 1930s did not imagine the possibility of creating several such beehive units, spread over a larger airport ensemble.

At the same time, and in a radically different approach, Berlin's famous Tempelhof II terminal was under construction (1936–9), a building of unprecedented size. The exceptional dimensions of this building, planned for six million passengers a year, are to be explained, however, not merely in terms of highly optimistic forecasts of traffic development and passenger movements. The terminal was to be the architectural gateway to the capital of the new authoritarian regime; its dimensions are an expression of the Reich's political ambitions. On the airside of Sagebiel's ensemble, the impressive curving façade, measuring 3,870ft (1,180m), is reminiscent of a coat-hanger when seen from the air, and shelters all the hangars under a single overhanging roof. At the centre of the composition, under the same roof, a zone 1,246ft (380m) long is for use by passengers and for the servicing of aircraft in preparation for flight. The American writer, John Walter Wood, who visited all the major European airports in 1939, did not find Tempelhof's scale excessive: 'Extremely large installations are

construction, this protective shelter was useful. The metal aircraft of the 1930s, however, were far less fragile and less in need of protection from the elements. But dry boarding was not the only aim pursued with this huge roof structure. As at Hamburg's Fuhlsbüttel airport, Tempelhof was also conceived as an 'air stadium', where rooftop spectators could admire air shows and acrobatic displays as well as military demonstrations by the Luftwaffe. Tempelhof's roofs were designed to accommodate 80,000 such spectators.

One of Tempelhof's less well-known features is its elegant airside elevation at the back of the boarding zone. For the first time, an airport terminal aligns numerous gates – twenty in all – corresponding with parking spaces for several waiting aircraft and enabling large numbers of passengers to embark or disembark simultaneously. Accentuating its horizontality, the continuous windows at the upper level of the building are punctuated by these gates, ten for departure and ten for arrival, each with a steel staircase leading down to the sheltered part of the apron and the waiting planes. The gates are placed at regular intervals, each one surmounted by a rectangular projecting window. These probably had no other function than to mark the gates visually and to give an overall rhythm to the façade.

For the history of civil aviation and aeronautical architecture, these two very different buildings at Tempelhof and at Gatwick represent monuments that we can appreciate today in their historical context. Although they did not serve as typological models as such, their functional characteristics make them the ancestors of post-war airport terminal design and of the principle of multiplying separate gates for ever-increasing numbers of air travellers.

Notes

1. As a contributor to the exhibition *Building for Air Travel* at the Art Institute of Chicago, I had the opportunity, during the mid-1990s, to do some research on the history of the architecture of European airports. Parts of the present text are adapted from my article in the catalogue of this exhibition: 'From the hippodrome to the aerodrome, from the air station to the terminal: European airports, 1909–1945', in Zukowsky J (ed), *Building for Air Travel. Architecture and Design for Commercial Aviation.* Munich and New York: Prestel/The Art

Top: *Birmingham (Elmdon), the terminal designed by Nigel Norman and Graham Dawbarn in 1938 (collection Wolfgang Voigt)*

Berlin-Tempelhof, gate and staircase under the canopy (photo Jürgen Hohmuth/ZeitOrt)

needed, since [...] the potential air traffic of the future is enormous.' Wood was critical, however, of the expense incurred in the construction of the roof: at Gatwick, 'dry boarding' had been achieved in a more practical and economical manner.

The roof at Tempelhof, supported by huge steel structures, protected not only the passengers but also the aircraft themselves that could park beneath the overhang. For the aircraft of the 1920s, of wood and fabric

Institute of Chicago, 1996, 26–49. This article gives references to the source material, which I shall not repeat here. For the period after 1945, see, in the same catalogue, the essay by Koos Bosma, 'European airports, 1945–1995: Typology, psychology, and infrastructure', 51–65. Another useful study of the subject is to be found in the older work by Alexander Wood Lockhart, 'Airport development and design: A new architectural problem'. Unpublished PhD thesis, North-Western University, 1972.

2 On the San-Niccolo airport, see the contemporary description published by John Walter Wood, *Airports. Some Elements of Design and Future Development*. New York: Coward-McCann Inc, 1940, 244–7. On the history of aviation architecture in Italy, see the rich documentation collated by Mariano Ranisi, *L'Architettura della Regia Aeronautica*. Rome: published by the historical office of the air force high command, 1991.

3 On the Reims-Bétheny meeting, see Robert Wohl, *A Passion for Wings. Aviation and the Western Imagination, 1908–1918*. New Haven and London, 1994, 100–10, and the recent publication by Stéphane Nicolaou, *Reims – 1909, Le premier meeting aérien international*. Paris: Musée de l'Air et de l'Espace/Addim, 1999.

4 On the air shows at Tempelhof and Johannisthal, see Werner Schwipps, *Riesenzigarren und fliegende Kisten. Bilder aus der Frühzeit der Luftfahrt in Berlin*. Berlin, 1984; Michael Hundertmark, 'Flugplatz Johannisthal – Wiege der deutschen Luftfahrt'. Museum für Verkehr und Technik (ed) *Hundert Jahre deutsche Luftfahrt. Lilienthal und seine Erben*. Berlin, 1991, 21–38.

5 See David van Zanten, 'Walter Burley Griffin's design for Canberra, the capital of Australia', in Zukowsky J (ed), *Chicago Architecture 1872–1922, Birth of a Metropolis*. Munich, 1988; on Agache's project, in particular, see pp 321, 332–3.

6 Vittorio Magnago Lampugnani (ed), *Antonio Sant'Elia. Gezeichnete Architektur*. Munich, 1992, 47, 180–2.

7 On the first international commercial flights, see Kenneth Hudson, *Air Travel, a Social History*. Bath, 1972, 62.

8 On the transformations at Le Bourget between 1921 and 1922, see Louise Faure-Favier, 'De Paris à Lausanne. Comment on inaugure une ligne aérienne'. *L'Illustration* (Paris), 19 November 1921, 462. On the history of Le Bourget, see Christelle Inizan and Bernard Rignault, 'Paris-Le Bourget'. *Années 30 Architecture des aéroports. Airport Architecture of the Thirties. Flughafenarchitektur der dreißiger Jahre. Berlin-Tempelhof, Liverpool-Speke, Paris-Le Bourget*. Paris: Editions du Patrimoine, 2000, 90–121, and the contributions by Bernard Rignault and Jean-Christophe Morisseau to this present publication, pp 73–82, 145–57.

9 On the buildings at Königsberg, and their architect, see Voigt, 'From the hippodrome', 33–4, and Gabriele Wiesemann, *Hanns Hopp 1890–1971. Königsberg, Dresden, Halle, Ost-Berlin. Eine biographische Studie zur modernen Architektur*. Schwerin, 2000, 65.

10 On the history of Tempelhof, see Helmut Conin, *Gelandet in Berlin. Zur Geschichte der Berliner Flughäfen*. Cologne, 1974; Frank Schmitz, *Flughafen Tempelhof. Berlins Tor zur Welt*, Berlin: be.bra verlag, 1997; Gabi Dolff-Bonekämper, 'Berlin-Tempelhof'. *Années 30 Architecture des aéroports*, 32–61; and the contributions by Manfred Hecker, Axel Drieschner, and Werner Jockeit and Cornelia Wendt to the present publication, pp 92–9, 100–111, 158–170.

11 On the first terminal at Tempelhof, see the analysis of the building's construction by Frank Schmitz, 'Das alte Hauptgebäude des Flughafens Tempelhof (1926–29)'. Unpublished thesis, Free University of Berlin, 1999.

12 On the construction of Fuhlsbüttel, see Wolfgang Voigt, *Vom Flugbahnhof zum Terminal. Flughafen Hamburg 1929–1999*. Sulgen (Switzerland), 1999.

13 At Tempelhof, by way of comparison, there were still only 113 passengers per day in 1928, a number which reached 678 in 1938. On the Hamburg statistics, see Werner Treibel, *Geschichte der deutschen Verkehrsflughäfen. Eine Dokumentation von 1909 bis 1989*. Bonn, 1992, 219; for Berlin, see Conin, *Gelandet in Berlin*, 350. These are average figures. On a busy day, however, during the summer months, the number of passengers passing through Tempelhof could reach 1,500, with 100 scheduled flights per day (figure given by Wood for the year 1939, *Airports*, 198).

14 For French companies, state subsidies represented between 60 and 80 per cent of turnover. See L Hirschauer, 'L'aviation commerciale en 1921'. *L'Illustration* (Paris), 10 September 1921, 219–21.

15 See Peter Fritzsche, *A Nation of Flyers. German Aviation and the Popular Imagination*. Cambridge (Massachussetts) and London, 1992.

16 See the report by John Dowers (secretary of the RIBA's Aerodromes Committee), 'Aerodromes'. *Journal of the Royal Institute of British Architects* (London), 30 April 1932, 501–17. A useful French overview of the debate is to

be found in a special issue of *L'Architecture d'Aujourd'hui* (Paris), no. 9, 1936.

17 A B Duval, 'Les Ports aériens'. *L'Illustration* (Paris), 17 August 1929, 155–8.

18 Reyner Banham, 'The obsolescent airport'. *The Architectural Review* (London), October 1962, 250–3.

19 See Lehigh Portland Cement Company (ed), *American Airport Designs*. Reprint of the 1930 edition, foreword by Dominick A Pisano, Washington DC, 1990. A German echo of this competition is to be found in H Gescheit and K Wittmann, *Neuzeitlicher Verkehrsbau*. Potsdam, 1931, 219–21, 236–40, 263–5 and 332–3.

20 Lehigh Portland Cement Company (ed), *American Airport Designs*, 18–19.

21 See the projects for Chicago's O'Hare airport and for Idlewild at New York in Charles Froesch and Walther Prokosch, *Airport Planning*. New York, 1946, 106 and 111.

22 Hans-Joachim Braun, 'The airport as symbol. Air transport and politics at Berlin-Tempelhof, 1923–1948', in Leary W M (ed), *From Airship to Airbus. The History of Civil and Commercial Aviation*, Vol 1. Washington and London, 1995, 45–53.

23 See L F Bouman, 'Droog Instappen'. *Het Vliegveld*, May 1933, 138–41.

24 See Froesch and Prokosch, *Airport Planning*, 107.

The evaluation of military aviation sites and structures in England

Jeremy Lake, Colin Dobinson and Paul Francis[1]

English Heritage's study of military aviation is the third, after barracks and naval dockyards up to 1914, in a series of thematic surveys that have been undertaken in consultation with the Ministry of Defence and other owners. This process of assessment has taken place against the background of English Heritage's work on 20th-century military sites, the aim of which has not only been to ensure adequate levels of record and protection, but also, at the same time, to broaden public understanding of the wider historic significance and educational potential of these sites.

Historical development

Military airfields have had an enormous impact on the landscape. There were 250 airfields and seaplane stations occupied by the Royal Air Force (RAF) in the summer of 1918, most of which were subsequently abandoned; nearly 100 airfields built in permanent fabric existed between 1923 and 1939, and the country's total of 150 expanded to 740 – mostly comprising temporary buildings and on dispersed sites – during the Second World War. In contrast to the combined hangar terminals associated with civil aviation of the 1930s, their planning demanded the integration of a wide range of requirements, from housing communities of flyers, technicians, administrators and their families to accommodating the functions of a technology-based service. The transition of air power from observation to offensive capability in only a decade – from when the Wright brothers had listed Japan, America and the European great powers as potential customers in 1906 to the first metal planes and strategic bomber forces at the end of the First World War – both mirrored the extraordinarily rapid growth of aviation technology and provided a graphic and alarming reminder of its potential. In the inter-war period, there was a growing realisation that, despite an awareness of the liberating and even peacemaking potential of air technology, air power had immeasurably increased the vulnerability of

civilians well away from the battle zone. The philosophy of offensive deterrence, which had its origins in the closing stages of the First World War, guided the policy of the Allied air forces in the Second World War, and formed the basis of the nuclear-based deterrence of the Cold War period. Although the image in the mind's eye of the mass destruction of civilian populations challenges our very notion of heritage, it is worth noting that the protection of historic buildings through listing was, indeed, propelled into reality (by the Town and Country Planning Act of 1944) out of a heightened awareness of the potential destruction of a nation's culture which aerial bombing brought in its wake, the need to identify what could be saved and the awareness of the opportunities presented to architects and planners by the tabula rasa of devastated city centres.[2]

Air power had been initially conceived as an adjunct of the army and navy, and the first military airfields (from 1912) were built for the army at Farnborough in 1905, around Salisbury Plain (at Upavon) and for the navy at Eastchurch on the Kent coast. Under R B Haldane, whose tenure of office as Secretary of State for War between 1906 and 1911 witnessed the triumph of the technology-based *matériel* school of warfare, aviation was placed at the heart of naval operations and a small Expeditionary Force. Popular enthusiasm for this new technology, and especially for private manufacturers, was greatly encouraged by the press (especially *The Daily Mail*) and found its voice in the Aero Club, the Aeronautical Society and specialist journals such as *Flight* (1909) and *The Aeroplane* (1911).

The training aerodromes at Larkhill on Salisbury Plain and Eastchurch in Kent, where hangars have survived, exemplified this fusion of government and popular interest in aviation's formative period. At Larkhill, for example, the British and Colonial Aeroplane Company established the first of a series of civilian schools where army officers received their initial flight training. A measure of the site's importance

Top: *The 1910 hangars at Larkhill, probably the earliest surviving aircraft hangars in Europe (photo Jeremy Lake)*

The officers' mess of 1913 at Netheravon (photo Jeremy Lake)

was that 53 of the 109 pilots who qualified in 1911 were Bristol-trained and flying schools on the Bristol pattern were established in Spain, Germany and Italy in 1912.[3] The creation of the Royal Flying Corps, in April 1912, was marked by the formation of a Central Flying School at nearby Upavon, followed by the selection of Netheravon – planned from the outset with a strict separation between technical and domestic sites – as the first new squadron station selected and developed by their Military Wing. In this early period the War Office issued specifications for building types, against which contractors submitted tenders, the aim being to achieve a degree of standardisation. Fragments of the technical site at Netheravon have survived, leaving its domestic site as the most remarkable early example in Britain from the entire period up to November 1918. The remaining key sites associated with army flying before August 1914 are Farnborough and Montrose in Scotland, built to provide air cover for the naval stations at Rosyth and Cromarty and where a uniquely well-preserved group of hangars have survived.

Air stations witnessed a major expansion and impact on the British landscape in the First World War. This period saw the completion of coastal stations for the Royal

Naval Air Service (founded in July 1914) and Home Defence Stations for the Royal Flying Corps, both underway from 1912 and the latter integrated by the end of the war into a complex infrastructure linked to searchlight and anti-aircraft gun provision. Air station planning became highly standardised and marked by a strict separation between domestic and technical sites. By 1918, standardised type designs for every aspect of airfield operations and life proliferated, from bomb-storage, synthetic training, motor transport and storage to accommodation for every rank, recreational facilities, cinemas and barber shops, all reflective of the divisions of functions and hierarchies within these sites.

When the RAF was formed as the world's first independent air force in April 1918, and during the period of retrenchment that lasted from the Armistice until the early 1920s, its founding father and first Chief of Air Staff, General Sir Hugh Trenchard, concentrated upon developing its strategic role as an offensive bomber force. Trenchard's expansion of the air force, given Parliament's blessing in 1923, was centred upon the building of offensive bomber stations in East Anglia and Oxfordshire, behind an 'aircraft fighting zone' some 15 miles (24 kilometres) deep and extending round London from Duxford in Cambridgeshire to Salisbury Plain. This principle of offensive deterrence, although subject to fluctuations which reflected events on the world stage and varying degrees of political support, continued to guide the siting and layout of stations after 1933, when Hitler's rise to power and the collapse of the Geneva disarmament talks forced the British government to engage in a massive programme of rearmament. The continuing development of existing stations (some dating from the First World War) and the building of new stations was thus concentrated on the establishment of training and maintenance stations behind a fighter belt and an eastern front line of bomber stations – extending from Yorkshire to East Anglia – facing Germany.

The choice of the Modernist style as a means of 'underlining the modernity and progressiveness' of the air stations[4] of newly independent Finland serves as a reminder of how the consideration of architectural style needs to be placed against its broader historical context. In Britain, the marked improvement in the quality of buildings designed after 1932 and associated with the post-1934 expansion of the RAF provided a direct response to public concerns over the issues of rearmament and the pace of environmental change. The design and planning of Trenchard's stations – which for the first time integrated the principle of dispersal against air attack – owed much to the army background of the designers who worked from the office of the Air Ministry's Directorate of Works and Buildings (DWB). The DWB had already come in for stringent criticism over its conservative handling of Croydon airport (1928), and it was in the context of popular resistance to rearmament and the pace of environmental change that Ramsey McDonald, as Prime Minister, had instructed that the newly established Royal Fine Arts Commission (RFAC) be involved in air station design. A process of consultation with the Air Ministry was initiated with visits by commissioners – three distinguished architects (Sir Edwin Lutyens, Sir Reginald Blomfield and Giles Gilbert Scott) and the planning authority Professor S D Adshead – to Upper Heyford and Abingdon in November 1931. Despite the obvious clash of cultures that ensued, particularly over the dispersed layout which the Air Ministry stressed was an essential component in airfield design, there is no doubt that the period of mutual consultation following the submission of the summary report in February 1932 resulted in improvements to individual and standard designs between 1932 and 1934. This can be observed not only in the individually varied administration, mess and barracks buildings at Cadet College Cranwell, the seaplane station at Lee-on-Solent and Henlow, all stations with unique functions, but also in some of the standard designs produced by DWB in this period.

The ratification of the first phase of post-1933 expansion, in June 1934, resulted in renewal of collaboration between DWB and the RFAC, resulting in the creation of the new post of architectural advisor to the Directorate of Works and Buildings, first occupied by A Bulloch. Lutyens was deputed by the RFAC to liaise over layout and other matters, although the exact extent of his involvement remains unclear.[5] The impact of new airfields on the environment had also concerned another newly founded environmental group, the Council for the Preservation of Rural England (CPRE), who invited the Air Ministry to consult its local advisory panels. The chair of the Wiltshire panel of the CPRE had been invited to present their views on the planning of a new

Flight Training School at Hullavington near Chippenham, where all the buildings were faced in local limestone.[6] The site also, as the other Scheme A stations where the results of RFAC consultation were most immediately felt, displays a skilful reconciliation between operational and aesthetic requirements in the placing, for example, of the station headquarters as the focal point at the site entrance, with the barracks square to the rear, extending to the water tower on the same axis with the entrance and the hangars with their accompanying stores and other technical buildings. The married quarters for officers, warrant officers, sergeants and airmen manifested a notable departure from earlier married quarters designs, with separate living rooms and kitchens. A clear stylistic distinction was made in all stations of the 1930s Expansion Period between neo-Georgian for domestic buildings, exhibited most dramatically in the officers' mess designs by Bulloch and his successor P M Stratton, and a more modern horizontal emphasis for technical buildings. From 1938, new buildings and stations made increasing use of concrete and flat roofs in order to counter the effects of incendiary bombs and minimise bomb damage. The decontamination centres which appeared on stations from 1937, and which, with their encircling blast walls, bore a superficial resemblance to new designs for operations blocks, were designed and built with the fear of gas attack in mind.[7]

During the Second World War, new airfields were constructed for a variety of purposes, from the fighter stations built in England's south-west peninsula in reaction to the German occupation of France, to the Advanced Landing Grounds which provided tactical support in the period preceding and after D-Day and, the most substantial in terms of cost and environmental impact, those built in support of Bomber Command and later United States Army Air Force (USAAF) operations. From 1940, with the completion of the last of the eighteen permanent stations underway, the Air Ministry had been forced to abandon its dislike of temporary hutting. In September 1940 the Air Ministry took Trenchard's principle of dispersal to its extreme in a ruling that the technical and domestic sites of all new airfields should be laid out in dispersed 'clutches'.[8] As a consequence, and in contrast to the grass airfields, permanent structures and tightly defined sites characteristic of the inter-war period, the temporary structures of wartime airfields are spread across many square miles of land, in line with a policy to disperse all station facilities well away from the airfield and each other.

Hangars and the flying field

The key developments of the Second World War serve as a reminder that the character and development of the flying field, and its relationship to the hangar apron, is fundamental to an understanding of military aviation's infrastructure. Until the late 1930s, hangars, built for the shelter of aircraft and repair personnel, directly mirrored both aircraft technology and the complement of aircraft accommodated on any one station. In March 1916, for example, it was decided to increase the number of aircraft in a squadron from twelve to eighteen, which led to a complete change in shed design and the adoption of the Anderson Belfast truss, which the company had been advertising since 1914 in *Flight* magazine. The dimensions of the steel-framed A-type shed, the standard hangar type for Trenchard's Home Defence Expansion Scheme designed in 1924, were based on the need to accommodate the RAF's largest projected twin-engined bomber, the De Haviland DH9A.

The adoption – as protection against an enemy 'knock-out blow' – of perimeter 'dispersal', executed for the first time in the Aircraft Storage Units (ASUs) that were built from 1936 for the storage of essential reserve aircraft, broke the relationship between aircraft and hangar planning. Hangars on ASUs were grouped in pairs around the perimeter of the flying field, and designed as low parabolic vaults. In their clear relationship to developments in France and Germany, for example, in the adoption of the Junkers *Lamellendach* design,[9] they comprise the most advanced examples of engineering construction designed by the Air Ministry. The increasingly widespread adoption of dispersal meant that the standard designs for hangars from this period ceased to relate in such a direct manner to aircraft technology.[10] This stood in contrast to the planning of the flying field, which had witnessed an average increase in size as engine technology progressed.[11] The development of radio communication, and the increasing need to organise the flying field into different zones for take-off, landing and taxiing, brought with it an acceptance that movement on the airfield needed to be

controlled from a single centre: control towers thus evolved from the simple duty pilot's watch office to the tower design of 1934 and integration of traffic control and weather monitoring in the Art Deco horizontality of the Watch Office with Meteorological Section of 1939.[12]

The ability of airfields to disperse and shelter aircraft from attack and ensure serviceable landing and take-off areas was first adopted in 1939 by the RAF for its most essential fighter sector airfields, whose perimeters were provided with fighter pens for parked aircraft. Climate[13] and operational disruption were the principal factors that had inhibited the construction of concrete runways until the Second World War, the deployment of four-engined bombers and the intensity of the bomber offensive of 1942–5 underpinning the remodelling and construction of airfields with concrete runways. During the Second World War, prefabricated surfaces of wire mesh (Sommerfeld Track, Square Mesh Track) and steel plank (Pierced Steel Plank, the most popular choice of surface) enabled rapid runway provision.[14]

The assessment of significance

It is considered that, in view of the character, great number and diversity of military airfields, the identification of the most complete, historically important and strongly representative sites will constitute the most effective and historically valid method of protecting standardised building types which are otherwise well-represented in other, more altered or less significant, contexts. The assessment of groups and individual structures outside these key sites rests on their intrinsic historical or architectural importance. Where there is a role for statutory protection, the form of protection selected is designed to encourage the type of management that will best ensure the site or structure's long-term future. Scheduling is used where the future of sites as monuments is the preferred option; listing where continuing or new use of built structures is both desirable and feasible. Airfield buildings are structures that fall most easily within the framework for listing, whereas the earthworks and pillboxes – both concrete and hydraulic – associated with airfield defence in the Second World War can be most suitably managed as monuments through the scheduling legislation. In recommending sites for scheduling or buildings for listing our role is advisory, and each recommendation we make to the Department for Culture, Media and Sport must be compelling and demonstrate the site's national importance (in the case of scheduling) or the structure's special interest (in the case of listing). Sites of this nature also demand specialist input into the drafting of guidelines for management,[15] which will significantly reduce areas of uncertainty relating to crucial issues of maintenance and adaptation: these are being piloted on one site (Bicester), in partnership with the local authority and the Ministry of Defence. As we shall see, in some cases it is not so much individual structures that are important, but the landscape of which they are a part. Here, Conservation Area designation can have a significant role, especially when built into a conservation strategy within local plans, thus acting to maintain the character of extensive monuments or the areas in which they lie.

The assessment of airfields and other military sites by English Heritage has thus increasingly come to reflect a unified approach to management, designation and recording. A thorough statistical analysis of what has survived, comparison with original populations and a critical analysis of importance or otherwise in a typological and national context, has been compiled by Paul Francis, author of *British Military Airfield Architecture* (1996) and the acknowledged national expert on the subject. Colin Dobinson has undertaken archival research, exploring certain themes relating to airfield planning and architecture, particularly from 1923: this study, entitled *Airfield Themes,* has been circulated as one volume of the *Twentieth Century Fortifications in England* series, otherwise commissioned by the Monuments Protection Programme (MPP) as a key element in its evaluation of defence sites of this period.[16] This has enabled us to gain a fresh overview of the subject at a strategic level and understand the rationale and forces which determined the typology, distribution and development of military sites. Dobinson's report on airfield defences was published as a volume in this series, and the MPP assessment of the pillboxes, battle headquarters and fighter pens associated with airfield defence has also been based on material drawn together by Paul Francis.

It is clearly important to identify a range of sites which, as a consequence of events on the world stage, military imperatives or varying degrees of public and political support, reflect the development of military aviation from 1910 to 1945. The eligibility of military aviation buildings for listing, indeed, depends less on intrinsic architectural merit (which is rare), than their rarity (in the case of the period up to 1918), completeness, historical importance and their inclusion within outstanding groups. This makes the following *desiderata,* in addition to the degree of completeness of individual buildings or groups, of critical importance to an evaluation of the relative significance of buildings and sites:

- rarity and the degree of survival
- architectural importance
- the relationship of built fabric to the flying field, its character and development
- international context
- identification of individual structures and sites with key campaigns of the Second World War, namely the Battle of Britain, the Strategic Bomber Offensive and the Battle of the Atlantic.

The consideration of rarity and completeness in a national context is a fundamental criterion. The vast majority of buildings erected in the period 1914 to 1918 – of temporary materials designed to last for the duration of the conflict – were either cleared after 1919 or have since decayed. Attention is consequently drawn to complete aircraft hangars (individual examples only surviving on eight sites) and especially the principal hangar groups, of which seven (Calshot, Duxford, Henlow, Hooton Park, Lee-on-Solent, Old Sarum and Yatesbury) survive in England, and one (Montrose) in Scotland. These exemplify their aviation use more clearly through their plan and form than isolated survivals of domestic or technical buildings; the latter have generally only been recommended where they relate to these groups. The available evidence indicates that unaltered pre-1918 survivals are of extreme rarity in an international context. No hangar or other buildings, for example, are known to have survived in Germany from the period before 1914, with the notable exception of Schleissheim, sited just to the north of Munich and established in 1912 as the station of the Royal Bavarian Flying Corps.[17] In this context, the survival of hangars dated 1910 at Eastchurch and Larkhill is especially important, even more remarkable being the good survival of structures at nearby Netheravon and Upavon

The hangars of 1918 and associated workshops and technical buildings at Duxford, now managed by the Imperial War Museum, comprise the best-preserved groups in Britain (photo Mike Williams)

which make the Salisbury Plain area the cradle of British aviation and these sites of outstanding importance in an international context, joined in the course of the 1914–18 conflict by two other significant surviving sites at Yatesbury and Old Sarum.

Inter-war air stations have survived in a far better state of preservation than those of the 1914–18 and 1939–45 conflicts. They comprised the bulk of those stations retained for use by the RAF and USAAF after 1945, and the completeness or otherwise of inter-war stations is closely linked to the nature and intensity of post-war use. Upper Heyford, for example, which was the test bed for the planning of Trenchard's Home Defence Scheme stations, was greatly extended and adapted as a key USAAF site in the Cold War period. Less intensive use – at present for administration, storage and glider training – has ensured that Bicester is the most complete group representative of developments on bomber airfields for the period up to 1939. It retains, better than any other military air station in Britain, the layout and fabric relating to the development of Britain's strategic bomber force in the period between 1923 and 1939. The grass flying field still survives with its 1939 boundaries largely intact, bounded by a group of bomb stores built in 1938–9 and airfield defences built in the early stages of the Second World War. Hullavington in Wiltshire, faced in Cotswold stone further to representations by the Council for the Protection of Rural England, is in every respect the key station representative of the improved architectural quality of post-1934 expansion. Duxford in Cambridgeshire survives as the most outstanding multi-period site and fighter station in Britain, with

buildings of both inter-war expansion periods added to a uniquely well-preserved suite of hangars and technical buildings of 1918. Of the twenty-four Aircraft Storage Units built by the Air Ministry up to 1941, Kemble in Gloucestershire survives as the site with the greatest cross-section of these important hangar types.

The fragmentary survival of Second World War sites, which hold very limited potential for conservation, can be regarded as part of the archaeology of transient settlement, such as contemporary prisoner of war (POW) camps, Napoleonic militia camps and the labour camps associated with the railway construction programmes of the previous century.[18] Many surviving groups are now in agricultural use, with consequent adaptations, and others are in an advanced state of decay, leaving only the remains of runway strips and ruinous control towers. Those currently in good repair are likely to be so only through extensive modification, and little consistency of treatment has been found in the post-war treatment of those belonging to any one station: none have retained its full complement of technical and domestic buildings.

An examination of the inter-relationship of hangar buildings, aircraft technology and airfields – similar to the relationship between a mill building and its associated weaving sheds and workshops – is also fundamental to a proper understanding of the dynamics that underpinned military airfield planning. Old Sarum in Wiltshire, now designated as a conservation area, is the only survival in Britain where hangar buildings relate to an airfield characteristic of the period up to 1918, and the grass flying field at Bicester uniquely relates to the

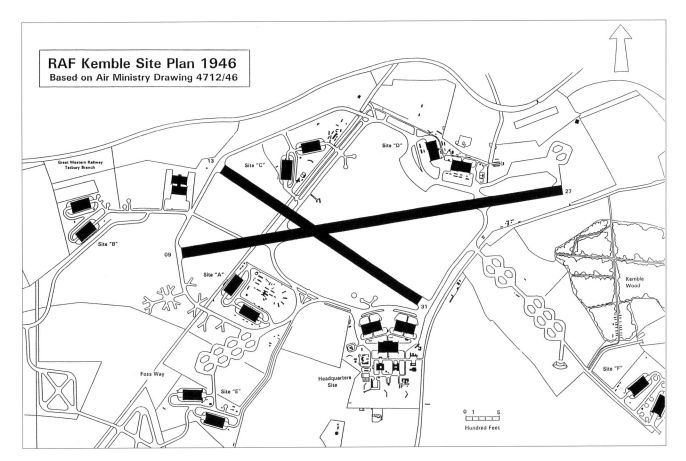

best-preserved bomber station representative of both phases of inter-war expansion. Of the key sector stations remodelled for Fighter Command in 1939–40, Kenley survives as a uniquely complete landscape. It is now largely used for amenity purposes and under consideration as a conservation area, and the uniquely complete survival of Dunkes- well in Devon as a landscape characteristic of Second World War airfields in relationship to hangars, control tower group and operations block has served to underpin their recommendation for listing and the consideration of the site as a conservation area.

Certain buildings and sites have strong associations with key historical developments and episodes of the Second World War. The uniquely well-preserved group of seaplane hangars at Calshot in Hampshire stand on the only site dating from the First World War whose built fabric can be associated with air defence, specifically with anti-submarine activity in this case. During the Second World War Britain's entire layout of military airfields was involved in the war effort, there also being a diverse range of nationalities associated with these sites. Fifteen per cent of Fighter Command's strength in the Battle of Britain came from overseas pilots, Czechs and Poles making up the largest European element, and training units such as Bicester took in many thousands from overseas. Some sites, however, can be more readily associated with key military episodes than others.

The Battle of Britain involved a limited number of sites, mostly concentrated in 11 Group in the South-East which took the brunt of the Luftwaffe attack: significant building groups have survived at Biggin Hill (designated as a conservation area in 1993) and Northolt, an airfield landscape at Kenley and the command bunker at RAF Uxbridge, preserved exactly as it was described by Churchill in 1940.[19] Duxford's distinguished wartime associations related to its role as a sector station in 12 Group to the north and a USAAF fighter station in support of the daylight bomber offensive. These stations continued to play a key role in air defence and activities over occupied Europe during the conflict; West Malling, for example, being the only site identified in this survey which played a key role in Operation Diver's

Kemble, by virtue of its range of five different hangar types including structurally advanced ones of parabolic form, is the most strongly representative of the twenty-four Aircraft Storage Units planned and built by the Air Ministry for vital reserve aircraft in the period 1936 to1940 (photo Jeremy Lake; plan drawn by Paul Francis, reproduced with his kind permission)

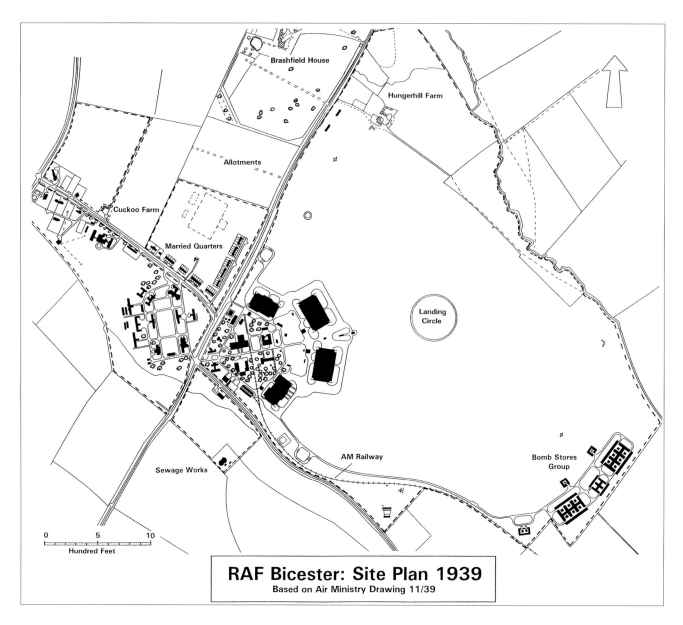

RAF Bicester: Site Plan 1939
Based on Air Ministry Drawing 11/39

This 1939 plan of Bicester clearly shows the functional division of airbases into domestic, technical and airfield sites. The entire area, including the former married quarters to the east, is now designated as a conservation area (drawn by Paul Francis, reproduced with his kind permission)

defence against the V-1 flying bomb from 1944. The decisive role of air power in the Battle of the Atlantic finds reflection in three important English sites (Calshot, Dunkeswell and Hooton Park, in addition to the single seaplane hangar surviving at Mount Batten) buttressed by two in Wales and one in Northern Ireland. In contrast, the strategic bomber offensive was longer, less focused, and involved a much larger number of stations, mostly 1930s Expansion Period stock, plus many wartime temporary airfields. Scampton's association with 617 Squadron's raid on the Ruhr dams in 1943 is an exception to the general rule that the scale and diffused nature of the bombing campaign does not warrant a special historical distinction to be applied to specific sites, in contrast to the Battle of Britain's involvement of a relatively small number of airfields. There is a case for the statutory protection of control towers on Second World War airfields with distinguished operational histories, both as their operational

nerve centres and as memorials to the enormous losses sustained by American and Commonwealth forces in the course of the Strategic Bomber Offensive.

Conclusion

At present, thirty-one buildings on military airfield sites are listed at Grade II; six items are already listed at Grade II★, five of these (at Calshot and Yatesbury) resulting from research conducted for this project and one (The Wind Tunnel at Farnborough) being sited on a military site which was evaluated in 1996. As a result of the thematic study, more than 300 buildings have been recommended for protection through listing (including six to be upgraded to II★) on thirty-nine sites and recommendations for upgrading and the revision of existing listings have been made on a further eleven sites. The site-based approach, where the full range of means for protection are brought to bear on those sites judged to be

of the first importance, represents a radical departure from the original, and largely typologically based, list of 145 recommendations made to Listing Team in a report of 1994,[20] and fewer listings on fewer sites will be the undoubted result of this approach. It thus has to be accepted that many building types cannot achieve the statutory protection that more locally based surveys would recommend. Awareness of the educational potential and wider historic significance of airfield sites, including those not recommended for protection, must instead rest upon the body of research and publication which this thematic survey has generated. Critically, this body of research – which will result in the production of CD Roms in addition to a major book on the subject by Colin Dobinson (*Building for Air Power. Britain's Military Airfields, 1905–1945*) – will also provide a framework for assessment against which all future proposals for reuse and development can be placed.

List of key sites

The following list represents the military aviation sites from the pre-1945 period in England which retain the best-preserved airfield landscapes and/or most historically significant groups of original buildings.

Bicester, Oxfordshire[21]
Bicester was built as a bomber station from 1924. It retains, better than any other aviation site in Britain, the layout and built fabric relating to both the first Expansion Period of the RAF and subsequent developments up to 1940. The grass airfield survives with airfield defences, bomb stores, perimeter track and some hardstandings added during the Second World War.

Biggin Hill, London Borough of Bromley
Britain's most celebrated fighter station. It retains a particularly fine officers' mess of 1934 and a good group of technical and domestic buildings (mostly 1930–4). The latter include the best-preserved married quarters group associated with a nationally important site. The flying field, with later runways, retains defence posts and fighter pens from 1939.

Calshot, Hampshire
Opened in 1913, Calshot is the best preserved of a chain of contemporary seaplane bases. The surviving group of hangars of 1913–18, now listed II⋆, exemplify the

development of military aviation during this period in Britain.

Catterick, North Yorkshire
Originating as a Home Defence Station in 1914, Catterick is the best-preserved fighter sector station in the north of England. It retains a group of First World War hangars and Expansion Period buildings dating from the 1920s and 1930s. Fighter pens and defences were added around the airfield at the beginning of the Second World War.

Cranwell, Lincolnshire
The development of the Cadet College at Cranwell, begun in 1929, was a cornerstone of Britain's independent airforce. College Hall (1929–33) and its formal setting form the most architecturally impressive set piece designed for the RAF. Although best known for the Cadet College, Cranwell has in addition a long aviation history dating back to 1918.

Debden, Essex
Opened as a fighter station in 1937, Debden retains much of its 1930s character. It is also noted for the largely intact preservation of its flying field and defensive perimeter. Its

The seaplane hangars at Calshot date from between 1913 and 1917, and range from a small wooden-framed hangar for the housing of early flying boats (Sopwith Bat Boats) to this immense range of steel hangars built in 1917 for housing Felixstowe F5 flying boats. The group exemplifies the remarkable development in aero engine and aircraft technology in this period better than any other site in Britain, and is now used as an Outward Bound Adventure Centre (photos Mike Williams)

The officers' mess at Biggin Hill, one of a small number of uniquely-designed mess buildings and built to Bulloch's plans in 1935. As one of the sector stations in 11 Group during the Battle of Britain, Biggin Hill occupied a pivotal role in the air defence of south-eastern England. Few buildings have been demolished on the technical site since 1945 (photo English Heritage)

historical importance largely resides in its role as one of the essential 11 Group sector stations during the Battle of Britain.

Dunkeswell, Devon
This is the best preserved of all the sites in the west of Britain associated with the strategically critical Battle of the Atlantic. Begun in 1941, the US Navy Fleet Air Wing was based here from 1942 until 1945. Dunkeswell exemplifies the highly dispersed planning and temporary fabric of contemporary airfields. Among the surviving original buildings are the operations block and control tower.

Duxford, Cambridgeshire[22]
A famous fighter station noted for its Battle of Britain associations and later used as a USAAF fighter station. It retains the best-preserved technical fabric remaining from a site up to November 1918, including three paired hangars. The station was mostly rebuilt in the 1930s, with architecture representative of both expansion periods remarkably well preserved, and the airfield largely intact.

Farnborough, Hampshire
Farnborough is one of the key sites in Europe relating to the development of aviation technology and aeronautical research. Originating as the base for the Royal Engineers' School of Ballooning in 1906 and the Royal Engineers' Air Battalion from 1911, the site was later occupied by the Royal Aircraft Establishment. It closed as a military research establishment in 1999. Although much altered, the site retains a small number of historically significant buildings including two wind tunnels of 1934–45 and 1939–42.

Halton, Buckinghamshire
Halton was established as the centre for technical training for the Royal Flying Corps in 1917. After the First World War the site was developed to house the Aircraft Apprentice Scheme. The domestic site retains an extensive and well-preserved group of buildings from the 1920s and 1930s including the Groves and Henderson Barracks.

Henlow, Bedfordshire
The five General Service Sheds at Henlow comprise the most complete ensemble of hangar buildings on any British site for the period up to 1923. The domestic site retains an extensive group of married quarters, executed in the Garden City tradition, and barracks and office buildings dated 1933–5. These display unique architectural treatment for a military air base.

Hullavington, Wiltshire
Hullavington, which opened in 1937 as a Flying Training Station, embodies to a unique degree the improved architectural quality associated with the post-1934 Expansion Period of the RAF. Most of the original buildings have survived and form a particularly coherent and well-ordered ensemble. The flying field remains, bounded by groups of hangars.

Kenley, Greater London/Surrey
One of the key sector stations famous for its associations with the Battle of Britain. Although most of the original buildings have gone, the officers' mess and institute buildings survive. These relate to a uniquely well-preserved airfield completed at the beginning of the Second World War, with runways, fighter pens and perimeter tracks.

Kemble, Gloucestershire/Wiltshire
Kemble is the most strongly representative – by virtue of its range of hangar types – of twenty-four Aircraft Storage Unit sites planned and built by the Air Ministry between 1936 and 1940. The hangars are dispersed in pairs around the airfield and include the most advanced Air Ministry hangar types of parabolic form and concrete construction.

Lee-on-Solent, Hampshire
(HMS Daedalus)
The best-preserved seaplane base in Britain, with three seaplane sheds of 1918 grouped around the original slipway. A major

rebuilding took place after 1931 including the addition of a particularly fine officers' mess of 1934.

Manby, Lincolnshire
After Hullavington, the most complete and architecturally unified of the post-1934 Expansion Period stations in Britain. Both the technical and domestic buildings show a meticulous attention to layout and detail. The airfield is now in agricultural use.

Netheravon, Wiltshire[23]
Begun in 1912, Netheravon is the most complete of the sites that relate to the crucial formative phase in the development of military aviation in Europe, prior to the First World War. The domestic site retains a remarkably well-preserved group of single-storey barracks and mess buildings dating 1913–14. The grass airfield remains intact.

Northolt, Greater London
Northolt was one of the 11 Group sector stations that played a significant operational role in the Battle of Britain. Although parts of the site have been subject to post-war redevelopment, most of the original buildings of the 1920s and 1930s survive. Among these are the officers' mess, four barracks blocks, two hangars, the station workshops and the operations room. A fine memorial commemorates the contribution of Polish airmen to the Allied war effort.

North Luffenham, Rutland
Opened in 1940, North Luffenham is representative of the bomber bases built under Scheme M, retaining two J-type hangars as well as a coherent group of contemporary technical and domestic buildings. The runways, perimeter tracks and dispersals were added in 1944 and are one of the most complete landscapes of that period. The site was adapted in the Cold War period as a Thor IBM Headquarters with facilities for two Mark 1 Bloodhound squadrons.

North Weald, Essex
North Weald was a fighter sector station with Battle of Britain associations, and after Kenley and Debden it retains the best preserved of the landscapes put in place by Fighter Command at the beginning of the Second World War.

Old Sarum, Wiltshire
The best-preserved flying field of the First World War period, bounded by one of the most complete suites of technical and hangar buildings of the period.

Scampton, Lincolnshire
Opened in 1936 as a bomber station, Scampton's association with the Dambuster Raids make it Bomber Command's most famous base of the Second World War. It also played an important role in the Strategic Bomber Offensive and the daylight raids in support of the Allied offensive in Europe. It continued to evolve as a landscape for the projection of deterrent power against the Soviet Union in the Cold War period.

Upavon, Wiltshire
Founded in 1912 as the Royal Flying Corp's Central Flying School, Upavon comprises one of three sites around the Army training ground at Salisbury Plain which relate to the crucial formative phase in the development of military aviation in Europe, prior to the First World War. Several buildings of the 1913–14 period survive here among later development.

Uxbridge, Greater London
This site was developed as a major armaments training school at the end of the First World War and then as a recruit-training centre for the RAF in the 1920s. An impressive cinema building, barracks and other structures survive from this period. The site was developed in the grounds of Hillingdon House, which still stands. The underground bunker of 1938 contains the Group Operations Room from where the key 11 Fighter Group was commanded during the Battle of Britain.

West Malling, Kent
A barracks square, officers' mess and control tower survive at one of the RAF's key front-line fighter stations. Opened in 1940 it has a long and distinguished wartime record.

Wroughton, Wiltshire
Opened in 1940, and after Kemble the best example of a landscape built as one of the Air Ministry's twenty-four Aircraft Storage Unit sites, with hangar types of parabolic form and concrete construction dispersed in groups around the flying field. No recommendations for protection.

Notes

1 This paper was drafted by Jeremy Lake, building on the results of research undertaken by Paul Francis and Colin Dobinson. See J Lake 'Thematic survey of military aviation sites and structures'. Unpublished report for English Heritage Thematic Listing Programme, 2000. Other works of reference on this subject include Hollis, B and Willis S *Military Airfields in the British Isles, 1939–1945*. Newport Pagnell, Enthusiasts Publications, 1987, and D Edgerton, *England and the Aeroplane. An Essay on a Militant and Technological Nation*. London: Macmillan, 1991.

2 A Saint 'How listing happened', in Hunter, M (ed), *Preserving the Past*. London: Routledge, 1996, 115–34.

3 N South Parker 'Aviation in Wiltshire'. *South Wiltshire Industrial Archaeology Society Monograph* **5** (1982).

4 A Makinen 'Hygiene, technology and economy: The 1930s architecture of the Finnish defence forces'. *Docomomo Conference Proceedings*. Barcelona: Docomomo, 1994, 135–40.

5 Colin Dobinson 'Airfield themes'. Unpublished report for English Heritage Thematic Listing Programme, 1997, 136–8.

6 Colin Dobinson 'Airfield themes', 142.

7 Paul Francis *British Military Airfield Architecture, From Airships to the Jet Age*. Sparkford: Patrick Stephens, 1996, 186–93.

8 Colin Dobinson '*Airfield Themes*', 198.

9 J S Allen 'A short history of "Lamella" roof construction'. *Transactions of the Newcomen Society* **71** (1999), 1–29.

10 Great quantities of portable hangars, mass-produced with interchangeable parts permitting rapid erection and dismantling, were produced from the late 1930s. The Hinaidi shed of 1927 was designed for quick assembly overseas (thirty-eight examples were built in Britain). In 1936, its designer, the DWB's N S Bellman, conceived a hangar constructed on a unit system of lattice steel girders of which 400 examples were built. In total, 906 examples of 'Type T' hangars, designed by the DWB in collaboration with the Teesside Bridge and Engineering Company, were built on RAF stations at home and abroad from 1940. Hundreds of arched sheds, called Blister hangars, were also built on airfield dispersal points during the war years. Robins Hangars, distinguished by their pitched roofs, were chiefly built on the dispersals of Aircraft Storage Units and Satellite Landing Grounds.

11 A survey of Lincolnshire airfields established that whereas the average size of airfields in the 1914 to 1918 period was 167 acres (67ha), this had increased during the 1930s to 400 acres (162ha) and by 1945 to 640 acres (259ha); see Blake, R, Hodgson M and Taylor, B *The Airfields of Lincolnshire since 1912*. Leicester, 1984, 210.

12 Paul Francis *British Military Airfield Architecture*, 118–24.

13 As Henry Lewis-Dale, one of the key planners of military aerodromes from 1923 pointed out, 'climatic and other conditions in this country are favourable to the production of good turf on many aerodromes', the principal remaining factors being landing speed, weight and intensity of use: Lewis-Dale, H A 'The construction of aerodromes'. *Minutes of Proceedings of The Institution of Civil Engineers*, Vol. 236 (1934), 182.

14 R A Betts *The Royal Air Force Construction Service, 1939–1945*. Ware: Airfield Research Publishing, 1996, 19–22.

15 English Heritage, *Historic Airfields: Guidelines for Management*. London: English Heritage, 2001.

16 Colin Dobinson 'Airfield themes'.

17 See the contributions by Christina Czymay and Günter Braun in this publication, pp 50–8, 121–6.

18 J A Hellen 'Temporary settlements and transient populations. The legacy of Britain's prisoner of war camps'. *Erdkunde (Archive for Social Geography)* **53/**3 (1999), 191–211.

19 J Lake and J Schofield 'Conservation and the Battle of Britain', in Addison P and Crang J (eds), *The Burning Blue. A New History of the Battle of Britain*. London: Pimlico, 2000, 229–42.

20 Paul Francis and Julian Temple, 'New guidelines for listing military airfield buildings in England'. Unpublished report for English Heritage Listing Team, 1994.

21 Paul Francis, 'RAF Bicester'. Unpublished report for Cherwell District Council, 1996.

22 Paul Francis, 'RAF Duxford. Historical appraisal'. Unpublished report for Imperial War Museum, Duxford, 2001.

23 Colin Dobinson 'RAF Netheravon, a short structural history'. Unpublished report for English Heritage Thematic Listing Programme, 1998.

Aviation architecture and heritage in France

Bernard Toulier

Aviation architecture, an emblematic feature of 20th-century history, can be defined as a civilian or military installation that forms a specific landscape around an airfield, consisting of infrastructures and buildings linked in a network to produce a complex. These complexes can vary greatly in size, some of them covering up to several thousand hectares. In addition to their use value, they come to acquire heritage values when they are identified and studied, recognised and designated as such by the various players in society.

Unlike the 'flying machines' that are collected, catalogued and sometimes even flown by various amateurs or groups of passionate enthusiasts such as the Aéro-club de France, a comparable procedure does not exist for aviation's structures on the ground. There are very few studies of the subject, which, to a certain extent, lies at the fringes of the recognised fields of industrial or military heritage. These sites are associated more readily with the memory of the heroes of aviation, celebrated by countless monuments, than with the achievements of their builders and engineers. This architecture, however, bears witness to an adventure of the modern age that has marked our history and our environment and revolutionised the way in which we live and travel.

Examples of this architecture are abundant. Hundreds of airfields associated with industrial, commercial or military activities have shaped whole new landscapes. Thousands of hangars and other structures, often built using new materials and innovative techniques, have been erected to meet ever-changing economic and social needs. But how can such structures be 'consecrated'? How can the buildings produced be made sacrosanct? How can we preserve architecture which was not always intended to last without changing its meaning and its characteristics? How can buildings and structures that were often temporary and fragile be turned into rigid and sustainable objects? In view of the rapid obsolescence of infrastructures designed for flight, and in view too of the present-day demands of urban

development and the redeployment of the military programmes, how can this architecture be handed down to future generations and find new uses that are compatible with the preservation of its heritage values?

As for all forms of heritage, aviation architecture can only be preserved when we know enough about it to be able to identify it correctly, when we know how best to protect it, and when we have defined criteria for its restoration and future development. But this transmission depends, above all, on a shared recognition of its interest by all the players involved: owners and managers of the sites, State departments, local planning authorities, users and citizens.

Knowledge and identification

In France, it is only recently that this type of heritage has generated any interest. In 1986, the Inventaire général entrusted Marie-Jeanne Dumont with a study of aviation architecture.[1] An initial inventory of sites dating from before 1940 was drawn up, based on a survey of published sources such as architectural, civil engineering and aviation periodicals: 127 sites were identified by this research. An illustrated typological study covered airship and aircraft hangars, airport terminals and air clubs, aircraft construction factories, test centres as well as the various laboratories, offices and schools. The list of sites was checked by the regional offices of the Inventaire général and served as a useful reference for some of the structures subsequently protected as historic monuments. Some regions, such as the Midi-Pyrénées or Provence-Alpes-Côte d'Azur, carried out more in-depth investigations in the field. But, as far as France as a whole is concerned, the results still remain fragmentary.

Launched in 1999, the 'L'Europe de l'Air' project gave a new impulse to the preparation of a national inventory. Another study, carried out by Nicolas Nogue, was based on aerial navigation atlases published between 1913 and 1969. This has identified some 593 airport and airfield sites that still remain to be studied in the field. To pursue

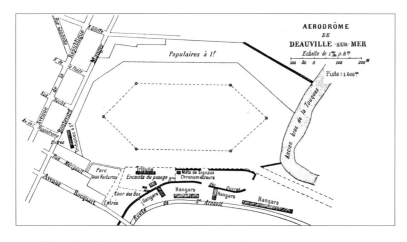

PLAN DE L'AERODROME

ECHELLE: 1/25.000

Top: *Deauville, plan of the aerodrome created at this fashionable seaside resort for the 'Grande Quinzaine d'Aviation de la Baie de Seine' in August 1910 (Musée de Trouville).*

Plan of the airport created nearby at Saint-Gatien in 1929 (Direction des Bases aériennes, atlas 1946)

inventory of the aviation sites that are of historical and archaeological interest and that includes various isolated structures that still dot the landscape should focus first and foremost on the remains of the early days of aviation and indicate the current use of the site.

The airport sites

The 600 or so airport sites identified by the research programmes carried out under the aegis of the Ministry of Culture are 'official' sites that feature in air atlases published up until the end of the 1960s. They do not include the sites of the temporary military airfields scattered throughout northern France and used during the battles of two world wars. Some of these sites, little more than fields, have disappeared completely even from local memories. With the help of archives and aerial photographs, several researchers are today trying to pinpoint their exact locations. In 1939, according to the historical services of the Air Force, more than 500 military airports were in activity. The Second World War left us with a further legacy of aerodromes created by the Luftwaffe, while the post-war years bequeathed new or rebuilt military bases, used within the framework of NATO agreements.

These sites are laid out in a network in accordance with technical requirements (range of the aircraft), military requirements (proximity to the theatre of operation) or commercial requirements (flow of passengers and merchandise) and in connection with the other transport networks (road, rail, sea). These networks extend far beyond metropolitan France, following commercial strategies initially inspired by France's colonial interests.

But how can a distinction be made between civilian and military aviation, which often used the same sites, either at the same time or successively, and often shared the same facilities on the ground (weather services, control towers, various other technical facilities)? Several generations of buildings have been built on these sites, overlapping each other and forming extremely heterogeneous complexes.

During the First World War, military Bessonneau-type hangars and Adrian-type barracks – structures in wood and canvas – were moved from one airfield to another according to needs. Airship hangars were also transferred from the Eastern Front to the Atlantic coast in the West. Nearly all

this inventory work, contacts have been made with various partners outside the Ministry of Culture: the department of civil aviation at the Ministry of Equipement, Logement et Transports (Planning, Housing and Transport) and the four special airbase services, the Ministry of Defence (Committee of Air and Space Heritage and the Central Department of Aviation Infrastructures), the Aéro-club de France, the historical services of the French Air Force and the Musée de l'Air et de l'Espace at Le Bourget. The departments of the three Ministries in question are becoming better aware of the importance of their built heritage and are drawing up their own inventories of the buildings and structures for which they are responsible.[2] A complete these military structures have disappeared; only the archival documents and a handful of photographs bear witness to them.

How can the actual perimeter of the airbases be delimited? The infrastructures can include lighting systems, beacons and radar installations that are far from the site of the flying field itself. On the site itself, various buildings house maintenance and logistical services, defence installations, storage and safety facilities, as well as the barracks and the accommodation for men and officers, and in addition to pilots' training schools. Any thought about this question of perimeters must also take into consideration the ancillary functions present on the civilian sites: customs, offices of the airline companies, restaurants and hotels, staff accommodation.

And how are we to deal with the sites of industrial production linked to aviation? Aircraft factories were often situated alongside an airfield. The capacity and the uses of these production sites had to keep apace of the constant evolution of each of the elements used for the construction of a plane, requiring facilities adapted to each production line. The first aircraft manufacturers were also the first builders on these sites. Historic production processes are difficult to identify on the site, a problem familiar in the study of industrial heritage.

Answers to all these questions are indispensable, not only for the necessary inventory work, but, above all, in order to evaluate correctly the interest of the sites and buildings and to find appropriate solutions, when necessary, for their reuse.

The airport site must be perceived as a complex where all the functions are linked by the airfield, the essential common denominator. Located in the middle of the countryside on open spaces, the flat land is sown with grass or equipped, from the Second World War onwards, with hard-surfaced runways. As far as seaplanes are concerned, the airfield also comprises a waterway with, in some cases, access to the sea.

The airport increasingly has taken on the appearance of an autonomous town with its own access roads and connections with various other means of transport and with different areas set aside for various activities. The buildings erected on the site can be considered as functional elements that lend themselves to typological classifications. Hangars, originally simple shelters in wood and canvas, were designed to cover large spaces using construction techniques that did not require intermediary supports.

Engineers, vying with each other for ever larger column-free spans, made the hangar a test bed for new ways of using reinforced concrete or steel.

Until the 1930s, the facilities for passengers, such as those at Le Bourget, for example, consisted of individual pavilions: customs services, weather-forecasting services, a restaurant, and the airport commander's accommodation. The first French terminal to integrate all these functions under one roof was at Lyon-Bron, built in 1930 according to German models. For the organisation of the passengers and freight processing, the first terminals were inspired by the examples of the railway and maritime stations. The building was designed around the route followed by the passengers, between the airside and the planes and the landside, linked to the land transport networks. It was racecourse stands, however, that served as an architectural model for the terraces and tribunes, making it possible to observe the planes during air shows.

Lyon-Bron, terminal built in 1930 to the designs of Antonin Chomel and Pierre Verrier, and destroyed during the Second World War (Transports en Commun, Aéroports. *Paris: Editions Albert Morancé, 1938)*

Orly, interior view, taken in 1929, of one of the airship hangars built by Eugène Freyssinet in 1922, destroyed in 1944 (photo Musée de l'Air et de l'Espace, Le Bourget)

Protection and restoration

Inventories and preliminary studies are indispensable in order to compile all the necessary information relating to the subject. Their results make it possible to judge whether the buildings to be protected meet the defined criteria and then help to draw up specifications for the restoration of the buildings. The number of aeronautical buildings currently protected under French legislation is very modest. The protected sites are not the result of a national policy and only the region of Toulouse can boast anything close to a coherent research and protection strategy.[3]

A well-thought-out policy could take inspiration from the selection criteria for the works to be protected, following the recommendations of the Council of Europe on the protection of the 20th-century architectural heritage, ratified by the French Council of ministers on 9 September 1991:

> The opportunity to recognise the value of significant works taken from the whole range of styles, types and construction methods of the twentieth century ...

On this point, we have already underlined the shortcomings as regards the acquisition of comprehensive information, in particular in the field of military aerodromes. While certain aeronautical sites from the inter-war period today enjoy legal protection, it is also necessary to consider the buildings and sites of the second half of the 20th century, such

as the Orly terminal, opened in 1961 or that of Roissy-1, dating from 1974.

> The need to protect not only the works of the most famous designers and architects in a given period or style, but also to protect less well known examples which have significance for the architecture and history of the period.

In France, the work of engineers such as Eugène Freyssinet or Bernard Laffaille is gradually becoming better known, but other figures such as the engineers Albert Caquot, Fernand Aimond, Vladimir Bodiansky, Simon Boussiron or Nicolas Esquillan still await in-depth study.

> The importance of including among the selection criteria not only aesthetic considerations but the contribution made in terms of the history of technology, and political, cultural, economic and social development.

Among aeronautical buildings, there are many superb examples of thin vaulting in concrete, of shell structures, of self-supporting steel structures, suspended structures and so on.

> The crucial importance of extending protection to every aspect of the built environment, including not only independent structures but also duplicated structures, planned estates, large ensembles and new towns, public spaces and amenities.

The aeronautical site should not be considered as a collection of individual buildings but as an ensemble. The urban dimensions

of these ensembles must be taken into consideration, not only the flying field itself, but also its service areas, its access roads, the accommodation associated with it, the housing of the sizeable workforces associated with the airport's activities, whether civilian or military. In France, one of the most effective protection instruments, which takes into account these sites in their entirety, is the *Zone de Protection du Patrimoine architectural, urbain et paysager* (ZPPAUP), akin to the British designated conservation area.

To the protection criteria outlined above, it is also worth adding the notion of 'places of memory' featuring in the heroic history of aviation. One such example is the Hôtel du Grand Balcon in Toulouse, associated with the pilot-author Saint-Exupéry and with the Aeropostale Company. Places of memory also include the memory of war, such as the Junkers test beds in Strasbourg. Other more 'usual' criteria should not be neglected either: the structure's mere age or the archaeological and architectural legibility of a site and its potential as an educational tool. These basic criteria should make it possible to pinpoint the sites that have left their mark on the history of the 20th century and that are eligible, in France, for the 'Twentieth-century Heritage' label, created in September 2000 by the Minister of Culture.

Alterations and new uses

Clearly, the best means of conserving these sites is to perpetuate their use by aeronautical activities, ensuring that the airfield remains in running order. The Bloch aircraft construction factory at Déols, near Châteauroux, continues to be used for industrial activities and the site of Montaudran, near Toulouse, is still used by Air France for aircraft maintenance. Both these sites have managed to preserve their airfields and runways.

Beyond the cultural interest of conserving historic remains, the numerous sites identified can present various economic interests in the coming century and be used in urban planning projects. In the past, airfields were isolated and at a certain distance from the town they served. Well served by road networks they have come to acquire greater economic potential. They are spaces that can be used for economic and industrial development. To meet environmental concerns, the land can be landscaped to create green spaces within urban areas. Investments made in the past for the needs of military

defence can be turned to peaceful uses.

The new uses to be found for these sites are numerous and varied. They can entail the implantation of permanent industrial, commercial or business parks, as was the case for the *Avord aeropole* close to Bourges. The building of the Aéro-club du Touquet, designed by the architect Louis Quételart, has been transformed into a restaurant. The land can be used for the organisation of temporary, sports, musical or cultural events, the advantage in the case of these large gatherings being that they are far away from town centres and built-up areas. The

Top: *Avrillé, near Angers, the pilots' school, built by the architect Ernest Bricard in 1938, viewed from the airfield (photo Bernard Renoux/Inventaire général Pays-de-la-Loire)*

Avrillé, interior view of the main hall. The mosaic decoration is by Isidore Odorico (photo Bernard Renoux/Inventaire général Pays-de-la-Loire)

land can also be laid out as open-air sports centres.

Furthermore, there is a strong demand for redevelopment for cultural purposes. The pilots' school of the French Aviation Company, situated at Avrillé close to Angers, designed in 1938 by the architect Ernest Bricard, had been abandoned for thirty years and left to go to ruin. It is now going to be transformed into a *Maison de l'Architecture*. Another trend is the conversion into museums or memorials dedicated to civilian or military aeronautics. In addition to the network of existing museums devoted to this theme, such as Le Bourget or Biscarosse, projects are also underway for a naval aviation museum at Ecausseville or even a glider museum at Fayence in the Var. The transformation of these sites into museums also has implications for their restoration. Two sites are at a preliminary study stage: at Meudon, the Y hangar is to be transformed into a European aerostation centre and Le Bourget's terminal is to be restored within the framework of a reorganisation of the Musée de l'Air et de l'Espace.

To ensure the preservation of these aeronautical ensembles and to make sure that they are put to the best possible use, it is essential for the inventories to be pursued and developed and to include analyses of their potential for reuse. The national inventory cannot be carried out by the Ministry of Culture alone and must call on partnerships, in particular with the ministries responsible for planning and for defence, and with the local authorities. Before any protective measure is enacted, it is necessary to carry out studies into possibilities for reuse. As far as the military heritage is concerned, assistance can be provided by the Ministry of Defence's *Mission pour la Réalisation des Actifs immobiliers* (MRPAI), which should give more attention to the aeronautical heritage of its airbases currently being decommissioned. The preliminary studies into the renovation or reuse of these sites, launched by local authorities or Chambers of Commerce, can also be carried out by specialised research centres.

Historic airports served as a backdrop to numerous constructive innovations, such as hangars covering ever-larger surface areas, demonstrating the technical potential of metal and concrete. But air transport generated greater ensembles and specific landscapes that must also be handed down as heritage. Our common aeronautical heritage represents one of the major challenges for conservation in the 21st century.

Notes

1 Marie-Jeanne Dumont, 'L'Architecture de l'Aéronautique en France, 1900–1940'. Unpublished research report, Ministère de la Culture et de la Communication, Inventaire général des Monuments et des Richesses artistiques de la France/CILAC, 1988.
2 Inventory of the infrastructure of aerodromes up to 1947, compiled up by Jean Sauter, General Inspector of Aviation.
3 Research report by Philippe Gisclard, Les bâtiments de l'aéronautique à Toulouse avant 1950. Toulouse: Direction régionale des Affaires culturelles, 1996.

Monuments of aviation in France

Paul Smith

France today has about 40,000 monuments that enjoy statutory protection according to practices which date back to the first half of the 19th century and which are codified in a law of 1913. These monuments are either *classés* – the minority, classified as historic monuments, or *inscrits* – the majority, which are inscribed on a supplementary list of historic monuments. The differences between these two grades of protection are of little importance here; both seek to preserve buildings for their 'public interest, from the point of view of history or art', and both engage the State, its authority, its heritage inspectors and its finances.

Among these 40,000 monuments, fewer than twenty are related in one way or another to the history of aviation.[1] Unlike Parisian bakeries at the turn of the 19th century or the built heritage of the French railway network – stations, roundhouses, viaducts, tunnels – aviation architecture has never been the object of a concerted campaign of study and protection. In the absence of major works designed by the major architects of the Modern Movement, aeronautical sites were ignored by campaigns of the mid-1960s and mid-1970s launched by the Ministry of Culture to catch up on the protection of the 'modern' architectural heritage, since 1850. With only two exceptions, statutory protection for aviation sites was introduced only after 1984, a turning point in the history of heritage conservation in France, when initiative was decentralised to the cultural authorities in France's twenty-two administrative regions.[2]

Consequently, this modest corpus of French aviation monuments can be viewed as the result of an accumulation of regional conservation preoccupations and local priorities, with no Cartesian programme of 'reasoned' assessment and selection nor any overall national vision based on detailed historical research and survey work in the field. This corpus includes a handful of sites of European significance, but does not offer a coherent or representative account of the history of aviation architecture in France.

Probably the best known and most frequently cited structure in that history, the twin airship hangars built at Orly by Eugène Freyssinet in 1922, are excessively well documented, filmed during their construction, photographed in black and white and in colour, from the ground and from the air.[3] They were never used for their original purpose and were destroyed by American bombs in 1944, destruction which was filmed too.

In France, knowledge about the built aviation heritage is still largely based on documentary evidence, and bears little comparison with the thematic surveys undertaken for English Heritage on civil and military aviation sites. Unlike England, however, and the home counties' fields which saw Spitfires and Hurricanes taking off during the Battle of Britain, French airfields played no heroic role during the Second World War. The country's historic sites are the various 'birthplaces' of aviation or other aerodromes associated with its interwar exploits: the playing fields at Bagatelle, near Paris, which saw Santos-Dumont's first powered flight in 1906; the parade ground at Issy-les-Moulineaux, also in the Paris suburbs, for Henry Farman's 1-km circuit in 1908; Port-Aviation, the 1909 aerodrome created near Juvisy to the south of Paris; the field of Pont Long near Pau, where Wilbur Wright opened a school in 1909; the Montaudran airfield near Toulouse, home of the Aéropostale; Le Bourget where Charles Lindbergh landed in May 1927.

Focused originally on the work of Georges Hennequin, architect of several aircraft factories built during the 1930s, the research undertaken in 1986 by Marie-Jeanne Dumont for the national inventory service[4] provides a preliminary typological analysis on aviation architecture in France, from the origins up to the Second World War: hangars for airships and aircraft, aircraft factories, airports and their terminal buildings, clubhouses, laboratories and wind tunnels, administrative offices, flying schools, etc. This research was carried out largely in the documentation centre of the

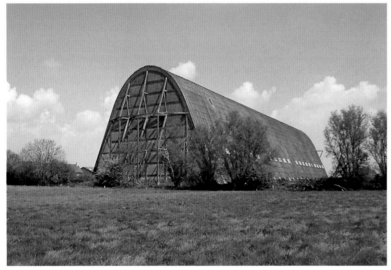

Top: *Meudon, the 'Y' airship hangar of 1879 (photo Paul Smith)*

Ecausseville, the airship hangar designed by Henry Lossier in 1918 (photo Paul Smith)

Musée de l'Air et de l'Espace at Le Bourget and in the national airforce archives at Vincennes, places where flying machines are usually to the fore, but where the built infrastructures can sometimes be analysed in the background. The inventory of sites which accompanies this exploratory study – 127 references in all – was based on the architectural, civil engineering and aviation periodicals of the time; it is far from exhaustive and has still to be completed by field research. Within the framework of the 'L'Europe de l'Air' project, this systematic inventory work has been taken up again, on behalf of the Inventaire général, by Nicolas Nogue, whose database of 621 sites is founded on aerial navigation atlases published between 1913 and 1969. Here then is another point of departure for the sites still to be studied on the ground.

The absence of comparative perspectives has not prevented the recognition of the significance of a certain number of sites, presented here in a succession of brief notices. These are arranged by building type and draw attention to the contexts in which the 'public interest' of the monument was first recognised.

Hangars

The 'Y' hangar at Meudon (Hauts-de-Seine)

This hangar, first protected (*inscrit*) in 1981, is thought to be the earliest airship hangar in the world and is certainly the oldest in existence.[5] It was from this hangar, on 9 August 1884, that *La France*, the world's first navigable airship, powered by batteries, left for a round flight of some 7km and 23 minutes over Villacoublay. The hangar was erected in 1879 for the recently created Etablissement central de l'Aérostation militaire. It was constructed using the lattice-truss iron portal frame of a machine hall dismantled after the Paris Exhibition of 1878 and offering a clear span of 24m in width, 26m in height and 70m in length. The trusses were originally designed by the engineer Henri de Dion and were manufactured by the Moisant-Laurent-Savey firm. This airship and balloon hangar remained in use up to the First World War.

The recognition of its interest in the early 1980s focused on its structure, attributed at the time, as many 19th-century metallic structures in France, to Gustave Eiffel. The hangar is the property today of the Ministry of Culture and is provisionally used as a shelter for the stands erected on the Champs-Elysées for the military parades of 14 July. Since 1991 two restoration campaigns have been undertaken on its roof structure and on the corroded iron bases of the portals.[6] Various adaptive reuse projects have been envisaged – a centre for the history of the circus, or, more appropriately, a centre for the history of ballooning – but for the time being the hangar remains unused and rarely visited.

The Ecausseville hangar (Manche)

This reinforced concrete hangar was built at the end of the First World War for airships employed in the surveillance of the French coast against German U-boats.[7] It is the only surviving element of an airship base comprising a hydrogen production plant, ancillary technical buildings and barracks. Designed by Henry Lossier, an engineer of Swiss origin, and constructed by the firm of Fourré and Rhodes, the structure measures 150m long, 24m wide and 28m high. It was completed in 1920 and, as with the hangars at Orly, never actually sheltered airships. Its owners, the French navy, used it as a depot for submarine parts (it is situated not far from the naval dockyards of Cherbourg), and it was used after the D-Day landings by the Ninth US Air Force. It owes its survival today largely to its isolated situation in the middle of the Cotentin peninsula, surrounded by grazing cows inside a regional nature park. It is one of the last such hangars extant out of a dozen First World War airship bases on the Atlantic and Mediterranean coasts. Recognition of its interest dates back to the end of the 1980s. In 1993 the department's general council envisaged its purchase for the creation of an aeronautical museum, but a year later, after an analysis of the structural condition of the building and the estimate of the costs necessary to open and run the museum, this project was abandoned. In December 1999 it was purchased by the Association Franco-Américaine des Aérodromes Normands de la Neuvième Air-Force, a private association of which the president, Madame Bouvier-Muller, is Henry Lossier's granddaughter. This change of ownership and a new project for some sort of aeronautical museum facilitated the protection of the hangar that was finally designated (*inscrit*) in August 2000.

Factories
The Marcel Bloch Factory at Déols (Indre)

This factory was built from 1936 to 1937 on a 157-ha site situated 5km north of Châteauroux.[8] Far from the capital and the country's frontiers, it was part of the rearmament effort of the latter half of the 1930s, marked by the nationalisation of the war industries in August 1936. Flanking an airfield, the Déols factory was used for the construction of fighters, bombers and reconnaissance aircraft designed by Marcel Bloch, better known by his *nom de guerre*, Dassault. The factory was designed by the architect Georges Hennequin, a schoolfriend of Bloch's. The architectural press of the time applauded his design largely in terms of what the factory was not: 'Not too like a palace, not too industrial, not too like an exhibition hall, nor an airport terminal'.[9]

The buildings were badly damaged by allied air raids in March 1944, but were rebuilt in identical form. From 1951 to 1967, the airfield was used first by the US Air Force and subsequently by NATO. It is still used by aviation today as part of an industrial and business park run by the Indre department's Chamber of Commerce and Industry, owners of the site since 1988. The factory's entrance lodges, its office buildings around the main courtyard, and two large erecting shops were all protected (*inscrits*) in 1992, a measure justified by their varied architectural qualities. This protection, however, does not extend to the flying field.

Test beds of the former Junkers Flugzeug- und Motorenwerke AG, Strasbourg (Bas-Rhin)

At the beginning of the Second World War, the Mathis motor-car factory at Strasbourg-

Top: Déols, near Châteauroux, the entrance to the Marcel Bloch factory (photo Mariusz Hermanowicz/ Inventaire général-Centre)

Strasbourg-Meinau, the Junkers test beds in the early 1950s (collection Comité d'Etablissement de l'Aérospatiale, Châtillon-sous-Bagneux).

Meinau, dating back to 1911, was requisitioned by the Junkers firm and converted to wartime use for the production and testing of aircraft engines, notably the 'universal' Jumo-211 and 213. Known as the *Werk M*, a group of test beds (*Prüfstände*) was constructed in 1941 at the edge of the site.[10] These test beds comprise six identical U-shaped blocks arranged three by three along a central alley. The chambers are lined inside with perforated bricks designed to attenuate the noise of the engines being tested. The building survived air raids in 1944 and was used after the war by the French Arsenal de l'Aéronautique.[11] It is occupied today by a public works company (Société Schell) which uses it as a garage and workshop. The test beds were 'discovered' in 1992 during a survey of the industrial heritage of the Strasbourg region, undertaken for the regional inventory service by Chip Buchheit. They were protected (*inscrits*) in 1993. The measure was justified both by the building's 'historic context' and by its striking architectural forms. The fact that the Junkers firm and engineers were based at Dessau led some to discern a Bauhaus influence in the strict brick functionalism of the design.

Blockhaus, Eperlecques (Pas-de-Calais)

Also dating from the German occupation of France, this huge and practically indestructible concrete complex was built from December 1942 to November 1943 as an assembly plant for V-2 ballistic missiles and a factory for the production of their liquid oxygen fuel. The plans are signed by Xavier Dorsch, the regional head of the Todt organisation. The blockhaus was bombed in August 1943 and November 1944 and abandoned in March of that year without having being put into use. It was protected (*inscrits*) in September 1986 as a vestige of the war and a place of memory: more than 2,000 forced workers were employed in its construction.[12]

Airports and terminal buildings

Le Bourget airport (Seine-Saint-Denis)

The Paris 'air port' at Le Bourget was the birthplace of civil aviation in France, during the spring of 1919, becoming famous between the two wars as the scene of many aeronautical exploits.[13] Charles Lindbergh landed here on 21 May 1927 after his 33-hour transatlantic flight in the *Spirit of Saint Louis*, a crowd, estimated at 150,000, greeting his arrival.[14] The first passenger buildings of the mid-1920s were replaced in 1937 by a grand new terminal designed by the architect Georges Labro. Despite considerable damage suffered during the war, when Le Bourget was occupied by the Luftwaffe, the terminal was rebuilt to the same plans and continued to serve as one of the capital's airports until 1977 and the opening of Roissy-1. Since 1987, it has housed the most prestigious pieces from the collections of the Musée de l'Air et de l'Espace, the world's first aviation museum, founded in 1919. The terminal, one of the last of its generation to survive in France, was protected (*inscrit*) in June 1994. The protection covers Labro's prestigious building inside and out, but does not extend to other historic structures on the airport site, notably a series of 1917 metallic hangars taken from Germany as war compensation, five vast concrete hangars built for civil aircraft by Henry Lossier in 1922, and still in use, and two pavilions which survive from the first airport ensemble of the 1920s. The terminal building has been considerably modified and added to since its reconstruction but its viewing platforms (now closed to the public) still look out over an active airfield landscape, where the earliest concrete runways are a German legacy of 1942. Today, the airport is one of the busiest in Europe for private business flights, and every two years Le Bourget hosts an international air and space show which is a major commercial event in the calendars of the world's aeronautical and arms manufacturers.

Montaudran airport, near Toulouse (Haute-Garonne)

Situated to the south-east of the city, this airfield marks the origins of Toulouse's present-day association with aviation and the aeronautical industries. It dates back to the end of the First World War and to the workshops originally intended for railway carriage construction but used for assembling aircraft – a military order for 1,000 Salmson two-seater reconnaissance planes – after 1917. Pierre-Georges Latécoère, owner of these works, pursued aircraft construction after the war and founded his own civil aviation company, based at the flying field created in front of the workshops along the Toulouse-Sète railway line. This company,

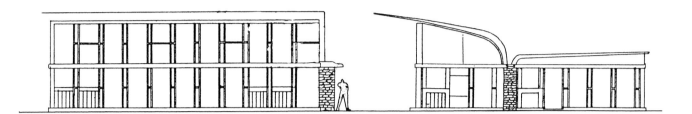

L'Aéropostale, inaugurated services to
Casablanca and subsequently to South
America, and counted among its intrepid
pilots Jean Mermoz, Didier Daurat, Henri
Guillaumet and Antoine de Saint-Exupéry.
In 1933 it was one of the companies
absorbed in the creation of Air France, the
national company that, for the time being at
least, still uses the Montaudran site for
maintenance operations on its short-haul
aircraft. The protection of certain elements
of the ensemble, seen regionally as 'a landmark in the history of aviation', was decided
in 1997, following a general survey of the
built aeronautical heritage of Toulouse and
its region.[15] It covers a late-18th-century
chateau purchased by Latécoère in 1918
and used as administrative offices for his
company, a small building used as a waiting-
room, part of the 1917 workshop buildings
and a 500-metre length of the runway (out
of a total of 1,800m). Laid down in 1956,
this is the only airfield runway in France to
enjoy historic monument status and its protection is an encouraging sign of the intention to preserve the airport landscape as a
whole.

V-1 launch ramp at Equeurdreville-Hainneville (Manche)

Situated to the west of Cherbourg, this V-1
launch site was built by the Luftwaffe
towards the end of 1943, close to a network
of underground galleries used by the French
Navy before the war for stocking fuel, and
occupied by the German army. The ramp
constructed for the V-1s was oriented
towards the port of Bristol. It is comprised
of two massive parallel walls in reinforced
concrete, 75m long, a diagonal slot inside
each wall indicating the angle of the catapult
ramp. A thick concrete protective cover was
planned but not in place when the site was
taken by American forces in June 1944. It
was protected (classé) in February 1995 as a
particularly well-preserved example of a
supposedly invulnerable Nazi missile site,
unique in France of its type. The ramp,

which belongs today to the Ministry of
Defence, was surveyed during inventory
work on the regional vestiges of the Atlantic
Wall, carried out in anticipation of the 50th
anniversary of the D-Day landings.

Aero-clubs

Aero-club building at Doncourt-les-Conflans (Meurthe-et-Moselle)

This clubhouse, known as 'Cap Doncourt',
was designed in 1953 by Le Corbusier, in
association with the architects Jacques and
Bernard Ogé and the constructor Jean
Prouvé.[16] It replaced the earlier clubhouse
and hostel of a popular flying club,
destroyed in 1944. The building comprises
two aluminium shell structures placed back
to back against a central stone partition
wall. The public part, opening onto the airfield, has two levels while the rear part, of
one level, is reserved for private use. This is
less a monument to popular aviation than to
the collaboration – the only official one –
between Le Corbusier and Prouvé, two
major figures in the history of 20th-century
architecture. When the clubhouse was protected (inscrit) in April 1999, it was one of
the last remaining French buildings
designed by Le Corbusier not to enjoy statutory protection.

Laboratories and research centres

Buildings of the Etablissement central de l'Aérostation militaire, Meudon (Hauts-de-Seine)

The domain of Chalais-Meudon, situated
above a bend in the Seine to the west of
Paris, was designed at the end of the 17th
century for Louis XIV's minister Louvois,
and has been associated with lighter-than-
air experimentation since the French Revolution and the creation, in the Year II of
the Republic, of a national military balloon
school. A new central establishment of

Doncourt-les-Conflans,
Aéro-club de Doncourt
(drawing by Le Corbusier,
1953; Fondation Le
Corbusier/Plan 7958
© FLC)

Paris, Gustave Eiffel's 1912 wind tunnel, a cross-sectional drawing from a contemporary technical review (reproduction in the protection file, Conservation régionale des Monuments historiques, Ile-de-France)

military aerostation was created by Léon Gambetta in 1877 and placed under the direction of Colonel Charles Renard. In 1946, this research establishment became the ONERA (Office nationale d'études et de recherches aéronautiques[17]). In September 2000, when the ONERA's 1930s wind tunnel was protected (see below), the protection of the 'Y' hangar (see above) was upgraded from *inscription* to *classement*, and three other buildings from the Renard period were also given statutory protection (*inscrits*): two houses, dating from the early 19th century and used by Renard as his home and office, and a curious, wooden-framed workshop erected in 1898. This chalet-like building, used for various experiments on balloon tethers, propellers and so on, still retains its original decor and is highly evocative of the aeronautical research of the late 19th and early 20th centuries.

Gustave Eiffel's wind tunnel, Paris

Towards the end of his long career, Gustave Eiffel became interested in aerodynamics, using his famous tower in Paris for his first experiments in this realm, carried out in the open air. In 1912 he built a laboratory in Paris (rue Boileau, in the 16th arrondissement) which is considered to be one of the first aerodynamics laboratories in the world, used by such aviation pioneers as Blériot, Farman and Voisin. Eiffel designed a straight tunnel through which air was drawn by ventilators at speeds of up to 100km per hour. This type of wind tunnel became a model for others constructed in France in succeeding years. It is still in use today, notably for wind-trials on models of large new buildings such as the Grande Arche at La Défense. The laboratory building is a simple metal-framed hall that was first protected (*inscrit*) in 1984. In 1997 the ensemble, including all its surviving technical equipment, was

designated (*classé*) as a monument to 'French industrial genius'.

Hispano-Suiza wind tunnel, Bois-Colombes (Hauts-de-Seine)

This wind tunnel, of the Eiffel type, was built by the aircraft firm of Hispano-Suiza as part of their factory at Bois-Colombes in the Paris suburbs, created in 1913 and employing up to 4,500 workers.[18] The wind tunnel was erected in 1937 by the Haour Frères building firm to designs established by the Compagnie Electro-Mécanique. Its aerodynamic tunnel was 55m long and wind speeds above 360km per hour made it one of the most advanced private wind tunnels of its time. The building was converted into offices in 1960 and retains none of its original technical installations. Its outer reinforced concrete structure is intact, however, and its profiled 'anti-vortex' concrete filters make it a monument that is still recognisably aeronautical. The building was protected (*inscrit*) in April 2000 and a project, conceived by the well-known architect Philippe Robert, plans to install a school inside the building, now in the heart of a residential zone where the Hispano-Suiza factory used to be.

ONERA wind tunnel, Meudon (Hauts-de-Seine)

This wind tunnel at Meudon was built from 1932 to 1934 at the instigation of Albert Caquot, technical director at the Air Ministry.[19] It was designed by the aeronautical engineer Antonin Lapresle and built under the direction of Gaston Le Marec by the Limousin Company, specialists in reinforced concrete construction. It was intended for use by full-sized aircraft, with pilots in the cockpits and engines turning. Rendered obsolete, after the war, by larger aircraft, higher speeds and by the progressive development of computerised modelling techniques

for aerodynamic research, the wind tunnel was moth-balled in 1976. Its owners, the national French office for aerodynamic and space research finally accepted its protection (*classement*) in September 2000, as one of the most significant inter-war structural engineering achievements in France and an exceptional example of the architectural freedom afforded by reinforced concrete construction techniques. The comparison with similar 1930s wind tunnels elsewhere in Europe, made possible by the 'L'Europe de l'Air' project, helped considerably in the recognition of the historical significance of this stunning structure, now under consideration as a candidate for UNESCO's lists of World Heritage.

The Banlève wind tunnel, Toulouse

This wind tunnel was built in 1936 at the instigation of the Air Ministry, destined for use by the aeronautical industries concentrated in the Toulouse region.[20] It was constructed on a site alongside a lateral canal of the Garonne where a centre for hydraulic studies had been in existence since 1920. The wind tunnel, of the Eiffel type, was put into service in 1938, functioning at first in the open air. In 1940, in order to be able to use it in all weathers, it was encased inside a building designed by the Parisian architect René Krieger. The striking rounded façade of this building, with its serried fin elements in concrete, corresponds with the air outlet of the diffuser. Today the wind tunnel is part of an institute of fluid mechanics and is still used for training purposes and for some industrial research contracts. The heritage significance of the building – 'an exceptional monument to the history of aeronautical techniques' – was identified during the survey of Toulouse's aviation heritage and the wind tunnel, with its encasing building, were protected (*inscrits*) in November 1997.

Other monuments

Low-cost housing estate, 212 avenue du Huit-Mai-1945, Le Blanc-Mesnil (Seine-Saint-Denis)

This low-cost housing estate was built from 1933 to 1936 to the designs of the architect Germain Dorel for the Société du Foyer du Progrès et de l'Avenir, a social housing company of which the architect was one of the directors.[21] From 1931, this company purchased land in the commune of Le Blanc-Mesnil, situated directly opposite the

airport of Le Bourget. Known as *Les Carrières*, the ensemble originally comprised about 500 flats of between 18 and 54 sq m and met the hygiene and comfort standards defined at the time for low-cost housing (*HBM, Habitations à Bon Marché*). The five-storey parallel ranges that make up this ensemble have vaulted central passageways reminiscent of those of the famous Karl-Marx-Hof in Vienna, designed by Karl Ehn in 1927 and recognised by Dorel as his inspiration. Located opposite the airport, the estate housed many of the employees working there. It was protected (*inscrit*) in 1996 as an 'exceptional example of the Viennese influence on French social housing during the 1930s'. It has recently been refurbished by the Efidis company, with grant aid from the Ministry of Culture.

Domaine du Vivier, Henri Potez Villa, Albert and Méaulte (Somme)

A far cry from social housing in the northern suburbs of Paris, this villa, constructed near his factory for the famous French aircraft builder Henri Potez, was protected (*inscrit*) in 1990. It was built from 1927 to 1930 to the designs of Raoul Minjoz, aeronautical engineer and architect for the Société des Aéroplanes Potez. The protected ensemble comprises not only the villa itself, but also the guardian's lodge at the entrance, some farm buildings, the garage and chauffeurs' accommodation, the gardener's house, a pergola, a former gaming room and a turbine building on the Ancre river which runs through the estate. The aeronautical interest of this villa lies in its association with Potez, born at Méaulte, but it is also an interesting example of the architecture of the reconstruction after the First World War. Its interior decoration is intact and of remarkable stylistic coherence; the basement gaming room has a bar that is something of an Art Deco masterpiece.

Meudon, the 1930s wind tunnel, showing the exhaust air ducts, covered in 1976 when the installation ceased to be used (photo Paul Smith)

Toulouse, the Hôtel du Grand Balcon on the Place du Capitole (photo Paul Smith)

Two other residences belonging to inter-war aircraft magnates, also protected as historic monuments, can be mentioned here in passing. At Rayol-Canadel-sur-Mer, in the Var, the Rayol estate was purchased by Henri Potez in 1939. The villa, dating from 1910, was enlarged by his architect Raoul Minjoz and protected in 1994. The Montpensier chateau at Seuilly, in the Indre-et-Loir department, was acquired by Pierre-Georges Laté-coère in 1930. Parts of the chateau date from the 14th century. Latécoère set about restoring the chateau and its gardens with the help of the architect and landscape designer Albert Laprade, the ensemble being protected (*inscrit*) in 1995.

Hôtel du Grand Balcon, Toulouse

Part of a mid-19th-century brick building located at the corner of Toulouse's Place du Capitole, and run, from 1925, by the Marquez sisters. This modest hotel was frequented by the pilots of the Aéropostale company; room 32 on the second floor was the one occupied by Antoine de Saint-Exupéry. The hotel as a whole and this room in particular were protected (*inscrits*) in 1999 for their association with the Aéropostale adventure. The lounge of the hotel is decorated today with ageing photographs and posters recalling this adventure, subject of a 1949 film entitled *Au Grand Balcon* directed by Henri Decoin and with screenplay by Joseph Kessel.

Conclusion

The protection of historic monuments is a never-ending story founded on the accumulation and sharing of new knowledge and the emergence of new perceptions of interest. To conclude this rapid survey of France's aviation monuments, mention can be made here of a certain number of sites put forward for statutory protection on a national list of significant 20th-century buildings published by the Ministry of Culture in September 2000:[22] the 1961 Orly terminal built by Henri Vicariot for Aéroports de Paris; the Air France administration buildings of 1950 to 1958, also at Orly, designed by the architect Edouard Albert; Paul Andreu's Roissy-1 terminal of 1974; the 1921 Latham aircraft factory at Caudebec-en-Caux (Seine-Maritime); the pilots' school built at the Avrillé airfield, near Angers, in 1939 by the architect Ernest Bricard, with decorations by the famous mosaïcist Isidore Odorico; the 1919 aviation hangars constructed at Istres (Bouches-du-Rhône) by the Eiffel company, and the 1951 hangars at the nearby Marignane airfield, designed by Auguste Perret in collaboration with Nicolas Esquillan and Eugène Freyssinet; a reinforced concrete hangar dating from 1938 at the airfield of Varennes-Vauzelles (Nièvre); the 1938 terminal buildings designed by the architect Jacques Sonnet for the airport at Nevers; a double hangar, dating from 1937 at the Thise aerodrome, near Besançon.

Notes

1 This paper, presented at the Liverpool workshop in October 1999, was brought up to date in June 2001. The documentary files on France's protected monuments are centralised at the national heritage Médiathèque (4 rue d'Aboukir, 75002 Paris) and contain copies of the decrees along with their considérants, the historical or artistic arguments justifying the measure of protection. Brief notices on all the country's protected monuments can also be consulted on the Ministry of Culture's web site: see the Mérimée and Archi-XXe databases (www.culture.fr/bases de données). Launched in June 1999, the Council of Europe's site (www.european-heritage.net) gives details on the heritage protection policies of a selection of European countries.

2 On the evolution of historic monuments legislation in France and on the various protection campaigns mentioned here, see the introduction to Bernard Toulier, Paul Smith and Fabienne Chaudesaigues, Mille monuments du XXe siècle en France, le patrimoine protégé au titre des monuments historiques. Paris: Editions du Patrimoine, 1997.

3 The film was shown at the 1997 exhibition at the Centre Georges Pompidou in Paris, L'art de l'ingénieur, constructeur, entrepreneur, inventeur, a picture of the Orly hangars featuring on the cover of the exhibition catalogue. On 27 February 1932, the popular review L'Illustration reproduced what it claimed were the first ever colour photographs taken from the air, including a view of the Orly hangars.

4 Marie-Jeanne Dumont, 'L'Architecture de l'Aéronautique en France, 1900–1940'. Unpublished research report, Ministère de la Culture et de la Communication, Inventaire général des Monuments et des Richesses artistiques de la France/CILAC, 1988. This document was disseminated throughout France's regions and served as a guide for further inventory work, notably in the Midi-Pyrénées region.

5 The hangar's name comes from an alphabetical index of buildings on a plan of the site drawn up in 1886.

6 See Pierre-Antoine Gatier (Historic Monuments Architect), 'Le Hangar Y, analyse et restauration des appuis de portique'. L'Archéologie industrielle en France 37 (December 2000), 25–8.

7 See Yannick Lecherbonnier, 'Un hangar aux champs'. L'Archéologie industrielle en France 37 (December 2000), 29–35.

8 The Bloch factory features among the fifty exceptional sites presented in Jean-François Belhoste and Paul Smith (eds), Patrimoine industriel, cinquante sites en France (Images du Patrimoine no. 167). Paris: Editions du Patrimoine, 1997. In 2001, a thesis on the history and architecture of the factory was submitted at the University of Tours: Nelly Alletru, 'L'Usine d'aviation Marcel Bloch de Châteauroux-Déols (Indre), Histoire et Architecture'. Unpublished thesis, Université François-Rabelais, Tours.

9 La Construction moderne, 19 February 1939.

10 See Dominique Toursel-Harster, 'Les bancs d'essais et d'entretien de moteurs d'avions de l'usine "Junkers Flugzeug- und Motorenwerke A.G." à Strasbourg, vestiges de l'industrie de guerre nazie'. Cahiers alsaciens d'Archéologie, d'Art et d'Histoire 39 (1996), 171–6. The German firm employed 3,500 workers at the Strasbourg plant but also had workshops at the Struthof camp at Natzwiller (Bas-Rhin). This concentration camp, the only one on French soil, was protected (classé) in 1950.

11 This aeronautical arsenal, created in 1936 at the time of the nationalisation of the war industries, built its own test beds – a direct

copy of the German installation – at Gâtines, near Paris, in 1947. See Paul Smith, 'Comité d'établissement de l'aérospatiale, Châtillon-sous-Bagneux'. Mémoire d'Usine, 60 ans à la production d'avions et d'engins tactiques. Paris: Syros, 1985.

12 The site, in private ownership, attracts several thousand visitors a year.

13 On the history and architecture of Le Bourget, see Christelle Inizan and Bernard Rignault, 'Paris-Le Bourget', in Berlin- Tempelhof, Liverpool-Speke, Paris-Le Bourget, Airport Architecture of the Thirties. Paris: Editions du Patrimoine, 2000, 90–121, and the different contributions by Bernard Rignault, Jean-Christophe Morisseau and Didier Hamon in the present publication, pp 73–82, 145–57, 219–21.

14 Le Matin, 22 May 1927; see Christiane Degrain, 'La Figure de l'Aviateur dans l'Entre-deux-guerres'. Unpublished thesis, Université de Paris-X, Nanterre, 1998.

15 Philippe Gisclard, 'Les Bâtiments de l'Aéronautique à Toulouse avant 1950'. Unpublished report, Direction régionale des Affaires culturelles de Midi-Pyrénées, 1996.

16 See Catherine Coley, Jean Prouvé en Lorraine. Nancy: Presses universitaires de Nancy/ Archives modernes de l'Architecture lorraine, 1990, 17, and the Jean Prouvé website: www.jean-prouve.net/

17 'Aéronautiques' became 'aérospatiales' in 1963. See Onera, Cinquante ans de recherches aéronautiques et spatiales. Paris, 1997. On the history of the Chalais-Meudon site as a whole, see Monique Mahaux and Paul Smith, 'La S1 Ch'. L'Archéologie industrielle en France 37 (December 2000), 6–24.

18 See Hélène Jantzen, 1860–1960, Cent ans de patrimoine industriel, Hauts-de-Seine (Images du Patrimoine no. 163). Paris: Service régional de l'Inventaire général Ile-de-France, 1997, 30.

19 See Mahaux and Smith, 'La S1 Ch'.

20 See Annie Noé-Dufour, Les quartiers de Toulouse; l'île du Ramier (Itinéraires du Patrimoine no. 176). Toulouse: Accord, 1998, 14–18.

21 See Pierre Meige, Mémoire de la Cité du 212. Le Blanc-Mesnil: La Maison du Chemin Notre-Dame, 2000.

22 Direction de l'Architecture et du Patrimoine, Ministère de la Culture et de la Communication, Patrimoine du XXe siècle, Liste indicative d'édifices du XXe siècle présentant un intérêt architectural ou urbain majeur pouvant justifier une protection au titre des Monuments historiques ou des Zones de Protection du Patrimoine Architectural, Urbain et Paysager (en totalité ou en partie). Paris, September 2000.

Military aviation sites in Berlin-Brandenburg

Christina Czymay

Is flying an expression of the desire for unlimited freedom? Has the world become too small? Are unrelenting pressures and environmental pollution some of the reasons why we feel this need to escape from the daily drudge, the misery and the worries? Is the urge to fly a form of escape? Taking to the skies is an active process for which pilots, 'flying like birds', are much admired, as were pilots during the First and Second World Wars. But does this mean the invention and development of aircraft, which has transformed the dream of flight into reality, is a positive chapter in the history of the human race?

Some publishers bring out endless volumes in which fighters, bombers and aerial warfare play an undeniably prestigious role. The military are aircraft enthusiasts, but are less interested in the buildings that were erected to house and service them. The technical evolution of equipment and accessories and the resulting size of the flying machines dictate the dimensions of the aircraft hangars and workshops on the airfields. Hence hangars cannot be understood without giving due consideration to the aircraft themselves. The technical equipment and size of an aeroplane is also dependent on its function. The military quickly recognised the usefulness of the civil invention of flight and encouraged its development.

The majority of pre-1945 German airfields were created for military uses: the so-called Fliegerhorste or 'flight eyries'. Civil airfields were also frequently used for military purposes. After the First World War this made it possible to find a way around the ban on military aviation imposed by the Treaty of Versailles. Many of Germany's surviving historical airfields therefore served primarily military ends: wartime reconnaissance and conquest from the air.

Recent developments in research

German research in the history of architecture has paid little attention to airfield buildings and structures. During the past few years, however, there has been a clear increase of interest in surviving aircraft hangars dating from the mid-1930s. It was only after the reunification of Germany and the consequent withdrawal of the different occupying forces that it at last became possible actually to visit and survey such sites. Since the barracks and aerodromes built for the military were located on land acquired by the Ministry of Defence, the Federal Republic became the owner of these sites, commissioning development companies in the individual Länder to look after their administration and assessment. Each Land is trying to find new uses for these properties, or at least to assess their values for the future.

For the heritage departments in the Länder that have responsibility for assessing the heritage value of all types of buildings, this meant that it was necessary to carry out rapid surveys before or during planning procedures. But even if it is possible to designate a building as a heritage structure relatively rapidly, there is still no firm guarantee that the future of the building is assured. The search for suitable new users, who will maintain the structure of the airfield installations and, if possible, the airfields themselves, is very complicated, especially in view of the sheer numbers of these installations dating from between 1934 and 1939 in the area of former Prussia.

Research into military installations and aerodromes is predominantly based on contemporary contributions to specialist journals of the 1930s, devoted to the main representative sites. Drawings of aircraft hangars in construction journals are rarely accompanied by references to their location. In historical maps and plans – even in modern ones – military installations are often denoted by white patches. This makes it even more complicated to identify and map out the built installations and their historical development. The military airfields in Berlin-Brandenburg were used by the Luftwaffe only for about ten years. After the

Second World War, many sites continued to be used as military installations by the forces of occupation – in this case the Soviet Army – and sometimes saw new developments, along with decorative murals and commemorative monuments. Such traces of the Cold War period have so far received even less attention than those of the 1930s.

In Germany today there is no national inventory of surviving pre-war airfields. Thanks to the pioneering work carried out by the photographer Johannes Bruns,[1] a survey has been drawn up of the surviving airfield hangars in the Land of Brandenburg. This photographic inventory, along with the dissertation written by Andreas Skopnik on aircraft hangars in Brandenburg,[2] is an extremely useful document for assessing the heritage values of these military aviation sites. Surveys of these sites must be continuously updated and further inventory work is needed for other airfield ensembles, in particular the barracks and living quarters that are associated with the military airfields. This task is too vast to be carried out by a single civil servant in the heritage department of each Land.

The first airfields in Germany

Any available open space could serve as a landing field. Over 200 years ago, in 1788, when the Frenchman Pierre Blanchard made an ascent in a hydrogen balloon in Berlin, he used an exercise ground in front of the Brandenburg Gate.[3] From 1826 to 1828, the Prussian Defence Treasury purchased a large area of arable land in Tempelhof, near Berlin, the Tempelhofer Feld, and turned it into an exercise and parade ground. It was not only used for military parades, however, but also for horse races, athletic meetings, sport festivals, and also as an airfield.[4] In 1883, the newly formed Prussian Airship Squadron was stationed at the western perimeter of the Tempelhof parade ground. In 1887 this became the location of an early balloon hangar. The first heavier-than-air flying attraction on this site was the two hops achieved by another Frenchman, Armand Zipfel. A few months later, in September 1909, Orville Wright became a hero for Berliners following his successful demonstration flight at Tempelhof. 'European powered flight was born on the 23rd of October 1906 in

France with a sixty-metre flight by the Brazilian Santos-Dumont.'[5] The first German airfield for powered aircraft was officially opened on 26 September 1909 with a 'Flying competition between the first aviators in the world' at Johannisthal, south-east of Berlin.

As early as 1910, five airfields were already mentioned in an aviation yearbook, *Jahrbuch der Luftfahrt*: Johannisthal, Bork, Schulzendorf, Teltow and München-Puchheim. By the end of 1911 the number of airfields had risen to seventeen, covering between 0.7 and 3.5 sq km, each surrounded by several tents or simple wooden sheds to shelter the aircraft. The first permanent hangar was built in Weimar in 1911 for the Weimar Air Transport Association by the Otto Hetzer Company and boasted four hangar doors.[6] In a 1914 publication on the development and current status of hangar construction in Germany, the Imperial Government's former 'Master Builder and Chief Engineer', Richard Sonntag, claimed that the first purpose-built hangar was completed in 1912 by the Prussian Military Authorities on a military airfield. Following these initial developments, a few more hangars or workshops for the repair and maintenance of aircraft were built without the support and influence of the military.[7]

The evolution of flight technology and aircraft construction was boosted by the use of powered aircraft. More airfields and hangars became necessary. A survey dating from 1914[8] lists 31 civil airfields and a further 14 military airfields, and gives a comprehensive summary of 37 locations identified in a register of landing fields with hangars: 'On the eve of the First World War, there were 87 airfields within the territory of the German Reich (excluding the colonies) and another 31 were under construction or being planned.'

Two of the most important installations at this period were to be found in Döberitz and Jüterbog. At both sites, situated to the west and south of Berlin, the airfields were completely dismantled after the war, in accordance with the provisions of the Treaty of Versailles, but after 1933 other extensive military installations took their place.

Due to several exceptional circumstances, six aircraft hangars of the first generation survive today. They are to be found in an outlying district south-east of Berlin and are of considerable interest from the point of view of construction history.

Berlin-Karlshorst, landside elevation of the 1917 hangars (drawn in 1991), which are occupied today by the research department of a federal water service (Bundesanstalt für Wasserbau)

The airforce installations at Berlin-Karlshorst

At the beginning of the First World War, concerted efforts were made to create a garrison in the municipality of Friedrichsfelde-Karlshorst. In 1917 the municipality bought a total of 152 hectares of land[9] from the owners, Siemens, von Treskow and Pahl, on a site that had seen the first rotating airship hangars on the Continent, dating back to the end of 1909. In April 1917, the first plans for the Berlin-Friedrichsfelde installation were drawn up. A ground plan of July 1918, drawn by Friedrich, building advisor for the Air Force Directorate, shows the airfield with four distinct units on the site, situated between the communities of Biesdorf and Friedrichsfelde:[10]

1 In the north-west corner there was a unit for aerial photographic and film reconnaissance comprising four double hangars and one single one, an officers' mess, staff and crew barracks and other working and living quarters.
2 To the south-west there was an aviation unit and experimental unit with a workshop, six aircraft hangars, various sheds used for railway carriages and vehicles and barracks, including the offices of the Military Planning Department and the sentry house. There were plans to build the crew's living quarters with all the necessary secondary facilities, and a training barracks farther to the east, some distance from the hangars and test beds.
3 A balloon unit was to be built to the south-east, and plans for a balloon tent and sheds for balloon equipment and winches had already been drafted in January 1919.
4 A training unit was located to the north-east with crew's barracks and offices, classrooms, training buildings and other

buildings for non-commissioned officers, and four hangars.

A ground plan of this Berlin-Friedrichsfelde airforce installation,[11] submitted by the Military Development Department on 15 January 1919, shows an ensemble covering a total of 150 hectares and marks the paths between the units and all the other buildings. A map dating from 1920[12] shows the large, almost square-shaped airfield surrounded by extensive woodlands and the communities of Biesdorf and Karlshorst, located to the north and to the south. One can clearly make out the L-shaped building of the aerial reconnaissance and film units on the boundaries, the hangars of the aviation and experimental units with a works siding and the connecting roads. Even on a ground plan dating from 1934,[13] the buildings of both units appear almost in their entirety. Surprisingly, the 135-metre-long Siemens-Schuckert airship hangar is not shown on any of these ground plans. It was only dismantled in 1920 as a result of the demilitarisation provisions of the Treaty of Versailles and traces of the rails of the track-rotation bed, measuring 39 and 93.4m in diameter, are visible on an aerial photograph of 1928.[14] The Siemens-Schuckert airship SSL I that was developed there did not use the Karlshorst site after April 1912.

Three units of the Friedrichsfelde installation are shown on the plan dating from 1919 along with hangars for the storage of aircraft of every description. On the northern boundary, four double aircraft hangars and one single one were built; at the western edge of the field, there were six other hangars and, close to the training unit situated to the north-east, six Valanciener-type hangars.

The most important unit on the site was the one accommodating the experimental services. This not only had its own railway sidings and a direct road connection next to

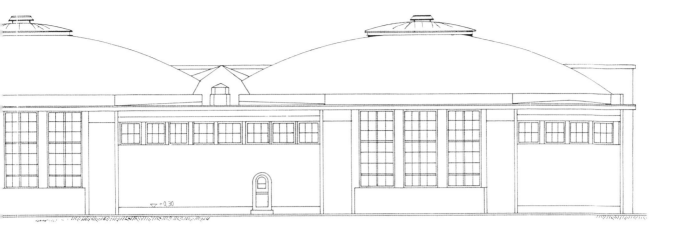

Querschnitt C-D

the workshop, but it was also equipped with a motor test bed structure. Compared to the six hangars of this unit, the other buildings around the airfield seem less important. With the exception of the workshop building, these hangars have survived up to the present day and we can note that, roughly in accordance with the standards for aircraft hangars, they have a footprint of 22.70 x 66.50m. The aircraft and workshop hangars designed in April and May 1917 were reinforced concrete constructions.[15] They are identical structures, developed by the Munich-based construction company Gebrüder Rank.[16] In a volume published for this firm's 125th anniversary,[17] reference is made to four hangars built for the Military Planning Department in Berlin at the Friedrichsfelde (Karlshorst) airfield, each hangar roofed with three rounded domes measuring 23m in diameter, as well as a workshop construction with a hangar measuring 50 x 30m. As the southernmost hangars were built first, this explains why only four hangars were mentioned. Only a

few months later, the two northern hangars followed as an extension to the workshop facilities. In the same commemorative publication, further airfield constructions built for the Military Planning Department are mentioned, dating from 1917. The workshop structures have survived in Schleißheim and Fürth.[18]

The hangars at Karlshorst represent a special type of construction, developed by the Rank brothers' firm in the early days of reinforced concrete. Similar structures of this period, with the same type of domed shell roof, are not known to construction history specialists, nor has it been possible to ascertain the existence of any comparable hangars elsewhere in Germany.

Each hangar consists of three vaulted parts, linked together without supporting pillars. The roof construction of the three domes is supported by the masonry of the outer walls and by two reinforced concrete arches, anchored in the ground using a tie-beam.[19] The upper parts of these arches jut out above the roof between

Berlin-Karlshorst, cross-section of one of the 1917 hangars (drawn in 1991) with the airfield to the left (Bundesanstalt für Wasserbau)

Top: *Berlin-Karlshorst, the southern group of hangars viewed from the west (photo Wolfgang Reuss/ Landesdenkmalamt Berlin)*

Berlin-Karlshorst, the southern group of hangars viewed from the south (photo Wolfgang Reuss/Landesdenkmalamt Berlin)

personnel. Every second hall is equipped with a low workshop extension on the northern side, comprising a coal store, boiler room with chimney, lavatory and equipment room.

Hangars that were used to accommodate completed aircraft differ considerably from the manufacturing hangars of the aircraft industry, as they are subject to different operating conditions.[21] But minor cleaning and maintenance work, necessary to ensure the starting capacity of the aircraft, had to be carried out in all aircraft hangars. The equipment for this was stored in the small extension. It was necessary to heat the hangars not only in order to carry out this kind of maintenance work but also in order to prevent the build-up of condensation and the resulting damage to equipment.[22] It sufficed to maintain temperatures inside the hangar at 8 to 10 degrees Celsius, that is to say frost-free. The first generation of aircraft hangars was equipped, as were storage hangars, with flat radiators placed against the walls. In the surviving hangars at Karlshorst, the heating pipes were placed under the floor, with the return pipes in the ceiling area, above the window bands. In 1938 the head of the Government Planning Department, Werner Spillhagen, wrote in *Der Flughafen* that now aircraft hangars are always equipped with hot-air heating systems:

> While previously, due to the lack of suitable apparatus, it was necessary to heat the air for the central heating system and then conduct it through floor channels or sheet metal pipes and the individual discharge openings into the room in order to achieve a regular distribution of heat, in more recent times so-called hot-air systems have been used almost exclusively, mainly composed of a ventilator for the mechanical circulation of air and a heater to warm the ambient air.

The Karlshorst aircraft hangars are rare survivors from the beginning of an evolutionary process that led to the aircraft hangars constructed during the 1930s. Large hangars free of internal supports were also needed for the storage of aircraft, which were still relatively small. After all, the hangars always serve the aircraft and have no end in themselves, nor are they built for aesthetic purposes. But just as storage hangars differ from the erecting halls of the aircraft industry, there are different requirements for aircraft hangars of military and civilian sites, because of differing operating conditions.

the domes. The domes rest on annular beams supported by the arches. Comprised of 120-mm-thick hollow blocks, the steel reinforcements probably placed on either face are coated in concrete: the moulding of the form-work is still clearly visible today. The corner pieces around the domes are lined with masonry and plaster. A skylight is situated at the apex of each dome, measuring 5.60m in diameter, with concrete ribs. The original glazing, using glass bricks, has survived in the southernmost hangar.

The airfield side has a band of four windows that were originally situated above the hangar doors, which no longer exist today.[20] Inside, these small windows are integrated into the structure of the dome beneath a low arch with reinforced concrete braces. Further daylight comes from the surrounding window bands and, at the middle of each of the hangar sections, there are three rectangular openings which occupy almost the entire height of the walls. On the longitudinal side, away from the airfield, there are also smaller entrance doors intended for

Improvements in the technical performance of aircraft construction, however, went hand in hand with new developments in building construction and materials. Up until the end of the First World War, the majority of hangars were built of wood and steel. Compared with these materials, concrete not only offered a higher degree of solidity but also better protection against fire. The superior thermal insulation properties of concrete also made the heating of aircraft hangars more efficient. In combination with their steel armatures, arched shell roofs were constructed with ever-increasing spans.

Various investigations were carried out to develop structures better able to withstand damage from air raids and comparisons were made with hangar construction in other countries. In *Der Flughafen* dated 1938,[23] reference is made to a 'bomb-proof hangar' from England, designed by Diagrid Structures Ltd. In the same article it is reported:

> The effect of a high-explosive bomb is in inverse proportion to the size of the room in which it detonates. The shock wave of the detonation therefore does not often have the force to destroy the whole construction when it hits the inside wall of a high and large hangar, but can instead push the light building components to the outside. These therefore function as a security valve and are known as evasive surfaces. It is therefore important to select the largest possible evasive surfaces for the doors and the windows, etc, in order to ensure the solidity of the construction in the event of an explosion. A hangar structure of rigid frames and arches could also resist the detonation of high-explosive bombs. A vapour seal of reinforced concrete also increased resistance to the effects of incendiary bombs.

The connections between military and building activities is vividly demonstrated at Berlin-Karlshorst. Both world wars played a part in the development of new construction techniques that cannot be analysed independently of the larger framework of German history.

Jüterbog-Damm: the flying school and 'Fliegerhorst'

Another remarkably well-preserved and self-contained installation of considerable architectural interest is to be found at Jüterbog-Damm, near the medieval town of Jüterbog, which became a garrison town as long ago

as 1748. Its development as a military centre was given a further boost when an artillery unit was stationed there in 1832.[24] Jüterbog's economy was closely bound up with its expansion as a garrison town. In 1860, a permanent garrison was established and, in 1864, a firing range was set up to the west of the old town, followed by a large barracks development during the military build-up that followed the foundation of the Reich. Seven former military sites still survive today in the town's vicinity.

Military aviation began at Jüterbog during the reign of Wilhelm II when an artillery air corps was deployed for the surveillance of enemy troops, first from balloons and airships and later from aeroplanes. 'A reconnaissance aviation school was then established with the setting up of the Artillery Air Corps Base in 1916, to the south of the municipality of Damm. This school trained artillery officers to become aircraft pilots and reconnaissance officers.'[25] At a junction in the road leading out of Jüterbog to the south-west, near an existing windmill, living

Top: Berlin-Karlshorst, interior view of the hangars; the wall replaces the original hangar doors on the airfield side (photo Wolfgang Reuss/Landesdenkmalamt Berlin)

Berlin-Karlshorst, interior view of the hangars, showing the strip windows to the left, on the airfield side (photo Wolfgang Reuss/Landesdenkmalamt Berlin)

Jüterbog-Damm, interior view of one of the reinforced concrete shell hangars built in 1934, showing the inner ribbing of the construction (photo Paul Smith)

quarters, vehicle hangars and other technical buildings were constructed for this school, along with ten aircraft hangars and a workshop, laid out in a semicircle around the airfield.[26] Following the ban placed on military aviation after the First World War, the school and its airfield were dismantled. The workshop, however, along with some of the buildings parallel to the old aircraft hangars, appear to have been occupied for a few years as commercial premises.[27] These buildings are still visible on a ground plan dating from about 1935.[28] The airfield, however, had been returned to agricultural uses.

In the early 1930s, plans were already underway for a new airfield, one-third larger than the original. 'In 1934, a new aerodrome installation was built on the site of the former airfield under the code name "German Air Transport School", complete with three aircraft hangars, a workshop, living quarters and the accompanying infrastructural buildings such as training facilities, mess and hospital.'[29] Here again, the division of the aerodrome into different functional areas is clearly marked: the main entrance, to the north, leads directly to the living quarters built to the north-east, where the accommodation, training and administration buildings, kitchen and refectories, sick bay, telephone exchange, cinema,

officers' mess and smaller residential buildings are laid out in an east–west direction. To the south-west, along Dennewitzer Straße, are the mechanical service areas with various garages and workshops, a petrol station on two reinforced concrete mushroom-shaped pillars, the vehicle administration offices and a warehouse located along the former railway siding.

The southern area comprises the airfield proper and the buildings for aircraft maintenance. The three aircraft hangars and the workshop are arranged alternately with the oil storage depot, an electric power plant, administrative facilities and air-traffic control and a fire station, all arranged in a semicircle on the northern perimeter of the airfield. The workshop, 50 x 40m in size, was built in 1934 to a design by Dyckerhoff & Widmann AG. It is a reinforced concrete shell construction with two arches and a tie-beam. This impressive workshop type was described in the magazine *Der Baumeister* in 1937. The aircraft hangars have a rectangular footprint and at each extremity, a curved-sided extension houses the functional areas. The concrete shell vaulting of the three identical hangars, each trussed with four projecting ribs, forms an open span from the door supports down to the floor at the rear.

The former aerodrome at Jüterbog-

Damm, together with its airfield, was used for its original purpose for about ten years, up to the end of the Second World War. The Soviet Army, which took over all military property after 1945, including Jüterbog, stationed a missile unit there with hardly any subsequent structural changes. The now abandoned airfield was walled off. It was only in April 1994 that this last Russian garrison withdrew from Jüterbog.

Thanks to its continued military use, the entire installation has been preserved in a state of completeness that make it today a rare 'document' bearing witness to the workings of a German military aerodrome of the 1930s. It would be wishful thinking to anticipate new civilian uses for the site that can respect the overall structure and make it possible for all the buildings and the airfield to be preserved. This former military installation, however, needs to be better studied and documented before any of its buildings are demolished.

Notes

1 Johannes Bruns, *Militärbauten und Denkmalpflege. Vortragstexte zur Fachtagung Militärbauten und Denkmalpflege, am 8. und 9. Dezember 1998 in Mülheim a.d. Ruhr*, Reihe Arbeitsheft der rheinischen Denkmalpflege, no. 54. Essen: Verlag Klartext, 2000.

2 Andreas Skopnik, 'Flugzeughallen in Brandenburg, Ingenieurbauwerke unter Denkmalschutz – schutzwürdige Ingenieurbauwerke'. Dissertation, Fachhochschule Potsdam, Civil Engineering Department, June 1998.

3 *Luftfahrt in Berlin-Brandenburg, Stätten deutscher Luftfahrtgeschichte im Wandel der Zeit.* Berlin: Verein zur Bewahrung von Stätten deutscher Luftfahrtgeschichte eV, Berlin-Schönefeld, 1992, 11.

4 'Flughafen Tempelhof'. Leaflet *Berlin wird ...*, Senatsverwaltung für Stadtentwicklung und Umweltschutz (eds). Berlin, [1997].

5 *Luftfahrt in Berlin-Brandenburg*, 22.

6 Richard Sonntag, *Über die Entwicklung und den heutigen Stand des deutschen Flugzeughallenbaues*. Berlin: Verlag Deutsche Bauzeitung GmbH, Berlin, 1914, 1.

7 Sonntag, *Über die Entwicklung*, 1–2.

8 See Joachim Grenzdörfer and Klaus-Dieter Seifert, *Geschichte der ostdeutschen Verkehrsflughäfen*. Bonn: Verlag Bernard und Graefe, 1997, 11.

9 Helmut Eikermann, 'Luftschiffahrt in Karlshorst', in *100 Jahre Karlshorst*. Berlin: be bra verlag, 1995, 137.

10 Bundesarchiv Berlin, 1:2,500 ground plan of the Berlin-Friedrichsfelde airfield, Intendantur der Luftstreitkräfte, Berlin, July 1918.

11 Bundesarchiv Berlin, 1:2,500 ground plan of the Berlin-Friedrichsfelde airforce

Jüterbog-Damm, the rounded roofing of a workshop at the end of one of the 1934 hangars, its windows bricked in (photo Paul Smith)

installation, Militär-Neubauamt Berlin-Friedrichsfelde, Karlshorst, 15 January 1919.

12 Landesarchiv Berlin, Cartography Department, 1:25,000 situation plan of 1920.

13 Staatsbibliothek Unter den Linden: Stadt Berlin, Verw. Lichtenberg, about 1934.

14 Bezirksamt Lichtenberg, Berlin: aerial photograph, 1928.

15 Landesarchiv Berlin, Cartography Department: projects for an aircraft hangar and workshops for the air force installation at Berlin-Friedrichsfelde, Intendantur- und Baurat, Berlin, 4 April and 20 June 1917.

16 Skopnik, *Flugzeughallen in Brandenburg*, 5–6.

17 *125 Jahre Rank*, Baugesellschaft Gebr. Rank & Co Munich (eds). Munich, 1987 (see Skopnik, *Flugzeughallen in Brandenburg*, 5).

18 According to Skopnik, at the aerial reconnaissance school in Schleißheim, a 90-metre-long aircraft hangar was built, even though a 70-metre-long one had been built only a year before. In fact, the workshop hangar in Schleißheim measured 51.40 x 27.50m and has therefore roughly the same dimensions as the workshop in Friedrichsfelde. At the airfield at Fürth, again according to Skopnik, citing the Military Planning Office: 'At the airfield: five aircraft hangars and a workshop building also with a hangar measuring 50 x 30m.'

19 K O Kalisch, Report ZLK no. 90.84 on the corrosion of the roof construction of the hangar at Berlin-Karlshorst, commissioned by the VEB Forschungsanstalt für Schiffahrt, Wasser- und Grundbau, Fachdirektorat für Versuchswesen, Berlin, 7 June 1984, 2 (Archives BAW Karlshorst).

20 1917 outline plan with five windows.

21 Werner Spillhagen, 'Die Beheizung von Flugzeughallen'. *Der Flughafen* 6th year (1938), Vol 9–10, 25–6.

22 Spillhagen, 'Die Beheizung von Flugzeughallen', 25.

23 'Hallenbau und Luftschutz'. *Der Flughafen* 6th year (1938), Vol 9–10, 23.

24 Marie-Luise Buchinger and Marcus Cante, *Denkmaltopographie Bundesrepublik Deutschland, Denkmale in Brandenburg, Landkreis Teltow-Fläming, Part 1: Stadt Jüterbog mit Kloster Zinna und Gemeinde Niedergörsdorf.* Worms am Rhein: Wernersche Verlagsgesellschaft, 2000, 34–53.

25 Buchinger and Cante, *Denkmaltopographie Bundesrepublik Deutschland*, 48.

26 See the aerial photograph of the airfield about 1918, Municipal Museum of Jüterbog, Repro F 91/1129.

27 In 1923, a flax factory and in 1925 a road haulage contractor gave the airfield as their address. See the collection Jannek, Municipal Museum of Jüterbog.

28 Plan at the Municipal Museum of Jüterbog.

29 Buchinger and Cante, *Denkmaltopographie Bundesrepublik Deutschland*, 187.

Aviation buildings in the Netherlands: monuments under pressure

Marieke Kuipers

The first real 'Flying Dutchman' took to the sky in 1910, thanks to initiatives taken by the army. The impetus for the launch of civil aviation in the Netherlands was given by the first aviation exhibition in Amsterdam, which was held in 1919. A small part of the military airfield at Schiphol, located within the *Festung* (fortification division) of Amsterdam, was set aside for civil aviation purposes, paving the way for what is today the main airport in the Netherlands. At the same time, many smaller airfields were developed for military and/or civil purposes. A fierce debate took place in the Netherlands as early as the 1920s as to the location, the accessibility and safety of these airports. This debate has been rekindled in recent years as a result of new economic conditions and the growth of an ecological awareness. Since the 1990s, besides such environmental issues as birds, noise and air pollution, the debate has also addressed the significance of airfields as historic monuments and cultural landscapes. The air transport industry and its constructions are faced with an increasingly acute shortage of space; airports are calling for desperately needed extensions in order to meet the constant growth in air traffic. The very survival of certain historic aviation buildings is under threat, even when they enjoy statutory protection as historic monuments.

An inventory of historic airports in the Netherlands

Any study or inventory of these still relatively recent installations has to come to terms with the consequences of the Second World War for the historic aviation structures in the Netherlands. Very few pre-war aviation buildings actually survived the war or the modernisation programmes that followed it; conversion for military use also meant that some pre-war installations have been modified beyond recognition. At the same time, a large number of German military buildings and structures have survived from the period of the Occupation. They are

to be found on air force bases or at civil airports that are either still in use today or have been closed down only recently. Today, this contradictory legacy also fulfils the minimum age requirement of fifty years laid down by the present Dutch Historic Buildings and Monuments Act (*Monumentenwet*, 1988), a law which stipulates that buildings of aesthetic, cultural, historic or scientific significance are to be protected in the general interest. At least three out of some twenty aviation sites surveyed, as well as various individual structures on other sites, meet the necessary criteria to be preserved as historic monuments.

Until the 1980s, Dutch airports were mainly considered as places of progress at the service of constantly developing air travel, rather than as monuments to the history of technology and transportation, as

Airfield sites in the Netherlands

Ypenburg, the airport clubroom in 1936. The veranda window frontage offers a panoramic view over the flying field. The original interior fittings are completely lost. Today, the terminal building is used as an information centre for the new housing estate (Collection M Kuipers)

was the case for about twenty railway stations that had already been officially protected as historic monuments. Between 1987 and 1994, the Monumenten Inventarisatie Project (MIP) established a national inventory of the cultural legacy of the so-called 'steam era' (1850–1940). This was followed by the Monumenten Selectie Project (MSP) which has recently been completed and which is intended to secure statutory heritage status for a selection of the sites identified by the inventory. For the first time, these campaigns are giving due consideration to aviation constructions, with assessments being carried out to ensure that they qualify for heritage status and listing in the MIP documentation. The year 1940 was chosen as a logical cut-off date, corresponding, on the one hand, with the interruption caused by the war and, on the other, with the fifty-year clause of the 1988 heritage act. The authorities and certain colleagues had to be convinced that even these relatively recent constructions were eligible for protection as heritage. But, with time, interest in structures dating from the Occupation has increased and, gradually, sites from the 1940s have been included in the MIP and MSP programmes. Without any doubt, one of the reasons for this is that the employees of the inventory services are mostly young, belonging to the post-war generations that have a more impartial attitude towards these sites.

Within the framework of the MIP campaign, ten historic aviation sites were initially selected. Most of these were built in the 1930s for civil aviation purposes and consisted of relatively modest installations.[1] Unfortunately, by this time, the earliest airport buildings at Schiphol, of considerable interest in both architectural and historical terms, had already disappeared and Waalhaven, in Rotterdam, was also completely destroyed in 1940. But the buildings of the third most important airport of this period,

Ypenburg near The Hague, have survived in their entirety. Built out of wood, the KLM passenger buildings at Leeuwarden have also resisted the passing of time, as have the KLM terminals at Eelde and Welschap (near Eindhoven), although all are much modified.

The extensive survey work carried out as part of the MIP and MSP programmes was divided up geographically and enlisted the help of almost every single expert available; there was little opportunity to carry out thematic research. Nevertheless, in 1994, an application submitted by a local historical association to protect Ypenburg airport as a historical monument provided the impetus to set up a nation-wide survey of civil aviation sites of historical interest. Prior to this, a 'Quick Scan' was undertaken to compile a list of all the military complexes built on airfields and dating from the 1930s and 1940s. A small working group was set up consisting of two representatives from the Ministry of Defence, two conservationists and an independent art historian. We visited a total of twenty sites, eleven of which are still in use for military purposes.[2] This rapid survey was encouraged by the large number of applications for the protection of barracks built by the German air force, submitted by the Dutch Federation for Aviation Archaeology (NFLA).

The Dutch Monuments Act stipulates that all buildings and structures which are the object of an application submitted in accordance with the regulations are entitled to legal protection until the Minister for Culture decides whether or not they are to be officially 'classified' as historic monuments, or otherwise. In practice, our national *Monumentenzorg* service takes this decision on behalf of the State Secretary for Culture. This means that social forces are at work that are difficult to control and can have a considerable influence on privately owned property and even affect military properties. The air force bases and the civil installations must also respect town and country planning regulations as well as labour and environmental ones. With towns expanding at the same pace as the airports, initially located at a respectable distance from them, both are gradually encroaching on one another. The enlargement of Schiphol airport poses a threat not only to some archaeological remains but also to various other historic monuments in the vicinity. In other places, urban growth or military renovations are endangering the survival of historic airports.[3]

Ypenburg from the airport to the VINEX-district

As already mentioned, most sites dating from before the last war – buildings, grass runways, technical facilities – have either been destroyed or considerably modified. With the exception of Schiphol, the few completed civil airfields in existence were reconverted for military use and enlarged either shortly before the war or during it. After their restitution by the Allies, the installations often continued to be used for military purposes. One example of this is Ypenburg airfield, close to The Hague. Its functionalist terminal building and steel hangar for twenty-five to thirty aircraft was designed in 1935 by the architects Jan Brinkman and Leen van der Vlugt, in co-operation with the local architect, Maarten Zwanenburg. From 1939 onwards and after the war the site was used as an air force school, although it was originally created for The Hague and Rotterdam flying clubs as a sporting and demonstration airfield. Compared with Tempelhof, for example, Ypenburg was a very modest airport, but in its time, with a surface area of some 200ha, it was the second largest in the Netherlands, after Schiphol, and was larger than Waalhaven. Unlike other airports, its construction was mainly financed by private capital. For a while, it was also a very popular airfield, where it was not unusual for as many as 1,800 spectators to gather to watch aeroplanes taking off and landing. The roof of the terminal building comprised a viewing terrace for visitors and there was also a spectator stand on the south-west side of the airfield. During the economic crisis of the 1930s, the grass runways were drained by the unemployed as an emergency labour measure with central government financial backing. Without these almost invisible measures of technical improvement – a total of 80km of earthenware drainage pipes, two reservoirs, ditches and a pumping station – the marshy flying field could not have supported even the lightest of aircraft.

During Ypenburg's occupation by the Luftwaffe and its role as the airport of The Hague, several new drainage ditches were dug and a wooden landing strip laid down. Nothing remains of these today. Nor have the V-1 launch ramps or the food dropping campaigns of the *Manna* allied operation left any tangible traces. In the course of the airport's reconstruction, in 1955, tarmac runways were laid down and the originally

Above: *Ypenburg, near The Hague, an air show in the late 1930s. The terminal building, designed by L C van der Vlugt and J A Brinkman, was inaugurated in 1936 (Collection M Kuipers)*

Amsterdam-Schiphol international airport in 1928. The control tower is part of the asymmetrical terminal building, in front of the hard-surfaced apron. The building was destroyed in May 1940 (Collection M Kuipers)

white buildings, riddled with bullet holes, were partly plastered over in camouflage (beige-green). Subsequently, the windows, the entrance and the control tower were modernised and the hangar was taken over by the Fokker company and enlarged. The functionalist interior fittings of the terminal building were almost completely removed. Only a few features of the kitchen fittings and the fireplace in the former clubroom remained. At the beginning of the 1990s, it was decided to abandon the airport; the city council of The Hague needed the site for urban development. Whether Fokker could or wanted to stay was not yet decided. With the threat of demolition looming over the entire site, including the terminal building, gate houses, hangar and Dutch national flying school, built by H F Mertens in 1939,

Welschap airport (later the Meerhoven military site), near Eindhoven. The terminal building, designed in 1934 by Dirk Roosenburg, was recently restored by Jan van den Burg. As at Ypenburg, the building today serves as an information centre for the new housing estate (photo Norbert van Onna)

the local historical association submitted an application for these four structures to be protected as historic monuments.[4]

This led to a study of the significance of the historic architecture and technical aspects of the buildings. The airfield, however, in its modernised form, with the 2,400-metre-long runway, was not included in this heritage assessment. Only a few publications were available on Ypenburg's architecture, although Brinkman and van der Vlugt were already acclaimed nationally and internationally as the architects of the famous Van Nelle factory at Rotterdam, completed in 1931. It was thanks to the intervention of one of the directors of the Van Nelle firm, Dick van der Leeuw – the younger brother of Kees van der Leeuw, a passionate pilot and member of the Rotterdam Aero Club – that they were awarded the commission for Ypenburg.[5] It was van der Vlugt's last construction. He died four months before the official opening.

Although the Ypenburg buildings were in a bad state of repair in the early 1990s and although their functionalist appearance had been disfigured, their demolition would have been unthinkable. Their preservation could lead to a conversion project and create the right conditions for a subsequent sale.

The whole site was located within the area set aside for the Haaglanden city development project, designated as a so-called VINEX zone, on which a large housing estate was to be built. VINEX stands for *VIerde Nota ruimtelijke ordening EXtra*, a planning directive that stipulates the nature and extent of urban expansion. It is a magic word for architects and estate agents, since these areas can be intensively developed. At Ypenburg, 11,000 of a total of 43,000

planned homes were to be built on the airfield site, where an additional 85ha were set aside for a business park.

The town-planner Frits Palmboom was entrusted with the overall control of the project. His task was not only the preparation of the building plan and the creation of a specific identity for the new housing and business districts, but also to draw up a report relating to the impact of the new housing estate on the environment. One of the results of this report was that the four airfield buildings were saved instead of being 'left to the mercy of nature', as was initially and euphemistically suggested, in order to justify demolition and the use of the space for housing. Although it was badly damaged by the effects of damp and vandalism, the former terminal building was successfully renovated and used first of all as a design office for the VINEX district. Today, it serves as an information centre for potential homebuyers. Despite the legal preservation order, the last of the interior fittings were lost during the renovation. Only the control tower, the stair tower, the overall silhouette and a veranda survive in their original state. The building was also rendered in white again, to symbolise its return to civilian use.

The 63-metre-wide steel hangar was dismantled after Fokker went bankrupt and, with the authorisation of the heritage department, it was rebuilt on a new airfield in Hoogeveen for use by a club that restores historic aircraft. Clearly, it would have been preferable to put the hangar to this use at its original location, but because of financial requirements and urban development, this was no longer possible. So Ypenburg airport lives on today mainly in street names and the three reconverted buildings.[6] The runway

can still be made out along the main artery of the estate, cutting a straight line through the recent 'forest' of homes. At Ypenburg, however, it was too late and too expensive to preserve a part of the airfield and to find a suitable new use that could reflect something of its aviation past.

Demolition or reconversion

A similar development can also be seen on a site close to Eindhoven. This military base of Meerhoven – a training station for pilots and tank infantry – was sold in 1998 as building land and granted VINEX zone status. As a result, 300 structures, including 124 buildings, were surveyed and their historic and cultural significance evaluated, at the same time as their structural condition was assessed. Assessments were also carried out of various possible new uses for these buildings, involving an estimate of their current market value. Only sixteen buildings were finally declared to be worthy of preservation. The most significant of these is without doubt the former Welschap terminal building, designed in 1934 by Dirk Roosenburg, KLM's house architect. Although this edifice is no longer fully preserved in its original form, it was given protection as a historic monument within the framework of the MSP campaign. It is destined to be used temporarily as an information and exhibition centre. Here again, the original use has been lost, as the training centre was transferred to an installation close to Eindhoven.

Although our knowledge of the historic airfield installations of the 1930s might have improved, we do not always succeed in taking the appropriate measures to save the constructions. One example is the Westenschouwen airfield (near Haamstede on the island of Schouwen-Duiveland, province of Zeeland), the site of a remarkable terminal building with a control tower dating 1932/3. It was put into operation when a new air connection was established with the Belgian seaside resort of Knokke. After the war, the two side wings were rebuilt in a modified form, in order to house a restaurant. The building was included in the MIP inventory but in its existing form it had no future. A new and larger hotel has been built around the former control tower in a way that makes the original function hardly recognisable. Only the nearby field for gliders, a grass runway in the dunes, serves as a reminder of the historic airfield of the pre-war era. The

sporting airfields near Hilversum and near Teuge have also kept their grass runways and still operate almost as they did before the war, though on a smaller scale and for leisure purposes only.

In the overpopulated Netherlands, hardly any complete civil airfield from the 1930s has survived up to the present day. Even military airfields face uncertainty as to their future. They are either being abandoned and sold, or falling victim to urban development projects. One example of this is the Valkenburg naval airfield near Katwijk and Wassenaar, which is still in use, in particular by the Dutch Royal Family. But it has already been designated as building land for the future Valkenburcht housing estate. This strategically located airfield was not completely finished in May 1940 and during the war it was extended as a German airbase. The simple Luftwaffe buildings stand on either side of a road that runs along dunes that are protected by a conservation order for nature and water-supply. These constructions could be integrated into the

Top: *Westenschouwen airfield near Haamstede in the 'golden thirties', when the links to Rotterdam and Knokke (Belgium) were KLM's cheapest air routes. Only the control tower of the terminal building survives, surrounded by a new hotel complex (collection M Kuipers)*

Gilze-Rijen air force base, inspection of the relics of a compass adjustment table. At the rim of this circular construction, triangular stones indicate the compass points (photo Jan van't Hof)

development project, but this possibility has so far generated little enthusiasm. It is also doubtful whether its original use as an airfield will remain visible if most of the site is developed; the historic structures would disappear along with the runways. There is also talk of surrounding the new housing estate with canals. Only the remains of the Atlantic Wall nearby (anti-tank trenches and bunkers) might be saved, although their spatial and visual relations to the airfield are difficult to understand today, as the central provincial road has been widened and garden sheds and greenhouses have been built between the air force constructions.

In other cases, only archaeological traces remain; everything else has been destroyed or rendered unrecognisable by post-war alterations. An interesting example of these archaeological vestiges are the compass-adjustment tables, which are totally overgrown with vegetation today. Examples of these tables have been preserved at Gilze-Rijen and, partially, at Deelen. They are demagnetised circular constructions with a diameter of 12m. The cardinal points of the compass are indicated on the edge of the concrete basin, which has a wooden floor that can be rotated either manually or by means of an electric motor. Aircraft were placed on these platforms in order to adjust their compasses. Thanks to our 'Quick Scan' survey programme, assessments are currently underway, in collaboration with the Dutch Air Force, to see whether these structures can be preserved within the framework of planned developments.

At the De Mok naval airfield on the island of Texel to the north of the Netherlands, a historic hangar dating from 1917 has entirely disappeared, but the tracks of its sliding doors still survive in the concrete floor, today the surface of a tennis court. At Bergen (between Alkmaar and the North Sea coast), some large hangars from the 1930s were replaced by new warehouse buildings, designed for mobilisation purposes during the Cold War. Only the old door tracks of the hangars and a pumping installation bear witness to the pre-war installation. This former military base close to the Atlantic Wall, however, is still strongly characterised by standard German concrete constructions. A bunker was painted to resemble a house for camouflage purposes, a technique that was also used for Dutch bunkers. The bunkers on this abandoned airfield survive, but development plans are also on the cards here.

A common European heritage

Despite the fact that the painful legacy of the war was systematically destroyed for decades, we should not today make the opposite mistake of protecting all the sites dating from the German Occupation, merely because they have survived and for reasons of political correctness. Our attitude must remain critical and selection criteria need to be better defined. The new knowledge gained at national and international levels must be applied, in particular to assess the significance of such structures from architectural, historical and typological points of view. Furthermore, our heritage policies should not be restricted only to the buildings, but should also take into consideration the empty expanses of the airfields. The Ypenburg example shows how protecting historic aviation buildings without their adjoining airfields is only half a protection measure. The monuments become obsolete in a newly created environment, even if efforts are made to conserve some free space around the terminal buildings. In principle, our Monuments Act makes it possible to include in protection measures open, 'green' areas as integral parts of a historic monument, for example, the historic layout of a garden of a country seat, where the entire site is protected as an ensemble. At Ypenburg, this possibility was not exploited. We then had little experience in this field and it was difficult to demonstrate the historic and cultural significance of an open surface which had been frequently modified and which had already been singled out as highly valuable building land.

Curiously enough, Twenthe and Deelen airports in the east of the Netherlands preserve their historic transport landscapes and are still in use, possibly because the pressure of urban expansion is not as strong here as in the west of the country. Twenthe opened as a civil airfield in 1928 and was extended in 1940 as an airbase for the German air force. During the Occupation, several new buildings were put up. On military and aesthetic grounds, shatter-proof barracks in the regional style of Saxon farms were built, grouped around small grass squares. Windows were painted onto the 550-mm-thick, brick-clad concrete walls in order to camouflage them. The architects of this Dutch variant of the *Heimatstil* have not yet been identified but, even in the detailing, they went to great lengths to respect regional building traditions.

During the post-war years, the airfield was modernised for the Dutch air force. Ever practical and thrifty, the Dutch removed the ruins of war and took over the other complexes built by the former forces of occupation, adapting them to meet new requirements, for example for NATO, during the Cold War. Some buildings were even embellished. This was the case, for example, of the building that houses both a chapel and a mess. Stained glass was installed in the windows in order to underline the return to peace. The survival of this building is threatened today by new building regulations concerning efficiency, energy-consumption and health and safety. It is not yet certain whether heritage values can prevail against the plethora of other regulations. Despite the objections at first shown by the site's commanding officer towards civil servants (especially representatives of the Netherlands department for Conservation), our field research rekindled interest in the history of the airfield and its buildings.

Deelen airfield, created in 1914 on a heath near Arnheim, was also the object of an in-depth study. The landscape of this area is of considerable interest not only for aviation history but also for archaeologists, on account of the crop-marks that are to be found there. The airfield was decommissioned in 1996, but is still used temporarily by a mobile air brigade. To the south of this airfield, where some German runways can still be seen, laid out in the form of an 'A', are based the camps of Vrijland, Klein and Groot Heidekamp, comprising more than eighty structures, including a fully preserved workshop and hangars of various types.

On a sandy plateau to the north of the airfield lies the so-called Kop van Deelen, with twenty-seven constructions, including a boiler house. This isolated complex, no longer air force property, is currently used as a centre for immigrant asylum-seekers, similar to the former air force housing estates of Burmania (Leeuwarden), Chaam/Prinsenbosch (Gilze-Rijen) and Oirschot (Eindhoven). Here, an inexpensive, if controversial, reconversion has been found for the burdensome legacy of the German Occupation.

South of Deelen lies the former Diogenes district command post, dating from 1943. During the war, massive air raids were conducted from this central command post. Inside the huge bunker, a vertical glass sheet measuring 14 x 11m was installed to plot the positions of the German fighters and other aircraft, using light projections at

night. This piece of military technology was in advance for its time, but was destroyed by the Germans during their withdrawal.

However evocative of conflict their origins might be, the wartime constructions in Deelen, Twenthe and elsewhere are part of our common heritage today. They are built witnesses of the occupation period and, to the east of the Netherlands, offer examples of military architecture trying to imitate regional building traditions. The Diogenes bunker, although empty today, is a remarkable construction of considerable significance for military history; it has been protected by law despite its grim function and history. Not all surviving German buildings, however, merit protection as historic monuments, simply as witnesses of history. And even constructions that do deserve protection, such as the headquarters in Deelen, are not always easy to save from demolition.

Within the framework of the 'Quick

Top: *The Kop van Deelen, originally part of the air force base at Deelen, which is still in use. The living quarters date from the Second World War and imitate the region's farmhouses; the brick cladding conceals a reinforced concrete construction. They currently serve as a centre for immigrant asylum-seekers (photo M Kuipers)*

Deelen air force base, the Junker hall of the Vrijland division, a rare and relatively well-preserved example of this German type of hangar, built from prefabricated elements (photo M Kuipers)

This imposing building at Hilversum, known as the 'Cathedral', was probably used as a parade hall during the Second World War (photo M Kuipers)

Scan' survey, we are attempting today to make a selection among the surviving sites. In collaboration with the local authorities, the air force and the provincial administrations, we hope to investigate the possibilities of applying preventive measures that will manage further development in such a way as to keep the historic 'infrastructural' landscape, with its installations, understandable to the visitor. To do so, a committee must be set up under the direction of the provincial administration responsible for town and country planning. The task implies respecting both military history and the architectural significance of the sites, as well as the importance of the airfields as cultural landscapes and nature reserves. A common policy is to be developed in order to achieve this aim.

Our 'Quick Scan' has shown us how diversified the architectural legacy of the German air force actually is. Thanks to our co-operation with the Ministry of Defence, it was possible to discover two extraordinary complexes in Hilversum that were highly atypical for the Netherlands. They were built near the occupied airfield, close to the Zonnestraal sanatorium, where the naval camp of Korporaal van Oudheusdenkazerne is installed today. Surrounded by high trees, there is a remarkable building, apparently known as the 'Cathedral'. Its original function is unknown; the lofty, undivided interior space possibly served as a parade hall, although the intricate details and the relatively rich materials suggest a more prestigious use. With its impressive concrete arches, it is now used as storage space for training materials for emergencies. The second building is the former command post, which has an unusual ground plan for the Netherlands with two inner courtyards and a monumental staircase. Once again, its architect is unknown. Further research is necessary to understand these unique pieces of military architecture, and to gain a more coherent picture of the diverse architectural legacy of the 1940s.

In the area surrounding the airfield, where more than 750 German soldiers were stationed during the war, various bunkers that served to defend the airfield have also survived. Some shatter-proof living quarters in the style of the German architect Paul Schmitthenner can be found on the site of the neighbouring Zonnestraal sanatorium. These are now used as apartments after having been converted immediately after the war into the Zonnepark rehabilitation clinic. Today, a new heritage assessment must be undertaken for the structures within the Zonnestraal complex, as only the buildings of the architects Jan Duiker and Bernard Bijvoet were taken into consideration for protection in the 1980s.[7]

Dynamism and heritage values

Besides technical advances and economy drives, land shortage in the densely populated Netherlands increasingly represents a major threat for historic aviation buildings. To conclude, I would like to return to civil aviation, still in a process of constant growth. From the outset, the international airport of Schiphol was a symbol of modernity and dynamism. Not only were its buildings constantly brought up to date and enlarged to meet the new requirements, but its surroundings also changed rapidly. Schiphol has long since been at the centre of discussions about air traffic control, economy, safety, the environment and architecture, although economic interests pre-dominate. The construction of a fifth runway, to the west of the present-day airport, in particular, is highly controversial. Recently, heritage values have also been taken into consideration in the debate, for the aviation constructions and other historic buildings nearby.

Schiphol is situated in the municipality of Haarlemmermeer on the polder of the same name that was first drained in 1852 for agricultural purposes. One of the small villages, Hoofddorp, has developed over the last decades into a boomtown. In the debate surrounding the constant extension of the airport, the local planning authority is not making the most of its influence. Schiphol is still considered as the airport of the city of Amsterdam and decisions about its future lie in the hands of central government and not with the local town council or the provincial administration, which plays an important part in the planning processes for

areas outside the jurisdiction of the local authorities.

Various farms are to be demolished in order to make way for the extension of Schiphol. The construction of the fifth runway is forcing ten families to abandon their homes. It is mainly city-dwellers, however, living farther away from Schiphol, who are protesting against growing environmental pollution. In 1995, 360 people jointly bought a potato field and planted it with trees in order to obstruct possible expropriations. Despite its strategic location, this small wood has recently been expropriated, following a court ruling. The Wilgenhof cemetery is also located close to the airport. It was established during the 19th century and later extended to the south-east for war graves and to the north-west for Jewish graves. Today it is no longer a tranquil haven, a green oasis in the open polder. Its willow trees have been cut down to their stumps and, nearby, excavators are already at work, even though the official authorisation for the fifth runway has not yet been granted. No solution has yet been found to ensure that the 13,000 grave-owners are

guaranteed safe access to the cemetery and to deal with the question of the Jewish graves, that cannot be moved.

Until the completion of the fifth runway in 2002, the cemetery should continue to exist. The fate of the transparent chapel designed by Gerrit Rietveld is also in the balance, even though it was designated as a heritage site by the local authority. This small building, designed in 1958 and completed in 1966, after Rietveld's death, under the direction of J Dillen and J van Tricht, will probably be unable to survive for very long the vibrations of the jumbo jets landing nearby. The single glass panes, the wooden frames of which are slowly rotting, will shatter unless they are repaired and reinforced. In the meantime, the local authority has decided to build a copy of the building at a new cemetery in Zwaanshoek, although the report of the Netherlands Department for Conservation recommended another solution and the local authority initially considered moving the building.

The construction of the fifth runway is also triggering fierce protests on account of the measures taken to combat noise

Schiphol East, the restored 'old' control tower. This tower had already been lowered, but was saved from complete demolition and restored by Wessel de Jonge Architecten in 2001. The operation involved not only the complete reconstruction of the upper levels but also the tower's adaptation to a new use. On the evening of its inauguration, the Minister for Transport arrived by air in an authentic Dakota-3 (photo Ruud Taal/Capital Photos) pollution on the north side of the airport. The inhabitants of the village of Assendelft (Zaan region) are refusing to install double glazing in their historic farms and country houses and are rejecting the stipulated insulation measures. Conservation and preservation do not always go hand in hand.

In the quest for a certain balance between the necessary development of Schiphol and the preservation of its history, a private initiative unexpectedly came to the rescue of an endangered monument of aviation. A group of companies decided to restore the 'old' control tower, dating from 1946 to 1949 (today at Schiphol East), a symbol of the reconstruction of the airport, which was badly damaged during the war. Irony of fate: this functionalistic control tower was built only as a temporary structure, out of steel, concrete and glass. Even back in 1949 it was expected that Schiphol would have to be enlarged. After lengthy political discussions, it was only in 1967 that the new airport was opened, at last equipped for modern air travel in jet planes (today Schiphol Centre). This was one of the first terminals with piers, designed by M F Duintjer and the NACO Office (Netherlands Airport Consultancy). The modest complex to the east, dating from the post-war reconstruction, continued to serve only small aircraft and various service areas. The practically freestanding control tower, built by the architect J H Groenewegen for the city of Amsterdam, gradually lost its function and also its characteristic feature: the wedge-shaped control platform. Despite this 'decapitated' state, the group of businessmen wanted to retain the tower for its historical significance and rebuild its control platform as a café, a club and conference centre. Furthermore, the tower, which had become an obstacle for new constructions and lorries, was to be moved by 30m (only a short distance compared to the move of the terminal at Copenhagen Kastrup). On the evening of 2 February 2001, the Minister for Transport, Tineke Netelenbos, landed in an original Dakota-3 in order to inaugurate the completely restored control tower (at least in its outside appearance). The reconverted tower has become a monument to dynamism and at the same time a good example of recycling in terms of environmental protection policies. The rapid growth in air traffic, which is reflected in ever-bigger terminals and ever-taller control towers, represents a permanent threat for the historic sites and buildings that gradually fall victim to it.

Without these historic monuments, however, it is no longer possible to grasp the true scale of the progress made by aviation.

Notes

1 These ten sites are Bergen (1938), Eelde (1931), Eindhoven (1931–4), Haamstede (1933), Leeuwarden (1937), Soesterberg (1911), Twente (1931), Valkenburg (1937–40), Venlo (1932) and Ypenburg near Rijswijk (1935–6).

2 Alongside the ten sites mentioned above, these include the following installations: Deelen (1914), Gilze-Rijen (1910), Den Helder (De Kooy), Hilversum (1934), Teuge (1934), Texel (De Mok, 1938), Volkel and Woensdrecht (1935); at Drachten, Hoogeveen and Havelte almost nothing has survived from the 1940s.

3 See *Cultuurhistorie en vliegveldlocaties: een archeologische en historisch-geografische verkenning en waardering tern beheove van project TNLI* [...]. Hoorn, 1998.

4 As already mentioned, Dutch law stipulates that any application for the protection of a building as a historic monument, submitted in accordance with the regulations, must be given consideration. Usually, the Minister for Culture only protects sites (under the terms of the *Monumenten Registratie Procedure* or preservation procedure) when these have been identified within the framework of the MSP campaign. In exceptional circumstances, however, emergency protection measures are also possible. An exceptional circumstance is deemed to exist when the significance of the construction for the public interest is undisputed and when its survival is threatened. The heritage department ensures that the construction in question fulfils these two criteria.

5 M A G (Dick) van der Leeuw died in an air crash in Waalhaven in December 1936, his brother, J J van der Leeuw, meeting the same fate in Africa in 1934.

6 New roads on the housing estate were named after famous pilots such as Anthony Fokker and Jan Olijslagers.

7 The memories of the Occupation were considered to be troubling at the time, and the living quarters – another 'layer' of history – were consequently not included in the preservation order. During the Second World War, Hilversum was an important military citadel. In 1943 a unique, three-storey concrete construction was built to house the commander of the German army in the Netherlands. Located to the north of the town, it had walls over 30m long. This terrestrial counterpart of

the Diogenes air force bunker served as the headquarters of the Atlantic Wall in the Netherlands. At the end of the 1990s, the well-situated site was purchased by a construction company which planned to build ten luxury villas after dynamiting the concrete colossus. This so-called 'Blaskowitzbunker' was preserved, however, on the one hand because of its uniqueness and on the other because of its significance for military history. The last commander of the German armed forces of the Netherlands, General J A Blaskowitz, had prepared the German capitulation of the 25th Army here. It is doubtful, however, whether the historical significance of the construction will still be discernible once it is surrounded by villas.

Select bibliography

MIP collection *Architectuur en stedebouw in Nederland 1850–1940*
NRC-Handelsblad
RDMZ Nieuwsbrief

Bremmers, J, Machielse, M and Sakkers, H 1998 *De commmandobunker van Hilversum, Hoofdkwartier van de Atlantikwall in Nederland.* Nieuw Weerdinge

van den Burg, J 2001 'Luchthavengebouw Eindhoven'. *DOCOMOMO NL Nieuwsbrief 002*, 10–11

'Een nieuwe toekomst voor een oud knooppunt'. 1999 Brochure *De oude Toren*

van de Graaf, H 1992 *Het vliegveld Oostvoorne.* Bernisse

Groenendijk, P and Vollaard, P 1998 *Gids voor moderne architectuur in Nederland*, 5 edn. Rotterdam

van der Klaauw, B 1982 *Luchthaven Schiphol.* Alkmaar

Kuipers, M C 1996 'Aviation architecture and its message of "Modernity"', in *Proceedings of the Third International Conference DOCOMOMO, Barcelona, 1994*, 131–4

Kuipers, M C 1997 'Erkend als monument, nieuwe beschermingsthema's in de monumentenzorg', in *In dienst van het Erfgoed, Jaarboek Monumentenzorg, Rijksdienst voor de Monumentenzorg 1947–1997*. Zwolle/Zeist, 131–57

Loeff, K 2000 'Quick Scan Historische vliegveldcomplexen (1910–1950) in Nederland, in opdracht van de Rijksdienst voor de Monumentenzorg, Laren/Zeist'. Unpublished manuscript

Molenaar, J 1994 'Het Sportpark en Vliegveld Ypenburg'. *Kroniek/Historische Vereniging Rijswijk* **3–4**, 5–17

Monumenten in Haarlemmermeer 1994 Haarlemmermeer

NFLA 1996 'Het belang van Deelen'. Unpublished manuscript, Arnhem

Schuurman, J H 2001 *Vliegveld Bergen NH 1938–1945, De aanleg van het 'vliegpark', de Duitse aanval in mei 1940, de verbeten strijd van de Fokkers, de geallieerde offensieven gedurende de oorlog.* Bergen

Swart, R 1997 'Vliegveld Deelen als luchtvaartinfrastructuurmonument'. *Cuypersbulletin* **3**, 13–16

Venema, H (ed) 2000 *Buitenplaats Ypenburg, een bevlogen bouwlocatie.* Bussum

Wattjes, J G 1938 'De gebouwen van het vliegveld Ypenburg'. *het Bouwbedrijf* **2**, 11–14; and **3**, 19–22

Historic Airports

Paris-Le Bourget: history of an airport site

Bernard Rignault

Despite being considered as early as 1910 as a potential location for air shows, which were becoming increasingly popular at the time, it was only four years later, at the beginning of the First World War, that the plain situated 7km to the north of Paris, close to the village of Le Bourget on the route de Flandre (Route nationale 2), was to enter aeronautical history. In September 1914, the army established an Air Reserve on the site, closer to the front than its existing depot at Saint-Cyr. During the following months, a proper military airfield was created, intended to provide Paris with an efficient defence against German air raids. Work started on requisitioned agricultural land with the construction of seven Bessonneau-type hangars in timber and canvas, followed by barracks and huts to house workshops and administration offices. About fifteen aircraft, almost half of which were prototypes, comprised the first squadrons of the Paris military region. The first pilots were airmen whose names were already familiar to the public from the pre-war air meetings.

The missions of these squadrons consisted of monitoring specific areas around the capital and of making day or night attacks on targets indicated by lookout posts. In 1915, the efficiency of these squadrons against night attacks over Paris by Zeppelins proved inadequate and resulted in the loss of some of their autonomy: in rotation, a third at a time, the personnel was sent to the front. Despite the absence of any heroic victories capable of justifying the use of the base, the site's infrastructures were nevertheless extended, mainly into the territory of the commune of Dugny,[1] where the Air Reserve Depot continued to expand, reaching a total of 500 aircraft. At the same time, the capability of the squadrons of the Paris military region was increased from 45 planes in 1915 to 116 in 1918. The base, close to Paris, also offered ideal conditions for inventors and industrialists, who used it for their aeronautical experiments.

As the war effort was stepped up on the front, the Le Bourget site came to be seen by the military authorities as of little real use and on 30 August 1918 the aviation services of the Paris region, described as a 'vain and illusory defence', were closed down by Clemenceau. The site retained its infrastructures and facilities, however, and continued to manage the equipment of the Air Reserve, after the Armistice.

Civil aviation takes off

As soon as the war came to an end, all the former belligerents saw the creation of air routes for passengers and freight as a serious prospect for aviation. Four years of warfare had seen aircraft manufacturing develop from small-scale workshops into major industrial complexes and the aircraft produced in 1918 had little in common with pre-war designs. As for personnel, while some of the trained pilots and ground mechanics stayed with the army, most returned to civilian life, providing a ready supply of experienced men for the commercial companies.

The changeover from a state of war to a

Aerial view of the military aviation camp in 1917, with the route de Flandre to the top and the northern part of the village of Le Bourget to the right. The Bessonneau hangars of the Air Reserve line the road leading to the village of Dugny (Musée de l'Air et de l'Espace, Le Bourget)

Top: *The boarding area of the civil airport in 1921. A simple wooden fence separates the flying field from the space open to the public; behind it, preparing for departure, a Breguet 14; in the distance, the military aviation hangars at Dugny (Musée de l'Air et de l'Espace, Le Bourget)*

The airport in 1927. From right to left: the pavilion housing the waiting rooms and the restaurant, with its terraced rooftop open to visitors, the pavilion of the airport control, the pavilion of the meteorological services, and the five hangars built by Lossier in 1922 (Musée de l'Air et de l'Espace, Le Bourget)

state of peace caused some delays in the reorganisation of the services and in the creation of new ones. In France, the air navigation service (Service de la Navigation Aérienne) was set up on 6 June 1919 with the task of defining air traffic networks and overseeing their creation and operation. Creating new aerodromes required time and money and, since Le Bourget was the only site in the Paris region capable of being opened quickly for regular commercial routes, the military authorities put the northern part of the airfield, along the route de Flandre, at the disposal of the nascent civil aviation industry. Although they were very rudimentary, the existing facilities – canvas hangars and timber barracks – were used to house the first private airline companies, the navigation service, the customs, the police and waiting rooms for passengers. The airport had a grass landing field. During the summer, landing at and taking off from Le Bourget could be a pleasant experience, but the same could not be said for rainy and windy days!

From 1919 onwards, the first international air routes from Le Bourget connected

Paris with London[2] and Brussels, soon followed by other connections to Prague, Warsaw, Vienna, Constantinople, etc. The bombers left over from the war and hastily adapted for passenger transport were gradually replaced by planes designed specifically for this purpose. Their development was encouraged by competitions for commercial aircraft designs, which the State and the Aéro-club de France endowed with large prizes. Between 1921 and 1924, all the practical trials associated with these competitions took place at Le Bourget.

Colonel Saconnay, a leading figure of military aviation, was put in charge of the Service de la Navigation Aérienne. He quickly grasped the importance of the coming boom in commercial air transport and realised that the rather basic control and reception facilities at Le Bourget would have to be rethought. The site had to be provided with infrastructures and buildings worthy of the airport serving the French capital. These new facilities, designed by the engineers Terrisse and Rumpler in collaboration with the architect Henri Decaux, were built as an extension of the existing ones, along the route de Flandre. They were essentially comprised of five hangars in reinforced concrete, each conceived to house six commercial aircraft. These hangars were designed by the Swiss engineer Henry Lossier, who, in 1918, had designed the airship hangar at Écausseville, on the Cotentin peninsula.

Administration, weather and telegraph services, public reception facilities (customs and a restaurant), the airport commander's living quarters and a large centre for pilots' medical examinations were distributed between several individual pavilions, laid out around an ornamental garden. The architectural style of these pavilions was not unlike that of hospital complexes of the same period. This 'air port', which entered into full service in 1922, was completed by the installation to the south of six metallic hangars from American army surplus stocks, some of them erected as early as 1920, and by five other hangars of German origin, recovered by France as war damages.[3] Although decried by some as being too large, these facilities proved over the following years that forecasts had been far from ambitious. The number of passengers passing through Le Bourget rose from 6,800 in 1920 to 45,000 in 1929.

Despite this boom in commercial aviation, the military presence on the site remained far more important. In 1920, the

34th Air Observation Regiment was created, installed at the southernmost point of the site, close to the village of Le Bourget. The infrastructures were still those left over from the war: Bessonneau hangars and standard timber structures. The entire western fringe of the site, running along the road linking Le Bourget to Dugny, was also occupied by military aviation buildings, which spread across the road, with the construction of warehouses. More land was expropriated in 1923 in order to provide barrack accommodation for the families of the 34th Regiment and for the personnel of the other services. By this date, the 34th 'mixed' air regiment comprised three night fighter squadrons, three observation squadrons and two reconnaissance squadrons.

A new terminal

From 1926 onwards, Le Bourget became the point of departure and arrival for planes trying to set new distance records. On 8 May 1927, Charles Nungesser and François Coli took off from Le Bourget in their ill-fated attempt to cross the North Atlantic, a crossing that Charles Lindbergh completed successfully, in the opposite direction, thirteen days later, landing at Le Bourget to the rapturous welcome of a huge crowd. Other 'raids' followed, pioneering new air routes to Asia, Africa and America that the companies soon followed. In 1932, Le Bourget airport handled 70,000 passengers.

While cohabitation between civil and military aviation continued without any major difficulties, in the face of this unprecedented development in commercial air transport, it soon became clear that the capacity of the facilities, as well as the airfield itself, would soon be inadequate. An extension was planned to the north, requiring the expropriation of 40 more hectares of the commune of Dugny, up to its limits, marked by the River Morée. This extension also needed land from the neighbouring communes of Bonneuil-en-France and Gonesse, and here development came into conflict with the plans of the City of Paris for the creation of a large municipal cemetery. After some polemical exchanges, this new cemetery was finally relocated to the south of the capital.

Hailed as innovative in 1922, fewer than ten years later, the 'air port' of Le Bourget appeared obsolete in terms of its dimensions and design. In the meantime, Germany in particular, but also other European countries, had been building better-designed

airports. In 1931, in order to meet growing needs, a project for a new terminal design based on these recent European models was launched by the Air Ministry. But the work, supposedly to be completed by 1934, never properly started, due to the bankruptcy of the contracting company.

In 1933, following a visit to Le Bourget, the new Air Minister, Pierre Cot, reaffirmed the official decision to create a new terminal building. An architectural competition was organised in June 1935 by the Ministry's Service des études et de la signalisation. Very tight deadlines were imposed since it was hoped to open the new terminal for passengers flying in for the International Exhibition, due to be held in Paris in 1937.

At the end of the competition procedure, which elicited protest from certain unsuccessful candidates, the architect Georges Labro, in association with a building contractor, the Société Nouvelle de Construction et de Travaux, was declared the winner. His project was a building of sober architectural character, 233m in length, integrating

Top: The landside entrance to the airport in the spring of 1932. In the foreground, to the right, the 'Paul Bert' pavilion; in the background, the pavilion of the airport direction, surmounted by a clock, and the waiting-room and restaurant pavilion next to it (Musée de l'Air et de l'Espace, Le Bourget)

Three of the five hangars transferred from Germany as war damages and used as maintenance shops by the Société Franco-Roumaine; photo taken in 1924 (Musée de l'Air et de l'Espace, Le Bourget)

Top: *Construction of the new terminal in 1936 (Musée de l'Air et de l'Espace, Le Bourget)*

View of the apron during the winter of 1938/9; arrival of a Swiss Airlines DC-2 (Musée de l'Air et de l'Espace, Le Bourget)

planes, passenger embarkation and the loading of freight in all weather. By 1939, Le Bourget, with 21,000 flight movements per year and 138,000 passengers, was the second busiest airport in Europe, after Berlin-Tempelhof.

Le Bourget at war

At the beginning of the war, the operational units stationed at the 104 Airbase at Dugny-Le Bourget were redeployed throughout the Paris region and the Somme, from where they operated during the Battle of France. After the order for withdrawal, on 10 May 1940, the aircraft still on the site and the base's administration and technical services were evacuated to Pau. On 3 June 1940, a massive German bombing raid damaged both the civil and military buildings, claiming several lives. Ten days later, the Luftwaffe occupied the site, to remain there until August 1944 and the liberation of Le Bourget by the Forces Françaises de l'Intérieur and General Leclerc's Second Armoured Division.

During the Occupation, the German military authorities carried out the extension of the site – envisaged since 1933 but always put off – thus increasing its total area to 420ha. In record time, two hard-surfaced runways were laid down as well as a network of shelter pens for fighters, built at the edge of the site close to the villages of Bonneuil-en-France, Garches and Dugny, under the protection of a complex of anti-aircraft defence batteries.

Le Bourget was a strategic objective for the Allied Forces and was the target of several air raids in 1942 and two more in 1943, the second of which claimed 200 civilian lives in the village of Dugny, which was almost entirely destroyed. The runways were made unusable, the hangars damaged and the terminal hit in several places. The following year, in April, May, June and August, the air raids started again. On 27 August 1944, the battle to recover the airfield came to an end and on 30 August, units of the 9th Engineering Command of the American Army took possession of the airport, rapidly putting it back into working order.

The buildings had suffered considerably. Labro's terminal, on which several large bombs had fallen, presented a spectacle of desolation with vaulting ripped open and windows blown out. The concrete hangars, whose structures had resisted the blast of the sabotage explosives left behind by the

all the functions of passenger handling and airport management. The building was not totally finished by the time of the opening of the Exhibition in June. It was officially inaugurated on 12 November 1937.

This new terminal considerably changed the image of the airport. The vast esplanade that opened out onto the Route Nationale meant the disappearance of the old hangars that bordered it. Almost all the buildings of the first airport were demolished with the exception of Lossier's large hangars, dating from 1922 and extended in 1932. Now with a new terminal clad in white stone, the complex as a whole acquired a new coherence.

The landing field still consisted of two grass runways, the first lying in a north-westerly direction, measuring 1,800m in length, and the second, oriented east to west, measuring 1,200m. Only the approaches to the large hangars and a broad apron in front of the terminal were paved in concrete to facilitate the movements of the

German troops, had lost all their glazing and their concrete roofing tiles.

American troops took over the command of the airport. In 1945, in unending rotation, Le Bourget was to witness the return of many prisoners of war and deportees. The British Royal Air Force then took over from the Americans, occupying most of the buildings.

Rebuilding Le Bourget

Civilian traffic resumed quickly, first of all under military control and then, at the end of 1945, under the aegis of Aéroport de Paris (ADP), a public body created by a decree on 24 October for the exploitation and development of all civil air transport facilities within a radius of 50km around Paris. Within the space of two years, ADP had Le Bourget up and running again.

By 1948, the terminal had been restored, in accordance with its original design, but with some additional amenities. It came into full use as the Paris airport while waiting for the completion of the capital's second airport, planned to the south of Paris, at Orly. In 1945, 360,000 passengers passed through Le Bourget. By 1950, it had two paved runways, an east–west runway of 1,960m and a north–south runway of 2,395m, and covered a total of 570ha. Aprons for planes, 180,000 sq m in extent and capable of supporting aircraft of between 60 and 65 tonnes, and almost 10km of taxi strips were created.

Close to the terminal, to the south, a freight centre was created while to the north, new buildings were put up to meet the developing needs of the commercial fleets based at Le Bourget. In 1949, a vast hangar, the HO hangar, was built with war damage funding and in 1954, the structure generally known as Le Building was erected for the Union Aéromaritime de Transport (UAT).[4]

On the Dugny side, the airbase was returned to French command in February 1945. Known as Base Aérienne Equipée no. 104, it included the 64th transport squadron that participated in the repatriation of prisoners of war and deportees before specialising in liaison missions with Northern Africa and French West Africa, these kinds of long-haul missions making up its main activity. As military reorganisation was carried out, the base at Le Bourget also became the temporary home for a variety of services. In particular, it welcomed a section of the Base Transit Air 250 of Paris.

Labro's terminal building after the air raids of 1944 (Musée de l'Air et de l'Espace, Le Bourget)

The military use of the site generated dense traffic: 800 to 900 flight movements per year, involving 36,000 passengers and 2,000 tonnes of freight. This was the last military function to remain on the site when the number 104 base was decommissioned, in 1984. In 1954, the Maritime Transport Squadron (ETM) took up its quarters in Dugny after being transferred from Orly. Ten years later, its air transport activities were handed over to the Air Force, which meant that the naval airbase at Dugny was left only with its own logistical liaison activities.

The 1950s saw a meteoric rise in civil air traffic. Between 1950 and 1953, Le Bourget witnessed a 20 per cent growth, the number of passengers rising from 541,000 to 647,000. The freight and mail activity experienced the same increase.

In June 1951, Le Bourget played host to an event that was to give it a new lease of life during the following years: an air meeting to display the most recent creations of the aviation industry, organised at the same time as the air show that had been held at the Grand Palais, in Paris, since 1909. This prestigious event was an immense success, despite makeshift facilities. In 1953, occupying a vast pavilion built to the south of the site, the International Air Show made Le Bourget its permanent home. Every two years, this show is one of the major events for aviation professionals throughout the world.

In 1952, with its facilities threatened with saturation, Air France left Le Bourget for Orly, where space was available for its growing fleet. Despite the activity generated by companies still based on the site – Aigle Azur, UAT and the Postale de nuit (the night mail) – Le Bourget saw a fall in traffic. By 1957, continued growth in air transport and the experience gained over the years made it clear that even with its new terminal

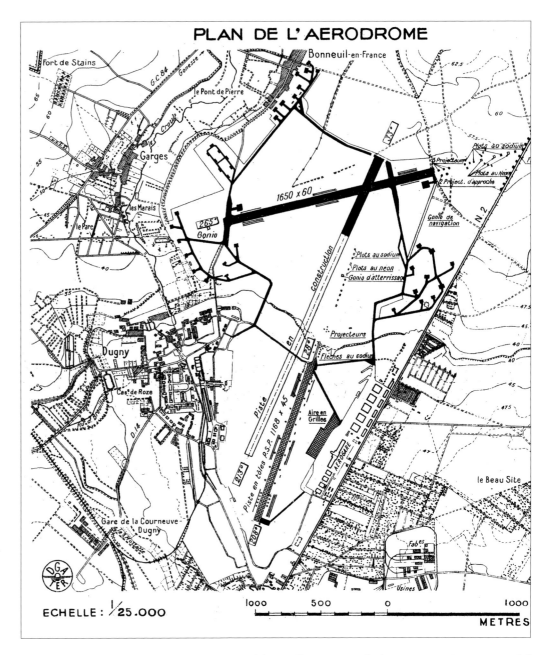

PLAN DE L'AERODROME

ECHELLE : 1/25.000

1000   500   0   1000

METRES

Plan of the airport taken from an atlas of July 1946. Note the hard-surfaceed runways built by the Luftwaffe and the network of pens for fighters at the periphery of the extended flying field.

planned to be opened in 1960, Orly could not absorb all the traffic. A redistribution was organised between the two airports, while 3,000ha of land were acquired to the north of Le Bourget, at Roissy-en-France, for the construction of a third Paris airport. The progressive closure of Le Bourget was scheduled for the 1970s.

In the meantime, and in order to cater to larger jets, extensive modernisation work was carried out. In August 1960, a new east–west runway of 3,000m in length, the 07-25, was opened to traffic and in the same year an immense hangar, known as K1, was developed for the UAT company. With its innovative design, this hangar provided 7,800 sq m of unencumbered space, capable of housing three large four-engined planes. Le Bourget was also the site of an assembly and test centre for the Sud-Aviation company, for its Alouette helicopters, as well as a maintenance company, SECA.

In 1963, of the 5,200,000 commercial passengers that passed through all of the Paris airports, Le Bourget only accounted for 22.3 per cent and 37.8 per cent of plane movements, which amounted to 154,000 for all of the sites. It had thus become an airport of only average importance. Most of the flights were short-haul and medium-haul connections to and from European cities. New facilities were nonetheless designed to reduce the time for boarding and disembarkation. Inside the terminal building, the reception and flow management installations underwent considerable modernisation and the building's internal decoration was brought up to date.

During the International Air Show of 1975, the Air Museum, originally created in 1920, began its transfer to Le Bourget with the opening of a display of historic aircraft. This transfer continued gradually over the next twenty years as more and more space

Arriving at Le Bourget airport in the late 1950s (photo J Feuillie/ © CNMHS)

was freed by the progressive departure of other services to Paris's two other airports. Le Bourget was finally closed to international traffic in 1977 and to regional traffic three years later.

Le Bourget today

This situation led some to believe that the airport at Le Bourget was doomed to abandon its aeronautical activities. To fill the spaces freed, various projects were put forward, such as 'a garden of the sky, air and space', 90ha of open spaces linking the park at La Courneuve to the Air and Space Museum.

But as well as the requirements of the military bases still active at Le Bourget, three factors played a decisive role in ensuring the aeronautical use of the site. First of all, every two years, the International Air Show continued to grow in size and popularity. Secondly, the northern part of the site was now occupied by a zone of industrial activities associated with aviation and aircraft maintenance. Finally, Le Bourget was

at the forefront of the expansion in private business flying, leading the development of this new form of traffic. On 17 March 1960, a corporate plane belonging to IBM landed at Le Bourget, inaugurating private business flights between France and the United States. Gradually, this new activity began to flourish over the following years. Several companies specialising in this type of transport, which saves time for passengers and guarantees them a certain degree of privacy, are based at Le Bourget.

The proximity of Le Bourget to the new airport at Roissy, opened in 1974, led ADP to effect considerable changes to ensure the safety of the air approaches. This meant that the 03-21 north–south runway that crossed the western approach axis to Roissy was abandoned and traffic diverted to the 07-25 east–west runway. The latter was in turn abandoned, apart from exceptional use, when the second Roissy runway was opened, after the entry into service of Terminal 2 in 1982. The former 'German' runway, dating from the war, was then extended for business traffic. This continued development, with

171,000 flight movements in 1991, made Le Bourget the leading business airport in Europe. The density of this traffic, restricted to the east–west runway, led ADP to build a new control tower in 1993, located in the airfield's northern sector, to replace the control tower at the centre of the terminal, dating from 1953. This now houses certain flight operation services, the runway control office and meteorological service. In 1995, a new east–west runway, the 09-27, 2,000m in length was laid out at Le Bourget, lying parallel to the Roissy runways.

Now, in 2002, the site of Le Bourget airport covers a total area of 560ha, 180 of which lie in the Seine-Saint-Denis department, spread over the communes of Dugny and Le Bourget, and 380 in the Val d'Oise department, on the territories of Bonneuil-en-France and Gonesse. At first glance, the airport zone, placed primarily under the responsibility of ADP, seems to be dedicated exclusively to aeronautical functions, but the diversity of the activities that have developed at Le Bourget over the past twenty years has made the technical and organisational management of the site more complex.

In the absence of any long-term project by the public authorities for the development of the entire site, it is thanks to the efforts of the various occupants and to the heritage of its past too, that today it retains such a varied personality. Le Bourget is not only a business airport, but also an industrial estate specialised in aircraft maintenance activities, an exhibition centre, a museum and a military zone.

This situation has evolved against a background of the de-industrialisation of the surrounding communities, where factories, set up at the end of the 19th century or the beginning of the 20th, have witnessed closures or relocations, all detrimental to the financial and social equilibrium of the local authorities. In this context, the airport zone as a whole looks rather shabby, an impression that is made worse by the lack of maintenance on access roads, unsatisfactory public transport links, the heterogeneous built environment and some poorly designed urban developments. This negative image is accentuated by the contrast with Roissy-Charles-de-Gaulle that has witnessed uninterrupted growth for the past twenty years.

During the past ten years, the neighbouring communes, the Department, the Ile-de-France region and the central State have all expressed their desire to see something done about this situation, but only succeeded in finding the necessary synergy when concerted action was finally taken by these institutional partners together with the users of the airport. The plan to develop the Air and Space Museum, which got off the ground in 1996 thanks to its regulating body, the Ministry of Defence, has focused the interest of these partners, who see this project as a means of revitalising the zone, and breathing new life into it, in the manner of the Plaine Saint-Denis after the building of the new Stade de France. At the same time, the planning contract, signed in 1999 between the State and the Region, recognises the need to reorganise the road network and to improve access by public transport. Finally, the management of ADP has also joined in general discussions on the overall reorganisation of the airport site. Any steps taken to improve its image will take into account Le Bourget's important historical and heritage characteristics.

The Air and Space Museum at Le Bourget

The decision to create a national air museum was officially taken in 1919, following a proposition to the War Minister made by Albert Caquot.[5] The first collections were displayed in 1921 in the buildings of the military air station, located since 1877 in the park of the Château de Meudon. Housed on a temporary basis, the museum remained there until the decision taken in 1973 to transfer it to Le Bourget. During the fifty years that preceded this decision, more than twenty different projects to install the museum in the capital were envisaged, without success. The only exception was the creation of an exhibition space in the new buildings constructed for the Air Ministry in 1936, on the boulevard Victor in Paris. But, after bomb damage in 1940, the collections were returned to Chalais-Meudon in 1945.

The transfer of commercial aviation from Le Bourget to the new airport in Roissy finally opened up the possibility for the museum to take advantage of covered surfaces and sufficient open spaces to present its collections under improved conditions, and on a site with a rich aeronautical past. The transfer took place over twenty years, according to the availability of resources allocated to the operation by the Air Force. A first hall opened to the public in 1975 but

Part of the collections of the national air museum housed at Meudon during the 1920s (Musée de l'Air et de l'Espace, Le Bourget)

it was only in 1986 that all the permanent exhibition spaces were inaugurated. The beginnings of aviation were then presented in the former Labro terminal, handed over to the museum in 1981.

The relocation of the collections in these new spaces enabled visitors to gain a better idea of their immense interest, their quality and the rarity of a large number of the exhibits. This 'revelation' was achieved at the same time as several other major museum development projects in Paris (the Musée du Conservatoire national des Arts et Métiers, the Grande Galerie du Museum d'Histoire Naturelle, etc) and led the Minister of Defence in 1992 to launch an ideas competition for a 'new air museum'. According to the terms of this competition, the projects for the general reorganisation of the museum's displays and the creation of reception and service areas had to take into account the existing historic infrastructures, particularly the former 1937 terminal.

When the competition was announced, the Heritage Department of the Ministry of Culture, preoccupied at the time with the 20th-century heritage, was concerned about the future of the terminal within the framework of this project and decided to give it statutory protection enacted on 30 June 1994. In the meantime, the Minister of Defence, faced with the high costs envisaged for the work, abandoned the new museum project.

But the dynamism that had been created provided the impetus to look for better conditions for the museum, conditions that were achieved in January 1994, when the museum changed its status to become a national public establishment with an administrative function, placed under the authority of the Ministry of Defence. In April 1996, the Board of Directors approved a new development plan. In addition to the reorganisation of the running of the museum, this plan defines new objectives for the management and promotion of the collections. The plan represents a coherent cultural project, its main objective being the adoption of a more historical approach within a framework of reorganised spaces and the identification of a range of partners capable of helping with the implementation of the project.

One of the main aims was the renovation of the esplanade in front of the former terminal. This area, modernised during the 1960s to satisfy the parking requirements of the airport site (then at its maximum capacity), was in a state of advanced disrepair. It provided a very unflattering approach to the museum and caused concern for the safety of visitors. The project for its renovation was drawn up in collaboration with the Architecture and Heritage Department of the Seine-Saint-Denis department and the Facilities Department of ADP, which acted as project manager. The programme set out to restore some of the coherence of the architecture of the terminal by reinstating the general axial plan of 1937, thus anticipating the future layout that will make the central part of the terminal the main access to the museum. The renovated esplanade was opened in September 1998.

According to the development plan, based on two preliminary studies in 1998 and 2000, the terminal will reassume its original function as a reception area for the public, by providing the support services required in a major cultural facility: a multi-media library, a food outlet, shops, conference rooms, a forum and temporary exhibition spaces. The characteristic and highly evocative architecture of the building itself will contribute to the museum's image and make the Air and Space Museum inextricably part of the historic site of Le Bourget.

In order to ensure that the programming studies of the terminal will make the most of its potential, while respecting the constraints imposed by its protection as a historic monument, the museum commissioned a historical and archaeological study of the building, undertaken in 2000. This study represents the museum's contribution to the 'L'Europe de l'Air' project and its conclusions and recommendations will serve as a reference for work to be carried out, in keeping with the historic values of George Labro's building.[6]

Urgency, however, sometimes makes it necessary to depart from initial plans. The storm of December 1999 revealed the state of disrepair of the stone cladding fixings of the central part of the terminal's main façade. A study, carried out by the architectural firm Daniel Lefèvre (Head Architect of the Historic Monuments Administration), concluded that it was necessary to remove the facing and the statues, and to replace them only after appropriate treatment. This takes priority over all other work. While awaiting its completion, safety measures have been taken by removing some of the stone cladding and by placing protective netting around the statues.

The terminal at Le Bourget is an important part of the built heritage of the 20th century at both national and international levels. But on the airport site, other buildings merit as much if not more attention: the Lossier hangars built in 1922, the maintenance workshops opposite them (identified during the international 'L'Europe de l'Air' workshop in June 2001 as German aviation hangars dating from 1917), as well as other buildings left over from the first airport or from more recent periods.

As a logical conclusion to the discussions and observations emerging from the Raphael programme, it is now necessary to undertake a detailed historical study not merely of the terminal building, but of the entire airport site, from its origins up to the present day. The research will be accompanied by fieldwork to identify and analyse all the site's buildings and infrastructures. It should be carried out in partnership with all of the keepers of archival and oral history, with past and present users and in collaboration with the future decision-makers of the site. Its results should be popularised by the various means at our disposal to make the reality of this pre-eminent place in the history of aviation available to as wide an audience as possible. Following the study, the preservation and interpretation of the heritage elements, recognised for their formal, structural and symbolic qualities, and properly safeguarded in their original location as the tangible landmarks of the site's permanent transformation should be made a primary objective.

Notes

1   Acquired by the French State on 24 November 1917, the airfield covered 115ha; three-quarters of the area of the rural commune of Dugny was affected by this expropriation.
2   The French and English quickly realised that the most important air route would be the connection between Paris and London. It was inaugurated on 25 August 1919, after a provisional agreement was signed by the two governments.
3   Situated behind the large Lossier hangars, these German hangars were converted into repair and maintenance workshops for aircraft.
4   Founded in 1949, the Union Aéromaritime de Transport became the Union des Transports Aériens (UTA) in 1963, following its merger with Transports Aériens Intercontinentaux. UTA joined the Air France Group in 1990.
5   Albert Caquot (1881–1976), an engineer of the French Highways Department (Ponts-et-Chaussées), is one of the leading figures in French aviation history. During the First World War, he designed a new type of captive observation balloon. As general technical director at the Air Ministry during the 1920s and 1930s, he was also the instigator of the Chalais-Meudon wind tunnel and designer of a large number of civil engineering structures: bridges, aircraft hangars, the Donzère-Mondragon dam and the docks at Saint-Nazaire.
6   For more on this study, see the article by Jean-Christophe Morisseau in this present publication, pp 145–57.

History of Speke airport, Liverpool

Roger Bowdler

The aim of this paper is to give a historical survey of Speke airport's construction, to outline the reasons why we regard it as such an important site, to set it in the context of inter-war attitudes to flying, and to ask some broad questions about the meaning of municipal aviation buildings. The 'L'Europe de l'Air' project has given us the chance to look in detail at Speke, and to follow the agreed project approach, which advances from the examination of specific sites to broader conservation conclusions.

From the outset it should be made clear that we are by no means the first people to study Speke airport's history. Phil Butler of the Merseyside Aviation Society wrote this history in 1983, a ground-breaking profile of an airport unsurpassed in terms of factual analysis.[1] Also of great benefit has been the listed building report prepared by Stephen Levrant for the owners of the site.[2] This unpublished report has shed much new light on the airport and is a balanced and penetrating analysis of the site, even if some of its conclusions are open to debate. These are two debts I wish to acknowledge straightaway.

Speke airport on the eastern fringes of Liverpool is generally regarded as the finest group of British aviation buildings of the inter-war period. Other sites might have greater claims to architectural fame, as pioneering examples of the heroic period of Modernism, but when it comes to a monumental array of aviation structures, Speke has few peers. Paris, Berlin and Liverpool: one is the odd man out, but Liverpool is nevertheless a worthy comparison for the two capital cities, and its airport is a supreme example of a provincial transport centre. The idea or image of the airport is nearly as significant to our understanding as a grasp of its practical functioning, and I will focus later on this notion of Speke as a symbolic site.

History

The story of Speke airport begins in 1928. Air Marshall Sir Sefton Brancker, director of Civil Aviation at the Air Ministry, embarked on a nation-wide campaign with his friend, the leading British flyer of his day Sir Alan Cobham, to promote civic air-mindedness. The idea was to encourage local authorities to establish landing grounds and hence create a flight network for Britain. The country is not large and is relatively well served by rail: there were not the political factors to encourage civil flight that there were, for example, in Germany, but nonetheless the crusade of Brancker and Cobham was to bear fruit. Nearly fifty municipal airports were opened in Britain between the wars. Liverpool was the twelfth to open, and by far the grandest.

The skeleton chronology of Speke airport can be told quickly. The City of Liverpool purchased the huge agricultural estate of Speke Hall in 1928. This Elizabethan manor house, one of the classic examples of half-timbering, survives today as a historic house run by the National Trust. But it is now an island amid a sea of noisy neighbours. The Speke development, of which the airport was just a part, included large estates of public housing, major new industrial zones and carefully planned road links. Four hundred acres (162ha) on the edge of the Mersey were set aside for a new airfield. Work on levelling the ground began in 1930, when an experimental service between London-Croydon and the business centres of Birmingham, Manchester and Liverpool was commenced. In 1931, Sir Alan Cobham, in conjunction with the eminent architects Sir John Burnet, Tait and Partners, published designs for an ultra-modern airport with provision for sea planes too, which would have required dredging the Mersey and providing for its considerable tidal fall. This plan was never adopted, but Cobham's dream remained in the mind of the city fathers. Cobham's main sponsor in promoting air-mindedness in Britain was an eminent Liverpudlian, Sir Charles (later Viscount) Wakefield, head of the Castrol oil empire. Quite what role he played in promoting an ambitious scheme in his home city is unclear, but his unseen

BUILD YOUR FACTORY HERE . . .

At Speke . . . the most up-to-date industrial site in the Kingdom. Efficient distribution of manufactures is assured because of the excellent geographical position of the Estate, but the added advantages of Liverpool's great Docking and Railway facilities reduce transport costs to the minimum. The Airport, which is a vital part of the Estate, is one of the best centres in the country and the natural hub for the operation of a network of Air Services.

A main link is in operation with the Continent via Hull, and services connecting Liverpool with London, Belfast, Glasgow, Isle of Man, Blackpool, Plymouth, Cardiff, and Birmingham, are proving most convenient and reliable assets to business men. Taking the economic point of view only . . . no manufacturer can afford to ignore the advantages to be gained by building his factory at Speke.

Write now for full particulars to the
LAND STEWARD AND SURVEYOR,
Municipal Buildings, Liverpool.

IDEAL INDUSTRIAL SITES
SPEKE ESTATE
LIVERPOOL'S *Great* **AIRPORT**

Advertisement for Liverpool's Great Airport, featured in The Story of the Mersey Tunnel, *officially named* Queensway, *published by the Mersey Tunnel joint Committee, 1934.*

influence probably goes a long way to explaining why Liverpool committed itself so deeply when it came to airport provision.

For immediate purposes, however, Speke's airport was decidedly humble. Existing farm buildings were adapted and a hangar created by roofing over the farmyard in 1932. In July 1933 the airport was officially opened by the Secretary of State for Air, the Belfast resident Lord Londonderry, who could now commute by air to Westminster. Some 30,000 Liverpudlians attended the gala, with its elaborate RAF displays. Avro Tutor training aircraft provided a warm-up for the more audacious acts of the day, which ended with a formal dinner in the City Hall and a gala ball at the Adelphi Hotel. In mid-1934 the international history of the airport began with a service run by the Dutch KLM fleet to Amsterdam. The Irish airline Aer Lingus also began a mail service to Dublin, and the despatch of mail was and remains an important element in the airport's traffic.

In July 1934 a delegation from Liverpool council, led by the dominant figure of

Councillor Sir Thomas White, chairman of the Speke development committee, visited the European airports of Amsterdam-Schiphol, Hamburg-Fuhlsbüttel and Berlin-Tempelhof. White was a wealthy brewer who believed in thinking big and spending freely. The members of his delegation were looking for a model to copy and found it in Dyrssen and Averhoff's Fuhlsbüttel airport, opened in 1929 and recently demolished. The symmetrical layout of terminal and hangars, the long, curving terminal building with central tower, the prominent decks for viewing terraces, here was a lucid, logical and brazenly modern approach to airport design which impressed the Liverpool party greatly. In planning and architectural terms, the debt was considerable as the comparison of the ground plans of Fuhlsbüttel and Speke demonstrates. Speke was substantially larger, however. Another powerful influence on the design of the Liverpool terminal was Oliver Hill's Midland Hotel at Morecombe, farther up the Lancashire coast. This was the smartest, most self-consciously *moderne* new building in the North-West of England, opened by the London-Midland-Scottish Railway. Like Speke airport, it serves as a reminder of the glamour associated with travel at this time. Opened in 1933, its curved body, glazed central stair tower and geometric austerity were taken up for Liverpool's air terminus. All the cachet and progressiveness of flying found their architectural equivalent in the chic new premises of the Midland Hotel, the most cosmopolitan structure in the Liverpool area and an obvious source of inspiration for all aspirant local designers.

The design of Speke airport was carried out by the municipal architects' department led by one Albert Jenkins, but the true designer, as discovered by Steven Levrant, was Edward Bloomfield (1898–1955). Speke is the masterpiece of this obscure figure, who trained at the Glasgow School of Art, and ended his career in charge of design at Liverpool's huge housing department. Published late in 1934, Bloomfield's proposals show how the dream of symmetrical monumentality, floated by Sir Alan Cobham, influenced the ultimate design. The hangars are no longer joined physically to the terminal building, but the composition is again dominated by the central control tower, rising up from the accentuated horizontals of the terminal with its glazed restaurant, waiting rooms and viewing platforms. Work began on Speke's new buildings in 1935. By 1937 hangar number 1 and the control tower were completed. The terminal building itself, wrapped around the Pharos-like control tower, was completed in 1939. Hangar number 2 was slower to rise, and was not completed until 1940.

The buildings

I now wish to consider the buildings of Speke in turn, starting with hangar number 1. This is far and away the most monumentally conceived aviation hangar of the inter-war period in Britain. It was opened for use by Lord Derby in July 1937 and described by the local newspaper as the largest hangar in Europe. When completed, all types of civil aircraft could be housed within its capacious interior, which was entered via vast folding wooden doors, electronically operated, located on the south end and west side. The hangar is a steel-framed structure, cased in pale brown brick, with relief sculptures of eagles flanking the wide window of the southern elevation. It is a measure of the ambition and monumentality of Speke airport that one encounters any sculpture at all in such a utilitarian context. The eagles have unmistakable echoes of Italian Fascist decoration, and there is an echo too of the Luftwaffe emblem, which decorated many German military installations at this date. Sculpture played an important part in the municipal classicism practised by the Liverpool City architects: a comparable image of flying bulls was incorporated on the Mersey Tunnel structures of 1934, and this tunnel's monumental ventilation shaft sported a fine sculptural relief entitled 'Speed: the modern Mercury'. A further emblematic decoration at Speke's hangar occurs in the main window of the southern elevation: the long, stacked horizontals resemble biplane wings or ailerons. The central upright can be read as a stylised airship, or, alternatively, as a tapering wing with an RAF roundel on it.

Before the completion of the terminal building, the lower side structures of hangar number 1 housed the young airport's landing facilities, the curved room on the tip serving as watch office for the airport. It is the sheer size of this hangar which impresses one today. In structural engineering terms it is difficult to make great claims for it. The hangar's power is nonetheless undeniable, with more than 1,000 tons of steel structure within. The prevailing aesthetic in current airport design demands expressed engineering, lightness of structural elements and

A 1937 press photograph of hangar number 1 (Liverpool Record Office)

explicit references to the mechanics of flight. Speke's hangar number 1 is a firmly land-based design, embodying the shelter and security that characterise the functions of such buildings: maintenance, inspections and protection from foul weather. The contrast between this vast protective barn and the relative fragility of the aircraft it housed would have been impossible to miss, and comparisons might be drawn with the well-mannered brick architecture of RAF aerodromes, which in character was far removed from the cutting-edge technology of flight and attack that their occupants sought to embody.

Hangar number 2 is utterly different in its design, although it occupies a symmetrical position to the east of the terminal and was obviously intended, at first, to match hangar number 1 in all aspects. The pressures of looming conflict put pay to that, and the resulting building, constructed from 1939 to 1940 by the Air Ministry, uses a striking latticed roof truss system of bolted steel members, at a cost of £50,000. This 'Lamella' roofing, was, ironically enough, a patented system originally developed by the Junkers aircraft company of Dessau and regularly employed by the RAF for its hangars. Other examples of this impressive technique survive in some numbers, as it was employed for RAF aircraft storage units across the country. The distance between the buildings at Speke is considerable, making it difficult to read them as a group. This lessens their monumentality, but it makes it possible to overlook the patent inferiority of hangar number 2 compared to its grander colleague. The presence of bas-reliefs of a winged figure suggest that these had been cast at an early stage, before the RAF took over. This figure has been said to represent

Speke's control tower, standing alone in 1937, prior to the construction of the terminal around its base (Liverpool Record Office)

against one of the maxims of airport design which placed a premium on low structures that did not present obstacles to flyers. Its height was an advantage, however, for overseeing the workings of a busy airfield.

The terminal building was added to the control tower nearly two years later, in 1938, at a cost of £80,000. One reason for this delay was a dispute with the Air Ministry, which had to approve all airport designs: they preferred a building with a convex footprint, sweeping away from the apron, rather than the design opted for at Speke. As well as being sleek, the completed terminal at Speke was carefully planned within. As the American architect John Walter Wood wrote in his 1940 book on airports, 'it is sometimes argued that architectural good looks at an airport are unimportant. Actually a building that is good-looking is one that is well planned'.[3] For Wood, handsome buildings attracted visitors and revenue; they provided new and welcome amenities for non-flying spectators; and they encouraged a greater interest in flying which could only be to the good of aviation. This propaganda aspect of airport buildings was not lost on the designers of Speke. The terminal served four distinct groups of users: passengers, pilots and aircrew, ground staff and spectators. The excitement of flight and the prestige of the airport buildings made the airport a popular destination for sight-seers: many who came to Speke airport were destined to travel no farther than the restaurant and viewing terraces. About 3,000 visitors were to visit the airport in August 1947 alone, and the restaurant did a fine trade, becoming a prestigious venue for wedding parties. Thus not only did airports become a new civic amenity on the edge of a new green space: the takings from the tea room could be set against the expenditure of the complex. Ground staff included airline personnel as well as air traffic controllers, customs officials, baggage handlers and managers. The interior of the terminal was organised around the need to separate the circulation routes of departure and arrival flights, and to ensure, for customs and immigration purposes, that incoming travellers were marshalled through the correct channels. In this, once again, the example of Fuhlsbüttel was a crucial influence.

Icarus (surely too ominous for a civilian airport; his more prudent father Daedelus is a more likely candidate) or perhaps an angel or a pilot. The 1930s were the golden age of flying, and the pilot as hero (or heroine) was a common image in the age of Amy Johnson, Charles Lindbergh and Antoine de Saint-Exupéry. These bas-reliefs embody such spirit, even if their setting is not quite up to such lofty and stirring concepts.

The control tower can be considered in isolation from the terminal building. For many months it stood alone, a pharos of the air sending radio and neon light messages out into the ether in order to provide homing aircraft with navigational assistance. Speke, incidentally, possessed the earliest set of the Marconi Standard Beam Approach system that enabled aeroplanes to home in on a destination by flying along a sound beam. Night flying and flying in poor weather were now possible, enabling regular scheduled flights to be maintained in all conditions. Floodlights were installed on the boundary, as well as perimeter lights. An illuminated wind indicator was also constructed which enabled pilots to come down into the wind, the only safe method of landing. Ninety feet (27.4 metres) high, the control tower is exceptionally tall, and goes

The runways came late to Speke. In this regard, European airports lagged behind those of America. An aerial view of Speke taken in the late 1930s shows the reality of a

muddy, scored landing ground but nonetheless one which was suitable for the smaller passenger and cargo planes that formed the bulk of traffic at Speke. Winter flying in such conditions – even at an airport as celebrated for its drainage as Speke – was less than ideal. A concrete apron had been constructed which protected the ground of the busiest area close to the hangars and terminal, but for the most part the former fields were left under grass. Speke's restricted site was a problem for heavily laden aircraft from the outset. As early as 1936, the American aviator Dick Merrill was obliged to take off on his Atlantic crossing from Birkdale Sands, a few miles to the north, because Speke's take-off area was too short for his fully-fuelled aircraft. The weight of aircraft was bound to go on increasing, which demanded ever greater take-off and landing strips, and the vagaries of English weather in the North-West made permanent runways an ever more desirable asset. The Air Ministry finally installed concrete runways in 1942, enabling the four-engined Halifax bombers constructed at the adjoining factory to take off. These runways were part of the greatest programme of civil engineering ever undertaken in Britain, as acre after acre of flat countryside was put under concrete for aerodrome use.

To digress briefly on this topic: runways, flat and uneventful in appearance, have a particular resonance as the truly essential land features for aeroplanes. Their sheer size

and lack of features make them particular challenges in terms of airfield conservation. Many are now being grubbed up for use as hard core. Flat surfaces cannot be listed in England, but some measure of protection is required. In this aspect at least, French designation of historic places is in advance of conservation legislation in England.

Speke's war

Speke had become an extremely busy airport by the outbreak of war. It was the centre for connections between Ireland, the Isle of Man and Glasgow, and the North-West's main connection point for flights to London and the Continent. KLM ran flights to Amsterdam via Manchester's new airport at Ringway, which later became Speke's greatest rival. Good road links and little road traffic meant that the air passenger could reach the city centre 6 miles (10km) away in a mere 20 minutes. Good road and rail links were crucial for airport planning if the time saved by rapid flight was not to be squandered in traffic jams after landing.

Speke airport was requisitioned by the government in September 1939 and only fully returned to municipal ownership in 1961. During the war it served several roles. The RAF had used the airfield since 1936. In 1940 several fighter squadrons were based here to protect Liverpool from the Luftwaffe. One of these, a Czech unit, was visited by President Edward Benes. In spite

American P-51D Mustangs being dismantled at Speke at the end of the war (Imperial War Museum)

of their presence, these units could do little to prevent the terrible bombing which Liverpool suffered, and which reached a climax in May 1941. In 1941 a remarkable outfit arrived: the Merchant Ship Fighter Unit. Liverpool was the principal port during the Battle of the Atlantic, and the Royal Navy's headquarters was located just behind the City Hall, in Derby House. Speke airport played its part by housing an experimental group that developed rocket-fired catapult launches for Hurricanes. Once the technique had been perfected, they were installed on merchant ships in convoys and used against long-distance bombers with some success. A number of wartime structures survived until recently at Speke, and it is now becoming possible to assess their rarity and significance thanks to the research and survey work commissioned by English Heritage in this field. Their temporary design and functionality contrasts with the monumentality of the original airport buildings. Overall, however, the government was said to have spent about £1 million on improving Speke for wartime use. Speke was a busy landing ground during the war. The huge Rootes plant just to the east of the airport opened in 1938 as a shadow factory producing Blenheim fighter-bombers and later Halifax heavy bombers, of which more than 1,000 were assembled. Later in the war the American Lockheed company used Speke as an assembly point for the hordes of aircraft being shipped across the Atlantic for use by the United States Air Force. At the end of hostilities, Speke became the principal place of dismantling aircraft such as P-51 Mustangs, for the victorious 8th and 9th Air Forces. It is important to focus on Speke's part in the Second World War: never again did events of such magnitude affect the site. Air travel brings countries closer together but also made it possible to bring war right to the heart of any country. Nowhere is safe from air assault, and an air of menace is thus attached to all aviation sites with a military past.

Post-war Speke

So much for war. Speke's architectural impressiveness cost Liverpool dear. It was the most expensive civil airport in Great Britain in its day, and the total cost, at some £435,000, far exceeded the average cost of £93,000. Two factors made this outlay appear increasingly over-confident. One was the rapid obsolescence of the constricted landing ground. The other was the position of Liverpool as a regional centre of a network of air terminals. The days of Liverpool's greatness as a port were drawing to a rapid close and the city's age-old rivalry with Manchester was played out by their airports. Civil Aviation had effectively been nationalised at the end of the war, and economic restrictions made it impossible to update all airports. A regional airport capable of receiving continental flights was needed for the North-West. In 1948 the Ministry of Civil Aviation carried out a comparative study between Liverpool-Speke and Manchester-Ringway. It decided that 'at the moment Speke is slightly better than Ringway. Potentially, however, Ringway is much superior. Speke has almost reached the limit of its development'. The report praised the 'excellent terminal building' at Speke, which greatly surpassed anything at Manchester, but now the price of building on a constricted site hemmed in by the River Mersey became evident. The possibility of seaplane travel had been one of the unknown quantities of aviation in the 1930s. It was thought to represent the way forward for intercontinental flight, and Cobham's proposals of 1931 included provision for a seaplane base at Speke, making the Mersey itself a new runway. What had been a potential new gateway to the air became, for land-based aircraft, a watery barrier to future expansion. After the war, a scheme was contemplated which would have lengthened the runways by building jetties out into the river, but this project was never carried forward. The terminal buildings remained greatly admired, however, one authority, Captain Olley, stating in 1945 that Speke had the finest airport terminal buildings in the country: 'No other building can even compete with it for general layout. It is a great advance on Croydon.'

Speke's post-war fortunes were in decline then. Manchester was preferred by a number of air operators, maintenance facilities once at Speke were relocated to Scotland, and the volume of traffic remained insufficient for the airport's considerable dimensions. In April 1946 the *Liverpool Echo* wrote optimistically of Speke becoming the Clapham Junction of the region's air and anticipated the opening of a major new facility for the new nationalised airline, British European Airways. This came to nothing and in 1949 the same newspaper reported that one City councillor, chairman of the Air Transport Committee, was 'ashamed' of the airport: it was semi-derelict and deserted, despite being one of the finest complexes in Europe. The outlook was increasingly bleak. The *Liverpool and Merseyside Digest* in 1953 declared that 'somehow Speke, although as well-equipped and as convenient as most other airports throughout the country, has not caught on with the public'. The *Liverpool Express* in 1953 was tougher: describing Speke as Liverpool's White Elephant, it put the matter bluntly: 'For fifteen years Liverpool has been kidding itself that Speke might yet become an international airport. The dream is over. It is time Liverpool faced the facts.' Newcastle overtook Speke as the regional number two airport in 1954. One glimmer of hope was the establishment in 1956 of the world's first regular scheduled helicopter service which flew from Speke to Cardiff.

If the 1950s was a slack decade, the 1960s were far livelier. The airport was denationalised under the Conservative government and returned to Liverpool in 1961. The Beatles returned from their German tour of 1963 and were met by thousands of screaming fans at the airport. Thereafter, substantial new investment was made: the hard surfaces were upgraded and the buildings modernised. In 1963 the decision to construct an entirely new runway parallel to the Mersey was taken. This involved acquiring land from the National Trust, owners of Speke Hall, in order to connect the new runway with the original terminal buildings. This new modern runway, 7,500 feet (2,400 metres) long, was opened in 1966. The distance from the new runway to the old buildings made new terminal facilities badly needed. Increasingly, from this period, the dual functions of the airport became apparent: maintenance was carried out at the original, northern site while passenger flights were served by the southern, newer runway. The huge increase in jet travel, ushered in by the rise of the package holiday abroad in the early 1970s, made the southern extension of Speke airport ever busier. In 1971 serious thought was given to closing the northern site altogether and releasing the ground for new housing. This would surely have resulted in the demolition of all the 1930s buildings, which only gained statutory protection in 1978. The oil crisis of 1974 even led to the temporary closure of the airport, but by then the decision to invest in a new terminal had been taken. Financial uncertainty prevented new buildings being erected for some time. Only in 1981 was a

new control tower built, partly funded by the European Economic Development Board. In 1983, the fiftieth anniversary of the airport's opening, an agreement for redevelopment partly funded by the private sector was set in place. Liverpool's main traffic came from tour operators, and nearly 630,000 passengers flew from Speke in 1995. This number reached nearly 2 million in 2001, making Speke one of the fastest growing regional airports in Europe. It recently received much attention when Yoko Ono formally renamed it Liverpool John Lennon Airport.

The old terminal and hangars entered their lowest period with the closure of the

Top: *Hangar number 2, temporarily converted into an international terminal in the early 1970s (Liverpool Record Office)*

Speke airport in 1997, prior to its restoration (BB97/02780 © Crown copyright. NMR)

Hangar number 4 at Speke, a transportable wartime hangar designed by N S Bellman in 1936, and recently demolished (AA97/03145 © Crown copyright. NMR)

terminal building in 1986. The site passed from the ownership of the Liverpool Corporation to British Aerospace and the buildings declined in condition. A dwindling amount of aircraft maintenance took place in hangar number 1, but little else. The future of the listed buildings appeared increasingly uncertain. The regeneration agency, English Partnerships, acquired the northern site in 1995 and established a dedicated development company for the whole Speke-Garston area. This commissioned a historical report in 1996, and in 1997 began discussions with the city planning authorities on the reuse of the site and alterations to the buildings. This was part of a grand strategy for the redevelopment of this blighted area of once-industrial Liverpool, assisted significantly – as was our project – by funds from the European Union. Elsewhere in this publication (pp 176), Bob Lane gives an account of how the Speke-Garston Development company has brought new life to the 1930s buildings.

Speke's significance

The story of Speke's 1930s airport buildings is a mixture of several themes. One is the grandeur and civic vision of the Corporation during the depressed years of the early 1930s. Led by Alderman White, the City committed itself to a hugely expensive programme of airport development which would further Liverpool's claim to be Britain's premier Atlantic port, with a fine capacity for the promising field of transatlantic flight.

Liverpool built big in these years, and the airport, along with the Mersey Road Tunnel, is the most splendid monument to this, the final heroic phase of municipal building in Liverpool. Perhaps inevitably, the most monumental group of airport buildings in the country looked over a flying field that could not live up to the expectations raised by them. Speke had an interesting war, but the speed of technological development in terms of the size and weight of aircraft during the 1940s meant that Speke's landing ground was soon obsolete. The expandability of an airport site had been one of the essential planning criteria laid down by all commentators on the subject. Liverpool had been meticulous in studying airport design, as its 1934 trip to the Continent demonstrated. But when it came to the zonal planning of the Speke estate, insufficient room for expansion was allowed. This led to governmental preference for Manchester as the principal airport of the North-West. Only the sustained commitment of the City of Liverpool to its airport and the carrying out of an extensive programme of enlargement and renewal has ensured the survival of Speke. The surrendering of the 1930s airport buildings to non-aviation purposes is the price that has had to be paid for their retention.

Paris, Berlin and Liverpool ... an odd trio: but why not? One of the great ports of the world, Liverpool had moved ahead of Bristol as the principal Atlantic port during the 18th century. A pioneer in terms of canal and railway transport too, home of the world's very first railway station in 1830, Liverpool had a tradition of innovation and enterprise. By the late 19th century the city authorities were also acquiring a reputation for their progressive commitment to public works, commitment which continued in the 20th century. The Great Depression resulted in an Act of Parliament, in 1930, which facilitated major programmes of public expenditure. The Mersey Tunnel, a great engineering feat with imposing architectural entrances, was completed in 1934 under this programme. Constructed at the same time as Roosevelt's Tennessee Valley Authority projects, this hugely costly public project embodied the heroic age of municipal expenditure. Merseyside was badly hit by the slump in world trade and the City authorities did what they could to stimulate short-term employment and longer term prosperity. Speke airport was the next major project undertaken by the City authorities. It represented another massive commitment to the idea of enhancing Merseyside's transport infrastructures, and thus helping preserve Liverpool's status as a great Atlantic port. Southampton, on the south coast and far nearer to London, was challenging Liverpool as the premier port for passenger liners. Both cities were engaged in a rivalry for pre-eminence. Civic buildings were one aspect of this municipal assertion, and the grandeur of Speke airport can be ascribed to this sense of municipal pride. Speke's buildings are much grander than they needed to be: compared with other municipal airport buildings, Speke's are immense.

Liverpool was accustomed to handling thousands of travellers being discharged at once from ocean-going ships. A city expert in transit, when it came to its airport Liverpool planned on a grand scale. Changes in aeroplane technology doomed future development of the restricted site, and the airport buildings, magnificent as they are, had a cloud hanging over them from early on. The chimera of sea plane travel also contributed to the future problems of Speke. By locating the airport on a hemmed-in site on the Mersey, future expansion of runways was ruled out. We are thus left with buildings with new uses, but ones which still embody the final heroic phase of one of the world's great ports and one of Britain's greatest cities. Airports are aviation buildings but they are civic buildings too. This duality greatly enhances their significance, and justifies their reuse, long after the last passenger has passed through their gates and the last aeroplane has left the runway.

Notes

1   Philip Butler, An Illustrated History of Liverpool Airport. Liverpool: The Merseyside Aviation Society, 1983.
2   Stephen Levrant (Heritage Architecture Ltd), Speke Airport Liverpool, Listed Building Report. English Partnerships, 1997.
3   John Walter Wood, Airports. Some Elements of Design and Future Development. New York: Coward-McCann Inc, 1940.

Berlin-Tempelhof: a city-airport of the 1930s

Manfred Hecker

Tempelhof airport at Berlin was designed in 1935 by Ernst Sagebiel (1892–1970), an architect who had served as the manager of Erich Mendelsohn's practice until the latter's emigration in 1933. Sagebiel's subsequent appointment as head of the planning department at the Reich's Air Ministry gives a clear indication of his ideological U-turn. His first independent design for the Air Ministry's headquarters in the Wilhelmstraße, completed in 1935, shows a complete break with Mendelsohn's style. This huge building is treated in a cold, traditional form with decorative details inspired by the Schinkel style. Julius Posener described this Ministry of Aviation building (today converted to house the Federal Ministry of Finance) as a 'textbook Nazi construction'.[1]

Overall, Sagebiel's design for the Tempelhof airport complex forms an open quadrant, suggesting that his style was not uniform, but influenced rather by the special significance of the project. This new airport was to reflect the modern, international style of the age and provide a striking example of this recent building type. Large enough to remain in use until the end of the 20th century, its spatial dimensions, thirty times greater than what was actually required at the middle of the 1930s, were expressive of the pretensions both of the architect and of the city's planning authorities. The fact that Sagebiel's architectural style was appreciated by the Nazis is confirmed by this commission from the government for the construction of the airport building in 1935. Prior to this, in 1933, a competition had been held that attracted entries from Germany's most respected architects, including Mies van der Rohe, Walter Gropius and Hans Poelzig. None of their projects met with the regime's approval.

A 'world airport'

It as Hitler's idea to keep Berlin's airport on the Tempelhofer Feld, inside the city limits and only 2.5km from the city centre.[2] Tempelhof was to become Europe's principal aerial cross-roads and, thanks to its location, to assert Berlin's status as the capital of the Third Reich. Because of aircraft noise and the risks of accidents, most other capital

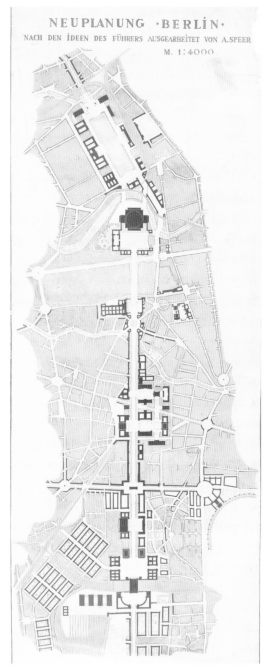

NEUPLANUNG ·BERLİN·
NACH DEN İDEEN DES FÜHRERS AUSGEARBEITET VON A.SPEER
M. 1:4000

Albert Speer's project for the north–south axis of Berlin, 1937. Tempelhof airport is situated at the eastern extremity of the west–east axis (Landesarchiv, Berlin)

The entire Tempelhof airport site in 1968; in the foreground, the Platz der Luftbrücke (Landesbildstelle, Berlin)

cities avoided locating their airports close to the city centre. Croydon, for example, is 14km from the centre of London. But Hitler had visions of Tempelhof as a prestigious international landmark and a major attraction for the masses. The airport, therefore, was placed at the eastern extremity of the prestigious east–west axis, crossing the major north–south axis of Albert Speer's plan for the centre of Berlin, dating from 1937. It is in this context that the architect designed a new urban space, the vast proportions of which offered an alternative to Mendelsohn's extension of the IG Metallhaus, never built but intended as a new centre for this neighbourhood near the Mehringplatz.

A surface area of 450ha was necessary for the new airport. This was acquired by integrating the site of the first Tempelhof airport, built between 1924 and 1929[3] on the eastern part of the airfield, and by taking over a part of the old garrison cemetery and the former 'people's park'.

As far as its layout and interior organisation were concerned, Sagebiel's Tempelhof was the most spacious and modern installation of its kind in Europe, designed to be more than just a 'normal' airport. Office buildings for aviation bodies, erected around

a circular plaza with a diameter of 120m – intersected by the Mehringdamm-Tempelhofer Damm from north to south and by the Columbiadamm from east to west – was to create a new urban focus at the same time as the airport. According to the original plans, four modern blocks were to be built to the west of this plaza, which would have entailed considerable demolition and redevelopment and incurred high costs. Because of the existence of a prestigious group of apartment buildings, designed in 1910 by Bruno Möhring, to the west of the Tempelhofer Damm, it was only on the eastern part of the plaza (today's Platz der Luftbrücke) that a new, semicircular construction was finally built.

The rapid construction of the ensemble demonstrates the mastery of civil engineers of the second half of the 1930s in the realm of high quality reinforced concrete buildings. Work started on the terminal in 1935 and by December 1937 the basic structure had already been completed. Construction slowed down considerably, however, following the outbreak of the Second World War in the autumn of 1939. Hitler lost interest in the airport's role as a manifestation of the international prestige of his regime. Building work subsequently progressed in fits and

The main building and courtyard of honour in 1999 (photo Wolfgang Reuss/Landesdenkmalamt Berlin)

starts. The north-eastern complex on the Platz der Luftbrücke, initially intended to house the offices of foreign airline companies (today accommodating the Federal Monopolies Commission, the Federal Debt Administration and the Head Customs Office for Berlin South), had already been completed in 1937. The airport buildings also had already been given their definitive form although some of the walls were not completely faced in stone.

On the city side, the airport complex opens out on the south-eastern perimeter of the Platz der Luftbrücke. Two symmetrical four-storey, concave front buildings are separated by the 80-metre-wide forecourt; a courtyard of honour that is 90m deep. Similar to the other airport constructions, these front buildings are faced with a type of shelly limestone with a yellowish hue; the surrounds of the windows, as well as the protruding cornice, are of a lighter-coloured limestone. This design is common to the façades of almost all the airport buildings, marked by the varying sizes of the window openings and other small details.

The concave buildings that flank the entrance to the forecourt each have nineteen vertical rows of windows comprised of two sets of eight, separated by a central group of three rows of larger windows. This part of the façade, where the windows, divided in two by a mullion, extend to the floor, draws attention to the staircase that lies behind. The street level entrance to this staircase is marked by a short flight of steps covered by a simple porch. The two outer series of windows have standard formats, corresponding with the office spaces inside. At either extremity of the two front buildings, the façades present a flat, windowless surface

above the entrance to a broad arcade surmounted by an eagle sculpted in relief. The forecourt area is enclosed by two three-storey wings forming passages to the terminal proper and each comprising a covered arcade. It was originally planned to occupy the spaces under these arcades with shops. The two floors above are offices. The façades are crowned by a rectangular protruding cornice, as on the front buildings. The flattened gable roofs of the wings join up with the airport building, the upper floors of the latter emerging above the roofs.

On either side of the concave front buildings, two more four-storey office buildings line the Tempelhofer Damm and the Columbiadamm, set back behind small lawns and ending, at the south and west extremities, with a long, slightly projecting part. On either side of these projections, broad passages link up with the curving underground supply road, via ramps. Two more inner constructions comprise the south and south-west boundaries of two closed courtyards. Sagebiel originally planned for the courtyard to the west to house the main post office, with the airport's administration occupying the buildings around the opposite courtyard.

The rear end of the central forecourt is comprised of the 180-metre-long reception and administration building, which is five storeys high at its centre and seven storeys high to either side, above the underground road. This exceptionally long and high building forms the main feature of the airport's reception and administration facilities. Flanked by its two forecourt wings, the central reception area has a monumental form, emphasised by the verticality of its lower windows reaching up from the first to

The departures hall in 1962
(Landesbildstelle, Berlin)

the second floor. The parts of the building to either side have twelve vertical rows of uniform windows, for the offices. On these side areas, the window surrounds are flush with the surface of the façade, whereas in the central area, the surrounds project slightly. The surrounds of the first and second floor windows are combined vertically, reaching up to a cornice at the top of the second floor. This central part of the façade is also marked at the ground floor by a long canopy with twenty-two rectangular supporting columns. This extended the covered space of the side arcades, thus ensuring that passengers coming to or leaving the departure hall were always protected from bad weather. Sagebiel situated the main entrance hall at the centre of the terminal building, rising up through three floors. This grandiose volume was also to serve as a memorial hall to the heroes of aviation, their statues placed against pillars punctuating the entire length of the hall. Because of its sheer height and its opening onto the forecourt through its twenty-one tall windows, an imposing spatial connection would have emerged between the hall and the forecourt area. This prestigious reception and memorial hall was not entirely finished by the end of the war, however. In the 1950s it was divided horizontally by a ceiling built above the level of the ground floor and corresponding with new aesthetic tastes of this era. The post-war years were less concerned with heroes of aviation. Nonetheless, the striking impression created by the memorial hall, as designed by Sagebiel, is today still perceptible on the façade, thanks to the combined window frames of the first and second floors. The windows of the two floors above also have projecting surrounds. The

summit of the building was originally crowned with a huge iron eagle, set on a pedestal, as a symbol of the airport. Only the head of the eagle, which was removed in 1961, has survived and is to be seen today on a pedestal on the lawn of the Platz der Luftbrücke.

The entrance hall opens onto the main departures hall. The floor of this hall is 5m lower than the entrance floor, and it measures overall 50m wide by 100m long. Rectangular columns divide the hall into a 32-metre-wide central nave with two 9-metre-wide side aisles forming balconies that are only accessible from the entrance hall via a staircase. Non-flying visitors, strictly separated from the passengers, look down over the departures hall from these side balconies. For the two longitudinal walls and the end wall on the airfield side, the architect used large glazed surfaces reaching right down to the floor and bathing the hall in light. The view from the departures hall onto the airfield's boarding area resembled a cinema screen and was left open, as the architect had separated the departure zone into two different spaces for domestic and foreign flights. In the 1950s, this transparent end wall was closed off by a new restaurant, built above the boarding area. The ceiling of the central part of the departures hall, designed to support the weight of a restaurant and banqueting hall for 2,000 people, consists of a 4-metre-thick reinforced concrete trellis-work structure, developed by the municipal engineer Dischinger in the 1930s and bearing witness to efforts to economise on steel in the building. The storerooms for the restaurant were accommodated inside the structure.

In keeping with the vertical separation of

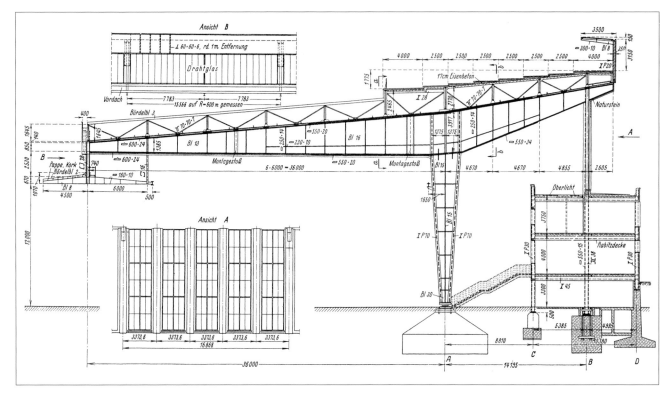

Structural cross-section of the boarding area (from Schleusner 1938, 58)

the visitors from passenger traffic and transport systems, Sagebiel relegated the baggage-handling facilities to the area underneath the departures hall. Items of luggage, already sorted onto electric trolleys in the departures hall, were transported by a lift. The baggage room is connected with the mailroom and cargo area, 10m under the level of the hall, via a ramp. The south-east end of this level has access to a railway tunnel, which meant that a direct connections were possible between rail and air transport. Still underground, the mailroom and cargo area are connected to the departures hall at the south-west and north-west. Via ramps, the two courtyards have access to the Tempelhofer Damm and the Columbiadamm and to the boarding area.

Facing onto the airfield, the 380-metre-long boarding area forms the centre of the immense concave building, 1,300m long, occupied on both sides by maintenance and workshop hangars, each 460m in length. Two large lifts at the ends of the balconies of the departures hall, along with the 14 stair towers at the rear of the complex, were installed to take visitors either to the gallery of the boarding area or up to the rooftop viewing platforms. Above the individual departure gates, the former departures gallery is used today as office space, with storage rooms beneath, on the ground floor. Flights of twenty steps lead down from the departure gates to the sheltered boarding area. Above each flight of stairs, projecting square bays, glazed on three sides, are reminiscent of the Bauhaus style, at the time still in favour for industrial buildings. Above, a glass wall closes off the back of the boarding area. This glass wall integrates vertical steel pillars which are attached to the shorter, rear beam of the steel girders supporting the canopy that overhangs the whole boarding area and side hangars. These steel pillars are extremely thin, but are not subjected to much tension even under excessive strain. The balanced cantilever construction of the canopy, with its remarkable 40-metre overhang, bears witness to the engineering skills of Dr A Schleusner. The slim pillars at the rear give anchoring support for the steel structures that serve as columns for the canopy. Schleusner, following Sagebiel's instructions, designed the roof to accommodate stepped viewing stands for 65,000 spectators. The construction work was carried out by the steel company Krupp-Druckenmüller. 'St-37' steel was chosen as the building material: 'After detailed preparation it was observed that a reinforced concrete construction with a cantilever of 40m, although possible, cannot be considered to be equivalent from an economic or aesthetic point of view.'[4] The steel-framed structure was welded rather than riveted, which represented a significant innovation in the field of steel construction at the time.

The far ends of the semicircular sweep of the boarding and hangar area comprise two six-storey cubic wings. Between them, a total of 14 stair towers give access to the roof, eight to the east and six to the south-west. Between each tower, slightly set back, stands the rear side of the gate gallery, with its glazed upper part. The two elements create a striking contrast and are reminiscent of outline sketches by Erich Mendelsohn.[5]

The post-war era

On the airfield in front, there is a 300-metre-deep apron the contours of which follow the sweep of the building, originally offering two side parking areas for aircraft. This is where the planes were prepared for flight, before taxiing beneath the covered area for boarding passengers and freight loading.

The elliptic airfield was surrounded by a 75-metre-wide taxiway with three semicircular take-off stands, each 140m in diameter. Thanks to these so-called 'start stumps', take-off was possible in any wind direction, starting from this paved surface. In general, however, until the Second World War, grass surfaces were still considered to make the best runway. Only the south-west half of the taxiway is still preserved today, with two of the take-off stumps.

The airport's power supply was to be as independent as possible of the city's energy resources. The water supply system, with four deep wells, was installed during the construction of the buildings. In the Schöneberg district of the city, a special electric power station was built for the airport and, inside the airport itself, an emergency power station was also installed. The airport was to be heated using urban heating, but two low-pressure steam boilers were also installed. These technical facilities for the reception and departures halls, as well as for the offices, lie under the mailroom and cargo level.

The airport was not completed at the outbreak of the Second World War and aircraft continued to use the 1920s terminal. Construction work on the new airport by the company entrusted with its management, the Berliner Flughafengesellschaft, continued at a less intensive pace under the direction of Werner Loebermann.

After war, the Berliner Flughafengesellschaft continued the work, mainly repairing war damage, under the control of the Allies. During the Berlin Blockade in 1948, with the technical help of the US Air Force, airlift aircraft landed at Tempelhof. Two east–west runways were laid down to accommodate modern air traffic. By May 1949, at the end of the Blockade, about 277,000 flights had been processed at Tempelhof airport.

In 1950, the American High Commissioner authorised the City of Berlin to use part of Tempelhof airport for civil traffic. As the main entrance to the airport was still being used by the Allies, the access for commercial air traffic was transferred to the Tempelhofer Damm, with a departures hall of only 250 square metres. The modifications were again entrusted to Werner Loebermann, who extended the boarding area by opening a restaurant at the end departures hall. In 1951, the civil airport area was

The boarding area, beneath the 40-metre overhang of the canopy (photo Wolfgang Bittner/Landesdenkmalamt Berlin)

opened to traffic. The constant growth in air traffic up until the end of the 1950s meant that a large part of the area used for military purposes was switched to civilian use. As a result of this, the original reception and departures hall was redesigned. In the reception hall, a massive ceiling was constructed over the ground floor. Today's coffered ceiling with its neon lighting and radiators was built to replace the badly damaged stucco ceiling of the hall. The glazed wall looking out over the airfield was closed up. In 1962 the airport was opened to the public in its current form.

The historic monument

Since 1994, the airport buildings and the adjoining apron area in front of them have been protected as a historic monument. Their preservation is justified by their historic, artistic, scientific and urban importance. Irrespective of its current status as a city-centre airport, Tempelhof is of considerable significance in terms of Berlin's history as well as construction history. Its location on the Tempelhofer Feld is closely bound up with the early history of aviation. At the beginning of the 20th century, in 1909, this field was used, for example, by the Wright brothers for their demonstration flights, heralding the use of the field as an airport. In 1923, it was the site of Berlin's first central airport. During the time of the Berlin Blockade of 1948 to 1949, as the focal point of the Allies' airlift, it became a symbol of the West Berliners' desire for freedom.

Alongside the importance of the complex as an outstanding example of Nazi architecture, clearly influenced by the international construction style of the age, its spacious internal organisation and the inclusion of offices, a post office and administrative buildings, make it an exceptional example of an airport building. The steel canopy over the boarding area and maintenance halls and hangars, and the reinforced concrete trellis-work of the ceiling over the central part of the departures hall are remarkable engineering feats of the 1930s.

Thanks to its central location, Tempelhof was a vital centre for the existence of the city during the Berlin Blockade and subsequently, during the economic boom of the 1960s. Since the opening of Tegel airport in 1975, Tempelhof has been closed to intercontinental air traffic. One of the conditions of the recent project for the large new airport at Berlin-Schönefeld is the closure of Tempelhof. This raises two crucial questions. What will be done with the disused airport site? And is it really worth closing this city-centre airport? After all, as far as its location and transport connections are concerned, Tempelhof is ideally situated to serve Berlin's government district. When the new plans were drawn up for London's docklands, the central location of a new airport was considered to be crucial.

Even though the suspension of air traffic at Tempelhof appears to be inevitable, other papers in this present publication make it absolutely clear that this site, which has made such a significant contribution to air transport in Europe and which is still operational today, cannot be closed down without further reflection.

Notes

1 Julius Posener, *Fast so alt wie das Jahrhundert*. Berlin: Siedler Verlag, 1990, 230.
2 'Der Weltflughafen Tempelhof, ein Blick auf das Werden eines großen Werkes'. *Monatshefte für Baukunst und Städtebau* **22** (1938), 82.
3 The first permanent hangars at Tempelhof were constructed in 1924 by Heinrich Kosina and Paul Mahlberg. The terminal building was constructed during two periods between 1926 and 1927 and 1928 and 1929 by the same architects, following a plan drawn up by Paul and Klaus Engler, whose project had come first in a design competition; see Laurenz Demps and Carl-Ludwig Paeschke, *Flughafen Tempelhof, die Geschichte einer Legende*. Berlin: Verlag Ullstein, 1998, 28 et seq.
4 A Schleusner, 'Die Flugsteighalle für den Neubau des Flughafens Tempelhof', in *Neuzeitliche Stahlhallenbauten*. Berlin: Verlag Wilhelm Ernst und Sohn, 1938, 57.
5 See the sketch for a factory building in steel and reinforced concrete in: *Erich Mendelsohn 1887 bis 1953. Ideen, Bauten, Projekte*, exhibition catalogue by S Achenbach, Berlin, 1987, 37.

Select bibliography

Berlin und seine Bauten 1984 Part 10, Vol A: *Verkehrsbauten*. Berlin: Verlag Ernst & Sohn
'Berlins neuer Flughafen' 1937 *Deutsche Bauzeitung* **20**, 343–4.
Conin, H 1974 *Gelandet in Berlin. Zur Geschichte der Berliner Flughäfen*. Berlin: Berliner Flughafen GmbH, 182–92.
Demps, L and Paeschke, C-L 1998 *Flughafen Tempelhof, die Geschichte einer Legende*. Berlin: Verlag Ullstein

'Der Weltflughafen Tempelhof' 1938 *Bauwelt* **9**, 193–208.

'Die Neugestaltung der Reichshauptstadt' 1938 *Die Baugilde* **4**, 98–100.

Schäche, W 1991 *Bauwerke und Kunstdenkmäler von Berlin, Architektur und Städtebau Berlin 1933–1945*. Berlin: Gebr. Mann Verlag

Schaper, G 1939 'Flughallen und Flugsteighallen des Flughafens Berlin-Tempelhof', in *Vom Werdegang der Stahlbauwerke*, Vol 1. Berlin: Deutscher Stahlbau-Verband, 126–35

Schleusner, A 1938 'Die Eisenbetonbauten des Welt-Flughafens Berlin-Tempelhof'. *Der Bauingenieur* **45/46**, 621–8.

Wasmuth, V E 1937 *Wasmuth's Lexikon der Baukunst V*. Berlin: Nachtrag A–Z, 204–5.

Ernst Sagebiel's Tempelhof airport: typology, iconography and politics

Axel Drieschner

The design of Tempelhof airport was the result of many different influences. In a unique historical context, the multi-faceted challenge of conceiving an airport in the form of a monumental piece of urban planning produced an ensemble that was highly acclaimed. The objective, however, was not merely the creation of a centralised structure for commercial air travel. Tempelhof was also an instrument of National Socialist propaganda, serving both as a functional building complex and as a symbolic political construction. The aim of the following paper, divided into four sections, is to draw attention to these different sorts of influence, focusing on the areas where the different factors overlap or are at odds with one another. It hopes to throw light on the political conditions surrounding the whole project, on the place of the airport in its international context, on the architectural motifs used and their significance, and finally on the aesthetics of the steel canopy of the covered boarding area, the airport's most remarkable feature.[1]

The political framework

From the 1920s onwards, Berlin-Tempelhof was considered to be 'Europe's aviation crossroads'.[2] The number of passengers rose from about 30,000 in 1926 to more than 200,000 in 1936,[3] making it the busiest airport on the Continent. By the beginning of the 1930s, this growth in traffic was already forcing the airport's operators to consider abandoning the existing, though still unfinished buildings and replacing them with an ambitious new design. After the National Socialists came to power in 1933, this project found a fervent advocate in Adolf Hitler himself. The eastern part of the Tempelhofer Feld, covering about four square kilometres, was to be set aside almost entirely for air transport. The existing airfield of 1923 covered only about half of this area.

Prior to its designation as the site of Berlin's main airport in the 1920s, this Tempelhofer Feld already had an illustrious past. Since the early 18th century, it had been used as a military exercise and parade ground. To mark the victory over France in 1871, for example, the Prussian monarch and new German Emperor staged a major military parade here. From the end of the 19th century onwards, the field also served as a multipurpose open space for sports contests, workers' demonstrations and Sunday leisure activities.[4] At the beginning of the 20th century, the Prussian army began to think about disposing of the site. This set off a fierce debate about the types of uses and buildings that would be appropriate for this, the largest open space within Berlin's city limits at the time.[5] Some were already considering using it as an airfield, especially after it was the scene of Orville Wright's first motorised flight in Germany in 1909.[6] While the smaller, western part of the site had been developed from 1912, the eastern part of the field was still intact as an open space. Until the new airport was built here in the middle of the 1930s, 'Berlin's Sahara', as one journalist described it, continued to be used for various events. The first airport was surrounded by sports facilities, allotment gardens and a festival ground.[7] Between 1933 and 1935 it was used by the National Socialists to hold their May Day mass demonstrations. The first of these ostentatiously staged marches played a significant propaganda role in Hitler's seizure of power.[8] The Tempelhofer Feld was subsequently marked by the topography of political terror: until work started on construction of the new airport, the Columbiahaus, one of the most notorious concentration camps of the early days of the regime, stood on today's Columbiadamm, at the periphery of the field.[9]

Hitler emerged then as one of the most fervent supporters of the airport project, becoming personally involved in its ambitious propaganda aspects. In October 1934, he issued directives to the airport company.[10] In view of ever-increasing air traffic, he demanded that the new airport should be large enough to remain in service for several decades. Imagining the world in the year 2000, when the scale of the proposed airport would be nothing special, he prophesied that 'in the near future, no one will even contemplate travelling distances of more than 500 kilometres by any other means than by air.' Hitler also wanted this new airport to complement the development plans for the capital of the German Reich that he himself had initiated. To have rail and road transport serve the airport, direct links were planned with the projected new railway station to the south of Berlin, as well as to the future central, north–south road axis. Alongside the new South Station, the airport was to provide a gateway appropriate for a major metropolis. According to minutes signed by the airport's director Rudolf Böttger, 'its beauty and size alone will silence any negative criticism directed against Germany.' Intent on being the envy of the world, Hitler wanted Tempelhof to become, in his own words, 'the best' as well as 'the largest and most beautiful civilian airport in the world.' Exactly how he pictured this airport in concrete terms was delineated, in his own hand, in a few rough sketches, that were soon overtaken, however, by the development of the project.

It was not only through its 'beauty' and 'size' that the airport was to play its propaganda role. Hitler also wanted the new airport to become a monumental stage for showing off the German air force, at this time still secret, and still illegal under the terms of the Versailles Peace Treaty. Annual air shows – possibly deliberate references to the field's prestigious military history – were to remind the population that it was the National Socialists who had resurrected Germany's air force. After the thin veil of secrecy shrouding the Luftwaffe was finally lifted, in May 1935, military demonstration flights were immediately organised, for example, at the party rallies in Nuremberg.

From the outset, therefore, the airport project was characterised by its 'paramilitary' duality. 'Military and civil air traffic belong together. They are to stimulate each other and the conversion of Tempelhof into a single airport is [...] part of the necessary rearmament effort', Hitler declared. Putting this theory into practice, in the late summer of 1935, the local authorities were obliged to hand over their planning responsibilities to the Reich's Air Minister, Hermann Goering. Consequently, from 1936 to 1941, the construction of the airport was financed by the Third Reich's arms budget.[11]

It should be noted, however, that the

Ernst Sagebiel's first project for Tempelhof airport, photo of a model, 1935/6 (Bundesarchiv, Berlin)

overlapping of civil and military 'air power', as it was then known, was not a pure product of National Socialist ideology. Well before 1933, civil air transport was considered as the cornerstone of the 'monumental expansion of the German dominance of the skies', and was thus described by party journalists.[12] The National Socialists in power, however, took this symbiosis further. Following Goering's remark in June 1934 that Germany had to become a nation of flyers, efforts were made to 'raise children with the idea of dominance of the skies' from an early age.[13] The new Tempelhof airport was intended to play a decisive role in this educational concept.

Tempelhof in its international context: logistics versus representation

In order to find the ideal solution to make it possible for the airport to last for generations, Berlin studied the wealth of ideas concerning airport design and construction that had emerged throughout the world during the preceding decade. Projects that existed only on paper were given particular attention. Above all, it was the British and American ideas dating from the end of the 1920s that influenced Ernst Sagebiel, the architect appointed by Goering, although to many observers, in 1935, their implementation did not appear at all practical.[14] These were the only schemes, however, offering the ambitious and comprehensive designs for a 'complete' airport installation of the kind required at Tempelhof, integrating urban development and transport connections, and which took into account the layout of the airfield as well as the planning and

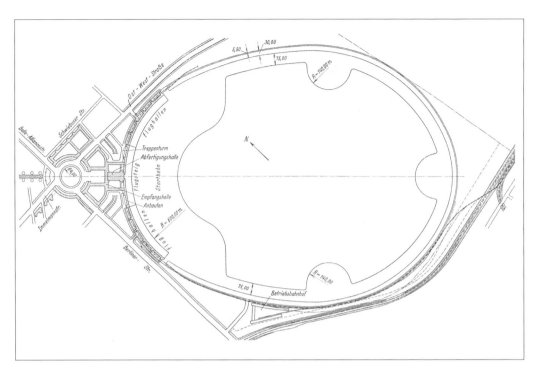

General plan of Tempelhof airport, 1938 (from Schleusner 1938, 89)

design of the building ensemble. As far as concrete examples were concerned, this kind of total creation as a 'unified whole' was without precedent. But, at Tempelhof, the themes of the English and American experiments were realised with such vigour and in such proportions that they exceeded the expectations of even the boldest visionaries.

Among these trends were the notions of 'dry boarding', generally made possible by the use of covered gates or passages, the isolation of the various traffic flows by their separation onto different levels inside the terminal building and in front of it, and the composition of extensive, geometrical ground plans, comprising the whole airfield, the buildings, the forecourts and the access roads. These ideas were put forward in spectacular form during the American Lehigh competition and, in many respects, the prize-winning design by A C Zimmermann and William H Harrison closely resembles the solutions found for Tempelhof. Another project put forward at this competition, by Wesley S Bessell, also inspired Sagebiel to imagine an alternative technical scheme, with gate piers extending sideways from the terminal.[15] Unlike Tempelhof, however, the geometry of these American plans was based on systems of hard-surfaced runways, the layout of which was inspired by Renaissance plans for the ideal town or by baroque garden design.

The 1928 winner of the airport design competition organised by the Royal Institute of British Architects demonstrated how a formal, closed composition could also be achieved using a round grass flying field encircled by a boundary path. This British competition also repeatedly put forward

bridge-type boarding passageways, which enabled travellers to reach their planes without getting wet. If we compare the ground plan of Tempelhof airport, as implemented, with these designs, the similarities are very obvious. Tempelhof probably represents the only example of the practical outcome of the 'ideal' projects dating from the period before 1930 when airports were considered as urban works of art.

Let us take a closer look now at the overall ground plan of Tempelhof airport. The oval airfield and the buildings assembled in the north-west corner are actually merged into a unified whole. The main symmetrical axis of this ensemble is the median line formed at the angle of the tangential boundary roads. The north-western extremity of this axis is marked by the memorial to the wars of liberation against Napoleon's rule – Friedrich Schinkel's Kreuzberg memorial – not far from the airport. This means that the buildings, the road network and the open spaces come together to form a comprehensive geometrical structure with one form replying to another. The surrounding taxiway gives the airfield its clear contour. Lining the grass-covered central area, this boundary strip opens smoothly out into larger apron areas and into the so-called take-off stands. Seen from the sky, the rounded contours of these bays contribute to the organic appearance of the overall design. The result is an outline of considerable emblematic force, vaguely imbued – why not? – with the potency of a mystical figure.

The work of Hans Poelzig is a good example of the creation elsewhere of comparably expressive outline figures making an indelible mark on the urban landscape.

Tempelhof is reminiscent in particular of Poelzig's plan for the Berlin exhibition centre at the *Funkturm*, drawn up in 1927.[16] Erich Mendelsohn, in whose practice Sagebiel had worked from 1929 to 1933, also understood how to blend multi-component architectural complexes into a single organic whole, a particularly striking example being his proposal for the renovation of the Alexanderplatz in Berlin.[17]

The way Sagebiel renders the abstract concept of 'expanse' tangible, thanks to the crescent form of his building opening out the space, is also reminiscent of Mendelsohn's work. Indeed, it is almost as if here – and here only – that Mendelsohn's precept of the 'domination and penetration of space' was put into practice. In the introduction to his essay *Reflections on New Architecture*, Mendelsohn wrote 'Architecture takes hold of a space, embraces it, is itself space. From the three-dimensional infinity of the universe – which in itself is unimaginable – via its determined limits, it brings the idea of space into the world.'[18] With the lines of force of the immense curve of the building joining up in the distance on the other side of the airfield, Tempelhof managed to achieve the expression of 'cosmic' spatial references that Mendelsohn sought after, and that lay at the heart of his creation.

We should not forget, however, that other references might also have influenced the vast curve of the Tempelhof airport building. From time immemorial, open spaces and elevated vantage points have been framed by ample exedras. A modern example was the exhibition building built by Adolf Abel on the Rheinufer in Cologne-Deutz between 1926 and 1928. This example was certainly familiar to Sagebiel, since at the time he lived in Cologne where he worked in the office of the architect Jacob Koerfer.[19]

Last but not least, this curve of the terminal and hangar building at Tempelhof is reminiscent of a rather naïve conception of a classic harbour. This can be illustrated by illustrations from the architectural treatise of Francesco di Giorgio Martini.[20] Evidence of the continued influence of this vision can be seen in a design by Boris Iofan, dating from the early 1940s.[21] This idea of the airfield as a stylised harbour, and the pictorial reference to the concept, common at the time, of the skies as an ocean, is already to be found in one of the many preliminary studies for Tempelhof, in which the curve of the building, then still subdivided into individual elements, forms a sort of sheltering harbour wall, further extended by the semicircular boundary path opposite.[22]

But as interesting as these conceptions might be from a 'structural' point of view, the practical applications of the airport's organic form proved to be rather problematic. Returning here to my earlier point: if Tempelhof's design is set against the standards that were emerging on the international airport scene by the middle of the 1930s, in many ways it appears anachronistic. For example, in contrast to the clear trend towards hard-surfaced runway systems and, consequently, towards groups of buildings pushing forward in convex forms towards the runway system, a grass airfield was chosen for Tempelhof, with a concave border.

Elsewhere, during the second half of the 1930s, a new generation of airports was rapidly superseding the preceding one. This took place in the United States soon after 1930. The project for an airport of world-wide importance is embodied, at the end of the 1930s, by the airport at New York's North Beach, with its provisions for seaplanes.[23] Comparably large airports were also being planned for Paris-Versailles and for London in 1936 and 1937. Versailles, for example, was to be equipped with 2,500-metre-long double runways, alongside a water surface for the flying boats anticipated for transatlantic crossings.[24]

At Tempelhof, by contrast, the attempt to achieve record proportions and to reach an exemplary solution that would last for generations was in fact a resounding failure. The principle – already a litany from the 1920s onwards and still valid today – according to which change is the only thing an airport planner can be sure of, was intentionally ignored. Instead of producing a flexible and extendable design, a definitive state was calmly 'wrapped in concrete'. This state

The model of the final project for Tempelhof, 1938 (from Gerdy Troost (ed), Das Bauen im neuen Reich. Bayreuth, 1938, 116)

Tempelhof, landside view of the hangar building today, with one of the projecting stair towers (photo Axel Drieschner)

could already be considered as technically obsolete when construction commenced in the spring of 1936. Even the airport's director Böttger, one of the key players in the project, promised in 1938 that the complex would soon be modernised by means of hard-surfaced runways.[25] This would have nullified the entire organisational underpinning of the concept, however: the oval airfield with the buildings bordering it. This is what actually happened at Tempelhof after the war.

It was not until after 1945 that these and other flaws in Tempelhof's design gave rise to open criticism. As early as 1937, however, two experts, Bilfinger and Rapp, had already anticipated future problems, even though Bilfinger, like Sagebiel, was also employed as an assistant secretary at the Reich Air Ministry. 'It should always be avoided', as he wrote in a specialist article, 'that flights take off and land directly over human dwellings'. Furthermore, 'the development of a transport facility in a makeshift fashion, with the traffic squeezed into it, no longer corresponds with the new perceptions'. This barely veiled attack on Tempelhof culminated in the phrase 'in the future, an airport without runways will be viewed as just as old-fashioned as using logs to lay roads.'[26]

And, in point of fact, a radical change of direction was already announced. Hitler himself, at the beginning of the 1940s, recognised the disadvantages of this city-airport and demanded its transfer beyond the city limits. This U-turn was also to have an effect on Albert Speer's plans for Berlin. He now wanted to shut down the still unfinished 'central airport' at Tempelhof, replacing it with a large new airport in Rangsdorf, located on the motorway ring road and equipped for sea planes. Aptly baptised 'Utopia', this project made little headway; as for the future of the Tempelhof site, as Speer wrote in his memoirs, it could have become 'an amusement park, like the Tivoli in Copenhagen.'[27]

Tempelhof's architecture and its meaning

The view of the airport from the city side falls into two distinct parts that are nonetheless indistinguishable in planning terms: the self-contained plaza and forecourt ensemble on the one hand, and, on the other, the terminal and hangar ensemble curving away beyond the boundary roads.

The landside façade of this curving hangar ensemble is regularly punctuated by powerful, projecting square towers, separated by tall windows and narrow pillars. Beneath the large windows, the façade comprises a base of several storeys. The consoles that emerge at the tops of the pillars seem to support a projecting, windowless band, but the majority of these pillars and consoles are purely decorative, attached to the roof construction of the hangars. Only one in five of these vertical supporting elements actually serves any load-bearing purpose, providing external stone cladding for the rear part of the steel hangar girders. The sections that are visible as consoles are here the rear, concrete-sheathed heads of the large roof trusses of the hall.

The cityside façade of the terminal has clearly been influenced by Erich Mendelsohn's futuristic studies of industrial buildings, dating from 1914 and 1915.[28] But it was Sagebiel who, in the end, turned out to be the interpreter and executor of Mendelsohn's architectural visions. Another reference, however, is of more significance in iconic terms: the long wall structure of the façade is an idea borrowed from contemporary stadium architecture.

One typical feature of the architecture of large sports stadiums, at the time, was the projecting stands supported by concrete consoles; the division of the external containing walls into structural elements is another. In both these respects, Tempelhof bears a close resemblance to the Olympic stadium in Los Angeles.[29] Other comparable examples are a stadium project by Pier Luigi Nervi for Rome, or the *Hallenstadion* in Zurich, built by Karl Egender.[30]

The roof of Tempelhof's terminal building was designed to accommodate viewing stands for more than 60,000 spectators and the entire airport was conceived as an air stadium for a million spectators: for the majority of this public, further stands were to be provided at the edge of the airfield.[31] At the same time, however, the stadium theme is both eclipsed and accentuated by motifs drawn from quite different references, those of fortifications. The series of towers containing the staircases that lead up to the rooftop stands thus takes on a defensive function. On the landside, they protrude from the body of the building as massive, self-contained blocks. Rising slightly above the rooftop level, their upper parts are also visible from the airfield side, forming a ring of sturdy 'watchtowers'.

Such protruding towers were seldom used for stadium buildings. In formal terms, two other different influences were at play here in Sagebiel's design. A competition entry by two of Hans Poelzig's disciples for the first, 1920s terminal in Tempelhof already anticipated the tower structure.[32] Sagebiel leapt at the chance to use this effective invention, especially as it had served Poelzig so well in his design for the IG Farben Haus.[33] But this bulwark-type of appearance given to the façade was also intended to convey a political message. From 1933 onwards, the tower motif was deliberately employed to propagate the idea of the *Volksgemeinschaft*, the 'folk community', understood in military terms. An early example is Klaus Müller-Rehm's design for a *Thingstätte*. His amphitheatre-type stand is surrounded by free-standing stair towers, reminiscent of siege towers.[34] The Zeppelin field on the Third Reich's rally ground in Nuremberg, the side stands of which are comprised of pylon-like tower stumps, can also be seen as belonging to this genre of fortification-type public arenas. More will be said later about another site used for party rallies, the *Märzfeld*.

Commemorative monuments of the 1920s paved the way for the specific semantics of the tower and fortress motifs. The castle-like Tannenberg memorial in East Prussia was the prototype here.[35] In this context, the image of archaic military constructions took on positively political and revanchist overtones. The suggestive effects of this chauvinistic 'atmospheric architecture' also drew on the fantastic sets of film and theatre, such as Fritz Lang's *Nibelungen*.[36] If this slightly speculative interpretation is pursued, then the roads running along the façade of the airport building could be read as moats, spanned by stone drawbridges.[37]

But why such martial garb for a commercial airport? As mentioned above, the annual air shows were intended to demonstrate to the world that the Germans 'had the most powerful air force in the world.'[38] Used by

the reserve air force, and to a certain extent in keeping with the military traditions of the field, Tempelhof was the aerial counterpart of the *Märzfeld*, the Reich's parade ground at Nuremberg. There, ramparts with towers almost 40m high were planned as an architectural shell.[39] As for example at the *Märzfeld* – the name of which marked the rearmament proclaimed in March 1935 – the airport's external appearance was also intended to serve as a memorial highlighting this double military and political event. At the same time as the announcement of conscription in March 1935, the dissimulation of the regime's air force was lifted. Both measures were repeatedly alluded to in propaganda as a means of shaking off the 'yoke of Versailles'.[40]

The assumption that the airport's architecture was to serve as a reminder of this patriotic date gives rise to another interpretative possibility around the alignment of the complex with the Kreuzberg memorial.[41] By choosing Schinkel's iron spire as Tempelhof's crowning viewpoint, a historical link was established between the contemporary fortification of the nation and German national self-assertion under Napoleon's rule.

At the outset, the opening towards the Kreuzberg memorial was to consist of a broad green sward, extending the Viktoriapark and leading from the front of the main reception building overlooking the plaza and a generously sized ceremonial courtyard.[42] The idea for this broad green space was abandoned and the courtyard reduced to a size more in proportion to the buildings. Under the influence of the redevelopment plans of the General Planning Department at the end of 1938, however, another truly imperialistic gesture was invented: the plaza in front of the airport was transformed into an ornamental square, similar to the 'Round Square' planned on the north–south axis. It now came to form part of a sequence of plazas in circular, rectangular or octagonal shapes that were to be aligned along an axis crossing over the north–south artery. An architecturally designed water feature, with sturdy obelisks as an added reinforcing gesture, was to decorate the trajectory leading to the Kreuzberg memorial, emphasising its meaning as a triumphal axis. At the beginning of the 1940s, after the change of plans as to the future of the airport, all these projects were scrapped. Speer's alterations meant that the broad composition lines

Top: *A 1939 model showing the monumental axis, with its decorative canal, leading from the airport's plaza to Friedrich Schinkel's Kreuzberg memorial (from Die Bauzeitung 49th year (1939), 6)*

Model of the 1935/6 project for Tempelhof airport, comprising the projected south railway station, in the background, to the left (Bundesarchiv, Berlin)

leading from the airport complex ended in nothing more than a turn in the road.[43]

It should be noted, however, that intentional associations between patriotic memorials and political or sports assembly points – which the airport, as an 'air stadium', was – had other precedents. At the turn of the century, there were plans to create sports fields in the shadow of large national memorials, such as the Kaiser-Wilhelm Memorial on the Kyffhäuser, with the aim of holding a German Olympics. The project for a national festival site for Goslar is a combination of a monument and sports arena, reminiscent of Tempelhof's ground plan as far as its shape is concerned.[44] During the 1920s and 1930s several other examples perpetuated this linkage between arena and memorial, one of the best known being the Berlin Olympic Stadium, where a memorial tower for the battle of Langemarck was added to the stands.[45]

Another motif used in the architecture of Tempelhof airport deserves to be mentioned here. It comes to the fore in front of the

heart of the complex, the departure area, where the buildings form a vast and impressive front, leading onto the plaza. Here, railway stations rather than airports spring to mind when considering whether the result is in keeping with a construction designed for transport. More than any existing airport, the large railway stations built in the late 19th century can be seen as providing a model for transport centres of international importance. The large European main line stations such as Leipzig or, later, Stuttgart and Milan, were prime examples of prestigious transport ensembles used by cosmopolitan clienteles.

Against the background of heightened national awareness in Germany, the climax was reached at the Central Station in Leipzig, inaugurated in 1915 as the largest complex of its kind in Europe and as the epitome of the grand railway station. Only this yardstick seemed to be adequate for the architects of Tempelhof; as Böttger proudly boasted, the new buildings at Tempelhof 'would in no way come second to Leipzig Central Station.'[46]

Outwardly, it is only from afar that this ensemble designed for air travellers bears any resemblance to Wilhelminian railway stations, in the massiveness of the volumes clad in cut stone, as well as in the shape of the broad façade on the city side. As far as its detailing is concerned, however, the airport closely imitates the railway station architecture of the early 1930s, especially the new passenger buildings of the Rhein-Ruhr line, with their sober, rectangular forms and abstract, ceremonious formulae such as the tall window formats used at Dusseldorf station. This feature appeared at Tempelhof on the façade dominating the formal courtyard, but earlier projects planned for broader windows. The final design was decided only after the construction of some examples of rows of windows.[47] Similarly, the definitive solutions for details such as the affixing of the decor and national emblems were found only by a process of trial and error.[48]

At this time, when airports were still sometimes referred to as air 'stations', its was by no means remarkable to regard Tempelhof in this tradition of large railway stations, and the airport was clearly seen to form a direct counterpart to the new South Station. The directive issued by Hitler, quoted above, already made this clear. In the early planning stages, it was envisaged to take this idea even further by linking the

One of the proposed designs for the departures hall, perspective drawing, 1938/9 (Archives of the Berliner Flughafengesellschaft)

airport and the South Station as part of a single urban development project. The park that was to stretch from the terminal would have been continued beyond Kreuzberg to the west, to reach the railway station. Their similar shape was to emphasise the unity of the two buildings for passengers.[49]

In general, the grand main line railway stations, thought by some to belong to a bygone age, were to experience a revival in Hitler's Germany. The plans drawn up at the end of the 1930s for Berlin South Station and for the new Munich Central Station provide compelling evidence of this development. It is not surprising therefore that even the interior of Tempelhof is influenced by representations of this type of construction in terms of pathos and scale. The passenger halls of the railway stations were perceived as prestigious gateways to cities. Borrowed from historic spatial forms, their colossal proportions guaranteed a sense of pomp and ceremony, underlined by carefully directed lighting. Examples of this are to be seen at Stuttgart and Leipzig. A proposal for Berlin's South Station, from the planning phase in 1938, also shows a departures hall that is similar to that of the airport.[50] The resemblance with railway station structures is most striking, however, beneath the vast canopied structure of the boarding area.

The boarding area

The departure gate area opening out onto the 'expanse and infinity of the air ocean' is the last and most spectacular space in the airport's sequence of spaces.[51] In describing it, hardly any reporters failed to make comparisons with metal-framed railway station sheds. In an unprecedented engineering achievement, this 380-m-broad area was entirely covered by a cantilevered canopy

some 36m deep.

The organisational logic of the departure and boarding areas indicates that the model of the railway station, or, more precisely, the railway terminus, was used in the airport in a novel way. The principle of a perpendicular platform connecting the individual platforms like so many teeth on a comb – here corresponding with the aircraft positions – was applied to the new purposes of flying, creating a new type of gate. The spatial characteristics of the railway station shed, with its intermediary status between inside and outside, was also repeated.[52] In both cases, like a 'house within a house', a bar-like building forms the rear of the boarding zone. In Frankfurt's Central Station, this rear building housed waiting rooms; in Tempelhof, the departure galleries lead to the openings of the individual gates.

The rigorously modernistic forms of the boarding area are somewhat surprising. On the landside, and in both of the large halls of the terminal building, the structural frame disappears behind architectural cladding. On the airfield side, on the contrary, structure rules. The frequently noted Janus-faced nature of the traditional railway station, characterised by this dualism between architecture and engineering, can be observed in the airport, in the deliberate formal contrast between the land side and the air side.

At the same time, however, functionalism as a generic style for industrial and transport buildings found its place in the Third Reich. Selectively used as a type of 'machine style', it was an architecture that was deemed particularly suitable to reflect the ideal of Germany's technical superiority, here epitomising technical progress in the air transport sector. The wealth of forms found in classical modernism could be presented without restriction at Tempelhof. Its

Construction of the building in March 1938. To the right, one of the massive trusses of the overhanging canopy, with the steel frame of a stair tower to its left (from Conin 1974, 192)

elongated structure was supported on slim columns in Le Corbusier's style and even the remarkable detail of the small oriel windows above the staircases leading down to the boarding zone can be related to the work of this architect.[53]

In his own words, Sagebiel had 'no hesitation' in displaying the hangars' supporting framework 'without any kind of cladding'.[54] The solution chosen was based on steel girders of a total length of about 50m, protruding 36m from the main vertical supports out towards the airfield. The rear part of each girder, about 14m long, was anchored in place by slim, box-type tension rods concealed between the windows in the wall of the hall. Despite appearances, the load was evenly distributed between the rear of the girders and their overhanging extension.[55] This surprising result is explained by the use of solid beams and by the heavy structure of the viewing platforms towards the rear, whereas the cantilevered area has open trellis-work and a lightweight steel covering. Furthermore, the entire glazed façade facing the city was suspended from the rear of the structure.

Despite its unprecedented dimensions, the result is not merely an extravagant piece of engineering but a solution that took advantage of steel construction techniques of the time. Direct precedents for this type of cantilevered truss are to be found in some contemporary industrial buildings.[56] The same types of truss was still in isolated use during the 1960s,[57] and Tempelhof clearly served as a model even for the famous airport hangar designed by Skidmore, Owings and Merrill at Los Angeles.[58]

Both generally and in detail, Sagebiel accepted the sober solution of the engineers, but tried to make the most of its specific qualities of form by means of a clear spatial arrangement. He left the massive, vertical supporting structures standing isolated in space like enormous steel sculptures. Their massiveness is further emphasised by the contrast with the building behind, to the rear of the boarding zone, on a completely different scale. Above all, however, the silhouettes of the girders remained unrestricted, thanks to the deliberate intervention of the architect, Sagebiel's only identifiable intervention in the work of the constructors, who, for static reasons, would have preferred to install the roof covering below the level of the main trusses.[59] In the final design, the impressive profiles of the girders are fully exposed, giving expression to the power that has been mastered. The outline of these steel girders would have stood out even more vividly had the open roof above been concealed by a plaster ceiling, as planned. Poelzig had already devised a similar design for the exhibition halls in Berlin, where some of the unfulfilled parts had also been designed within the context of a dynamic curving ground plan.[60]

The fact that solid steel girders rather than trellis-work beams were used for this structure, as was the case for Poelzig's halls, corresponds with a trend that started at the turn of the century, and which did not solely reflect practical considerations. Since Schinkel's time, iron construction had been criticised for lacking visually effective mass. The reaction was therefore one of delight when, thanks to solid girder forms, the steel-supporting framework could at last be expressed as a physical presence, making an immediate understanding of tectonics accessible. From the point of view of National Socialist ideology, this was seen as an opportunity to give engineering structures a 'cultural soul'. 'Form requires mass' observed Rudolf Wolters, one of the leading figures in Speer's General Planning Department.[61] The use of steel in the Munich station project, which included plans for a vast ribbed cupola made of broad-stemmed box girders, exemplified this attitude.[62]

The completion of this aesthetic purification process was made possible by the use of welding technology in steel-framed structures, developed about 1930. Such techniques made the girders appear to be joined together without any transition between the component parts. Like rolled steel sectional pieces, they seem to be fashioned in one single piece. The elimination of any evidence of the fabrication process brought a degree of material sublimation that was completely unknown at the time for constructional steel. Small joint sections, such as angular

The sheltered boarding area in 1951 (Landesbildstelle, Berlin)

steel gusset plates or brackets, became obsolete. Because of their smoother surface and texture, welded structures were considered to be aesthetically superior to riveted ones. Numerous articles appeared on this subject in specialist publications in the 1930s.[63] It was largely for this reason, as a visible demonstration of industrial progress, that such up-to-date technology was used at Tempelhof.

The solid, welded structure of the boarding area therefore celebrated the potential of cutting-edge technology while remaining true to the larger vocation of a massive, monumental state airport of dominating dimensions. Contemporary press reports celebrated it as a modern wonder of the world.[64] The boarding area was seen as an explicit and convincing incarnation of the 'incredible' power and will of the new Reich. This was based, however, on an understanding of technology that was hardly consistent with the emancipatory spirit of progress.[65] The form of the structure, deliberately intended to have an overwhelming effect on visitors, was inspired rather by the menacing Technology Cult of Albert Speer's *Lichtdome* (light domes). Goebbel's call for a new era in 'iron romanticism' appears to have found its direct expression at Tempelhof airport.

Notes

1 As reference works see: Helmut Conin, *Gelandet in Berlin. Zur Geschichte der Berliner Flughäfen.* Berlin, 1974; Frank Schmitz, *Flughafen Tempelhof. Berlins Tor zur Welt.* Berlin, 1997.

2 Conin, *Gelandet in Berlin*, 60.

3 Rudolf Böttger, 'Berlin Tempelhof'. *Der Flughafen* **6** (1938), 6 et seq. Reports of the Berliner-Flughafen-Gesellschaft.

4 Helmut von Pressentin, 'Das Tempelhofer Feld', in *Teltower Kreiskalender 1906*, 69–71; Günter Wollschlaeger, *Chronik Tempelhof, Teil 1. Das Tempelhofer Feld.* Berlin, 1987, 26 et seq; Peter Buchholz, *Tempelhof.* Berlin, 1990, 45–57.

5 Werner Hegemann, *Das steinerne Berlin.* Berlin, 1930, 449–57.

6 Martin Mächler, *Weltstadt Berlin. Schriften und Materialien*, Balg I (ed). Berlin, 1986, 17 and 22–4.

7 Karl Mischke, 'Bilder aus Neu-Berlin. Unsere Sahara', in *Der Bär. Illustrierte Wochenschrift für Geschichte und modernes Leben.* 1899, 601–3.

8 Wieland Elfferding, 'Von der proletarischen Masse zum Kriegsvolk. Massenaufmarsch und Öffentlichkeit im deutschen Faschismus am Beispiel des 1. Mai 1933', in *Inszenierung der Macht. Ästhetische Faszination des Faschismus.* Berlin, 1987, 17–50.

9 Kurt Schilde and Johannes Tuchel, *Columbia-*

Haus. Berliner Konzentrationslager 1933–1936. Berlin, 1990.

10 Documents on the development of Tempelhof, Berliner Flughafen, 31 October 1934, copy at the Bundesarchiv Berlin (R 43 II/1181, Bl 62 fol), cited in Jost Dülffer *et al*, *Hitlers Städte. Baupolitik im Dritten Reich.* Cologne/Vienna, 1978, 108–11.

11 Notes of the Reichskanzlei on the financing of Tempelhof airport, 18 and 26 March 1936 (Bundesarchiv Berlin, R 43 II/1181, Bl 144), cited in Dülffer *et al*, *Hitlers Städte*, 120 et seq.

12 'Deutsche Luftfahrt im Dritten Reich', *Der Flughafen* **9/10** (1938), 40; see also Karl-Heinz Völker, 'Die Entwicklung der militärischen Luftfahrt in Deutschland, 1920–1933', in *Beiträge zur Militär- und Kriegsgeschichte.* Stuttgart, 1962, 121–292.

13 Hans Rosenberg, 'Luftverkehr-Luftpolitik-Krieg'. *Der Flughafen* **1** (1944), 12–14, esp p 14.

14 *American Airport Design.* New York, 1930 (Reprint, New York, 1990); Hermann Gescheit and Karl Otto Wittmann (eds), *Neuzeitlicher Verkehrsbau.* Potsdam, 1931; John Zukowsky (ed), *Building for Air Travel. Architecture and Design for Commercial Aviation.* Munich/New York, 1996.

15 Bundesarchiv Berlin, R 4606/3753, Vol 3, Picture 28.

16 Theodor Heuss, *Hans Poelzig. Bauten und Entwürfe.* Berlin, 1939, 186; *Berliner Messearchitektur. Geschichte der Bauten auf dem Berliner Messegelände.* Berlin, 1995, 40–9.

17 Bruno Zevi, *Erich Mendelsohn. Opera completa.* Milan, 1970, 198.

18 Erich Mendelsohn, *Bauten und Skizzen.* Berlin, 1924, 3 (special edition of *Wasmuths Monatshefte für Baukunst.* 1924, 3–66).

19 Wulf Herzogenrath (ed), *Frühe Kölner Kunstausstellungen.* Cologne, 1981, 80; Klemens Klemmer, *Jacob Koerfer, 1875–1930. Ein Architekt zwischen Tradition und Moderne.* Berlin, 1987.

20 Codice Magliabecchiano II. I. 141, fol 86^v, in Francesco di Giorgio Martini, *Trattati di architettura ingegneria e militare*, Maltese C (ed), Vol 2. Milan 1967, tav 309 et seq.

21 Alexei Tarkhanow and Sergei Kavtaradze, *Architecture of the Stalinist Era.* New York, 1992, 103.

22 Bundesarchiv Berlin, R 4606/3753, Vol 3, Picture 42.

23 Zukowsky, *Building for Air Travel*, 119.

24 Bilfinger and Rapp, 'Über die Anlage von neuzeitlichen Verkehrsflughäfen im Auslande', in *Der Bauingenieur.* 1937, 780–7, 784.

25 Rudolf Böttger, 'Der Betriebsablauf im neuen Flughafen Berlin', in *Der Flughafen.* 1939, 145–52, 149.

26 Bilfinger and Rapp, 'Über die Anlage'.

27 Albert Speer, *Erinnerungen.* Berlin/Frankfurt a M, 1969, 92.

28 Erich Mendelsohn, *Das Gesamtschaffen des Architekten. Skizzen, Entwürfe, Bauten.* Berlin, 1930, 36, 39 and 59.

29 Werner March, 'Stadien', in *Wasmuths Lexikon der Baukunst*, Vol 5. Berlin, 1937, 528.

30 Giuseppe de Finetti, *Stadi. Esempi, Tendenze, Progetti.* Milan, 1934, 124–7; Rudolf Ortner, *Sportbauten. Anlage, Bau, Ausstattung.* Munich, 1953, 169.

31 Böttger, 'Der Betriebsablauf', 151.

32 Werner Hegemann, 'Ernstes und weniger Ernstes vom Berliner Flughafen-Wettbewerb', in *Wasmuths Monatshefte für Baukunst.* 1925, 447–53, 450. The project is signed by Ludolf von Veltheim and Peter Friedrich.

33 Heuss, *Hans Poelzig*, 112–17.

34 Irina Antonowa and Jörn Merkert (eds), *Berlin-Moskau, 1900–1950.* Munich/Berlin, 1995, 352 and 422.

35 Berthold Hinz, 'Das Denkmal und sein "Prinzip"', in *Kunst im 3. Reich. Dokumente der Unterwerfung.* Frankfurt a M, 1974, 104–9; Jürgen Tietz, *Das Tannenberg-Nationaldenkmal. Architektur, Geschichte, Kontext.* Berlin, 1999.

36 Dietrich Neumann (ed), *Filmarchitektur. Von Metropolis zu Blade Runner.* Munich/New York, 1996, 79; see also Dieter Bartetzko, 'Stimmungsarchitektur. Zur Theatralik von NS-Bauten', in Harten J *et al* (eds), *'Die Axt hat geblüht …'. Europäische Konflikte der 30er Jahre in Erinnerung an die frühe Avantgarde.* Düsseldorf, 1987, 82–90.

37 See Neumann, *Filmarchitektur*, 74.

38 Böttger, 'Der Betriebsablauf', 151.

39 Winfried Nerdinger (ed), *Bauen im Nationalsozialismus. Bayern 1933–1945.* Munich, 1993, 44.

40 See for example, Erich Gritzbach, *Hermann Göring. Werk und Mensch*, 2 edn. Munich, 1938, 158.

41 Michael Nungesser, *Das Denkmal auf dem Kreuzberg von Karl Friedrich Schinkel.* Berlin, 1987.

42 Bundesarchiv Berlin, R 4606/3753, Vol 3, Pictures 34 and 37.

43 Rudolf Wolters, *Stadtmitte Berlin. Stadtbauliche Entwicklungsphasen von den Anfängen bis zur Gegenwart.* Tübingen, 1978, 207.

44 Karl Arndt, 'Architektur und Politik', in Speer A (ed) *Architektur. Arbeiten 1933–1942.* Frankfurt a M/Berlin/Vienna, 1978, 113–35, 127.

45 Franz-Joachim Verspohl, *Stadionbauten von der Antike bis zur Gegenwart. Regie und Selbsterfahrung der Massen.* Gießen, 1976.

46 Böttger, 'Berlin Tempelhof', 7.

47 Bundesarchiv Berlin, R 4606/3753, Vol 7, Picture 51.

48 Bundesarchiv Berlin, R 4606/3753, Vol 4, Picture 39.

49 Bundesarchiv Berlin, R 4606/3753, Vol 3, Picture 31.

50 Antonowa and Merkert (eds), *Berlin-Moskau, 1900–1950*, 425.

51 Walter Zuerl, 'Neue Gesichtspunkte für den Flughafenbau', in *Deutsche Bauzeitung*. 1938, B 603–B 605, B 604.

52 Ulrich Krings, *Die Architektur der Großstadt-bahnhöfe. Deutsche Bahnhofsbauten des Historismus, 1866–1906*. Munich, 1984.

53 House in Vaucresson (France), 1922, in Le Corbusier and Pierre Jeanneret, *Œuvre complète de 1910–1929*. Zürich, 1937, 49 et seq.; in Berlin, Le Corbusiers' bay motif was already quoted in 1930 in Peter Behrens' Villa Lewin. Martin Wörner *et al*, *Architekturführer Berlin*, 4 edn. Berlin, 1994, 443.

54 Ernst Sagebiel, 'Die neue deutsche Architektur', in *Deutsch-Französische Monatshefte*. 1938, 275–82, 279 (shorter version in *Die Baugilde*. 1938, 1013–15).

55 Arno Schleusner, 'Die Flugsteighalle für den Neubau des Flughafens Tempelhof'. *Der Stahlbau* 11th year (1938), 89–94 and 160.

56 For example, a 1934 coal silo at the Berlin-Prenzlauer Berg abattoir; see Eberhard Günther Ermisch and Klaus Konrad Weber, *Richard Ermisch. Porträt eines Baumeisters*. Berlin/Munich/Düsseldorf, 1971, 37.

57 Bridge-restaurant near Montepulciano (Italy), in Franz Hart *et al*, *Stahlbauatlas. Geschoßbauten*. Munich, 1974, 108 et seq.

58 Zukowsky, *Building for Air Travel*, 141.

59 Schleusner, 'Die Flugsteighalle', 90.

60 Heuss, *Hans Poelzig*, 190; *Berliner Messearchitektur*.

61 Rudolf Wolters, *Vom Beruf des Baumeisters*. Berlin/Prague/Amsterdam, 1944, 41.

62 Hans-Peter Rasp, *Eine Stadt für tausend Jahre. München – Bauten und Projekte für die Hauptstadt der Bewegung*. Munich, 1981, 131–41.

63 For example, Gottwalt Schaper, 'Warum schweißen und wie schweißen?', in *Die Bautechnik*, 1936, 619–22.

64 *Völkischer Beobachter*, 9 October 1936.

65 See Jeffry Herf, *Reactionary Modernism. Technology, Culture and Politics in Weimar and the Third Reich*. Cambridge, 1984.

Antwerp-Deurne airport: the history and future of an aviation landmark

Jozef Braeken

Deurne airport, near Antwerp, is one of the second generation of city airports. These were built in the most important European centres during the 1930s to form a network for commercial aviation, then in full expansion. The airport was built according to the most revolutionary standards set for aviation architecture at the time. Most airport buildings from this period – those at least which survived the Second World War – were replaced by, or integrated into new building complexes during the jet age. Others were abandoned or transformed to fulfil new functions. Deurne, however, was left in suspended animation, to be gradually revived a quarter of a century later as a small-capacity business airport. To put a halt to the creeping decay of the building, a 'master plan' was commissioned in the year 2001 to manage its development. The 1930s terminal building will be protected as a historic monument in the near future.

The first stone

The foundation of the Aéro-club d'Anvers in 1909 marks the starting point for aviation in Antwerp. This was the year in which Louis Blériot made his legendary flight over the Channel and the year in which the first

Belgian pilot's licence was granted to Baron Pierre de Caters. It was also the year in which Antwerp hosted the first air show on Belgian soil. This was the age of the passionate pioneers, often combining, in one and the same person, an aircraft builder, a test pilot and a stunt flyer. Flying was an elite pastime for daredevils and a sensational new pageant for the masses until it lost its innocence in 1914.

It was not until May 1924, on Ascension Day, that the first airport in Antwerp was opened. Two years earlier, the Minister of National Defence, then responsible for aviation, had already begun to expropriate agricultural properties covering a total of some 80ha situated within the territory of the municipality of Deurne. A disused railway wagon was used as its first 'air station', replaced in 1926 by a wooden chalet. Meanwhile, the Belgian airline company Sabena, founded in 1923, had opened the first air routes to Rotterdam, Antwerp, Brussels, Strasbourg and Basle. In the following years, other connections to Cologne, Hamburg, Copenhagen, Malmö, Paris and London were also launched.

The first real air terminal in Belgium was opened in 1924, on the former military airfield at Haren, near Brussels. The building was an elegant Art Deco pavilion looking rather like a Mediterranean villa. Barely five years later, a new terminal was built next to it. This building was of a more clearly defined type, though on a scale and with the appearance of a rather second-rate railway station: the design was the anonymous product of the Railway Ministry, which had been responsible for civil aviation since 1925. Both buildings, incidentally, have been preserved up to the present day.

It is still not entirely clear whether it was the disappointing result at Brussels that made the Transport Minister, Maurice Lippens, decide to take a different approach at Antwerp. On 1 March 1929, however, a competition was announced for architects of Belgian and Luxemburger nationality for the design of a 'modern' airport on the existing flying field of Antwerp-Deurne.

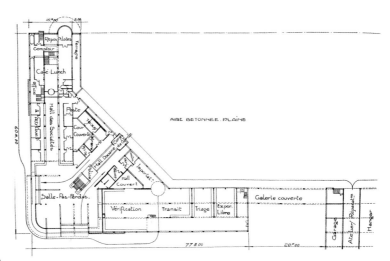

This new airport was to be built for the World Exhibition due to take place in Antwerp in 1930. When the competition came to a close on 15 May 1929, the jury gave prizes to only four of the nine entries. The first prize was awarded to the project by Van Riel and Janssens, the second prize being shared by the team formed by Gérard, Goffay and De Mey, the partnership between Victor Bourgeois and Emile Henvaux, and the project by Stanislas Jasinski. These were all young architects, most of them at the beginning of their careers. Only Victor Bourgeois, a co-founder of the Congrès international d'Architecture moderne in 1928 and one of the leading proponents of modernist architecture in Belgium, looked back on a longer career and enjoyed an international reputation. Goffay and Jasinski would subsequently make their names in the Belgian avant-garde.

We have been unable to locate the original plans for this competition and it is consequently difficult to compare the four prize-winning projects. All we have to go on are some imperfect reproductions taken from the architectural periodical *L'Emulation*. We know hardly anything about the five projects that did not win prizes. Common features shared by the four winning projects are the site of implantation of the airport terminal building and a modernist design. The project by Van Riel and Janssens is undoubtedly the most classic, presenting a completely symmetrical building which resembles the railway stations of the time. The rounded forms of the Gérard-Goffay-De Mey design give a particularly fluid impression and introduce the 'finger' on the apron, a feature never seen before. The design by Bourgeois-Henvaux is certainly the most impressive, with its clearly defined passenger hall and separate wings for hotel accommodation and freight handling. The most outstanding feature here is not a 'finger', but a vaulted passageway, the size of an aircraft, placed on the middle of the apron for passengers boarding their plane. The design by Jasinski stood out, however, as the most compact and efficient project in constructive terms. Apparently, the Minister Maurice Lippens was of this opinion, since he ignored the verdict of the jury (which mainly consisted of architects) and awarded the project to Jasinski, who had only won second prize in the competition. His decision was based on the advice of aviation experts, and was supported by one of the non-winning participants in the competition,

Jean De Ligne. In *L'Emulation*, De Ligne declared that the solution for airport facilities could not be reached on the basis of a one-day flight over Antwerp, the Channel and Croydon, but needed the everyday experience of pilots and airport commanders, experience which the members of the jury, as architects, could not provide.

On 30 December 1929, after the foundations of the building had been finished, the first stone of the new airport was laid officially. Less than nine months later, on 10 September 1930, the building was almost finished and had its first inauguration. The completely finished building was inaugurated on 1 May 1931 by Crown Prince Leopold and Princess Astrid. This inauguration coincided with the opening of the *Baltic Air Express* between Antwerp and Malmö.

The complex consisted of an L-shaped main building, with a command post at its axis and one large hangar. The architecture was clear and fluid, in keeping with the 'traditions' of international modernism: a construction of reinforced concrete with compact building volumes rendered in white, with rotundas, horizontal strip windows with steel fittings, canopies in glass-block concrete, mullions and canopy brackets in rough, dark-coloured concrete, terracotta mouldings and terraced roofs.

Stanislas Jasinski (1901–78)

Stanislas Jasinski studied at the Academy of Fine Arts in Brussels, where he was born, and was an apprentice with Victor Horta, the Parisian architect Maugue and with Henry van de Velde. In Amsterdam, he came into contact with the architects of De Stijl, while in his own country, he joined the avant-garde group '7 arts'. During his stay in Paris, he met Le Corbusier, after reading his work *Vers une architecture*. From that moment, Le Corbusier's thinking would have a profound influence on his career. This is illustrated by the futuristic design he

Ground-floor plan of the terminal building (from Jasinski, 1931)

offered in 1929 for an administrative quarter in the centre of Brussels, consisting of three colossal cross-shaped towers, inspired by Le Corbusier's *Plan Voisin*. In the 1930s, he made several study trips to the Soviet Union and the United States. One of his most important commissions from before the war, apart from Deurne airport, is the training hospital Institut Jules Bordet in Brussels, which he designed in collaboration with Gaston Brunfaut. After the Second World War, Jasinski concentrated mainly on projects for apartment buildings and housing estates.

With his prize-winning design for Deurne airport, and his subsequent commission to build it, Jasinski broke through into the small milieu of Belgian modernists. It is consequently surprising that this significant building was hardly given any notice by the leading architectural journals of the time. After all, it was a public building and one for which – exceptionally – an architectural competition had been organised. The comparison with Haren airport in Brussels, built practically at the same time, demonstrates how modern and ground-breaking Jasinski's concept was, even on an international scale. It was featured in a special issue of the French review *L'Architecture d'Aujourd'hui* in September 1936, devoted to airport architecture. But Deurne airport has been ignored by recent surveys of modernist architecture in Belgium and it did not even feature in the exhibition 'Building for Air Travel', held in Chicago in 1996/7, except for the mention 'now demolished?' Even today, the building is not well known and, as a result, disregarded by architectural historians and heritage specialists.

In 1930 Renaat Braem, who became a major figure on the architectural scene in Belgium after the Second World War, visited the recently finished airport. The twenty-year-old student was impressed by this majestic example of modernism, judging by his enthusiastic, 'aerodynamic' comments:

> Something unique in our building trade, constructed by order of a public administration, along sound, modern lines. Something to cheer! Has the time for reform arrived at last? Façades: horizontals, alternating layers in glass and concrete. Beauty? The beauty which belongs to an organism fulfilling its special purpose, that of plant and crystal, of dynamo and sunbeam. Architecture is the organisation of space in the service of society, in the most functional and economic way.

Pierre-Louis Flouquet, one of the leading critics within the Belgian avant-garde, counted Deurne, together with Berlin-Tempelhof and Hamburg-Fuhlsbüttel, as one of the best airports in Europe.

An airport for the future

We are relatively well informed about the ideas behind Jasinski's design for the airport, thanks to his comments published in the architectural periodical *La Technique des Travaux* in July 1931. In 1933, an interview with Pierre-Louis Flouquet appeared in the architectural review *Bâtir*, in which Jasinski explained his theories in more detail. The concept was based on a number of fundamental principles which all anticipated an exponential growth in commercial aviation. With the enthusiasm of his age – he was then thirty-two – and his absolute confidence in technical progress, he saw aviation as one of the major issues of modern civilisation and a turning point in the history of transport. Aviation was so new that its terminology was not even in the dictionary. And if any rules for aviation could be fixed, they were sure to be replaced sooner rather than later by new ones, with no idea of what the future had in store. Jasinski was certain, however, that the international airport of his day would evolve towards the intercontinental and global airport of tomorrow.

When asked about his ideas on the perspectives for commercial aviation, Jasinski unfurled a plan in which road, rail, seagoing and air traffic would all link up with each other in one big and coherent transportation network. Following the example of the railways, he considered the separation between passenger and freight transport to be an absolute necessity. The needs of passengers would lead to the creation of 'intra-urban' terminals, situated in or near the heart of the city. Here, relatively modest resources would suffice to build runways on the roofs of existing, large building complexes. Other possibilities included the building of runways as raised platforms in concrete or steel above broad traffic thoroughfares. The aviation industry, he thought, should encourage this development by building helicopters and aircraft that needed no more than 200m to land or take off. Existing airports were located too far from the city centres, making them inappropriate for passenger traffic, but were highly suitable for cargo carrying, which was precisely what they would be used for in the future. With safety and regularity as absolute requirements for the greater democratisation of air travel, an intricate, global network of scheduled air routes had to be established between the major metropolitan airports. These would be connected with each other by secondary bases for tourism, and by flying fields for emergency landings at fixed distances. Future perspectives on aviation such as these were not unique at the time. They also underpinned Gescheit and Wittman's *Neuzeitlicher Verkehrsbau* of 1931, part of which deals with aviation. Jasinski was fascinated by speed, efficiency and rationality and expresses himself as an ardent defender of modernism. His plea sounds like a pragmatic echo of more inspired visions such as those given form by Le Corbusier in *Urbanisme* and by Fritz Lang in *Metropolis*.

From Jasinski's point of view, the design of the airport was not limited to architectural considerations. The airport terminal building had to be designed in its complex relations to the flying field, in keeping with the constraints imposed by aviation. He mentioned four main conditions for the siting of the airport. First and foremost, the location and altitude of the flying field had to be chosen to be as free as possible of fog. Second, this field had to be as flat as possible, with 2% as a maximum degree of inclination. Drainage was necessary to prevent mud forming and to create a resistant landing platform. Turf was regarded as the most appropriate covering, thanks to its drainage capacities, its elastic qualities under pressure and because it prevented the formation of dust. A third requirement was an open location, free from obstacles, so that air routes in different wind-directions could be used. Finally, the airport should not be too far from the city centre and had to be integrated into its urban planning. A good, direct access road and regular public transport – best of all an underground line with direct access to the terminal building – were essential in order to keep time loss on the ground to a minimum. After all, this was the reason why 55% of the travel time between Paris and London route was spent on the ground. In Antwerp, however, this last condition was never properly respected, despite the fact that the airport is relatively close to the city centre. The railway line that passed the terminal had no station there and even the post-war motorway infrastructure ignored Deurne airport, which by then was no longer of any importance.

Jasinski had to accept the existing Antwerp flying field as a given fact, but he was free to design the whole new airport complex. It was of considerable importance to him to make the most adequate use of the existing facilities. Jasinski declared that he had long been intrigued by the way in which architecture could serve the emerging aviation industry. In the solutions he proposed, he showed himself to be well informed about the technical demands of air traffic. His participation in the competition followed a comparative study of the major European airports of the time, although we do not know if he actually visited them. In the comments and the interview mentioned above, he refers mainly to the airports of London-Croydon and Hamburg-Fuhlsbüttel, completed shortly before. These, and other airports such as Berlin-Tempelhof, Lyon-Bron, Amsterdam-Schiphol and Rotterdam-Waalhaven, are also shown in the illustrations that accompany the interview. He also claims to have studied the modest bibliography available on the subject, but only mentions the article by the French engineer A B Duval, *Les Ports aériens*, published in the popular French magazine *L'Illustration* in August 1929. From this overview, Jasinski concluded that an airport could be designed according to one of three different typological models: the 'island' or 'core' type, the 'linear' type, and the 'wedge-shaped' type, none of which he considered entirely satisfactory. He rejected the 'island' or 'core' type – a pavilion isolated in the centre of the flying field – as the least suitable, since the longest axis of the field would be interrupted, necessitating four shorter landing strips around the terminal building. The building itself would not only limit landing possibilities, but would also compromise safety: from the control tower, it would be impossible to watch the four directions at the same time. The building would obstruct the pilots' view on the ground and, as a result, would increase the risks of accidents. The biggest problem with this type, however, was the fact that no extensions could be built. The more preferable 'wedge-shaped' type, pointing towards the centre of the airfield was also inappropriate. Here too visibility on the ground would be obstructed by the sides of the building. The 'linear' type – a bar-shaped building at the side of the airfield – emerged as the most elementary form but, from a creative point of view, was also the least interesting. Besides, it implied that the distances between the different

Airside view of the terminal (from Jasinski, 1931)

services would become greater, resulting in a loss of valuable time both for staff and travellers.

The type which Jasinski himself put forward as the best solution, on the basis of these reflections, was an L-shaped airport terminal building, or in his words *'l'angle mort'* or 'dead corner type'. Visually speaking, flight movements made by aircraft when landing and taking off in different wind directions form a circle. Jasinski concluded that the circle was the ideal shape for the flying field. It is surprising how many entries for the Lehigh Airports Competition, organised at the same time, were also based on this principle. The airport buildings had to be constructed in the area outside this circle's circumference, the so-called 'dead corner' that would never be used by aircraft. The circular shape of the flying field also suggested the ideal form for the airport building, that is to say a curved amphitheatre, as at Hamburg-Fuhlsbüttel. Jasinski admitted, however, that he had abandoned this formula because of the considerable economies he could achieve by building in straight lines, as opposed to curved ones. The combination of a circle and a 'dead corner' was necessarily influenced by the urban context in Europe at the time, where valuable open space at the edges of built-up areas were inevitably encircled by factories, railway embankments, telephone cables, church spires, and so on. Suburban Deurne was no exception to this. This limited the possibilities of extending the airport. In aviation, landing and taking off were, after all, the main activities. Safety, and the avoidance of unnecessary manoeuvres were of primary importance in every architectural design. However elegant and light the aircraft might look at full speed in the air, on the ground it became *'un oiseau pataut, l'albatros de Baudelaire'*, a 'clumsy bird, Baudelaire's albatross', as Jasinski put it. For this reason, airports with a clear layout were preferred by pilots.

The concept of a modern airport was inevitably subject to the unforeseeable technical advances in flying machines. The boldest predictions made during aviation's short history had proved valid only for a short time. Bearing this in mind, Jasinski decided to break with the tradition that, in the past, had always favoured a monumental scale, particularly for public architecture, based on a 'definitive' concept. But he did not see the alternative as 'provisional' or 'temporary', but, rather, as 'future-oriented'. How could a definitive form for the airport infrastructure be decided if that of an aircraft had not yet been fixed? His design for the air terminal at Antwerp-Deurne brought an organic and a functionalist perspective to architecture. The resulting building was a construction which Jasinski liked to call a *vertébré*, referring to its embryonic and modular character, designed to expand from an original 'backbone', at the same pace as the city and air traffic. This formula, proposing a permanent but extendable structure offering flexible solutions for the demands of the time, was a response to a requirement explicitly stipulated in the competition programme.

Basically, the Deurne terminal is a triangular structure, consisting of three elements spread over three floors corresponding with three functions. The central module is where the airport is 'commanded', the place from which the flows of passengers and all flying activities on the field are supervised. The module to the left is passenger territory, with all its related services. The right module houses the services for freight. The different spaces are grouped according to a functionalist circulation system. Following his image of the building as a *vertébré*, Jasinski referred to its internal subdivision as the 'breathing function'. Let us follow the footsteps of a passenger in the early 1930s, from the moment he enters the building up to the moment he boards his plane. Covered porches at the rounded apex of the building give access to the main hall, which is the centre of internal circulation. The axial location of the stairs gives this space a polygonal appearance. This shape is pursued in the circulation galleries on the upper floors, closed off by a continuous glazing with thin, steel profiles. The hall is covered by a skylight, formed by a framework in the same proportions filled with translucent glass blocks. The generous daylight, the straight lines and the reflections in the glazing create an optical effect giving a peculiar, 'cubist' sense of

space. In the left wing, the hall continues towards the check-in counters, where the different airline companies flying from Antwerp-Deurne have their offices and sell tickets. In the adjoining café, or in the restaurant above, passengers and visitors can sit and wait while enjoying the view of the busy flying field. The central corridor passes either side of the stairs in the main hall and forms the only passage to and from the flying field, with separate directions for departing and arriving passengers. In the middle of this corridor and on either side there are the usual police, customs, boarding and tax checkpoints. Antwerp-Deurne was an international airport with strict regulations to prevent smuggling and illegal passengers. Having gone through customs and passport formalities, our 1930s traveller would reach the concrete boarding area or apron, which was tastefully decorated with geometrical flower beds. There, the aircraft would be waiting, probably a three-engined biplane of the Handley Page W8 type, or a Fokker F-8.

The first floor of the middle, hypotenuse wing on the airside is only accessible to staff and is entirely occupied by the command post, the nerve centre from which all the airport's activities are controlled. Above the command post, the glazed dome of the control tower accentuates the axial composition of the building. The command post is surrounded by the meteorological and radio services, and is connected to the whole complex by a pneumatic network. The long, high-level-bridge with its glass front (regarded as something totally new at the time), links the command post directly to the hangar, over an open passageway, making it possible to check the aircraft at all times. The first floor of the passenger wing forms hotel accommodation: seven rooms, offering stranded travellers a place to stay. The second floor, limited to the space above the corner rotunda and the main hall, houses the Antwerp Aviation Club, which had a large bar there. Our historic visit ends on the terraced roof of the building, which is entirely conceived as a viewing platform that can be reached via individual staircases on the outside. As at Croydon and Fuhlsbüttel, these roof terraces formed a spacious and safe stand for the air shows which were frequently held at Deurne and always attracted huge crowds.

Two other factors directly related to the techniques and evolution of flight had an influence on the architecture of the building.

Deurne airport was built at a time when air traffic control by radio did not yet exist. Pilots still used maps for navigation and had to land by eye. It was extremely important for the airport to be easily recognisable from the air. The runways were marked out day and night according to international regulations. In the middle of the flying field, there was a circular sign displaying the letter code of the city in characters 6m high, as well as a pivoting arrow that indicated the landing direction according to the wind. But the architectural design of the airport building itself could also contribute to its visibility from the air, something of which Jasinski was fully aware. The most important feature here was the intentionally compact L-shaped design. This was further reinforced by its fluid lines which avoided superfluous details and unnecessary relief, and by the building's white rendering. Here, the credo of modernism as a fusion of shape and function was put into practice. Furthermore, the roof of the hangar was covered with aluminium that created an enormous light-reflecting surface. Serving as a beacon at night, the control tower was like a lighthouse, equipped with a rotating floodlight visible from a distance of up to 70

A landside view of the terminal in the 1930s (collection Afdeling monumenten en Landschappen, Brussels)

Detail of the landside entrance at the apex of the building (from Jasinski, 1931)

The main hall of the terminal building, with the staircase to the right, opposite the entrance (from Jasinski, 1931)

or 80km. Above, a red lamp indicated the Antwerp letter code in Morse. Finally, the roof terraces comprised several L-shaped bands in translucent glass blocks, which let the interior light shine out from the terminal towards the sky.

As already mentioned, the competition rules explicitly required that the design of the airport building should anticipate an expansion of air traffic. In Jasinski's concept, this was clearest in his plan for the hangar, which consisted of fixed bays, each 50m long. Extra bays could be added if necessary and the end façade was designed as a movable membrane which could serve as a temporary closing wall every time a new bay was added. In practice, however, only one module was actually built. But, in two directions, provision for further growth was organically integrated into the structure of the airport building itself. Thanks to its location in a corner, it was possible, on the one hand, to extend the L-shape on the left of the passenger wing. Secondly, the hypotenuse formed by the central wing could be pushed forward towards the flying field. Jasinski made a passionate plea here for the use of standardised materials and construction techniques.

A part of Jasinski's design for passenger comfort had been rejected by the aviation administration. Instead of the usual canopy to protect boarding passengers, he chose to build a tunnel that would lead from the arrival and departure hall to the open field. There, the tunnel would be closed by hydraulically operated hatches, opened shortly before take off or landing. This was only one of the period's many experimental proposals to keep passengers safe and dry when boarding and leaving aircraft.

A sleeping beauty

After barely ten years of activity, the scheduled flights from Antwerp were cancelled in 1939 because of the threat of war. During the German occupation of Belgium, the flying field was used from 1941 as a test and transit base for the Erla factories situated nearby, where Messerschmitts were repaired and prepared for flying. The airport's field was extended and a concrete runway built. Deurne also served as an operational base during the Battle of Britain. During the war, the airport building was camouflaged with false façades and pitched roofs to make it look like a row of houses. When the Germans retreated in 1944, they blew up the hangar, and its steel truss structure was completely destroyed. The Royal Air Force then used the field as a base from which to control the airspace above the Netherlands, still under German occupation, and as an intermediate landing field for aircraft flying to and from Germany. In September 1946, the airport was finally returned to the Belgian state. Necessary repair work was finished in 1949 with the reconstruction of the hangar. The following years witnessed a succession of initiatives to revive the airport but these met with varying degrees of success. The government's centralisation policy was only concerned with the expansion of Belgium's national airport at Zaventem, at the expense of local airports such as Deurne. Due to its short runway, only 1,500m long, the airport was unsuitable for jets. The chronicle of the site's ups and downs during almost half a century is too long to go into here.

Since 1992, however, the airport has been placed under the authority of the Flemish Region. There are now sixteen scheduled flights a day, alongside freight and business flights, resulting in passenger numbers of 300,000 per year. Different clubs and societies of aviation enthusiasts, from plane-spotters to amateur flyers, have their offices in the airport premises. Recently, a museum pavilion was opened. Several types of old RSV biplanes, built in the nearby Stampe-Vertongen factory, are on display, ready to fly. All these initiatives have raised public awareness of the site and enhanced its cultural value.

Until the early 1980s, the terminal building remained largely intact. The control tower was replaced by a more modern one in 1951 and it was probably at the same time that the translucent glass blocks of the skylight above the main hall were removed. When the control tower was modernised again recently, the original light beacon with its floodlight and Morse lamp was saved at the last moment, and will be given a museum setting after restoration. During the last twenty years, other repair work has had an insidiously negative influence on the original fabric. The most destructive changes are the replacement of the steel window-frames by dark-coloured aluminium ones with thicker profiles and different proportions, as well as the removal of the terracotta window sills and mouldings. Other interventions, such as the coating of the concrete canopies and a lot of prefabricated extensions added here and there, are reversible. The overall structure of the interior has been preserved, but rearranged and considerably redecorated. The central elevator in the main hall is a disturbing element, as are the new decoration of the cafeteria and restaurant, the excessive wiring, tubes, signs and commercial displays. Except for a few light fittings, the original interior furnishings with flexible walls and counters disappeared long ago, as had the interior cabinetwork and the flooring.

In the near future, Antwerp airport intends to adopt a new identity as a fast and comfortable local airport, characterised by its small-scale, punctual, rapid and customer-friendly services. It hopes to attract passenger and business traffic throughout Europe, particularly for the 25,000 companies in greater Antwerp, among which 1,500 are concerned with the diamond industry. To achieve this, the Architectural Office of the Flemish Government has commissioned a master plan for the development of a terminal with a capacity of 500,000 passengers per year. The architect was selected in accordance with standard procedures for public building projects. The Deurne project was included in the 'open appeal' for all building projects to be carried out under the aegis of the Flemish government during 2000/1. Ten architectural firms were first selected by the Architectural Office of the Flemish Government and five of these were then retained by a selection committee: Samyn and partners, Baumschlager-Eberle-Grassmann, Architectengroep Rijnbout-Ruijssenaars-Hendriks-Van Gameren-Mastenbroek, Atelier De Bondt and Studiegroep Omgeving. These were then given the task of developing a master plan for the airport. All the projects kept the airport building, in most cases restored to its original state and given an appropriate function. Unfortunately, this is not true for the hangar, however, which is only reused in one design (Atelier De Bondt) as an aircraft museum. In the other designs, the hangar is replaced by offices,

The main hall of the terminal today (photo Jo Braeken)

intended to free space in the old airport building. To compensate for lack of space even further, one design (Samyn and Partners) envisages the addition of a completely new, circular passengers' terminal on the apron. Another design (Atelier De Bondt), taking its inspiration from Jasinski's own concept for extension, proposes the addition of a light, tent-like structure in a reference to the way in which the first small aircraft were built. Finally, all five proposals stress the need for a thorough restructuring of the airport's surrounding area.

The committee's final choice was for the project by the architects Baumschlager-Eberle-Grassmann, whose design foresees an optimal reuse of the old building. All later extensions will be removed and the building itself will function exclusively as a departures hall. Arrivals will be accommodated on the ground floor of a new, twelve-storey office building on the location of the old hangar. We should point out here, however, that we are only dealing with general concepts, used as criteria for the appointment of a design team. The procedure which will lead to a definitive project is to start shortly.

With these developments in view, the government's Heritage department is currently preparing a proposal for the statutory protection of the airport building, including its hangar. Our aim is to ensure that the authentic, modernist appearance of this aviation landmark is properly preserved and restored. As for the interior, we feel that the parts accessible to the public, such as the main hall, the check-in hall and the cafeteria and restaurant, should be returned to their original state wherever possible, preserving the existing building fabric. A thorough architectural and historical investigation will be the first step. If, in the near future, Antwerp airport will be able to advertise with a slogan such as 'Back to the Thirties? Destination Antwerp airport!', then we will know we have achieved our aims.

Select bibliography

Braem, R 1930 'Bezoek Kring voor Bouwkunde aan Luchthaven Deurne'. KMBA **1**/6, 104

De Ligne, J 1929 'Le concours pour l'aéro-port de Deurne'. *L'Emulation* **59**/10, Suppl, 73–80

De Ligne, J 1931 'Quelques notes de notre rédacteur après sa visite à l'aérogare de Deurne'. *La Technique des Travaux* 7/7, 427–8

Flouquet, P-L 1933 'L'invitation au voyage; l'aéroport, gare mondiale'. *Bâtir* **10**, 376–83

Ghoos, J D 1984 *75 jaar Luchtvaart Antwerpen*. Antwerp

Goyens de Heusch, S 1979 *Stanislas Jasinski architecte 1901–1978, Exposition Galerie Claude Jongen, Bruxelles, 15 novembre–15 décembre 1979*. Brussels

Jasinski, S 1931 'Le nouvel aéroport d'Anvers'. *La Technique des Travaux* 7/7, 412–27

The airfield at München-Oberschleißheim

Günter Braun

München-Oberschleißheim airfield, established in 1912, was the first military airfield in Bavaria and is still used as a flying field today. It is also the site of an aviation museum. It is situated about 15km north of the city of Munich in the municipality of Oberschleißheim (commonly called Schleißheim), in the grounds of a large baroque country estate, which was to have a considerable influence on the layout of the airfield. The site is therefore closely bound up with local history.

The history of the airfield

In 1597, Duke Wilhelm V of Bavaria acquired property in Oberschleißheim and turned it into his residence. His son, Maximilian I, built the so-called *Alte Schloss*, or old castle. Between 1648 and 1726, the Elector Max Emmanuel had a baroque country estate laid out, encompassing two stately homes surrounded by extensive gardens with an elaborate canal system. Following Max Emanuel's death, Oberschleißheim sank back into political insignificance; the residence was turned into an art gallery and in 1821 the whole property was acquired by the Bavarian army and used as a stud farm. A railway station was built to the west of the estate in 1858.

In the autumn of 1911, the Bavarian military administration decided to use the land to the south of the estate as an aerodrome. The decisive criteria for this choice of location were the flatness of the land, its poor agricultural value, the fact that it was already army property, and the proximity of the railway network. The date given for the airfield's official opening is 1 April 1912. This same year saw work begin on the construction of two aircraft hangars and an administration building. This last building, designed as an airfield observation post, is the oldest aviation building in Bavaria.

The plans to install this Schleißheim flying station directly next to the chateau immediately came up against fierce opposition from the head stewards responsible for the management of the estate. This conflict

The first administration building with adjoining aircraft hangars; in the background, the Schleißheim estate. Aerial photo dating from 1913 (collection Günter Braun)

led to the setting up of an architectural committee to oversee the layout and design of the airfield buildings. This prestigious committee included representatives of the military administration, the estate's management and some well-known professors and curators of art and architecture. From this moment on, all building work carried out on the airfield had to be approved by the architectural committee. An important condition that governed its planning approval was that nothing should obstruct the historic perspectives of the estate. The aviation structures also had to harmonise with the chateau's architectural style. In 1913, barracks, two further aircraft hangars, garages for motor vehicles and a central water supply plant were added. The First World War led to considerable extension of the airfield, the site almost doubling in size during this period. Four new standard hangars were built, along with one larger hangar, as well as a new maintenance workshop. A primitive flight simulator, engine test beds, an air force radio school, motor vehicle hangars, a fire station, a mail dispatch building, two underground fuel tanks and beacons for night flying were also set up, to name but a few of the new structures. Each construction entailed lengthy committee

The first administration building with its airfield observation post and maintenance workshop. Aerial photo dating from 1930 (Bayerische-Flugzeug-Historiker archives, Oberschleißheim)

discussions, which in some cases led to delays of up to a year.

After the First World War, on the instructions of the victorious powers, most of the technical facilities were dismantled. The four standard aircraft hangars and the large hangar were handed over to France and Italy as war reparations. Alongside the maintenance workshop, only the two aircraft hangars dating from in 1913 were left standing.

In the years following the First World War, the airfield was first used as a technical base for developing civil air traffic and subsequently as a location for several flying schools. The best known of these was the *Deutsche Verkehrsfliegerschule*. About 30% of the trainee pilots at this school, however, were former members of the armed forces, who, as civilians, received further training before joining the air force again. This ploy was a means of getting round the ban on all military aviation in Germany, imposed by the Treaty of Versailles.

Prior to 1933, the airfield saw no new development of interest, but the intensive training activities and larger aircraft soon made it necessary to build two new hangars at the south-west edge of the airfield. Two identical, triple Junkers hangars were built, Junkers at this time being specialised not only in aircraft manufacture, but also in hangars. They consist of column-free, arched trusses, assembled in the manner of a construction kit from prefabricated, standard steel elements. The façades were covered in corrugated iron, characteristic of these Junkers hangars.

With Adolf Hitler's rise to power in 1933 and the rearmament of Nazi Germany,

Schleißheim airfield was considerably enlarged from 1934 onwards. This comprised the construction of new barracks, paved aprons in front of the hangars, five more underground fuel tanks, firing ranges, an armoury and a new command building. The airfield was levelled, partly paved and sown with special grass.

When war broke out in 1939, another construction programme was begun. To the north of the site, a huge bunker was built at the edge of the estate to house a fighter command unit for day and night aerial warfare in southern Germany. On the southern part of the airfield, five new aircraft hangars as well as two temporary barrack ensembles were built to accommodate the men. Part of the barracks was also used for prisoners of war. According to the plans, the barracks were eventually to be replaced by permanent accommodation and a sixth aircraft hangar was also to be erected. Germany's military reverses, however, slowed down the construction work; by the end of the war in 1945, only the foundations of the hangars had been completed.

During the Second World War, the site was badly damaged by nine heavy air raids. As well as several barracks and technical buildings, the two hangars dating from 1913, the two Junkers hangars, as well as two of the five hangars to the south were destroyed by bombing. Oberschleißheim's cemetery became the last resting place for 22 Allied airmen shot down over the area, including four British pilots and two Canadians.

In 1943, a 600-metre-long, 48-metre-wide concrete runway was laid down in an east–west direction, lengthened to 800m in 1944. After the war, the Americans occupied

The renovated workshop building and the new exhibition hall; behind them, the grounds of the estate and the railway station (photo Günter Braun)

the airfield and, in the summer of 1945, extended the runway to a total of 1,600m. This runway had a load-bearing capacity of 60 tonnes. Parallel to it, two paved taxiways were built with sixty hard standings. The two Junkers hangars were rebuilt to a slightly different design and the buildings that had not suffered too much damage were repaired.

In 1953, a radio mast was built on an isolated eastern part of the airfield for Radio Free Europe and Radio Liberty. In about 1958, the United States Air Force built a new control tower and 1964 saw the construction of a new hangar, on the southern part of the airfield, for the German Federal Border Guard. In preparation for the stationing of French troops, living quarters and two administration facilities were built, but these were abandoned in 1966 after France's withdrawal from NATO. The living quarters have survived to the present day and are commonly known as the 'French bungalows'.

The period following the Second World War, however, was primarily characterised by demolition. In 1967, the remains of the partially damaged 1913 Bavarian barracks were pulled down; in 1971, the bunker of the former fighter control unit was dynamited and in 1975 the ruins of an aircraft hangar as well as the motor vehicle workshops were demolished. The withdrawal of the United States Air Force in 1973 and the departure of the German army in 1981 each led to further demolition. At the same time, a campaign began to save the airfield and in particular the maintenance workshop dating from 1918. In 1981, this workshop, along with the airfield observation post built in

1912, were protected as historic monuments and thus saved from demolition.

The efforts to preserve the installation gradually met with success. The former workshop building was taken over by the Deutsches Museum in Munich and renovated between 1987 and 1991. With this workshop, a new exhibition hall, opened in 1992, provides the museum with a total of 7,800 sq m of exhibition space for about fifty historic aircraft. Since its inauguration in September 1992, more than a million visitors have visited the Flugwerft Schleißheim museum.

At the end of the 1980s, the two Junkers hangars and two other aircraft hangars at the southern edge of the airfield were also protected as historic monuments and in 1999, the airfield was authorised for use as a special landing field with a maximum of 10,000 flight movements per year.

The airfield today

The original surface area of the airfield has been fully preserved, practically the whole site being designated as a nature reserve. In the years following the final withdrawal of the army in 1981, the site was divided up into small sections as a result of property exchanges and sales. This explains its wide range of uses today. The central part of the airfield is a special landing strip. Aircraft not based at the airfield could only fly into Oberschleißheim after obtaining prior written authorisation. Following a court ruling, the number of flight movements authorised for these external aircraft is limited to 1,000 a year. Of the 1945 runway, a length of only 800m is still in use. The maximum take-off

The two Junkers hangars seen in August 1996. Originally, in 1933, there were two, identical triple hangars. Their current form results from the reconstruction in 1945 (photo Günter Braun)

The 1958 control tower with the adjoining command building of 1934; in the foreground the mail dispatch building of the Bavarian Air Corps, 1918 (photo Günter Braun)

weight is restricted to 2 tonnes, although 60 tonnes remains technically possible.

The wartime command building, the new control tower, the former Bavarian mail dispatch building and a part of the site are used by an organisation for refugees forced to leave former East and West Prussia in 1945. On the site of the former Bavarian air force barracks allotments are to be found today, along with an instrument office run by the German meteorological service. The northern taxiway and a hangar apron are used by a company as a brake testing circuit. The northern part of the site accommodates the aviation museum, which receives about 125,000 visitors a year. Munich city council runs a youth camp to the east of the

museum, while the municipality of Oberschleißheim has built a sports centre next to it. The area that used to be occupied by the air force barracks was transformed into parkland after the demolition of the buildings.

The part of the former airfield to the north of the runway is today used for agricultural purposes. The grassland to the east is intended to create an ecological balance for construction development elsewhere. The topsoil has been partially removed and special meadows have been created. Parts of these areas have also been reserved for the creation of biotopes. The forests surrounding the airfield are partly designated as nature reserves by the European Union. The hangars to the south of the airfield are the headquarters of the Southern Air Squadron of the Federal Border Guard. Of the two Junkers hangars, one houses a depot for the Deutsches Museum and the other accommodates six flying clubs as well as a small aviation technology company. Next to these hangars is a typically Bavarian feature: a beer garden.

Future perspectives

Some conservation organisations are calling for the entire site to be turned into a nature reserve and recreational area, which implies closing the airfield and levelling the surviving structures. Legal action was brought against the authorisation to use the airfield for flying, but the case resulted in a compromise. The number of flight movements was restricted, but air traffic was nevertheless guaranteed for the next few years.

A major problem is posed by road traffic connections. The current access road is only a temporary solution because of conservation concerns. A new access road is planned, but its construction is not envisaged in the foreseeable future, as the conservation organisations and the local population are expected to mount massive protests.

For the Air Squadron of the Federal Border Guard stationed here, there are even plans for a new hangar to be built to accommodate their new type of helicopter. A further extension of the aviation museum is not on the cards for the next few years in view of the funding shortages resulting from economy measures brought in by the government.

The refugee organisation has also been hit by the governmental budgetary restrictions. The continued existence of the new control tower and the command building is thus under threat. Ideally, these buildings should become part of the aviation museum, which should also be extended as far as the runway. But approximately 500,000 euros are lacking for the renovation of these buildings and their integration into the museum.

The Junkers hangars are also in a bad state of repair. Since their reconstruction in 1945, only minimum maintenance work has been carried out on them. The steel construction shows signs of serious corrosion. Their complete rehabilitation would cost about €3 million. Once again, government funding is unavailable and the flying clubs cannot finance the costly work to be carried out on a historic monument.

Of the airfield's original fabric, 63 buildings and structures have survived, out of which only the maintenance workshop and four hangars are currently protected as historic monuments. A written application for the statutory protection of the 1918 Bavarian mail dispatch building, the 1934 command building and the control tower built by the Americans in 1958, was submitted by the Association of Bavarian Aviation Historians on the 21 January 2002, but this application was rejected by the Bavarian Heritage Department on 28 February, arguing that 'in the opinion of the Bavarian Heritage department, in its current state and as an ensemble, the former airfield in Oberschleißheim does not have sufficient historical significance.' The Oberschleißheim municipal council also rejected the application on 12 March 2002. Consequently, all the unprotected buildings can be demolished or converted for other purposes, like the airfield itself.

Munich city council has already drawn up plans to demolish the control tower and the command building in order to replace them with an international youth centre and campsite. The former mail dispatch building, recently used as a restaurant, is to be converted into office and service facilities for this campsite, which will be situated only 170m from the runway.

Today it is our duty to raise the awareness of the general public and the authorities about aviation sites. Aerodromes and airports are not merely individual hangars and buildings, but are complex infrastructures that can only become a legacy for future generations if they are preserved in their totality. An airfield installation comprises taxiways, stands, fuel tanks, airfield beacons, flight safety installations and a lot more. Schleißheim offers the best possible conditions for a coherent conservation of an aviation ensemble and its landscape. Schleißheim could thus become a successful combination between a functioning airfield and a world-famous aviation museum. Protecting the entire site as a historic monument would be a crucial step in this direction.

Select bibliography

Carlsen, S and Meyer M 1998 *Die Flugzeugführer-Ausbildung der Deutschen Luftwaffe 1935–1945*, Vol 1. Zweibrücken: VDM Nickel

Carlsen, S and Meyer M 2000 *Die Flugzeugführer-Ausbildung der Deutschen Luftwaffe 1935–1945*, Vol 2. Zweibrücken: VDM Nickel

Chorley, B 1994 *Royal Air Force Bomber Command losses of the Second World War, Vol 3: 1942*. Leicester: Midland Counties Publication

Forsyth, R and Scutts, J 1999 *Battle over Bavaria*. Crowborough (East Sussex): Classic Publications

Geflogene Vergangenheit – 75 Jahre Luftfahrt in Schleißheim 1988 Illertissen: Verlag Flugzeug Publikations GmbH

Gundler, B 1994 *Deutsches Museum, Flugwerft Schleißheim, Museum für Luft- und Raumfahrt*. Munich, Deutsches Museum

Oberschleißheim, Von Slivesheim bis Schleißheim, Gemeindechronik 1985 Eigenverlag der Gemeinde Oberschleißheim

Passes in Review – 816 Engineer Aviation Battalion 1945 Munich: Bruckmann Verlag

Permooser, I 1997 *Der Luftkrieg über München*. Oberhaching: Aviatic Verlag

Pletschacher, P 1978 *Die Königlich Bayerischen Fliegertruppen, 1912–1919*. Stuttgart: Motorbuch Verlag

Ries, K 1970 *Luftwaffe, Band 1: Die Maulwürfe (Geheimer Aufbau 1919–1935)*. Mainz: Verlag Dieter Hoffmann

Ries, K 1988 *Deutsche Flugzeugführerschulen und ihre Maschinen, 1919–1945*. Stuttgart: Motorbuch Verlag

Zeidelhack, M (ed) 1919 *Bayerische Flieger im Weltkrieg*. Munich: Verlag der Inspektion des bayerischen Luftfahrtwesens

Under American skies: preserving the historic architecture of New York City's airports

Thomas Mellins

On 28 October 1963, many New Yorkers were shocked to find that an act of civic destruction, previously deemed a virtual impossibility, had in fact happened: the wrecker's ball had slammed into Pennsylvania Station. Based on the ancient Roman Baths of Caracalla, McKim, Mead and White's grandly imposing edifice had served, since its completion in 1910, as a noble gateway to a great city. A few architects and concerned citizens had protested its proposed demolition. But the station, dismissed by pragmatists as a waste of space on an increasingly valuable piece of real estate, would soon be replaced by a mixed-use complex distinguished only by its immense size and monumental banality. The tragic loss of Pennsylvania Station was not, however, without a positive dimension: more than any other single event it galvanised the incipient preservation movement and led to the establishment, in 1965, of the now extremely powerful New York City Landmarks Preservation Commission.

Today, nearly forty years after the station's demolition, another great transportation facility, Eero Saarinen's Trans World Air Flight Center of 1963, now referred to by the far less evocative name, Terminal 5, at John F Kennedy International Airport, stands vulnerable to the demands of business and the real estate market. Though protected as an official landmark since 1994, the building, in many ways the aeronautic match to Pennsylvania Station, still might be significantly altered and, many contend, mutilated. This precarious state has focused broad attention not only on Saarinen's masterwork, but also on all of New York's historic airport terminals and attendant buildings.

Even in a city with powerful legislative means for protecting its architectural heritage, the preservation of airports raises particular issues. Airport terminals, among the most emblematic building types of our time, are also likely to be among the most short lived, that is, the most likely to become outmoded and thus seen by many as expendable. Airports define technological

invention and efficiency. Yet, innovations in aeronautics, as well as sweeping economic and structural changes in the aviation industry, occur so rapidly that architects designing airports are perpetually planning on the basis of soon-to-be-outdated realities. Charles Dalluge, vice-president and managing principal of the Washington, DC office of Leo A Daly, an architecture and engineering firm that has designed more than $1 billion in airport facilities throughout the world since 1994, states that 'When it comes to airport design, the only thing you can absolutely count on is change'.[1]

For those concerned with architectural preservation, airports, particularly those built between the 1930s and the 1960s, constitute a conundrum. Many airport terminal buildings are among our finest exemplars of mid-20th-century Modernism, executed by some of that style's most gifted interpreters. As such, these buildings call out to be protected by legally mandated architectural preservation efforts. At the same time, airlines cannot be expected to preserve functionally archaic facilities if such action threatens their very economic survival. How then can airports be preserved?

I will focus here on New York City's two principal airports: John F Kennedy International and La Guardia, examining what already has been lost, what has been saved, and what the future might hold for their key Modernist buildings in the face of on-going and inevitable alteration and expansion. Before turning to a discussion of these airports, however, a look at the historic preservation movement in New York will serve to illuminate the challenges facing those seeking to protect airport terminals. The destruction of fine-quality buildings and their replacement with other buildings, usually larger, is nothing new in New York. As early as 1845, Mayor Philip Hone wrote: 'Overturn, overturn, overturn! Is the maxim of New York. The very bones of our ancestors are not permitted to be quiet a quarter of a century, and one generation of men seem studious to remove all relics of those which preceded them.'[2] Fourteen years later, the editors of the popular journal *Harper's Weekly* pointed out that in 'a city where new construction is constantly in progress, demolition of the old and excavation of the site are a commonplace to which New Yorkers have long been accustomed'.[3]

Architectural preservation was slow to gather support in New York, which throughout the 20th century prided itself on being the modern city par excellence. Preservation was to some extent viewed with suspicion nationwide, often being characterised as running counter to many main currents in the national experience and character: freedom, innovation, progress, and perhaps most critically, the right of the individual to own and control his own property. Ironically, the main exception to this anti-preservationist stance had a strong element of national chauvinism to it. By the 1920s, mass migrations, particularly from eastern and southern Europe, had forever transformed the nation. A collective xenophobia on the part of many Colonial descendants expressed itself in an intense interest in the Georgian style architecture of the colonies and young republic. During the interwar period, many of the remaining Colonial homes in New York City were saved through adaptive reuse programs that made them into public house-museums. Still, preservation remained the rather rarefied province of a social elite ridiculed by others as 'blue-haired ladies with white gloves' and campaigns were largely isolated responses to immediate threats of demolition.

While the destruction of Pennsylvania Station proved, as I have stated, to be nothing short of seminal, and forever broadened the scope of architectural preservation in New York to far beyond that of nostalgia-laden, white-painted-wood Colonial houses, the movement nonetheless remained grounded in anti-Modernist sentiment. The belief that a beloved old building would be replaced with something that was not only bigger, but also better, had evaporated, and Modernism, equated by some people with aesthetic monotony and poor craftsmanship, was viewed as the culprit. For a time, the preservation of Modernist buildings was not an issue simply because the New York City Landmarks Preservation Law specified that a building had to be thirty years old to be designated a landmark and thus no Modernist building qualified. In time, however, a whole generation of post-war Modernist buildings came under consideration. By then, the tables had turned. The once-young architects who had arrogantly thought Modernism would be the style to end all styles were confronted with the inescapable fact that it had become just another vocabulary, and one that seemed to many rather old-fashioned at that. If they didn't act fast, masterpieces such as Gordon Bunshaft's Lever House and Philip Johnson and Mies van der Rohe's Seagram Building might be destroyed or at least carelessly altered in an effort, perhaps, to bring them into the brave new post-modern world.

Modernist buildings, however, do not always inspire the same emotional response as traditional ones, or at least they don't for many at this moment. History has taught us that old buildings elicit nostalgia and new buildings spark debate, but the buildings of the recent past, particularly those about thirty or forty years old, often seem banal or awkward, and in any case, not worth preserving. In discussing the efforts of the international preservation group Docomomo (Documentation and Conservation of Buildings, Sites and Neighborhoods of the Modern Movement), Herbert Muschamp, the architecture critic for the *New York Times*, recently wrote 'The main challenge facing Docomomo is public education ... In no other country does Docomomo face greater ideological obstacles than in the United States. This should not be surprising. In no other country has modern architecture been so thoroughly reviled as the enemy of history. At the same time, no other country holds history itself in greater contempt.'[4] Thus, in New York, the preservation of Modern buildings requires a sea change in the preservation movement. It requires teaching people that it is best to take the long view and not be subject to every trend and fad in architectural fashion. It is, in a word, a hard sell.

Let's now turn to New York City's airports. In 1934, only seven years after Charles Lindbergh's pioneering solo flight from New York to Paris, New York City, under the stewardship of its colourful mayor, Fiorello LaGuardia, who had himself been a pilot bombardier during the First World War, began to plan a municipal airport in Queens. The city acquired 100 acres (40.5ha) at North Beach, on the East River just west of Flushing Bay, approximately 9 miles (14.5km) by road from midtown Manhattan. Once home to an amusement park, beginning in 1929, the site had served as a privately managed airport. After the Depression shut down that operation, the

waterfront site was enlarged as part of a massive municipally-sponsored land reclamation project undertaken in preparation for the New York World Fair of 1939. The airport was also part of La Guardia's highly ambitious transportation program, federally funded through the Works Progress Administration (WPA). The airport grew to cover 558 acres (226ha) and at the height of construction employed a force of 23,000 workers. Known by the time of its opening in 1939 as La Guardia Field Municipal Airport, the project, which cost more than $40,000,000, was not only, as the editors of *Fortune* magazine put it, 'the greatest single undertaking of the WPA', but also the largest airport in the world.[5]

The airport incorporated two passenger terminals, one for conventional airplanes making domestic flights, and one for seaplanes crossing the Atlantic. The land plane terminal was flanked by three hangars on each side, while a single hangar served the sea plane terminal. The architectural firm of Delano and Aldrich, widely known for designing elegant country estates and town houses for such wealthy and famous clients as the Rockefellers and Astors, as well as Lindbergh, designed all the buildings. Though William A Delano and Chester H Aldrich had both studied at the Ecole des Beaux Arts in Paris, and their residential work remained traditional throughout their careers, they nonetheless had experience with airport facilities, having designed the infrastructure for Pan American Airlines in Guam and other locations. For the airport in New York, Delano, who was apparently responsible for the project's design, chose a stylish Art Deco vocabulary that clearly expressed the modernity of the enterprise.

The land plane terminal building, which also contained the airport's administrative offices, was a two- and three-storey rectangular building that contained a semi-circular portion fronting on to the landing strips. Inside, a double-height circular room provided the main public space. A large information and ticket counter occupied the centre of the room, while restaurants, waiting rooms, and offices were located at the room's edges. Outdoor observation decks enabled visitors to watch planes take off and land. The building was demolished, without any organised public opposition, in the late 1950s and early 1960s.

The Marine Air Terminal, originally also referred to as the Overseas Terminal, was located close to Flushing Bay. The circular,

Top: La Guardia airport, Queens, New York. Main terminal and administration building, designed by Delano & Aldrich in 1940, now demolished (rendering by J Floyd Yewell, published in Pencil Points, *January 1938)*

La Guardia airport, Queens, New York. Marine air terminal, designed by Delano & Aldrich in 1940, now landmarked (photo Andrew Garn)

three-storey building contained three rectilinear, projecting elements, one of which contained the principal entrance. The building's main portion adopted a progressively stepped back, 'wedding cake' massing. At the second-floor level, a terra-cotta frieze playfully depicted golden flying fish against a blue, wave-filled background. A circular, marble-clad room, flooded with light entering through a skylight, dominated the building's interior. Wooden benches, designed by Delano, incorporated decorative stainless steel inlays in the shape of airplane propellers. Encircling the room, a mural titled *Flight* by the American artist James Brooks, later well known for his Abstract Expressionist work, portrayed the history of aviation.

During the 1950s, the terminal was renovated. Sadly, part of this effort involved painting over Brooks' fine mural. In the 1970s, as the Art Deco style became the focus of both serious scholarly re-evaluation and almost feverish popularity among the general public, the terminal building's aesthetic virtues were rediscovered. It is interesting to note that even the Art Deco Chrysler Building of

Top: *La Guardia airport, Queens, New York. Main terminal, designed by Harrison & Abramovitz in 1964, now altered (photo Bill Maris © Esto)*

La Guardia airport, Queens, New York. Main terminal, designed by Harrison & Abramovitz in 1964. Exterior staircase now demolished (photo Bill Maris © Esto)

extensive electronic retrofit complete with automated touch-screen ticket kiosks and publicly accessible computer data ports, left the architecture and decoration of the landmarked building intact.

By the 1950s, exploding demand was overtaxing La Guardia airport, despite the fact that in 1948 all international and transcontinental flights were moved to Idlewild, later known as Kennedy International Airport. In 1957, the Port Authority of New York and New Jersey, which had taken over both airports' management, proposed a major expansion scheme for La Guardia, including the incremental replacement of the land plane terminal. As designed by the firm of Harrison and Abramovitz, and completed in 1964, the new main terminal was a sleek exercise in International Style Modernism. The two- and four-storey, arc-shaped, glass-and-steel building, an impressive 1,250ft (381m) long, was efficiently served by a two-level roadway that adopted its sweeping, concave curve. Sculptural, open staircases provided pedestrian connection between the two levels. The building was surmounted by an open-air observation deck, which in turn was shaded by a slanted parasol roof. A twelve-storey concrete control tower containing round, porthole-like windows, gave the overall building group a decidedly futurist aspect. Contemporary response to the complex was lukewarm. In contrast to the comparatively flashy TWA Terminal at Kennedy Airport, which was written about extensively in both the architectural and general press, Harrison and Abramovitz's building group received little notice. The editors of *Progressive Architecture* rather matter-of-factly described it 'straightforward' and 'no-hokum'.[7] Almost four decades later, however, with International Style Modernism being reassessed, Herbert Muschamp stated that the building 'remains the most architecturally distinguished airport building in New York, not least because of the skill with which Harrison knitted the terminal into the context of urban transportation. With its raised roof canopy tilted toward the sky above the terminal's concave facade, the design deftly merges the highway's horizontal curve with an airplane's upward angle of takeoff.'[8] The building now stands unprotected by landmark designation. Already it has proven vulnerable to aesthetically ill-considered alteration, particularly the Port Authority's widening of the adjacent roadways, which sacrificed the

1931, which today is admired throughout the world as an iconic representative of New York City, was until the 1970s dismissed by many as a somewhat zany, if not downright embarrassing product of American capitalism at its crassest and most exhibitionist. In 1980, both the exterior and interior of the Marine Terminal were designated official New York City landmarks. By that time, the mural had been meticulously restored. The terminal is now used for shuttle flights between New York, Boston, and Washington DC. At the time of designation, the Landmarks Preservation Commission noted that 'The Marine Air Terminal is today the only active air terminal in the United States dating from the first generation of passenger air travel. That it has continued in effective operation, despite the great changes in commercial aviation during the past forty years testifies to the quality of its design.'[6] In 1999, Delta Airlines completed a renovation of the building that, while including an noteworthy staircases to the hegemony of the automobile. Additionally, a large parking garage now muscles in on the terminal, significantly blocking views of Harrison and Abramovitz's building from the principal approach road.

If La Guardia retains some important manifestations of aviation history, albeit compromised by alterations and additions, the big news, in terms of both buildings lost and buildings saved, is at Kennedy Airport. Mayor La Guardia had been determined that the city, which during the great age of ocean liner travel had been the country's busiest point of entry, would retain that status during the airplane age. He committed the city to building a second airport. Located on the shores of Jamaica Bay in the Idlewild section of Queens and completed in 1946, the airport was approximately six times as large as La Guardia. It was New York City's largest municipally sponsored construction undertaking ever, and with much of its 3,000-acre (1,214-hectare) site made of infill, Idlewild also constituted the nation's biggest land reclamation effort. Enough sand to cover every one of Manhattan's streets with an 8-foot-deep (2.4-metre) layer was brought to the marshy airport site.

Delano and Aldrich were principally responsible for an early design proposal that called for a single terminal and administration building, 1,700ft (518m) long. Another plan designed by the Port Authority in-house architect, Walter McQuade, called for a complex composed of four buildings: two terminals, an office building, and a hotel. Though the airfields were operating by 1948, for several years, with a few exceptions, including the world's tallest control tower, the airport housed only temporary buildings and structures. Wallace K Harrison, who between 1956 and 1962 served as the Port Authority's Coordinator of Exterior Architecture, devised a new master plan. He rejected the concept of a single mega-terminal in favour of a campus-like plan that he called Terminal City that incorporated eight discrete terminal buildings.

As designed by Charles Evan Hughes III and J Walter Severinghaus of Skidmore, Owings and Merril, and completed in 1957, the International Arrivals Building, joined to a redesigned and reclad control tower, was a sophisticated essay in International Style Modernism. The low-lying terminal and the comparatively soaring control tower, wrapped in the same glass-and-steel curtain walls, were visually tied

together by a sweeping steel-framed parabolic arch. Additionally, an elevated pedestrian walkway, designed by Harrison as part of the overall site plan, led from the complex across a roadway to a large landscaped mall, where two dramatically curving ramps swooped down to define a circular fountain. Inside, beneath the arch, an airy double-height main arrivals hall housed a brightly coloured and monumentally scaled mobile by Alexander Calder.

Beginning in 1997, the International Arrivals Building, deemed functionally outmoded, underwent a process of incremental demolition and replacement with new facilities, also designed by Skidmore, Owings and Merril (SOM). The buildings remained open for use throughout the logistically complex process. Writing in the *New York Times*, David Dunlap, described it as being 'not unlike performing open-heart surgery on a patient who is simultaneously running a marathon.'[9] SOM's original complex is now almost completely gone; only abandoned, partially demolished portions, eerie reminders of the past, stand beside SOM's

Top: John F Kennedy international airport, Queens, New York (originally Idlewild airport). International arrivals building, designed by Skidmore, Owings & Merril in 1957, now demolished (photo Ezra Stoller © Esto)

John F Kennedy international airport, Queens, New York. Tri-Faith Chapels Plaza. From left to right: Jewish chapel (Bloch & Hesse, 1966), Protestant chapel (Edgar Tafel & Associates, 1966) and Catholic chapel (George J Sole, 1966), all now demolished (The Port Authority of New York and New Jersey)

John F Kennedy international airport, Queens, New York. Pan American terminal, designed by Tippetts-Abbett-McCarthy-Stratton, in association with Ives, Turano & Gardner, in 1960, pending demolition (photo Ezra Stoller © Esto)

John F Kennedy international airport, Queens, New York. TWA terminal, designed by Eero Saarinen & Associates in 1962, landmarked but pending alteration (photo Ezra Stoller © Esto)

gleaming new Terminal 4. Additionally, Harrison's landscape was sacrificed to a redesigned infrastructure.

Lost also were three chapels that collectively formed Tri-Faith Plaza, facing a man-made lagoon. Each building was about 110ft (33.5m) deep, with a narrow principal façade facing the water, and rose to a height of approximately 40ft (12m). Edgar Tafel designed a Protestant chapel that adopted the profile of a capital letter 'A' with the sloping sides consisting of stone-clad slabs. George Sole designed a Catholic chapel that had an oval-shaped footprint and housed an aluminium sculpture of Our Lady of the Skies. As designed by Walter Hesse, the International Synagogue was a compressed hexagon, the principal façade of which was dominated by two slabs representing the tablets of the Ten Commandments. While the scale and siting of the chapels had a distinctly suburban tone to them, the inclusion of ecclesiastical buildings within the context of a vast airport gave the entire complex a level of urbanistic complexity and sophistication it would have otherwise lacked.

An arguably less significant, though nonetheless notable expected loss, is that of Kahn and Jacobs' American Airlines

Terminal of 1960. The rather straightforward building, principally distinguished by Robert Sowers' 317-ft-long (96.6-m), 22.5-ft-high (7-m), stained-glass window, reputedly the world's largest, has been slated for demolition. Reportedly, the airlines intends to save the abstract work of art, though how, when, and where it will be reinstalled remains unknown.

Currently, the prospects for two more terminals at Kennedy Airport are bleak. The Pan American Terminal, also known as Worldport, designed by Walter Prokosch of Tibbetts-Abbett-McCarthy-Stratton, in association with Ives, Turano and Gardner, celebrated technological bravura. As completed in 1960, an extensively glazed oval building supported a vast cantilevered roof. The great concrete and steel umbrella gave the building a memorable appearance, as it also served to shelter not only arriving cars and buses, but the airplanes that pulled up all along the building's circumference. The highly visible entrance and egress of planes elevated what soon became a routine event to the level of high drama. Dunlap notes 'Boeing 707s, those white-hulled, globe-girdling jetliners that Pan Am called "clippers", could nose in under the 4-acre [1.6-ha] elliptical

John F Kennedy international airport, Queens, New York. The lobby of the TWA terminal, landmarked (photo Ezra Stoller © Esto)

concrete canopy that covered the building, hung on spidery cables that resembled those of a suspension bridge'.[10] A 200-ft-long (61-m) glass screen shielded the terminal's main entrance from the wind and was decorated with bronze sculptures by Milton Hebald depicting the signs of the zodiac. Pending demolition of the building, the sole architectural replacement of which would be a bridge connecting two new terminals, the Port Authority is storing the zodiac sculptures in a hangar. In a history of Pan American Airlines, Barnaby Conrad III describes the terminal as 'the ultimate in jet-setting cool'. He further notes that at its peak in the 1960s 'Pan Am was the greatest airline in the world. The blue globe logo was the icon of America's imagination, power and global destiny … For Americans, the Worldport was the gateway to the world'.[11] Dunlap recently characterised the building as 'the most distinctive terminal at Kennedy' after TWA, and noted that its destruction 'would clearly mark the end of the first-generation of buildings that made up "Terminal City"' and were intended to 'serve the fledgling jet set'.[12]

Also endangered is I M Pei and Partners' National Airlines Terminal, completed in 1971, and just this year eligible for landmark status. As built, Pei's elegantly minimalist scheme incorporated glass mullions. The building marked the first American use of this feature, which required construction methods devised in Europe.

The big story at Kennedy Airport, in preservationist terms, is of course the TWA building. As designed by Saarinen, working with Kevin Roche, his associate, and completed in 1962, the TWA Flight Center was a boldly modelled building. Perhaps not surprisingly, Saarinen had studied sculpture in Paris prior to attending the Yale School of Architecture. Saarinen's TWA Terminal consisted of a reinforced concrete core, above which four piers carried a canopy of thin concrete vaults. The building also incorporated two low projecting elements, one containing facilities for check-in, the other for baggage handling, and a passageway, 125ft long (38m), leading to boarding lounges. Another such passageway was added later. The building's shape was undeniably dramatic. For the editors of *Architectural Forum* it looked like a bird in flight, and was an 'eye-stopping design … appropriate as a symbol of an airline'.[13] The critic John Jacobus insightfully pointed out 'What the architect sought was an updated architecture parlant, not a style but, in a curious return to eighteenth-century methodologies, a literary architecture that would arouse emotions and affect sentiments.'[14] Saarinen himself stated that he sought 'to design a building in which the architecture itself would express the excitement of air travel.'[15] Inside the building, visitors were confronted with a series of sensuously curvilinear forms defining sculptural spaces. The information desk and board more closely resembled contemporaneous sculpture than conventional furniture and signage. The white and pale gray concrete surfaces, as well as white tiled floors, were sharply contrasted by bright red upholstery and carpeting.

In 1993, the Landmarks Preservation Commission protected the TWA Terminal. The designation extended to a large portion, but not all, of both the building's exterior and interior. The terminal was among New York's first post-war Modernist buildings to be protected as a landmark, and its designation was highly significant not only in terms of saving a particular building, but also establishing the need to protect Modern architecture in general. TWA's designation contributed to building both public awareness of, and support for, such preservation efforts. Yet the decision was controversial. TWA strongly objected. Noting that the terminal served far more people and much larger planes than had ever been envisioned by Saarinen, the airlines argued that it needed to rebuild. Indeed, the terminal was designed for use by propeller planes; commercial jets did not yet exist when Saarinen worked on the building's design. Nearly from the first, despite extensive planning studies and innovations such as baggage-handling carousels and satellites housing clusters of passenger gates, planes of unprecedented size overburdened both the terminal and landing fields. The airlines' problems only increased with time. In 1994, Marvin B Mintzner, a lawyer for the firm of Davidoff and Malito, stated 'By extending the designation to all interiors and the wings of the terminal, it really prevents us from modernizing the terminal in a way we believe is necessary.' Malito further noted that Saarinen's plan 'precludes more than one large jet from navigating to it'. He concluded that the terminal required total reconstruction.[16]

Given the airline's stance, designation was critical in preserving the building. As David Dunlap recently noted 'When the dust clears, only one building may remain from the original Terminal City complex. ... Were it not an internationally renowned architectural icon and a designated landmark, there is little doubt that [the TWA Terminal] – woefully small and outdated – would have been swept away, too.'[17] But even with renown and official landmark status, the building is not fully out of harm's way. Because the terminal is not owned by a private entity, but rather, leased by TWA from a public agency, the Port Authority of New York and New Jersey, the Landmarks Preservation Commission's ruling legally can be ignored. At the time of designation, the Port Authority publicly welcomed it. Less than seven years later, however, New York State officials approved the agency's request to demolish the terminal's two passageways and the satellites to which they lead, to make way for a new, much larger terminal building directly behind the existing one. One passageway was included in the landmark designation; the addition was not. J Winthrop Aldrich, the deputy commissioner of the New York State Office of Parks, Recreation and Historic Preservation, which approved demolition, stated that 'We're very conscious, certainly, of the importance of the building as an icon of modernist architecture, and we're also aware that Kennedy is bursting at the seams. And those two things have to be taken into consideration.'[18]

Noting that in the future the Saarinen building might be used for extensive retail facilities, as well as an aviation museum, Herbert Muschamp has publicly opposed the proposed physical alterations:

> Nothing short of a private Gulfstream can bring back the days when jet travel was an invitation to romantic fantasy. But the alterations now being contemplated for the T.W.A. terminal do not even try ... Architecture is being left out of the loop ... At TWA, the functional shortcomings of the satellite pavilions far outweigh their aesthetic contribution to Saarinen's design. The umbilical tubes, however, are integral to the terminal itself. Their aesthetic should be fully integrated into that of the building's new offspring. An architect with sufficient talent should be able to rethink Saarinen's ethereal essay for our new century. What's missing now is any sign of rising to the occasion.[19]

Muschamp's comments raise interesting and difficult questions. The widespread destruction and significant alteration of older airport buildings cannot be explained solely as the result of profligate or capricious corporate behaviour. Reasonable practical consideration threatens, if it does not doom, the future of many airport terminals and attendant structures. Their preservation demands, I believe, a multifaceted approach. Firstly, public education regarding the quality and value of Modernist architecture is of fundamental importance; without it, a key element of our architectural inheritance will be lost. Secondly, legal protection is necessary if market pressures are to be resisted effectively. Thirdly, adaptive reuse might offer meaningful alternatives to demolition or disfiguring renovation, though alteration to suit new functions must be thoughtfully executed. Finally, and perhaps most importantly, those entrusted with designing expanded airport facilities should, whenever possible, also be given the opportunity to integrate the best of the existing buildings and structures into a comprehensive plan. In this way, airports, once seen as expressions of state-of-the-art technology, and increasingly viewed as a type of alternate city, physical distillations of the urban experience in the computer age, can themselves acquire the visible layering of history that is a core feature of all great cities.

Notes

1 Charles Dalluge, quoted in Thomas Mellins, 'The sky's the limit', Architectural Record 188 (July 2000), 147–9.
2 Allan Nevins (ed), The Diary of Philip Hone, 1828–1851. New York: Dodd, Mead and Co., 1927, 730.
3 Harper's Weekly, as quoted in Barbaralee Diamonstein, The Landmarks of New York. New York: Harry N Abrams, 1988, 10.
4 Herbert Muschamp, 'It's history now, so shouldn't Modernism be preserved, too?', New York Times, 17 December 2000, 2, 1, 40.
5 'Fiorello's windflower'. Fortune August (1940), 38–44, 84.
6 Landmarks Preservation Commission of the City of New York, LP-1109, 25 November 1980.
7 'La Guardia airport gets new terminal'. Progressive Architecture 45 (June 1964), 83.
8 Herbert Muschamp, 'Stay of execution for a dazzling airline terminal'. New York Times, 6 November 1994, 2, 31.
9 David W Dunlap, 'JFK enters the era of the megaterminal'. New York Times, 19 March 2000, 9, 1, 6.
10 David W Dunlap, 'Delta announces $1.6 billion expansion plan for Kennedy Airport'. New York Times, 19 October 2000, B, 1, 12.
11 Barnaby Conrad III, as quoted in Dunlap, 'Delta Announces', 12.
12 Dunlap, 'Delta Announces'.
13 'TWA's graceful new terminal'. Architectural Forum 108 (January 1958), 78–85.
14 John Jacobus, Twentieth-Century Architecture: The Middle Years 1940–65. New York: Frederick A Praeger, 1966, 159–61.
15 Eero Saarinen, as quoted in 'Eero Saarinen's flight center'. Architectural Record 132 (July 1962), 129–34.
16 Marvin B Mitzner, as quoted in David W Dunlap, 'TWA's hub is declared a landmark'. New York Times, 20 July 1994, B, 1–2.
17 Dunlap, 'JFK enters the era of the megaterminal', 12.
18 J Winthrop Aldrich, as quoted in Randy Kennedy, 'Airport growth squeezes the landmark TWA terminal'. New York Times, 4 April 2001, B, 1, 3.
19 Herbert Muschamp, 'Architecture hands off the baton to preservation'. New York Times, 4 April 2001, B, 3.

Gatwick's Beehive

John King

Few passengers arriving at or departing from the busiest airport in Europe, London-Gatwick, are aware that it has a listed building which was the first circular airport passenger terminal in the world in 1936. The terminal was used initially by the first British Airways Ltd. After 1956, it was not used by passengers and for many years its use was restricted to airport offices, but recently it was brought back into everyday use – albeit without passengers – by a British Airways franchise operator, GB Airways. In fact, Gatwick's history as an international airport is untypical in a number of ways. The airport was not planned, it just happened. From the outset and for more than twenty years it was privately owned during a period when state or municipal ownership was the norm. Its very existence was threatened on more than one occasion by geography, the River Mole, the streams of which flowed over or around it. It has always been dependent on the railway for its success. Without the persistence of certain individuals, it would not have survived. It has only had one runway since its redevelopment in the 1950s.

Gatwick was not planned in the way many airports were in the inter-war years, nor did it evolve from military or manufacturing activities. It just happened in 1930 when two young men who had just learnt to fly, Ronald Waters and John Mockford, decided to go into the aviation business with their own aerodrome. They started at Penshurst, an emergency landing ground situated on the route between Croydon and the Continent, subsequently purchasing farmland between the main-line railway and the main road between London and Brighton, next to the Gatwick Racecourse. Gatwick was licensed as an aerodrome on 1 August 1930. Its activities – pilot instruction, under the aegis of the Surrey Aero-Club, and the occasional private taxi flight – were not a financial success and in May 1932 Gatwick was sold to the Redwing Aircraft Company, the manufacturer of an attractive side-by-side two-seater aeroplane.

The flying club and social activities continued under Redwing while a School of Flying and Aeronautical Engineering was formed. But Redwing did not transfer its factory from Essex and eighteen months later, the company's owner tired of aviation and sold the Gatwick site to Morris Jackaman for £13,500. Jackaman, a young man with a civil engineering background, was an accomplished private pilot who had studied air transport. He believed Gatwick had potential as an international airport and envisaged scheduled services to Paris, on the hour, every hour.

Jackaman's task was not easy. He needed airlines, he needed a terminal building and he needed the co-operation of the railways as Gatwick was much farther out from London than Croydon or Heston. There was little chance of Imperial Airways or any of the major international airlines moving from Croydon or dividing up their operations. It was fortunate for Jackaman that in 1934 the Southern Railway agreed to provide a station alongside the airfield. Much of the cost, however, would have to be met by the company, Airports Ltd, which Jackaman had formed to develop the aerodrome. It was also fortuitous that Jackaman was able to interest an expanding little airline, Hillman's Airways, which was operating domestic and international services from a rather inaccessible airport in Essex.

Jackaman was particularly concerned about the design of Gatwick's terminal as a key to the airport's successful development. He did not want to copy the recent terminal building at Croydon, built in 1928 and criticised for its inefficiency. Eventually he arrived at a circular ground plan as the answer to the design problem but it is intriguing how this happened. In 1934 he was still living with his parents at a house near Slough to the west of London. One night he was working late in his study examining airport plans when his father came into the room. He suggested he should go to bed, as he was so tired that he would be 'thinking in circles'. Instantly Morris reacted: 'That's it, a circular terminal.'

With enthusiasm, Morris drew up a plan.

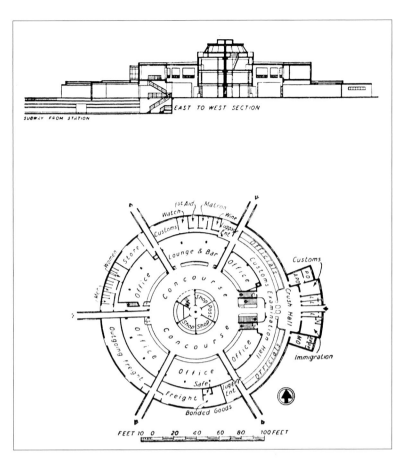

The building would not only be circular, but it would also be connected to the new railway station by an underground foot tunnel; and it would have telescopic covered passageways that would radiate out from the building on lines to the steps of waiting aircraft. Before the end of the year, Morris had obtained a provisional patent for this design. This was unusual for a building but was appropriate since it comprised moving parts. There was other good news that year for Airports Ltd. The Air Ministry recognised the potential of Gatwick, not as a terminal airport but for diverted flights, and would make annual payments for fifteen years.

Morris still needed an architect to interpret his ideas and it was probably at the beginning of 1935 that he came into contact with Frank Hoar who four years earlier had qualified as an architect at the Bartlett School of Architecture and was then working in the London County Council's Planning Department. When the young architect began to appreciate the challenge of interpreting Jackaman's circular concept, he contacted two other young men with whom he had been friends as architectural students. These were Bill Lovett, who was then working in the City of London's Planning Department, and Alan Marlow who was in private practice. The challenge of an airport terminal particularly appealed to the three young men who formed a partnership, Hoar, Marlow and Lovett. The brief included specifications that the building should be low, both in appearance and in reality, and white for easy recognition from the air.

The principal architect was Alan Marlow since his two partners had daytime jobs, but they all worked very hard, especially as the drawings were a difficult exercise in draughtsmanship because of the constant use of compasses. The first drawing was hexagonal but by June 1935 the first circular drawing was completed. More capital was required for the development and this was achieved by Airports Ltd becoming a public company with a board of distinguished businessmen and diplomats. The contractors moved in and at the beginning of July, the Gatwick airfield was closed. There were some difficulties with the local authority on planning matters, but these do not appear to have delayed the start of the building work after the drawings were completed; the first action was to mark the centre point of the building on the site. In addition to

the terminal there were to be three hangars. By August 1935 work had also started on the hangar, while the new railway station was nearly complete.

The central portion of the building was built of reinforced concrete, the floors being supported on two reinforced concrete ring beams, each supported at six points at the circumference. The remainder of the building was steel framed with brick in-filling to enable for future expansion. The roofs were of reinforced concrete with hollow tiles while the partitions were of hollow tiles and breeze blocks.

The building graduated in steps from one storey at the outside to four at the centre. On the ground floor the outer circle was devoted to customs, storage and freight activities. The next circle was to be offices while the inner concentric space, apart from the central block, was to be the assembly hall. The floor above was to be devoted to administrative offices, with a restaurant and balcony overlooking the airport. The glass-encased office at the apex of the building was to be the control point of the airport. There were seven points of access to the building, three to be used as exits and three as entrances, while the seventh corresponded with the tunnel entrance. The access points were all in the form of radial corridors which would extend outwards telescopically when the aircraft was in position by means of a moveable covered way, run out from the building on tracks set flush

*Cross-section and ground-floor plan of the terminal (*Transports en Commun, Aéroports. *Paris: Editions Albert Morancé, 1938)*

View of Gatwick from the air shortly before the completion of the development in 1936 (collection John King)

with the concrete of the apron. The aviation press likened the building to a wedding cake, but this was not criticism. In September work was completed on diverting the River Mole to a course alongside the railway

In October 1935 Hillman's Airways was merged with other small airlines to form British Airways Ltd, but fortunately the commitment to Gatwick was maintained. Some of the work on the airport took longer than expected on account of the mud in the winter after rain, while costs were higher than anticipated. By the middle of February 1936, the basic framework of the terminal was complete and the parquet flooring was being laid. At the end of March, the interior was still being fitted out. The building work included a concrete apron linking the terminal and hangars. There were concrete taxiways from the terminal and there was a defined landing and take-off area, but no concrete runway as this was still not considered necessary in England. By the beginning of May much of the work had been completed to the extent that a grand opening with an air show was planned for the beginning of June 1936.

In addition to British Airways Ltd, there were two other users of the new facility: Air Travel Ltd, a repair and maintenance company from Penshurst, and a newly formed two-aircraft charter operation, Air Touring. These companies moved into Gatwick at the beginning of May. On 15 May a contract was completed between Airports Ltd and British Airways Ltd which had been operating from Heston until Gatwick was ready.

Two days later the Air Ministry restored the airport's licence and British Airways operated its first service out of Gatwick, the 13.30 flight to Paris with a DH 86 hired from Jersey Airways on account of delays in aircraft delivery. The single fare between the two capitals was £4 25s which included first class rail travel from Victoria. The airline's Scandinavian service started the following day. With calls at Amsterdam, Hamburg and Copenhagen, Malmo in Sweden was reached just a little more than six-and-a-half hours later. Finally, on 25 May, the seasonal service to the Isle of Wight, which was operated jointly with the Southern Railway and which had been run from Heston the previous summer, was reopened.

By the end of the month, there was a change in the management of Airports Ltd. Morris Jackaman who had formed the company to develop Gatwick, withdrew and eventually resigned after becoming worried about the extra costs incurred in building work. When the formal opening took place on 6 June 1936, his place as Managing Director had been taken by his former Business Manager, Marcel Desoutter, an air pioneer of pre-war days. The airport was formally declared open before a large crowd by the Secretary of State for Air, Viscount Swinton. Displays followed of some of the latest military and civil aircraft while everybody who had anything to do with aviation was among the guests, many arriving by a special train from Victoria. The guests noted, however, when they transferred from the railway station to the terminal by way of the subway, that the advertisement panels did not carry the posters of West End stores, just those of a Horley chain of shops.

Gatwick's existence now seemed assured and there was expectation that its terminal design might be a portent of the future. This was not to be, however. The airline experienced a number of fatal accidents in 1936, some close to Gatwick; and there was friction between British Airways Ltd and Airports Ltd. Then, in March 1937, the flying field became water-logged following above average rainfall, whereupon the airline moved to Croydon. The fault was not with the terminal building, however, although there was always a misconception that the capacity of a circular terminal was greater.

The loss of scheduled services at Gatwick soon gave Airports Ltd financial problems and it was fortuitous for the company that Marcel Desoutter, a man of great energy and vision, was able to secure the establishment of an Elementary and Reserve Flying Training School. This was followed by companies associated with defence activities that were expanding as the political situation in Europe deteriorated. The terminal was no longer being used by airlines, but at least it did have tenants.

With the outbreak of war, the airport was requisitioned for military use and the terminal became the Station Headquarters of the RAF. Much of the flying activity was by Army Co-operation Squadrons, but Desoutter who, in 1940 was expelled from his own building on account of his slight European accent, never lost sight of Gatwick's potential. In 1943 he commissioned a report from the same consultants who had advised the Southern Railway ten years earlier. The report was very positive but it failed to interest the Air Ministry.

The RAF left Gatwick in September 1946. Still concerned about the future, Desoutter once again sought the support of the Ministry. He suggested Gatwick would make an eminently suitable base for air taxi and charter companies. This time the Ministry of Civil Aviation endorsed his views. He subsequently contacted the operators who were not affected by the nationalisation of the pre-war airlines that resulted in the formation, in October 1946, of British European Airways. Desoutter was heartened by the response from the charter operators who were soon more than sufficient to fill all the office accommodation in the Beehive and the available hangar space.

The companies that decided to operate from Gatwick included Bond Air Services

*Interior of the terminal in the late 1930s (*Transports en Commun, Aéroports. *Paris: Editions Albert Morancé, 1938)*

Ltd, Hornton Airways, Union Air Services Ltd and Ciro's Aviation Ltd. They were all formed in 1946 and by the end of the year were more-or-less established at Gatwick. Customs and immigration services returned to the building. Airports Ltd subsequently redecorated the interior and restored the restaurant. The new airlines expanded their activities in 1947 and were joined by others including the Windmill Theatre Transport Company.

The future of Gatwick, however, was still unclear. The Ministry was then reconsidering acquiring Gatwick for use as a secondary airport for London, but there was opposition from the new Ministry for Town and Country Planning that was projecting a new town at nearby Crawley. After the Chief Executive of the Crawley New Town sought an undertaking that the airport would only be developed as a charter base and would never become a major airport, Gatwick was again dropped from the Ministry's plans.

In 1948 aircraft movements increased considerably. That year Desoutter again took the initiative and published an attractive booklet to extol the virtues of his airport, particularly its railway connection. But

A British Airways Ltd departure in 1936 (collection John King)

in November the news for Airports Ltd was most alarming: the airport was to be de-requisitioned the following year. This would mean that Gatwick Racecourse and other adjoining land that had been requisitioned would revert to their owners, making the airport too small for air taxi and charter companies.

Charter activities continued much as before in 1949 but the political confusion continued. At the beginning of March it appeared to be the end for Gatwick when it was stated in Parliament that Stansted would be developed as the diversionary airport for London. Desoutter then acquired a new ally, British European Airways, which advised the new Ministry that Gatwick would be preferable as a diversionary and secondary airport because of its rail link and location south of London. Before the end of the year it was decided to defer de-requisition. Desoutter was now much happier about the future, especially when the BEA Helicopter Experimental Unit moved to Gatwick in 1951. The head office of BEA Helicopters/British Airways Helicopters was for many years to be in the Beehive. Desoutter did not live to see the changes, his death on 13 April 1952 removing one of the airport's visionary figures.

In 1953 two more airlines were operating from Gatwick: Silver City Airways, with a car ferry service to Le Touquet, and Jersey Airlines. With mounting opposition to the proposed development, a public enquiry was held in 1954. The Inspector reported to the Minister that a case had been established for Gatwick as a suitable base for an airport. A White Paper was published which stated that Gatwick would be developed as a

second main civil airport to serve London. The concept of the airport was gradually coming round to the inter-war visions of Jackaman and Desoutter. Agreement was subsequently reached with Airports Ltd on compensation of £350,000.

The plan for the airport was not dissimilar to that of the 1943 consultants, with a new railway station and terminal built over the old Racecourse Station. But this meant that the original passenger terminal would become obsolete, cut off from the main operational area of the airport by the diverted A23, the main road from London to Brighton. There was, however, no suggestion that the building should be demolished. On 31 March 1956 the airport was closed to permit the construction work to begin. The original terminal building soon had several empty offices.

The vision realised

Gatwick airport was reopened on 30 May 1958, the official opening by the Queen following on Monday 9 June 1958. The new airport had several significant and novel features that, in a way, were a repetition of developments two decades earlier. In particular, it was the first airport anywhere in the world to include a main-line railway station immediately beneath the terminal. There was also direct access to a trunk road that passed beneath the terminal building. It was the first airport in the United Kingdom to have a pier leading from the main building to the stands, to enable passengers to reach the aircraft without going out into the open. At last the visions of Jackaman and Desoutter were to be realised. Gatwick was an

international airport. Meanwhile, the 1936 terminal continued in use as offices for a variety of companies including some airlines.

The subsequent development of Gatwick did not bring the expected traffic for several years and it was to be some time before the airport was to be a major star in the international airport league. The airlines were slow to use Gatwick at first, although the formation of British United Airways at Gatwick in 1960 was a major step. During the ensuing years the 1958 terminal, runway and facilities were enlarged substantially and in 1966 ownership of the airport was vested in a new public corporation, the British Airports Authority (BAA). In 1970 British United Airways, the airline that during the previous decade had symbolised the airport's vitality, was absorbed by the charter operator, Caledonian Airways, to become British Caledonian Airways. The Beehive continued to be used as offices.

Jackaman and Desoutter would have been pleased, however, that the circular concept in airport terminal design was applied again in various parts of the world from the late 1950s, although it was not until 1983 that it was repeated in the British Isles, as a new satellite to the main terminal at Gatwick. By this time Gatwick was the second most important airport in the Britain and the fourth busiest international airport in the world. Jackaman and Desoutter would also have been pleased that their original terminal building was still being used by airlines such as British Caledonian, albeit as offices, nearly fifty years after its opening.

Recognition and listing

From the 1970s onwards, there were several suggestions that the Beehive should be listed and so permanently preserved as a building of outstanding architectural quality and historical importance. Successive government departments with responsibility for listing resisted such action however, ostensibly because of alterations that had been made to the building through the years. At the same time, officials at the BAA came to look on the Beehive as an important building of aviation heritage that should be retained. After the privatisation of the British Airports Authority in 1988, the company acquired the property development firm, Lynton, to bring expertise into the development of its land and buildings. In the early 1990s plans were prepared to conserve the building and at the same time convert it into small serviced office units,

but this did not happen. By this time the building was in need of major repairs and some limited work was carried out, but the Beehive still required more substantial investment if it was to survive; and it was still not listed.

As a result of a growing appreciation of the need to preserve significant aviation buildings of historical and/or architectural importance, English Heritage commissioned a survey of civil aviation structures in 1993. The resulting report recommended the statutory listing of a number of buildings, including Gatwick's Beehive. The recommendation was accepted and passed on to the Secretary of State for the Environment. The building was listed Grade II* in August 1996, only a few weeks after Gatwick had celebrated the Beehive's sixtieth birthday. The same year the original model of the airport, which had been displayed at the Royal Institute of British Architects in 1937, was flown to Chicago where it was much admired at the exhibition 'Building for Air Travel' at the Art Institute of Chicago.

The 1996 listing decision resulted in a closer focus on the building by the BAA with the result that major conservation work was undertaken with a view to bringing the building back to modern-day use. But one problem remained, the user of the building. The need to find an alternative use for the building coincided in 1999 with the search of GB Airways for new premises; the offices of GB Airways were then in the nearby Iain Stewart Centre. With the lease of the building, BAA Lynton, the Airport Authority's property department, was able to commit itself to expenditure to restore the building to its former glory. With the support of English Heritage, Crawley Borough Council,

Interior of the terminal after restoration work in 2000 (BAA Lynton)

West Sussex County Council and other partners, the building was carefully refurbished and at the same time enhanced. Many of the original features were retained, including the central concourse and the control tower at the apex of the building. Some of the rails on which the telescopic canopies once glided were subsequently restored. It was also proposed that at a future date the end section of the tunnel that linked with the former railway station building, along with its display cases, would be restored. The airline moved its offices and operational centre into the Beehive in October 2000. The official opening took place in the presence of His Royal Highness the Duke of Edinburgh and a number of guests on 1 December 2000.

With its move to the Beehive on a twenty-five-year lease, GB Airways was expressing confidence both in its own future and in a historic and distinguished building. In a surprise move at the beginning of 2001, the BAA decided that ownership of the building did not fit in with its core activities and sold it to GB Airways.

The return of the Beehive to modern-day use was a welcome development in 2000 but was not a total success story. For years the area surrounding the building had not been properly maintained; the 1930s hangars were still in use, but not to shelter aircraft. Gradually most of these hangars were removed, and in 1995, the former Southern Railway station was demolished after being purchased by the BAA. The final episode that was to detract from the success story of the Beehive was the development by BAA of the land between the terminal building and the A23 road. This was a retail and office development, Gatwick City, which at the very time that the Beehive was being brought back into airline use, was to obscure views of the historic building.

The visions of Morris Jackaman and Marcel Desoutter, together with their architects, might not have been fully realised but they would have been very pleased that from 2000 the Beehive building was being used by civil aviation again. They would have been delighted too to learn that in November 2002, BAA Lynton received a top award from the Association for Industrial Archaeology, in recognition of the adaptive reuse of the building which retains the architectural and structural character of its former use, while providing it with a new and economically sustainable future.

Airports in Mutation

Le Bourget's terminal building: historical and archaeological studies for its future restoration

Jean-Christophe Morisseau

The terminal building at Le Bourget, designed by the architect Georges Labro in 1937, is the last of its generation to have survived in France. Since 1982 it has been used to display part of the collections of the Musée de l'Air et de l'Espace, France's national Air and Space Museum. The building was protected as a historic monument in 1994. Traffic at Le Bourget airport is limited today to business aviation, although the site also comprises a military base, a centre for exhibitions and an industrial estate occupied by various aeronautical companies. An extensive reorganisation of the museum is planned in the near future, raising the question of the restoration of the terminal building itself.

This article summarises the conclusions of a study carried out between January and July 2001 on behalf of the Air and Space Museum by the architectural team of Catherine Frenak, Béatrice Jullien and Jean-Christophe Morisseau, with the help of Sylvain Le Stum. The study was followed by a scientific steering committee comprising representatives of the French Ministry of Culture and Communication, Aéroports de Paris, the Ministry of Defence and the association of the friends of the museum. It is divided into two parts: a historical and archaeological investigation, leading to the identification of a historic 'reference' state, and a series of recommendations intended to serve as guidelines for the team commissioned to restore the terminal.

From the creation of the site to Labro's terminal

The first buildings

From the first airfield at Le Bourget, set up at the beginning of the First World War, up to the installation of the Air and Space Museum, the whole site has witnessed constant change. Initially created as a military airfield, it was used for civil aviation from 1919, becoming the point of departure for the first commercial routes between Paris

and London. During this same year, a decree formalised the use of the airfield by civil aviation, attributing its eastern part, lining the Route nationale 2, to the Service de la Navigation Aérienne (the French Aerial Navigation Service).[1]

The earliest structures, dating from the First World War, consisted of temporary hangars and hutting made of timber, canvas and metal sheeting. Some of the wartime hangars were used subsequently for civil aircraft, but in the early 1920s work also began on the construction of more permanent hangars in order to cope with increasing air traffic and larger aircraft. These Lossier hangars, named after the engineer who designed them, were completed in 1922 and are still in use today. In 1924, the engineers Terrisse and Rumpler and the consultant architect Decaux designed several buildings to the south-west of these hangars to house the airport facilities. Laid out as individual pavilions and reminiscent of hospital designs of the time, they anticipated a building type yet to be invented, the airport terminal. The different functions, shared out between the various pavilions, represent the component parts of the terminal: administration, flight control, passport, baggage and customs services, a restaurant, an emergency power supply, meteorological and radio services and a special building for medical screening for pilots.[2]

Although generously sized at the time it was built, the new 'air-port' rapidly proved inadequate. From the end of the 1920s, only six years after its construction, this first ensemble was already obsolete in terms both of its dimensions and its organisation. Between 1926 and 1929, the construction of the first terminal at Berlin-Tempelhof inaugurated a new type of airport passenger facility, grouping together all the services in a single building. An international, modern architecture for aviation began to emerge. The terminal buildings at Lyons and Bordeaux airports, constructed at the instigation of these cities' chambers of commerce and opened in 1930 and 1936 respectively, bear witness to how this international model took form in France.

During the 1930s, at Le Bourget, one reorganisation scheme followed another, with ideas varying between reconstruction in situ and an entirely new site with the potential for extending the flying field. In 1935, the Air Ministry finally launched an architectural competition for the design of a new terminal building. Its inauguration was to coincide with that of the 1937 International Exhibition in Paris. In a country badly affected by economic crisis, this deadline served as a means of accelerating the decisions and the work.[3]

The Paris airport was therefore to remain at Le Bourget and its new terminal was to be built on the site of the earlier pavilions of the 1920s. This decision was governed above all by financial limitations. Many observers (including the architects Beaudouin and Lods) were in favour of moving the terminal to the other side of the airfield, thereby opening up a larger flying space in an east–west direction, but this move would have implied a costly reorganisation of the whole infrastructure of the site.

The architectural competition

As was the case for the buildings of the 1937 International Exhibition, the French State was the commissioning client. The construction of the French pavilions at this Exhibition was intended to contribute to the fight against unemployment while their design was to express a 'new order' in official architecture, combining academism and modernity. The new Le Bourget terminal should therefore be seen in the same context as the major official buildings erected for the Exhibition, in particular the Palais de Chaillot and the Palais de Tokyo; similar to the airport terminal, these two palaces were the result of architectural competitions.[4]

The Air Ministry drew up an outline brief which determined the precise location of the new terminal and a budgetary limit that would incur disqualification if exceeded. The brief also set out some precise design objectives: a building that would be representative of French national identity, which would group together all the necessary functions under one roof and which would serve as an instrument of 'aeronautical propaganda'. The competitors, operating within an 8-million-franc budget (with an 11-million-franc variant incorporating dry-boarding facilities) were to deliver a building capable

of being enlarged in the future. It was to be completed in time for the inauguration of the International Exhibition.

In order to respect both the budget and the tight timetable, the Air Ministry stipulated that the architects should join forces with a general building contractor. The competition was announced in 1935, leaving the candidates two and a half months to submit their proposals. The winner and prize-winning projects were announced on 24 December 1935. Out of twenty-two projects submitted, only fifteen were deemed admissible. Four were awarded prizes, those by the architects Toury, Gréber, Démaret and Labro.[5] Among the projects rejected for not respecting the budget or the proposed site were designs by well-known architects such as Beaudouin and Lods, a team associating Dondel, Aubert, Viard and Dastugue, and Rob Mallet-Stevens in partnership with Georges-Henri Pingusson.[6]

The deadline for the completion of the terminal was sixteen months away, as the opening of the International Exhibition was scheduled for June 1937. This deadline was partially met: the southern part of the terminal was ready in time to welcome the Exhibition's numerous visitors, but the official inauguration of the building only took place on 12 November, a month before the Exhibition came to a close.

Georges Labro's winning project

Georges Labro (1887–1981) was a brilliant pupil of the Lemaresquier-Laloux atelier at the Paris Ecole des Beaux-Arts and an excellent draughtsman. Largely faithful to his academic training, but with a few ideas borrowed from the Modern Movement, he was a capable builder, winner of the second Grand Prix de Rome in 1921. During the inter-war years, his output was prolific; his appointment as architect of the French Postal administration gave him regular projects in the capital, frequently published between 1926 and 1938. After the war, his activities are less well documented, though he is known to have been responsible for the rebuilding of the Le Bourget terminal and to have held several prestigious chairmanships (for example, of the Fondation Taylor and the Société des Artistes Français).

Familiar with public tendering, Labro formed a partnership with a general building contractor, the Société Nouvelle de Construction et de Travaux, coming up with a scheme that met the terms of the competition brief perfectly, respecting the chosen site and the budgetary limits, and committed to meeting the deadline. It was a literal interpretation of the idea of a single, linear building, a monolithic structure measuring 233m long by 30m deep, punctuated at its centre on the landside by a slight projection which corresponded with the projecting control tower on the airside. The entrance to the ensemble from the road was flanked by two symmetrical gate pavilions opening onto a vast esplanade. Seen from the sky, the complex was something like an aeroplane without its fuselage: the terminal spread its wings on either side of the control tower, reminiscent of a nose with a cockpit, the two entrance pavilions forming the tail unit.

In an article published in *L'Architecture* in January 1938, Labro described his terminal as follows:

> My project respected the desire for a simple composition, developing in a straight line slightly in front of the alignment of the hangars, and keeping the depth of the building to a minimum. It also made the most of the heights authorised for the building, the profile of which is intentionally low. In this way I could obtain the largest possible surfaces for the various parts of the terminal, maximising its potential. Furthermore – and this is very important – my design, articulated around a central feature or, if you prefer, around a kind of prow with long wings on each side, allows for the inevitable extensions of the future, with no obstacles placed at the ends of the wings. This makes future changes possible without any fear of compromising the overall order of the composition. As regards the structure, reinforced concrete made rapid construction possible, its simple skeletal framework offering various possibilities for its interior organisation with different and practical combinations of partitions. Finally, notwithstanding the desire to leave the elevations as open as possible, the pillars are faced externally with stone, in order to camouflage a structural material which can have a disgraceful appearance.

Overlooking the esplanade on the landside, the building had an imposing façade. On the airside, stepped terracing provided spacious observation platforms for the public. Large windows on the elevation facing the esplanade, along with translucent 'lenscrete'-type vaulting in the central part, lit up an immense hall inside, occupying the entire length of the building. Galleries led to the service areas and offices, housed on the

upper floor on the airside. Both elevations had extensive glazing, but are very different in appearance. On the landside, the public façade was academic in style, while the airside adopted a modernist vocabulary, closer to the International Style which had already influenced the Lyons and Bordeaux terminals. The terraces express this modernity and were justified in two ways. Their stepped profile reduced the encroachment of the building into the air space above the flying field. Above all, however, the platforms made available for the crowds watching these movements met the Ministry's demands for 'aeronautical propaganda'.

The reinforced concrete structure consisted of a succession of 'cellular bays', each covered by a low, hangar-like vault resting on two perpendicular beams. Between the vaults, these beams formed a gutter and also provided access paths to the viewing terraces from the staircases located on the esplanade side. The modular structural system was expressed on the landside façade, where the twin beams, alternating with the wider vaults, created a differentiation of design for the concrete grid that faced the upper part of the elevation. A continuous concrete canopy, situated at the upper level of the ground floor, emphasised the overall linearity of this façade. The slender, elegant steel window fittings divided the bays in a way that further emphasised the composition's horizontality.[7]

Materials for exterior finishes were chosen to give the building a prestigious appearance while remaining as inexpensive as possible. Both the landside elevation and the 'ocean liner' style airside were faced in marble-like white limestone, while the interior fittings were particularly sober. In the entrance hall at the centre of the building, stone was used parsimoniously, limited to the base of the walls, the eight ribbed columns and the central staircase of honour. This was decorated with wrought iron railings, the other staircases being fitted with simple steel handrails. The three vaults above the entrance hall were of translucent glass blocks. On the floor, sandstone paving was used only in the areas open to the public; the rest of the hall had painted cement flooring. Labro used facing stone for its durability and ease of maintenance, but also, in his own words 'to camouflage, in part at least, a structural material which can have a disgraceful appearance'. This was a far cry from the principles of 'read-

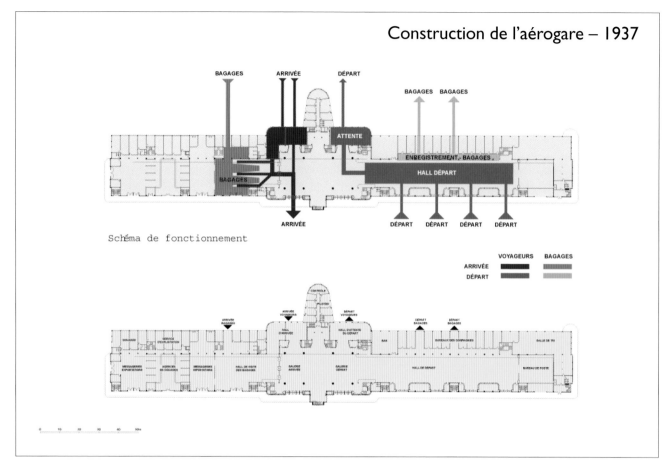

Construction de l'aérogare – 1937

Plan of Le Bourget airport, 1937.

ability' of materials expounded by the Modern Movement.

In his response to the architectural competition, Labro claimed that this modular building, with its monumental linearity, could easily be extended at either end, according to the requirements stipulated in the brief. And indeed, during the study phase, an extra bay was added to the north end of the building to house a post office, resulting in a slight asymmetry of the central projecting structure. This possibility of extension impressed the jury with its apparent simplicity and was characteristic of Labro's pragmatic approach that ignored the rules of academic composition as well as the rigours of functionalism.[8] In point of fact, the end extensions would have meant pushing the post office farther north and the freight offices and customs facilities farther south, as well as destroying the neighbouring hangars. The perpetual enlargements of the terminal – including those carried out by Labro himself after the war – never respected this initial concept: the extensions carried out always 'thickened' the building onto the apron, rather than lengthening it.

Construction work was completed very quickly. The first detailed drawings are dated February 1936, only a month after the announcement of the competition results. The structure, the outer walls and the interior layout were simply designed and easy to exe-cute. Cables and pipes, however, seem to have been fitted as an afterthought, without much prior consideration and without being integrated into the structure. Photographs of the building under construction document the successive appearance of different systems: drainpipes, electricity wiring, etc.

The main phases in the building's evolution

Few building types have had to evolve as rapidly as airports. It is not difficult to imagine how the growth in numbers of passengers and volumes of freight, the development of airline companies, the evolution of aerial navigation techniques and the levels of comfort expected by users all contributed to change at Le Bourget after 1937. The need for more space and new facilities was felt time and time again. Since its post-war reconstruction, the terminal has undergone endless modification and extension.

Four main periods in the terminal's history can be identified:

• the construction of the terminal in 1937
• the war and the reconstruction of terminal 1939–53
• the modernisation of the terminal, 1961–4
• the installation of the museum, 1982–5.

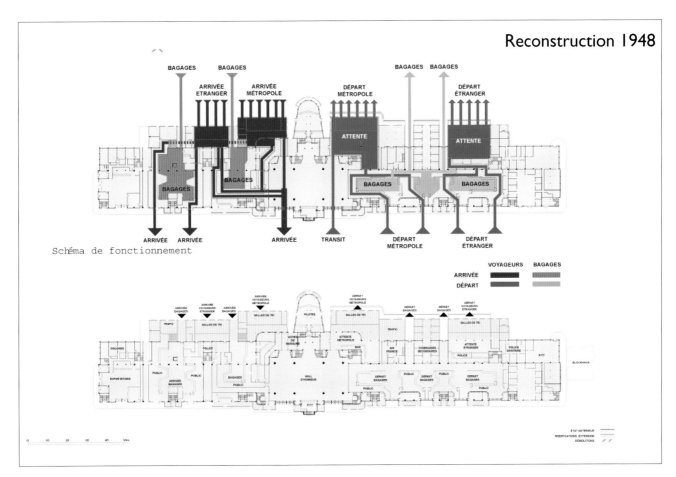

Reconstruction 1948

Schéma de fonctionnement

Plan for the reconstruction of the airport, 1948.

The construction of the terminal

The terminal built between 1936 and 1937 perfectly fulfilled its role as Paris's airport until the beginning of the Second World War.

The huge volume of the hall was divided into three parts: a central hall of honour and two side halls. The central hall concentrated the flows of arriving and departing passengers. From inside the terminal there was a direct view out onto the airfield. The baggage check-in facilities for departures were located in the north hall, in front of the offices of the airline companies, lined up on the airside. Above, a hotel and a restaurant, situated on the first and second floors respectively, were reached by open galleries inside the hall. The south hall was only partially accessible to the public; a vast freight shipping service and facilities for baggage reception for arrivals took up the ground floor. Apart from the restaurant and the hotel, the areas overlooking the viewing platforms were set aside for offices.

The war and reconstruction

During the Second World War, the airport was the target of several air raids. Following the first German attacks in 1940, the airport was occupied by the Luftwaffe. The flying field was enlarged to the north and two concrete runways were built, avoiding the necessity of flying over the terminal. The

building itself does not appear to have been modified. In 1941, British air raids targeted the runways. In July 1943, the airport was bombed by the American air force, and again by the British. In August 1943, operation 'Starkey' involved 169 British bombers in a mission to destroy Le Bourget. The terminal was badly damaged and the runways rendered unusable. The Germans evacuated Le Bourget to set up at Orly. In April, May and June 1944, more air raids took place. Immediately after the Liberation of Paris, the airport was used by American and British forces, who carried out rapid repairs on the runways. Civil flights resumed at the end of the war, as soon as the first repairs were completed.

By the beginning of 1945, the north wing and half of the south wing had already been repaired. In September 1945, Labro was commissioned as a consultant for the complete repair and reconstruction of the terminal. In 1946, in response to demands formulated by the airline companies, and Air France in particular, Labro proposed a new layout, requiring extensions both on the esplanade side and on the flying field. Another project under discussion at the time envisaged the rebuilding of the whole terminal farther to the north, with the existing terminal being remodelled into offices and passenger facilities. Consequently, the 1946 extensions were only temporary. On the apron, the new structures were built in

149

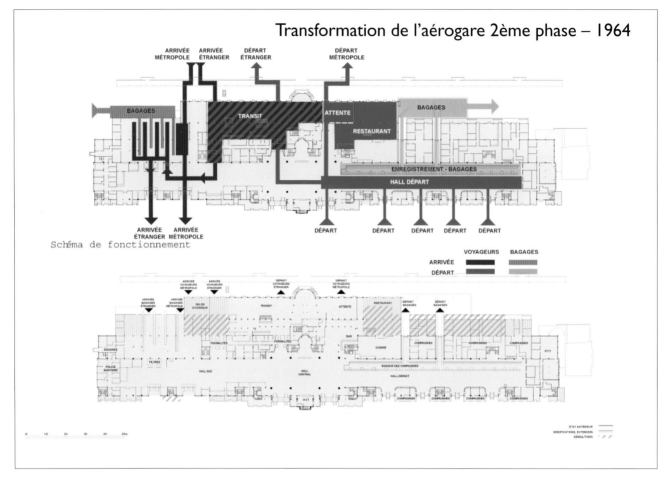

Transformation de l'aérogare 2ème phase – 1964

Schéma de fonctionnement

Plan for modernisation of the airport, second stage, 1964.

timber, while on the esplanade they were installed under the existing canopy, so as not to disfigure the building. Work started in May 1946 under Labro's direction.

The first temporary extensions carried out on the airside were designed to shelter waiting passengers and to house the offices of the airline companies. These structures gave direct access to the planes waiting on the apron in front. The extensions under the canopy on the esplanade side housed some of the airline reception offices, offices for interpreters and an area for passengers waiting for a coach, along with a bar. These alterations meant that the runways were now only partially visible from inside the hall. The base of the control tower was converted into a room for pilots.

The freight shipping office was moved to hangar S6 situated to the south of the terminal. For departing and arriving passengers, a distinction was created between domestic, transit and overseas flights. Because of this distinction, the various entrances were separated physically and the central hall consequently lost its status as a formal entrance concourse. But this organisation was abandoned from 1950 onwards: an operational layout closer to the original then made it possible to use the volume of the north hall again.

Independently of this extension work, the central roof glazing was repaired in 1951, a

new control tower was built in 1953 and in 1958 the first external portico was built, on the airside, to protect passengers from the elements.

The modernisation of the terminal

Ambitious plans for the renovation of the terminal date from 1958, and this modernisation programme was completed in 1964. It was a coherent and well-thought-out project, bringing Le Bourget up to date. The survival of the site as a commercial airport was at stake. Both inside and out, new facilities were installed. This period corresponds with the entry into service of the new Orly terminal, opened to passengers in 1961.

The elevation overlooking the flying field was unified by the construction of a broad new façade on each side of the control tower. A glazed portico was installed to replace the one dating from 1958. The window fittings of the north and south elevations were replaced by new metallic ones which no longer followed the original horizontality of the composition. Following more modernisation work, the landside elevation on the ground floor level now offered a balanced and articulated façade with display windows for the various airline companies.

The internal layout was also completely redesigned. Suspended ceilings with integrated heating and lighting systems were

Aménagement du Musée de l'Air et de l'Espace – 1985

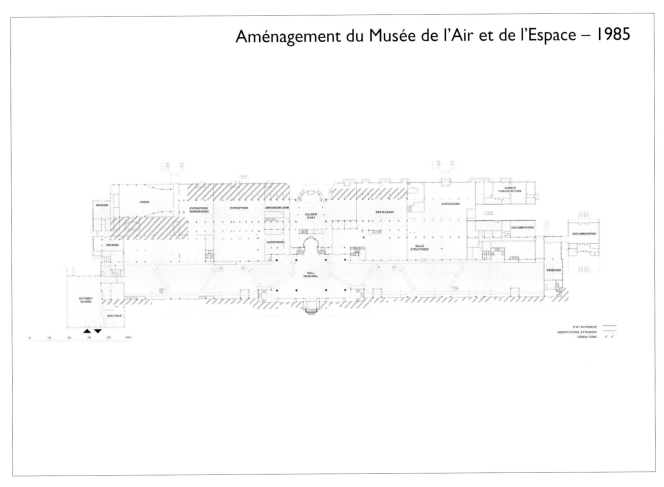

Development of the Air and Space Museum, 1985.

fitted in the side halls. The volume of the central hall remained unchanged, but the installation of an arrivals and departures display board along with new furniture gave it a new 1960s appearance. The check-in counters were modernised and increased in length, after the reduction in the space occupied by the post office. To the north, an independent pavilion was built for VIPs, replacing the former lounge inside the terminal, now used only for arriving passengers.

Extensions on the airside were mainly waiting rooms for passengers before departure or in transit. The covered glass portico was installed in front of the building and ran its entire length. The restaurant was refurbished and a special lounge created for passengers arriving on domestic and foreign flights. The offices of the airlines in the north part of the building were also remodelled. Foreign arrivals and departures were grouped together in the new transit zone in the south extensions. The baggage facilities were extended to the south. In the side halls, the area occupied by baggage handling was reduced by the installation of carousels. Other service areas also increased in size. The post office was reduced in size, enlarging the hall to the north and the offices of the airline companies. The central spur formed by the projecting control tower was now practically surrounded by new building.

At the beginning of the 1970s, further extensions were built on either side of the control tower, joining up the covered portico, which was reduced at its the northern end. To the south, a two-storey building was added, its ground floor used as an extension for baggage handling, the first floor for offices of airlines companies. Between 1971 and 1982 no significant modifications are to be noted.

The installation of the museum

In 1982, the Air and Space Museum, which had occupied some of the hangars to the south of the terminal since 1975, took over the entire terminal building to extend its exhibition areas. Between 1982 and 1985, major alterations were undertaken to transform the terminal into a museum, but these did not affect the load-bearing structure of the original building. To unify the whole, a new elevation was built on the airside. The elevation overlooking the esplanade was considerably modified; the extensions built under the canopy were removed but the ground-floor level of the façade, now walled up, did not recover its initial transparency. Above, the window fittings in steel were replaced with poorly designed aluminium ones that did not correspond with the original design.

A new hall, linking the south hangars to

the terminal building, was constructed to serve as a general entrance to the Air and Space Museum. Metallic staircases and gangways were installed inside the hall of the terminal to take visitors around the historic aircraft on display. In order to control the intensity of the lighting, a canvas awning was suspended as a false ceiling and the glazing of the façade was covered over. The upper galleries were concealed and, with the exception of the two main staircases of honour, the staircases giving access to the terraces were removed.

While not irreversible, these modifications are totally at odds with the initial spirit of the terminal building. Its architecture, considered to be too intrusive, was now concealed. The hall became a mere box to house the museum collection.

Since 1985, some refurbishment projects have been carried out, to meet maintenance requirements. A removable roof covering has been placed over all the vaults to limit water penetration. The watertightness of the terraces has been reinforced, but with a cheap and inappropriate material. The railings of the upper terrace have been re-installed in a spirit close to the original.

A 'reference' state for the restoration

For better or worse, the terminal at Le Bourget has thus witnessed many changes. Despite regular maintenance of the building, it is currently in a poor state of repair. Unless they are dealt with rapidly, the glass blocks of the three central vaults will soon be damaged beyond repair. The window fittings on the airside elevations and at the two ends of the building are also badly in need of repair. The complicated succession of airside terraces, corresponding to various extensions, can only lead to serious damp-proofing and structural problems in the long term. Inside the building, the museum installations created around the aircraft in 1985 have completely altered the spatial volumes of the 1937 interior. Only the main staircase and the eight ribbed columns still bear witness to the original decor. From the hall, the uninterrupted views towards the flying field and the esplanade, which were characteristic of the terminal as a building for air travel, have been obstructed. The museum entrance is no longer situated at the centre of the building, but has been moved to the side. Nonetheless, of all the historic layers that comprise the present-day building, the layer dating from 1937 still dominates in terms of volumes and structure.

At the beginning of the 1980s, the Air and Space Museum saw the terminal more as a container for its extraordinary collection than as a historic building to be interpreted and displayed to advantage. The building did not yet have historic monument status, being protected only in 1994. The issues are different today, however. The museum's intention is not only to carry out badly needed repairs on the building but also to restore it as a remarkable airport terminal. But restore it to what? A 'reference' state is necessary.

The Air and Space Museum is considering a far-reaching reorganisation of the entire site comprising the construction of new buildings for its reserve collections, the redeployment of the collections and the improvement of the reception areas for the public. The main objective is to restore to the terminal its role as a building designed to welcome the public, by freeing the hall of its historic aircraft, for which a new display area will be created elsewhere in the museum. With the restoration of its function as a reception building, the terminal will emerge as a feature of the museum in its own right, an exceptional example of aviation architecture of the 1930s.

The scale of this project, involving not only the terminal but also its functions within the context of the entire site, means that it can only be envisaged on a long-term basis. The detailed programme for the reorganisation of the museum is still to be drawn up and the nature of the changes that will be involved have still to be defined. As far as the terminal is concerned, it is essential to consider the restoration of the building in an overall perspective and not in isolation. In both architectural and management terms, it is imperative that one, or several, reference states be defined as a precondition for any intervention. A 'reference state' is understood here to mean the coherent state of the building at a given time, which is of strong architectural significance and satisfies the constraints of appearance, comfort and efficiency.

The rehabilitation and interpretation of the building will show how the Air and Space Museum is committed to this major monument in the history of aviation architecture and confirm its sensitivity to the building's role in aviation history, alongside the flying machines.

The reference state: the 1937 terminal

The various phases in the evolution of the structure, identified by means of archival research and on-site investigation, have made it possible to plot the successive layers of change. Each built component of the terminal has been analysed and dated in order to inform the decisions to be taken. A study of these plans of the successive modifications clearly shows the surviving traces of each chronological state. It is worth noting straight away that hardly anything remains of the 1948 extensions, which were intended to be of provisional duration. The modernisation programmes of the years 1961 to 1964 leave only the load-bearing structures and their airside terraces. All the 1960s additions such as interior fittings, the external portico on the runway side and the constructions on the esplanade side have disappeared. Moreover, this 'golden age' in air travel finds perfect expression in the aviation architecture of the Orly terminal (now Orly-Sud), which has recently been renovated and is still in service.[9]

The successive refurbishments and extensions that were carried out from the post-war reconstruction onwards had little respect for the architectural coherence of the terminal, and most were carried out as provisional solutions to urgent operational problems. The plans also suggest how one refurbishment partially eliminated the preceding one. The installation of the museum in the 1980s dealt the final blow in removing the evidence of earlier alterations and even destroyed several features of the 1937 terminal. It did not affect the structure of the building, however, in an irreversible way.

From the point of view of the coherence of the building and its historic interest, its 1937 form emerges as the only one that can be considered as a model for restoration. The considerable wealth of archive material held by Aéroports de Paris provides a comprehensive record of the 1937 Le Bourget, making its restoration both possible and authentic. In the case of certain features built at a later date, however, it will not be necessary to restore them to their 1937 state, either because of their own architectural value, their innovative qualities or simply because of the major difficulties that would result from a return to the original state. That is the case in particular for the control tower, dating from 1953.

Aviation architecture re-invents itself in response to permanently changing needs and technologies. As soon as it is completed, a terminal is already obsolete and, among other considerations, its qualities are judged in terms of its ability to evolve. With sixty years' hindsight, this question of ease of adaptation would give mixed answers at Le Bourget. From 1948 onwards, only ten years after its opening, the terminal was already out of date and there was talk of converting it to other uses such as a hotel or offices. Extensions with no overall coherence were built through the years to keep Le Bourget up to standard as Paris's airport, until the entry into service of Roissy, in 1977. Since this date, Le Bourget has only been used as a business airport. Despite continual modification, however, the building has remained intact as far as its initial volume is concerned. The 1930s terminal is still visible beneath the additions and modifications. As such, it represents a precious example of a specific era in the history of aviation architecture.

Furthermore, the site is still used for aviation. The museum continues to be associated with aviation activities, along with its noises and smells. The displays in the reorganised museum should make the most of this advantage, reflecting the relationships between the collections and air travel and restoring uninterrupted vistas through the terminal enabling visitors to look over the runways and watch planes taking off and landing. The era of 'aeronautical propaganda' might be over, but the fascination for flight remains.

Restoration to the 1937 state

Priorities

The work to be carried out on the terminal in order to return it to its 1937 state (with due consideration for the exceptions mentioned) can be broken down into five major phases, set out according to their degree of priority.

1. Restoration of the central projecting structure

In 2000, the central structure on the landside, with its three sculptures, was the object of a specific restoration study by an architect of the Historic Monuments administration. The renovation of this decorative element would be an ideal starting point for all future work.

2. Restoration of the façade overlooking the esplanade

Le hall central, dans ses prestations et son volume doit être réhabilité à l'identique de l'état 1937. Il faut retrouver la transparence, de part et d'autre de l'escalier central et restituer l'éclairage des voûtes verrières.

Certains éléments comme les verrières de 1951, le calepinage de l'escalier du hall, pourront toutefois être conservés.

Le Hall en 1937 - Cliché MAE

Le Hall en 1937 - Cliché MAE

Inauguration de l'aérogare - Cliché MAE

	PROJET 1⬛
Gros-oeuvre Cloisonnement	L'ensemble des ⬛ l'escalier d'honneu⬛ utilisée à l'extérieu⬛ paliers), plinthe d⬛ dimensions (jusqu'a⬛
Sols	Grés 12.5 x 12.5 c⬛ Les motifs noirs de⬛ de 1.625 m.
Peintures intérieures	Peinture appliqué⬛ poutres transversal⬛
Serrurerie	Escalier d'honneur ⬛ oiseaux + rose des ⬛ Escalier accès ter⬛ métalliques peints. ⬛ barreaudage 3 tube⬛
	Plan du dallage⬛
Verrières	Verrières centrales⬛ solidaire de la struc⬛ Etanchéité type "P⬛
Faux-plafonds	Pas de faux-plafon⬛
Menuiseries extérieures	Menuiseries fixes ⬛ vitrages simples fix⬛ - L pour le cadre ex⬛ - T entre deux vitra⬛ Les portes d'accès ⬛
Éclairage	Eclairage indirec⬛ incandescentes. ⬛ Caissons lumineux ⬛
Signalétique générale	Elle est constituée d⬛ lettre de métal mis ⬛ "FUTURA" ou dériv⬛ murs intérieurs, mai⬛ de cercle au dess⬛ départ). Type de tex⬛
Mobiliers fixes	Banques maçon⬛ d'Hydrequent, plan⬛ noire.
Chauffage Ventilation Électricité	Chaufferie en sous-⬛ Distribution par a⬛ placées sous les ⬛ locaux. Electricité : sans ob⬛

référence 1937	**ÉTAT DES LIEUX** voir état des lieux bât. actuel	**PRÉCONISATIONS**
y compris ceux de pierre d'Hydrequent 1.50 m au droit des es sont de grandes	Revêtement pierre de l'escalier d'honneur refait après guerre. Revêtement pierre de la façade intérieure parvis disparu. Volume concave créé au dessus de l'escalier, cloisonnement courbe en-dessous. Cloisons opaques montées de part et d'autre de l'éperon.	Retrouver le volume initial de l'escalier d'honneur (supprimer cloison vers le salon d'honneur + cloisons sous demi-coupole). Conserver calepinage datant de 1948 de l'escalier d'honneur. Retrouver le revêtement pierre de la façade intérieure ht 2 m parvis dito 37. Retrouver la transparence directe avec les pistes de part et d'autre de l'escalier d'honneur.
rrés noirs. ent une trame carrée	Peinture de sol sur chape. Rien ne permet de dire qu'il reste des vestiges des différents états de surface sous la chape. Si c'était le cas, il ne parait pas envisageable de les réutiliser.	Grés 12.5x12.5 cm avec motifs noirs dito état 1937.
arase inférieure des tres : badigeon.	Peinture bleu ciel dans la partie visible. Rampe escalier d'honneur noire.	Retrouver l'état de 1937, voir résultat des tests de couleur effectués.
ivragé avec écussons tifs cordages. npes + gardes corps m) encastrés au sol,	La rampe en fer forgé initiale est bien conservée, mais les sphères en tête de la rampe ont disparu au cours du chantier de réaménagement du musée. Passerelles-rampes construites pour la scénographie du musée. Les autre rampes et gardes-corps ont été remplacés par un système de cadres métal avec fils d'acier inox tendus.	Supprimer les passerelles-rampes. Refaire les rampes et gardes-corps dito 1937.

État actuel - Clichés JCM

Plan d'exécution de 1937 - Dessin des portes principales - Microfilm MAE A96

d de diamètre 12 cm avés de verre	L'état de la verrière correspond à la réfection entreprise en 1950-51 - voûte + coupole centrale : pavés 15x15 cm épais. 8 cm - voûtes latérales : pavés rond 12 cm épais. 6 cm Nombreux désordres (voir état des lieux)	Etat de 1951 conservé. Voir fiche de préconisation extérieur verrières voûtes.
	Faux-plafond en toile plastifiée tendue, posé lors de l'aménagement du hall en musée	Supprimer faux-plafond actuel.
du commerce avec l'intérieur) menuiseries métal.	Menuiseries aluminium ne correspondant pas au dessin initial. Porte d'accès vitrées remplacées par portes vitrées menuiseries aluminium.	Voir fiches de préconisation extérieur façades parvis et piste. Refaire les portes d'accès dito 1937.
rières par lampes accès.	Rampe néon en sous-face du faux-plafond	Retrouver système d'éclairage indirect des voûtes. Retrouver les caissons lumineux des entrées sur parvis. Compléter selon besoins avec technologie actuelle.
dimensions, réalisés en tilisée est de la famille général collées sur des ies en extérieur, en arc (voir auvent extérieur etc....	Sans objet	Retrouver les éléments de signalétique emblématique de la fonction d'aérogare (arrivée-départ...) Pour la signalétique propre au Musée : à l'appréciation du maître d'oeuvre.
latéraux en pierre ht 10 cm en pierre	Sans objet	Retrouver, suivant besoins, banques dito 1937, en fonction de l'implantation initiale.
haudière à mazout). alls (les gaines sont iteur pour les autres	- 2 sous-stations chauffage en sous-sol : dans l'aile nord sur ancien emplacement + aile sud. - 3 locaux de ventilation: 2 latéraux au sous-sol et 1 central au R+2 borne. Pas de rafraîchissement d'air.	Etablir un diagnostic de l'installation existante en fonction de la future configuration du musée, après analyse des besoins. Voir étude thermique réalisée, il y a environ 5 ans. Prévoir dispositif pour éviter les sas des portes d'entrée.

For the elevation facing the esplanade, it is necessary to replace the current, standard window fittings with slimmer metallic ones that are more faithful to the original design. The views through the openings at the ground floor level, a key to understanding the building as a terminal for flight, should be re-established. Appropriate facing materials might include either plaster rendering or stone cladding. Both would give the desired appearance of a smooth block.

3. Restoration of the façade overlooking the flying field and the transparency of the ground floor

This airside façade was designed as the passengers' first contact with Paris. It has a more modern appearance than the landside façade and is an essential part of the terminal's 1937 character. The role of the building as a filter for passengers must be recreated: the extensions encroaching on the apron that surround the control tower and obstruct the view from the hall towards the runways should be removed to restore the terminal's original visual permeability. As with the landside façade, the window fittings should be restored.

4. Restoration of the interior, in particular the hall and its galleries

The vast long hall with its ample volume and luminosity, covered by the vaulting of the bays and lined by galleries, is one of the major features of Labro's project. Once the museum's display installations have been removed, this hall will recover its original spatial qualities. It will also be necessary to reinstate the mezzanine to the north and the staircases giving access to the terraces, as well as to disencumber the galleries.

5. Access to the terraces

To envisage the 1937 terminal without its immense terraced platforms for the crowds coming to observe the daily spectacle of arriving and departing aircraft would be unthinkable. It is clearly desirable to reopen these terraces, although this poses considerable security problems for the present-day airport. Every effort should be made, however, to achieve this aim. The stairs should be made accessible to the public, the temporary roof covering should be removed, watertightness reinforced in asphalt and the railings reinstalled in conformity with current security norms.

Independently of the discussions currently taking place on the reorganisation of the museum, other studies must be undertaken to complement our own investigations, which focus on the terminal itself. These should deal with the entire airport site extending over the communes of Dugny and Le Bourget. The aviation landscape as an ensemble, including its constructions and infrastructural elements, needs further analysis, in particular the historic evolution of the runway system which accompanied the technological progress of aircraft, flight control, communications systems, etc. The airport's relations to its transport networks – the Route nationale 2 and the motorway – must also be taken into consideration. During the past few decades, the airport's urban environment has suffered from neglect. The Air and Space Museum has a truly remarkable collection that does not attract the numbers of visitors it deserves. Only when the conditions of access to the site have been improved will it find its rightful place among France's major national museums.

Recommendations

The last part of our study proposes a series of illustrated recommendation sheets as future design guidelines. For each space of the terminal, they present the reference state of 1937, the current state and the initiatives to be taken for the future rehabilitation of the building. They comprise archival material (Labro's execution drawings or photographs of the terminal in 1937), photographs of the current state of the building and other reference images which underpin the recommendations.

Notes

1 Marie-Jeanne Dumont, 'L'Architecture de l'aéronautique en France, 1900–1940'. Unpublished report, Paris, Ministère de la Culture et de la Communication, Inventaire général des Monuments et des Richesses artistiques de la France/CILAC, 1988.
2 Antony Goissaud, 'Le port aérien du Bourget'. La Construction moderne 18 (December 1927).
3 M S D, 'Les terrains – Le Bourget'. L'Aérophile, 15 September 1931.
4 See Jean-Louis Cohen (ed), Les Années 30, l'architecture et les arts de l'espace entre industrie et nostalgie. Paris: Editions du patrimoine, 1997; Bertrand Lemoine (ed), Cinquantenaire de l'Exposition internationale des arts et des techniques dans la vie moderne. Paris: Institut français d'Architecture/Paris-Musées, 1987.

5 Pierre Mathé, 'Le concours de l'aéroport du Bourget'. *L'Architecture d'aujourd'hui* February (1936).

6 Christian Bregi, 'Les trois conceptions en présence au concours de l'aéroport du Bourget'. *L'Aérophile* January (1936).

7 Charles-Edouard Sée, 'La nouvelle aérogare du Bourget, près de Paris'. *Le Génie civil*, 27 November 1937.

8 Charles-Clément Grandcour, 'La nouvelle aérogare du Bourget'. *La Construction moderne*, 24 October 1937.

9 See the contribution by Jacques Repiquet in this volume, pp 192–203.

Approaching the built heritage: the conservation plan for Berlin-Tempelhof

Werner Jockeit and Cornelia Wendt

Tempelhof airport was protected as a historic monument only in 1994. The assessment of its heritage values comprised the complete survey and documentation of the structure and fittings worthy of conservation, dating from the succeeding periods of construction and use of the airport. These were identified and evaluated within the larger framework of a conservation plan drawn up in collaboration with the various stakeholders concerned. This Tempelhof approach played an important part in the initial elaboration of the 'L'Europe de l'Air' project on aviation architecture.

Ironically, however, since the setting up of this European project, little or no progress can be reported at Berlin. A transfer of responsibilities, legal difficulties and errors, insufficient preparation, and the uncertainties of the political and economic climate in Berlin and in the Land of Brandenburg, have all put obstacles in the way of the clear and bold decisions that need to be taken. These decisions concern the continued use of Tempelhof, in keeping with its central location in the city and as part of a coherent distribution of air traffic between Berlin's existing airports, and the development of carefully considered and workable concepts for the airport's conversion to new uses. The present situation is that the bankrupt city now has a project for a future aviation hub at its outskirts, at Schönefeld, a project that is eagerly anticipated as part of Berlin's development as a major metropolis, but increasingly uncertain and of doubtful economic viability. At the same time, at Tempelhof, the city has a historic airport that (similar to the 1970s airport at Tegel) is soon to be closed. But Tempelhof's advantageous location, its popularity and its special atmosphere should be seen, by contrast, as precious assets for the city. Other European cities have succeeded in putting similar treasures to good use. In Rotterdam, the airport dating from the 1930s is now a business airport; Paris has converted the terminal building at Le Bourget into a museum; and the thriving city airport in the heart of London's docklands is used to supplement the capacity of the capital's other airports at Heathrow, Gatwick and Stansted.

The survey and inventory report on Tempelhof airport was prepared in 1995 by Arge Handrack/Jockeit. It seemed essential to develop this first report into a practical conservation plan for the whole site, setting out concrete and detailed conservation measures.[1] According to paragraph 8, section 3, of Berlin's heritage law,[2] such conservation statements – interpreting the existing historic fabric, analysing different degrees of interest and providing a basis for joint decisions by owners and heritage organisations – are considered to have binding legal force.

After lengthy discussions, however, the experts of the Federal Financial Directorate responsible for this airport property, the district administration and the heritage department of Berlin (the Landesdenkmalamt) were unable to reach an agreement about the legal consequences of the conservation plan. The jointly developed statutory document is now considered merely as 'Guidelines on the conservation of Tempelhof airport', even if there is a mutual acknowledgement of these guidelines as a basis for decision-making. The idea of simplifying the planning procedures for interventions at the airport complex, however, as originally intended, has now been practically abandoned.

The aim of the recommendations contained in the conservation plan is to preserve the whole construction as a historic monument – not only where its characteristic architectural elements are concerned, but also with respect to its complex mix of historic, town-planning and functional features – independently of the continuing political and economic discussions, at 'Land' and Federal levels, about the broader reorganisation of Berlin's airport landscape. Whatever future uses can be found for the airport buildings and the airfield, all decisions are to be evaluated in terms of their public interest and in relation to the cultural appropriation of the monument. This means respecting Tempelhof's multi-layered contemporary significance, among others for the surrounding neighbourhood of the airport, for the spatial and ecological structure of the city as a whole, for the history of the city, for architectural history, and for technical developments in air transport.

While this decision-making process is underway, even if air traffic is limited or entirely abandoned, the entire site should be kept operational, at least as far as its aeronautical and public facilities are concerned, or used temporarily in such a way as to ensure that air traffic can always be resumed, as was the case in 1985.

Within the overall form of the airport, including its spatial connections to the city's road network on the one hand, and to the open space of the airfield on the other, a distinction can be made, in terms of material appearances and details, between four very different zones of use: public areas, prestigious spaces or spatial sequences, administration areas, and technical areas.

With the airport's almost perfectly symmetrical layout and its planned hierarchy of carefully staged functional areas, these different logics are still easily recognisable today. At the same time, however, its unfinished construction history, its partial wartime destruction and post-war reconstruction, as well as the various layers of subsequent use have all left visible traces. It is the narrative that these traces bring together which makes the entire site such an essential and authentic place in Berlin's collective memory. This in turn means that protection measures cannot be limited only to the spatial and architectural characteristics of the construction – the mere realisation of the original plans drawn up by the architect Ernst Sagebiel – but must also encompass the site's subsequent existence and the ensuing phases of its construction and use. These too must be accepted as important historical documents, to be left in a comprehensible form.

Various possibilities can be envisaged for new uses for certain parts of the airport, uses that can be integrated into the existing structure. There is no reason why such partial conversion operations cannot use contemporary formal vocabularies. An important consideration for any decision either on these new uses or on the removal of intrusive alterations, is aesthetic quality, which should harmonise with the protected structure and the overall paradigm of the place, its functional distribution and the

materials and colours used. When alterations call for changes to original details or new additions, supplementary guidelines must be drawn up, or confirmed, to complete the conservation plan with new, binding standards.

The outside spaces of the airport – that is to say the open areas lined by the boundary roads, the courtyard of honour and the basic functional zones of the airfield – are explicitly considered as indispensable component parts of the historic monument. The structural and topographical vestiges of the first Tempelhof airport, dating from the 1920s, should also be included in the protective designation, for documentary and landscape reasons.

Building development on the rest of the airfield – the last major unbuilt area in Berlin's city centre – would eradicate about 270 years of urban history. It would also have a negative effect on the city's ecological equilibrium and seriously detract from the building complex that is preserved as a monument today. It would deprive the historic airport of what is certainly its principal functional element, turning it into something like a body deprived of arms and legs.

The conservation plan is intended to serve as a long-term management document. Based on the research carried out for the survey and inventory report, it comprises a summary of the building's history and construction phases, an inventory of what exists today, a description of the historically interesting elements, and an account of the airport's successive uses; detailed inventory forms are used to present and plot spatial alterations. One of the most important sections of the plan concerns the representation of the relative interest of the interiors and spatial sequences: these are identified, in red, yellow and green, as being of 'outstanding' or 'particular' interest, or simply 'interesting'. Finally, to recreate the original colours, a colour index has been included, based on architectural paint analysis. This has been undertaken for the most important spaces and details. In order to obtain a comprehensive picture of the original colour scheme, in particular in the access and circulation zones and the prestige spaces and spatial sequences, and in order to be able to restore them in keeping with the materials used, these studies must be systematically pursued. The conservation plan identifies the areas which merit such detailed analysis.

The results of these colour studies, as

Impression of Tempelhof airport with the planned circular plaza (drawing about 1935; Landesdenkmalamt Berlin)

well as those concerning other, unexpected, construction problems, were discussed in the course of regular co-ordination meetings between the airport's operators (the Berliner Flughafen Gesellschaft), the Tempelhof district heritage office, the Landesdenkmalamt Berlin and the authors of the conservation plan. In this way, the plan remains open and reactive, integrating new knowledge and accommodating demands by new users of the buildings.

History

Even on paper, the building complex of Berlin's Central Airport at Tempelhof assumed colossal proportions as an architectural creation of the Third Reich. In the vision of its planners, it was to provide a demonstration of Germany's might; linked to the north–south axis of the future world capital, 'Germania', it was to act as a majestic gateway to the city. Furthering these propaganda and ideological objectives, the monumental complex was also to serve as a showcase for the technical development of German aviation and to assert Berlin's role as Europe's principal air hub.

From a heritage point of view, the entire complex represents an exceptionally impressive architectural ensemble, combining rigorously functionalistic features with a built representation of the political and structural aesthetics of National Socialism. Bearing witness too to the high drama of Berlin's immediate post-war history, the site is still in active use as a busy transportation, administration and service complex; in infrastructural terms, it is one of the most important components of Berlin's urban landscape. In the public interest, then, this highly significant

'document' must be conserved intact, to be handed on to future generations.

Its location, the *Tempelhofer Feld*, was initially used during the 18th and 19th centuries as a military parade and exercise ground, subsequently becoming the scene for numerous events relating to the beginnings of aviation. The first, temporary airport buildings were constructed on the field from 1922 to 1923. An extension followed in 1924 and 1925, based on a preliminary plan by Otto Sauernheimer and designs by Paul Mahlberg, Heinrich Kosina and Fritz Bräuning. The conception of this terminal was strongly influenced by 'new objectivity' and the building was seen as an early example of this architectural style.

The technical evolution of aircraft design and guidance made a further extension necessary, carried out between 1925 and 1927 in two phases, based on designs by Paul and Klaus Engler. By the early 1930s, in terms of the number of flights, this airport was one of the busiest in Europe, stretched to capacity.

To keep up with rapidly developing air traffic, yet another extension of the airport was necessary. The huge expenditure incurred and the extremely short deadline made it possible for the opening of the new complex are to be explained, above all, by the Nazis' plans to resuscitate the air force that was to play a key role in their imminent war of conquest. In 1935, the commission for this extensive enlargement of the central airport was awarded to the architect Ernst Sagebiel by the Reich's Air Ministry.

Sagebiel's other airport designs at Munich-Riem and Vienna-Schwechat have already been extensively modified. The last original Sagebiel building at Stuttgart-Echterdingen was demolished in 2000.

Architecture

The airport buildings are conceived as a series of large, block-like structures and spaces fronting the sweeping curve of the hangar building, with the main departures hall, forecourt and projected central plaza on the landside. Its rigid compactness, exaggerated by the strict rhythms of uniform or similar geometrical features and an intentionally limited choice of construction materials, was intended to symbolise the indestructible stability and duration of the Reich's new social order. Further analyses of Tempelhof's architectural images are to be found in Axel Drieschner's contribution to this publication (pp 100–112).

The airport complex

The focal point of the airport's plan is formed by the open 'courtyard of honour' and a central group of buildings comprising the reception and departures halls. This backbone of the overall structure marks the principal symmetrical axis of the complex. The main group of buildings is followed by the boarding area, flanked by the hangars arranged in a vast open arc around the airfield, 1,200 metres in length. The rooftop of this building, reached via massive, bunker-like stair towers, was designed to hold viewing platforms for 65,000 people. Another million spectators were to be assembled along the grass verges surrounding the entire airfield to attend mass events such as march-pasts, demonstrations, political rallies, festivals and, above all, the *Reichsflugtage*, the Third Reich's air shows.

As far as the aeroplanes were concerned, a paved taxiway lined the periphery of the field, leading to two waiting areas. It broadened out into a deep apron in front of the central boarding area and the hangars.

Technical facilities

The new airport complex was to be equipped with the very latest technical facilities, to ensure its smooth and autonomous operation. These include, underground, an independent water plant, a power station, backed up by an emergency installation, as well as two low-pressure steam heating systems. Deep underground, a two-level cellar was probably used for storing top-secret aerial reconnaissance films and photos. A maze of connecting service passages, containing the heating ducts, electricity cables and water and sewage pipes, extends beneath the whole building and its courtyards.

Construction

On the landside, the monumental and archaic appearance of the buildings conceals a structure built according to the rationalised industrial techniques of the day and using the latest construction techniques. The load-bearing structure was designed as a steel skeleton with brick in-fill. Due to the shortage of materials caused by the war, in the later construction phases, steel was replaced as far as possible by reinforced concrete.

The trusses of the overhanging roof extending over the boarding area and the hangars are a cantilevered construction that is entirely column-free on the airfield side. The hangars and maintenance halls are closed by means of large, electrically operated sliding doors and bathed in light from both sides by elevated steel-framed windows.

Building materials

In choosing the materials for the façades and interiors, rigorous structural intentions were made apparent, underlining a hierarchy among the different areas of use. Various types of natural or artificial stone, wood and plaster, wall tiling, flagstones and, in certain spaces, decorative elements such as glass or stone mosaics, artistic stained-glass windows, etc, were all used to considerable effect.

Interiors

Alongside the departures hall, the interior spaces intended to impress include the main stairwells and various vestibules and larger rooms. These are fitted out with considerable opulence, using natural or artificial stone as well as wood panelling.

Bathed in light, the departures hall is divided by two narrow rows of rectangular columns into a broad central nave and two side aisles with raised galleries. The side walls and the end wall facing the airfield are almost entirely glazed. As soon as they entered this hall, at its far end, passengers and visitors could already see the aircraft on the apron. Above the departures hall, a large restaurant with a terrace covered by a sliding roof was planned, but this part of the project was never built.

In the administration wings, the overall

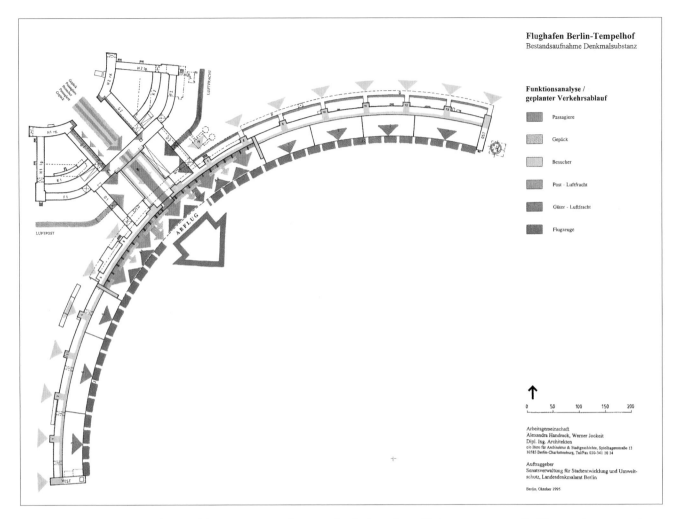

Functional analysis, projected traffic flows: (see colour-key at top right) passengers; luggage; visitors; mail-freight; merchandise-freight; aircraft.

plan and its sequence of spaces is designed in a modern, rational manner. Corridors divide the buildings along their entire length with standard offices on either side. These corridors, which are lined with built-in cupboards and fitted doors beneath overlights, comprise a washbasin, on the office side.

Exteriors

Different varieties of granite were used for the footways, the flights of steps and their strings, the cladding of the footbridges leading to the stair towers and the parapet over the 'Bunkerstraße', as well as for the base areas above this roadway and the foot of all the landside façades. The courtyard of honour was paved with large, regular flagstones forming a grid pattern, while the roads were surfaced partly in asphalt (the upper Bunkerstraße and the forecourt) and partly in basalt-concrete, or 'basaltin', slabs (the boarding area, apron, take-off stumps, taxiways and lower Bunkerstraße), with some paving stones, between the railways of the Bunkerstraße and inside the railway tunnel.

Operation

Marked by the building's demonstrative spatial effects, the airport was a highly efficient transport facility at the same time. For the first time, passengers, visitors and luggage were channelled in one-way flows and carefully separated from each other on different levels. This separation – an essential feature of airport planning today – was rigorously applied at Tempelhof as a basic planning principle, with important and visible consequences for the airport's overall appearance.

Passengers: Coming from the plaza, departing passengers reached the terminal via the rectangular forecourt, sheltered beneath the side arcades and the protruding canopy of the main entrance porch. A nearby underground station connected the airport with the public transport network.

Leading from the lofty reception hall at the entrance to the terminal, a broad flight of stairs led down to the departures hall, where the counters of the airline companies were aligned. From here, the passengers – sorted according to domestic or foreign destinations and separated from in-coming passengers – passed through the various gates and down the open flights of steps to the boarding area below, reaching the waiting aircraft on foot.

For the Führer, his high-ranking entourage and official state guests, a special

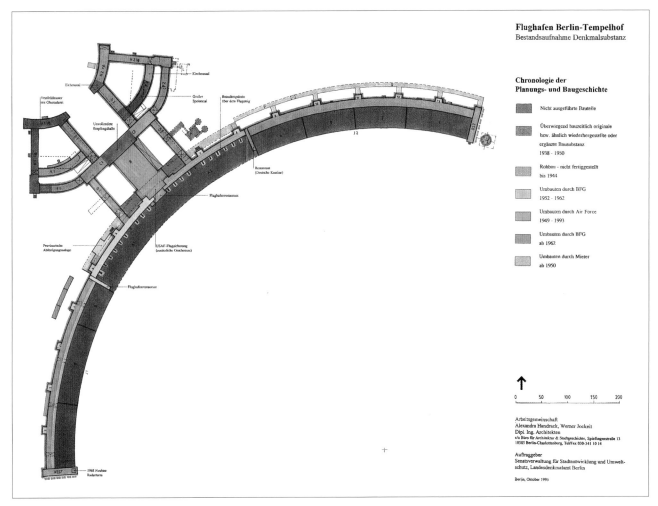

ramp (the *Führerrampe*) was created at the luggage level, leading up to the freight courtyard and thereby providing direct access to the streets; motor vehicles could thus pass through the whole building complex to reach the boarding area directly.

Visitors: Non-flying visitors to the airport could reach the side balconies of the departures hall via a flight of steps. The huge glass façade at the end of the hall gave them a view over the boarding area and the airfield. Lifts at the side led to galleries running along the departure gates and hangars and up to the planned restaurant over the departures hall and to the viewing platforms on the roof.

Luggage: Passengers' luggage, handed over in the departures hall and loaded onto electric chariots after being sorted according to the flight destination, was transported by lift to the luggage level beneath the hall and from here straight out to the boarding area and the aircraft.

Airmail and freight: The lowest level of the central building was on the same level as the freight courtyards, reached by ramps and comprising facilities for freight-handling and airmail. The airmail office had an underground connection to the main post office on the forecourt. The railways on the Bunkerstraße ran through the tunnel and enabled merchandise to be unloaded from railway wagons. Another railway line skirted the hangars, making possible the direct loading and unloading of aircraft.

Aircraft: Incoming aircraft taxied into the part of the boarding zone designated for arrivals, while empty planes and those being prepared for flight were lined up in the hangars or on the paved parking stands where they were held in place with loops fixed into the ground. Shortly before take-off, the aircraft taxied to their allotted position at the boarding area and from here to the relevant take-off position at the edge of the field.

When events and air shows were held, the parking stands for aircraft could be used by spectators in their own vehicles.

Building work

Apart from the urgent military and economic requirements, one of the main reasons for the extremely rapid completion of the gigantic project was a state-organised job creation scheme, with its accompanying propaganda. Construction work began shortly after the authorisation granted in

Planning and construction chronology: (see colour-code at top right) non executed elements; mostly original fabric, or elements rebuilt or completed, 1938–50; main structure, not completed in 1944; modifications by the Berliner Flughafen Gesellschaft, 1952–62; modifications by the United States Air Force, 1949–93; modifications by the Berliner Flughafen Gesellschaft from 1962; modifications by tenants from 1950.

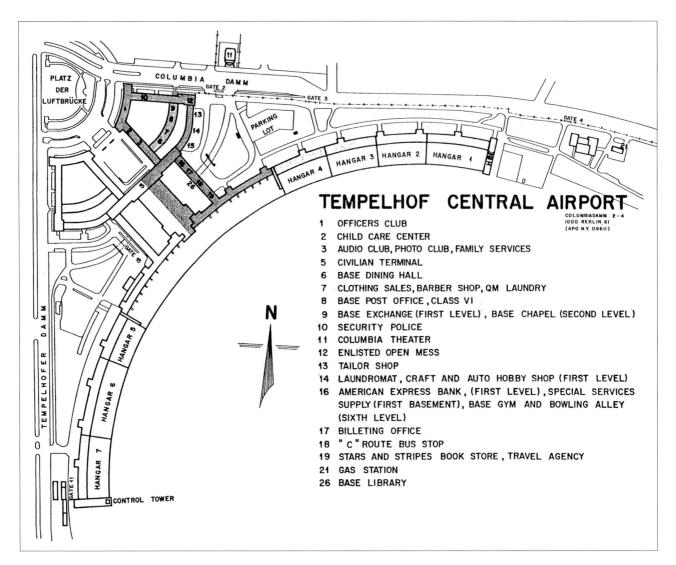

TEMPELHOF CENTRAL AIRPORT

COLUMBIADAMM 2-4
1000 BERLIN 61
(APO N.Y. 09611)

1 OFFICERS CLUB
2 CHILD CARE CENTER
3 AUDIO CLUB, PHOTO CLUB, FAMILY SERVICES
5 CIVILIAN TERMINAL
6 BASE DINING HALL
7 CLOTHING SALES, BARBER SHOP, QM LAUNDRY
8 BASE POST OFFICE, CLASS VI
9 BASE EXCHANGE (FIRST LEVEL), BASE CHAPEL (SECOND LEVEL)
10 SECURITY POLICE
11 COLUMBIA THEATER
12 ENLISTED OPEN MESS
13 TAILOR SHOP
14 LAUNDROMAT, CRAFT AND AUTO HOBBY SHOP (FIRST LEVEL)
16 AMERICAN EXPRESS BANK, (FIRST LEVEL), SPECIAL SERVICES SUPPLY (FIRST BASEMENT), BASE GYM AND BOWLING ALLEY (SIXTH LEVEL)
17 BILLETING OFFICE
18 "C" ROUTE BUS STOP
19 STARS AND STRIPES BOOK STORE, TRAVEL AGENCY
21 GAS STATION
26 BASE LIBRARY

Facilities in the eastern part of the airport as used by the United States Air Force (United States Installations, Berlin Command, telephone directory, 1989, 76)

May 1936 by the Reich's Air Minister, Hermann Goering, and its rapid progress was to demonstrate the capability and the orchestrated perfection of National Socialist Germany. What made this possible was the standardisation of construction elements, such as trusses, formwork, concrete reinforcements, concrete and natural stone blocks, delivered in shapes and dimensions as standard as possible.

By 1939, the basic structure of the airport was more or less complete. The first occupants moved into the administration wings and leases were signed with others. After the beginning of the war, however, construction work advanced at a much slower pace and, from 1943 on, it practically came to a halt. The opening of the new airport for scheduled air traffic did not take place during the National Socialist era; flights continued to take off and land on the site of the existing, 1920s airport.

War use and wartime destruction

During the war years, the boarding area, railway tunnel and other underground parts of the complex were converted into produc-

tion facilities for the assembly of fighter planes. Office space served as makeshift accommodation for personnel. At the end of the war, many of the underground cellars were used as air-raid shelters. Protection against bombs, by specially designed ceilings in the cellars and on the ground floor, was included in the original plans.

For lack of archives here, the extent of the wartime destruction of the airport buildings is difficult to ascertain precisely today; photographs show considerable damage to the structure. During the last phase of the war, bomb blasts damaged some parts of the building, façades were badly pock-marked by bullets and grenade splinters. During the fires that raged during the first months after the end of the war in particular, interiors and wall cladding suffered considerably and elements of the steel hangar construction were partially deformed by heat. Stains and marks of burning left by the flames leaping from the windows are still visible today.

At the end of the war, Soviet forces took over the site for nine weeks. During this period, the entire contents of the film bunker was also destroyed by fire, destroying all knowledge of what these films recorded. On 4 July 1945, American airborne troops took Tempelhof over for their own military uses.

The Berlin blockade

During the blockade imposed by the Soviet occupying forces on the Western sector of Berlin (24 June 1948 to 12 May 1949), the isolated city could only be supplied via air corridors, in the form of an airlift. Within a very short time, new unloading zones, maintenance installations and modern air traffic control facilities were installed at Tempelhof. New runways were built, with provisional paving.

Reconstruction

In accordance with changing uses and particularly during the first years after the war, individual parts of the airport were gradually rebuilt in their original state, while extensive structural changes were also carried out. These phases of reconstruction and alteration can be summarised as follows:

- 1945–93: repair to war damage and ongoing modifications by the United States Air Force
- 1950–4: first reconstruction by the Berliner Flughafen Gesellschaft (BFG), and creation of a provisional departures hall, the so-called 'Gate to the World'
- 1959–62: second reconstruction, comprising an extension of the departures hall and new runways
- 1975: closure to civil air traffic
- 1985: resumption of domestic flights
- from 1993: modifications following the departure of the US Air Force.

After the complete withdrawal of the United States Air Force in 1993, the entire site was handed over to be administered and exploited by the Berliner Flughafen Gesellschaft. According to recent legal clarifications about the ownership of the property, the Federal Republic of Germany (Higher Financial Directorate) is the principal owner of the buildings and airfield site, a smaller share, of about 20 per cent, belonging to the Land of Berlin.

About 30 per cent of the rented areas, in particular in the former American part, have remained unused up to the present day. Other parts have been rented out to various organisations and private companies, a process still in progress. Many of the building's interiors have been considerably

modified to meet the requirements of these new users. The resulting alterations to the historic fabric, often carried out in total ignorance of the historic significance of the airport complex and its original structure, have disfigured parts of the building, causing often irreversible damage.

Inventory

The present-day appearance of the airport, structuring the surrounding urban space, still speaks the language of the 1930s, but, inside and out, the complex also bears witness to the alterations resulting from successive post-war uses. It is still strongly marked, for example, by the almost symmetrical division, up to 1993, between the eastern, administered by the Americans, and the western half, run by the Germans. On the whole, both halves suggest that during work carried out to repair war damage, to complete the building complex and to repair the façades, efforts were made to respect the existing vocabulary of materials and forms.

This meant, for example, that facing work or new additions to the cladding in stone were carried out, as far as possible, using identical materials. Openings were only changed in exceptional cases. Windows were extensively repaired, often preserved in their original style or in a sympathetic modern version. A few, however, have been restored using other techniques, with glazing bars in aluminium or synthetic materials. These new windows show little respect for the dimensions and contours of the original window frames, for example, the struts of the windows in the former workshop areas.

In both halves, the hangars, with their steel truss construction, sliding doors, floor paving and façades between the workshops and administration offices and the landside glazing of the hall have remained unchanged, except where their colour scheme is concerned. In the eastern part, however, the former galleries have been almost totally disfigured with an additional office floor on the airfield side, leaving the original skylights in glass blocks above the lower levels with no proper function.

The open boarding area, with its sheltered façade to the rear, has been only slightly modified in terms of materials and appearance. Here again, as with the entire apron and the surrounding taxiway of the airfield, most of the original paving stones of

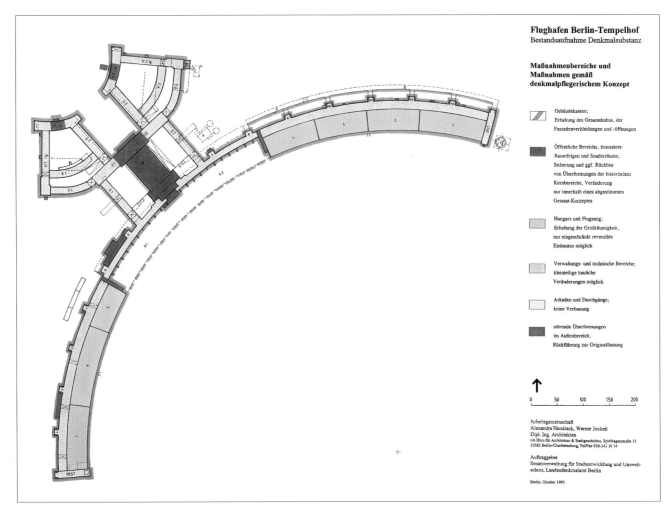

Flughafen Berlin-Tempelhof
Bestandsaufnahme Denkmalsubstanz

Maßnahmenbereiche und
Maßnahmen gemäß
denkmalpflegerischem Konzept

Gebäudekanten;
Erhaltung des Gesamtkubus, der
Fassadenverkleidungen und -öffnungen

Öffentliche Bereiche, besondere
Raumfolgen und Sonderräume;
Sicherung und ggf. Rückbau
von Überformungen der historischen
Kernbereiche, Veränderung
nur innerhalb eines abgestimmten
Gesamt-Konzeptes

Hangars und Flugsteig;
Erhaltung der Großräumigkeit,
nur eingeschränkt reversible
Einbauten möglich

Verwaltungs- und technische Bereiche;
kleinteilige bauliche
Veränderungen möglich

Arkaden und Durchgänge;
keine Verbauung

störende Überformungen
im Außenbereich;
Rückführung zur Originalfassung

0   50   100   150   200

Arbeitsgemeinschaft
Alexandra Handrack, Werner Jockeit
Dipl. Ing. Architekten
c/o Büro für Architektur & Stadtgeschichte, Spichagenstraße 13
10585 Berlin-Charlottenburg, Tel/Fax 030-341 10 14

Auftraggeber
Senatsverwaltung für Stadtentwicklung und Umweltschutz, Landesdenkmalamt Berlin

Berlin, Oktober 1995

Conservation plan, principal zones and recommendations.

Building contours: conservation of the entire mass, cladding and openings.

Public areas and specific spaces: conservation and, if necessary, removal of alterations in the central historic areas; modifications possible only within an agreed overall concept.

Hangars and boarding area: preservation of the large volumes; only reversible additions possible.

Administration and technical areas: structural changes involving minor components possible.

Arcades and passageways: no obstructing constructions. Removal of alterations to the outer façade: restoration to the original state.

basaltin have survived. The railway track that originally skirted the hangars to the rear, however, has been removed.

The addition of traffic lanes, bus stops, car parks, central lighting and a boundary fence has considerably changed the fore-court and its spatial appearance. Vestiges of the original, two-toned paving stones are only visible in the middle of the forecourt.

To the east, the lower Bunkerstraße has largely retained its original plaster and con-crete facing, the basaltin paving and the two parallel railway tracks, although these are no longer in use. The passageways in the lower parts of the stair towers have been walled up, as in the western part, and the interiors are partly used for other purposes.

The maze-like 'underworld' of the airport with its network of cellars, tunnels, water mains and sewage channels has seen hardly any change, just like the vast attic spaces above. Original equipment such as switch-boards and machines has also survived, especially in the technical areas.

Under the central part of the building, the railway tunnel, as well as the ceilings over some other areas (the upper Bunker-straße to the east, for example), show traces of serious deterioration of the concrete, resulting from insufficient covering of the reinforcements. Access to these zones has

been closed off. The concrete floors of the stair towers in the western part were also damaged and remain in their unfinished, pre-war state.

Recommendations

General situation

As far as its documentary values and its characteristic structural expression are con-cerned, the best way of ensuring the long-term conservation of a historic monument and its immediate surroundings is to retain its original use. This present text, however, is perhaps not the appropriate place to set out the political, ecological and economic argu-ments concerning Tempelhof's aeronautical future, its total or partial conversion, or the development of its airfield.

In the course of any repair or mainte-nance work on each of the airport's build-ings, the original fabric, along with the traces of its history, are to be respected and conserved as far as possible. If preservation of the heritage means replacing certain building elements and materials, every effort must be made to find identical qualities, or qualities that are as close as possible to the original, with appropriate craftsmanship as well as the original colours, insofar as this is financially feasible. Additions of modern elements (such as technical facilities or temporary fixtures in the hangars or changes to the layout of the boarding zone) should use recognisably contemporary forms that do not irreversibly compromise the original fabric or dominate it.

Recommendations, approved by the relevant planning bodies, should be drawn up by experts for the necessary and recurrent alterations to details concerning, for example, protection against the sun, suspended ceilings, light fixtures and air-conditioning systems on the façades.

The legibility of the various phases of use, such as the differences in terms of refurbishment between the eastern part used by the Americans in the decades after the war and the western part occupied by the Germans, should be conserved as historic traces as long as they do not detract from the original conceptual and aesthetic relations of the whole.

These recommendations basically come down to:

- the conservation of the original fabric and later historical alterations
- new additions and modifications being carried out in appropriate dimensions, materials and contemporary forms
- colours in accordance with those defined by paint analysis or according to an agreed design concept.

The heritage administration responsible for the airport should be informed of any intentions to change any elements defined in the inventory and, if necessary, a planning application is to be submitted. Other authorisations for the control of work that might be necessary remain unaffected by this stipulation.

Exterior

The façades of the buildings determine the airport's urban space and overall appearance, characterised by its sparse, almost minimalist use of carefully chosen materials and by the marked repetition of standard design forms. In order to preserve the coherence of this historic place in all its complexity, it is particularly important to maintain this appearance. This might require the reversal of certain alterations such as small extensions, repair work or replacements that have failed to respect this original state, for example, where window and door features are concerned, or natural stone details.

Interiors

From a heritage point of view, the clearly differentiated zones, divided according to the structural and functional organisation of the plan – public areas, special spaces and spatial sequences, administration areas, technical areas – are of varying significance and present different levels of priority for their conservation. The conservation plan includes a series of floor plans, on a scale of 1:500, indicating by a colour code the level of heritage interest of the different parts of the ensemble:

- A (red): areas of outstanding heritage interest, mainly the prestigious public areas, the technical monuments and historically important areas, along with some richly decorated rooms
- B (yellow): areas of special heritage interest; mainly the semi-public areas and particular technical features
- C (green): areas of less particular interest; mainly the offices, private areas and other secondary spaces.

Public areas

For both the past and the present, although social and political conditions are very different, these public areas are the centre of the complex, giving it content, meaning and prestige. They are awarded the highest priority.

With its boundary fence dating from the airport's military use, its central lighting, asphalt traffic lanes, bus stops, crash-barriers for the taxi rank and car parks, the courtyard of honour today retains few welcoming qualities for the visiting public. Even a dubious return to its original monumental layout would bring little improvement. For this courtyard, a new, sensitive solution must be found that integrates the original paving stones, the arcades and the façades of this area. With a drastic reduction of the surface occupied by parked cars, for example, arriving and leaving via this courtyard could become a pleasant experience.

At the end of the courtyard, the long colonnade of the porch was originally open, but, during the 1960s, its central part was enclosed to create a lobby.

Behind, the height of the original reception hall has been reduced to less than half by the creation of a false ceiling. How the upper part of this hall can be reintegrated in spatial terms and/or used as a particularly

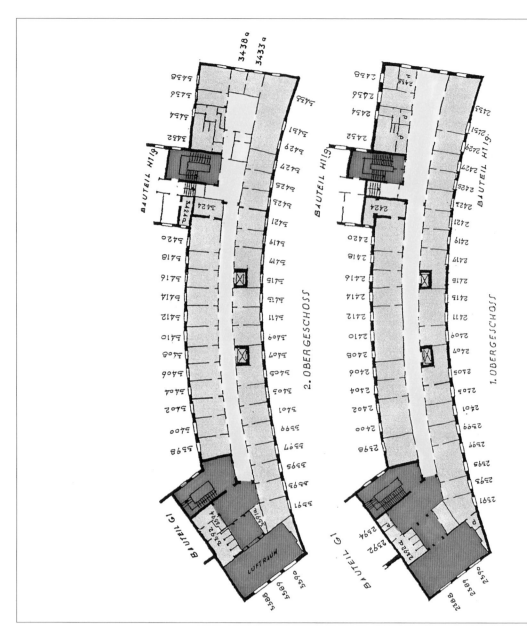

Conservation priorities; the example of the building to the east of the Platz der Luftbrücke; from right to left: second floor, first floor, ground floor and two basement levels. Key: Red – areas of outstanding heritage interest; Yellow – areas of special heritage interest; Green – areas of heritage interest.

striking history lesson in its still unfinished state must be the object of future discussions. This part of the hall is threatened today by serious dilapidation and should be structurally stabilised in its present state, including all its historical traces.

The departures hall is characterised by several successive phases of repair, refurbishment and alteration. Up to now, a satisfactory solution combining the hall's spatial and functional aspects, its aesthetic qualities and its historic perspective has not been found. Here, a better and less banal environment should be created, by means of new flooring, the reorganisation of the galleries, greater transparency towards the airfield, and the consequential modification of the passport control zone.

The boarding area has changed very little from its original state. In the former American part, the undersides of the staircases that were covered up should be exposed again, and the modified doorways and accesses to the underground level should be restored.

Special spaces and spatial sequences

These are important original or later interiors to which the public has only limited access and require particular attention because of the relative completeness of their historic fabric and their significance in each part of the construction or within the overall context. These areas illustrate one or several construction phases and can be read as a kind of architectural history book.

Alongside the various halls and large rooms that were completed during the war, the alterations carried out by the United States Air Force have been largely preserved. Like the uncompleted staircases leading to the planned viewing terraces, these represent significant phases of development, bearing witness to their time. The staircases,

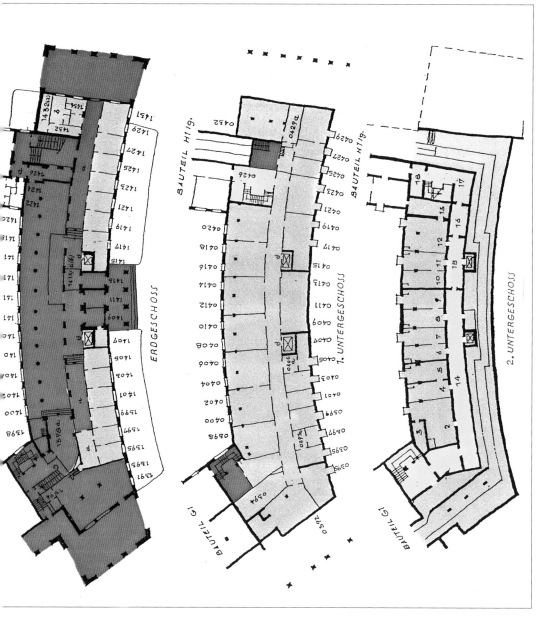

which are partly closed off today, should be left as they are, neither completed nor converted, but opened to the public during guided tours. The much-altered lower access areas of the stair towers should be redesigned accordingly.

Administration areas

These areas comprise the bulk of the available built surfaces and at the same time constitute the impressively monumental urban structure dominating the landside. The finishes of staircases, corridors, office and meeting rooms, as well as accommodation facilities, were complete down to the last detail: wall tiling, doors, handles, overlights in the corridors and fitted cupboards in the offices. In these areas, the refurbishments carried out by the United States Air Force and other users should be kept for their historical value, but at the same time a coherent concept must be defined anew to reveal the basic elements of the original design. This is particularly important with large numbers of tenants occupying the offices, each with specific, individual requirements.

Technical areas

The airside of the building is characterised by technical areas, by the roof structure of the hangars, the hangars themselves and the apron. The architecture here can still be seen as modern in terms of its response to functional and technical requirements, and particularly in contrast with the more ideologically modelled landside of the airport. For this reason, conservation planning ensuring respect for the original state is of particular importance, especially where the future use of the large, attractive volumes of the hangars is concerned. This means that the buildings to the rear which are still intact should no longer be disfigured by additional storeys and that new additions necessary inside the hangars should only be removable, inserted elements.

Beyond the hangars, on the landside, the ground floors of this 'coat-hanger' building are partly designed as two-storey workshops. This original function – documented by details such as doors and passages, workshop windows, flooring, gantry cranes and ramps – must remain recognisable. The same applies to the garage and technical areas inside the freight courtyards

The tunnel under the central areas, with its railway lines, gantry and other original components such as bare concrete and paving, etc, also has a lot to say about the airport's wartime use for aircraft manufacture. Similarly, the railway tracks and the original paved floors and concrete of the lower Bunkerstraße must be preserved as it is. Repair work on the degraded concrete ceiling and walls must be carried out in such a way as not to affect the original appearance.

Underground elements such as the water works, the power station, the 'film-bunker', technical and basement areas (for example, the luggage-handling floor), mains systems, tunnels and also the attics are essential components of the functional infrastructure and are of considerable historical interest. Original details such as control panels, electrical equipment, tiling and glazing should also be kept.

Aviation guidance devices and constructions such as radar antennae and the radar tower are functional expressions of the development of air traffic control systems and should be considered as structures designed to keep up with technological developments, grafted on to the original architecture.

Outside features

The outside areas cannot be dissociated from the buildings and should therefore be conserved in their original state, where this is still possible. The different types of paving stones (basalt, concrete) represent important functional features on the Bunkerstraße and, above all on the apron and on the surviving taxiways, with their large waiting areas at the southern edge of the airfield. This is also true of the drainage sewers, covered with cast-iron grids. Any alterations to the paved surfaces and roadways, the erection of new barriers, bollards or signs, as well as the layout of neighbouring green areas must take place within an agreed overall concept that respects the monument.

A single surviving building, marks on the ground, vestiges of old access roads, as well as tree and shrub growth, still provide visible evidence of the location of the first Tempelhof terminal, situated towards the middle of the present-day airfield. These traces should be preserved and included in the conservation plan for their documentary value and in order to respect the composition of the flying field's landscape.

The absence of real estate pressures on the site and buildings today, and in the foreseeable future, perhaps offers a unique opportunity for further reflection while awaiting developments. Officially, the political decisions taken at city and regional levels for the associated closure of Tempelhof and construction of a major new airport at Schönefeld by the year 2007 are repeatedly confirmed, although this project is increasingly uncertain and the economic arguments for giving Tempelhof an important future role for short-haul flights and business traffic remain strong. During this interlude, any measures that might destroy the essence of the historic monument, and which might impair a possible future function as a city-airport should be avoided at all costs.

Notes

1 The complete conservation plan, drawn up by the Büro für Architektur & Stadtgeschichte, Berlin (Werner Jockeit, Alexandra Handrack), can be consulted at the Landesdenkmalamt Berlin.

2 Paragraph 8, section 3, of the Berlin heritage law (DSchG Bln 95): 'For historic monuments, the preparation of conservation statements can be ordered by the authorised representatives of the heritage body responsible, when this is deemed necessary for the lasting conservation of the monument as well as for the dissemination of knowledge about the monument and its heritage values. As far as reasonably possible, historic monuments are to be kept and maintained in accordance with these conservation statements.'

The lessons of Speke airport: striking the balance between conservation, designation and regeneration

Bob Hawkins

When the Raphael project was only a gleam in the eyes of our colleagues at the French Direction de l'Architecture et du Patrimoine, the future of the first Liverpool airport site at Speke had been largely decided. By this time, the proposals for the physical and economic regeneration of the Speke-Garston area of Liverpool were well-advanced and already included proposals for the adaptive reuse of the terminal building, control tower and hangars of the old airport, the remodelling and redevelopment of surrounding areas, including part of the flying field, the demolition of redundant buildings and the development of a commerce park with a network of new roads, new buildings and attendant hard and soft landscaping. The proposals, developed as part of a coordinated and phased campaign, had evolved following the creation of the Speke-Garston Development Company and the £14.5 million tranche of European funding that was intended for a number of key sites within its operational area.

When we first began to discuss the 'L'Europe de l'Air' project, my initial feelings were that the principal contribution that we in England could make was by illustrating the extent of the missed opportunity at Speke so that, if similar opportunities occurred at Tempelhof, Le Bourget or other key civil aviation sites in Europe, they could be grasped at a sufficiently early stage in the proposals for change. For it seemed most important that the very special character of these first-generation civil aviation sites was not needlessly compromised or lost altogether as a result of ignorance, indifference or the absence of mechanisms to protect what is clearly emerging, in my view, as a highly significant part of a common European cultural heritage. As our project has progressed, however, I have become more optimistic about the possible outcomes at Speke and more convinced of the need to define, in agreement with our European partners, firstly what it is that characterises the special interest of historic civil aviation sites and, secondly, to develop a common strategy for evaluation and protection that

can be successfully expressed through different legislative and regulatory systems.

It is already apparent that the importance of Speke as the most complete site of its period in England is further enhanced by its association with Tempelhof and Le Bourget, recognised as the most important of each nation's civil aviation sites in their day. These associations, which express both the present-day relationship of the three historic airports and the former operational links between sites forming part of the earliest international air routes, are valued not only by those concerned with heritage issues, but also by organisations involved in the future development of Speke. Being placed alongside the airports of two capital cities is seen as an added cachet, something that can enhance the image of the regenerated complex of buildings at Speke. It is this shared perception that I hope will enable us to play a part in shaping the next evolutionary phase of Speke's history. Such involvement need not pose a threat to the general thrust of the redevelopment proposals or necessarily inhibit their scope. But we would like to ensure that the perceptions of significance that are developing through the project are given serious consideration as the detailed proposals for the airfield emerge.

For the partners in the Speke-Garston initiative, our aspirations are expressed at the very end of the eleventh hour. It is clear that their proposals were being developed at precisely the same time as English Heritage's thematic research programmes for civil and military aviation sites were being progressed. The initial impact of these programmes on the proposed developments at Speke was to demonstrate the significance of the surviving group of airport buildings and provide justification for the upgrading of the already listed buildings to Grade II*.

The buildings at Speke had been listed at Grade II in 1985. These upgradings and the listing of the sculptural gatepiers at the entrances to the airport, while helping to secure the future of historic structures at the airport, also demonstrate the limited effectiveness of a building-based system of

evaluation and protection; one that is not able to reflect the significance of an historic landscape created in the first half of the 20th century by the establishment of runways, taxiing areas, aprons to hangars and the terminal, alongside the rest of the airport's buildings. While the concepts of 'curtilage' – the area of land deemed to be associated with the functioning or usage of a building or group of buildings – and 'setting' are recognised in planning legislation as material considerations when considering changes likely to affect a listed building, their effect is usually limited to immediate surroundings and is not normaly held to apply to very large spaces extending a considerable distance from the building group. The curtilage of a listed country house, for instance, would not be held to include the whole of its parkland and its supporting estate, and generally such supporting landscapes, whether parks, factory yards or burial grounds, are indeed secondary in importance to the building they were created to serve. For an airport, however, the reverse could be argued; without the level field, the runways, the space to land and take off, there could be no airport and no need for terminal, hangars or gatepiers. The

airfield can be considered to be the primary historic component, a composite historic landscape in which the significant secondary components are located, which may themselves merit individual or group designation appropriate to their form, but which are also recognised as parts of a greater whole. In such circumstances, the principal designation needs to be that which recognises and protects the historic landscape.

When the buildings at Speke were first listed, the two designations of landscape protection that we have today were available, both of which can be deployed in recognition of extended or limited landscapes where appropriate. One designation, scheduling, is the responsibility of central government; the other, the designation of conservation areas, is carried out by local government. Both are discretionary. Scheduling is conventionally used in circumstances where archaeological sites and landscapes considered to be of national significance have been identified, and where there is a presumption against change and development. Conservation area designation offers much more flexible and locally-regulated means of recognising, protecting and enhancing valued landscapes, where the

preservation or enhancement of the 'character and appearance' of such areas is considered to be necessary and desirable. Originally used primarily for urban landscapes, the concept has been developed creatively in rural areas and in industrial landscapes, where the ratio of buildings to open space is very low and where the primary objective is the recognition of landscape distinctiveness. Within such areas are located significant landscape features such as field systems, ponds, plantations, spoil heaps, enclosures and buildings which, though not of listable quality, nevertheless illustrate how the landscape was used and the phases of its use. They also often have, as central features, transport systems and associated structures, canals, packhorse routes, railways, tramways, bridges, viaducts, and so on. While it has always been possible to list railway stations, canal bridges and tollhouses, it is only within conservation areas that such structures can be understood and treated in context, rather than, as has been the case with the Speke terminal and hangars, as structures of individual significance, without reference to their context and setting. We now have examples of conservation areas designated around industrial complexes and sections of canals. More recently, following our research on military aviation sites, proposals for conservation area designation as a means of managing change at Bicester airfield in Oxfordshire are being considered, as Jeremy Lake explains in his contribution in this book. Conservation area legislation provides for a less rigid management regime that can be tailored to the special characteristics of the area and can often accommodate levels of development and change considered unacceptable in or around listed buildings.

In England, the mechanisms of listing, scheduling and conservation area designation have been used individually and in combination to assign value to and regulate development affecting elements of historic transportation systems. The monuments of historic road, canal and railway networks are strongly represented in lists and schedules and rightly so, if we consider their contribution to our cultural development. The newly-defined importance of historic aviation sites that is emerging as a result of current thematic research is a challenge to the scope of existing designations. To be even partially effective these designations are perhaps best deployed in combination, to achieve both recognition and appropriate

levels of regulation in instances where comprehensive development proposals, such as those at Speke, need to be assessed from the different but complimentary perspectives of landscape management and building conservation.

All this is easy to say in hindsight. Although the listing of individual buildings has long been an accepted factor in planning terms, however unpopular or inconvenient, it would have been a very brave or innovative local authority that would have designated a conservation area at Speke airport at the precise moment in the region's economic history when a once-in-a-millenium funding package for redevelopment and regeneration had been negotiated. Such a proposal would probably have been seen as strongly anti-development and rejected as being an unjustifiable and inappropriate use of conservation area legislation. Yet at present, in different parts of England and particularly in historic industrial locations such as Ancoats in Manchester, the Jewellery Quarter in Birmingham or the Duke Street area in Liverpool, programmes of regeneration are underway using the existence of conservation

Top: *Landside view of the terminal building in 1999, prior to restoration work (photo Mike Williams © English Heritage)*

Restoration work in progress on hangar number 1 in 1999 (photo Mike Williams © English Heritage)

Interior of hangar number 2 in 1999, prior to restoration work (photo Mike Williams © English Heritage)

areas as their justification. They are not seen as areas where development and change are incompatible with conservation objectives but as places where legitimate and much-needed development strategies, involving substantial levels of change to both historic buildings and distinctive urban landscapes, are balanced and tempered by an appreciation of the special character of the areas in which they are to take place.

It is a lack of balance that most forcefully expresses the missed opportunity at Speke from the conservation perspective. The imaginative proposals for the reuse of the historic buildings on the site, developed as a significant element of a dynamic and positive regeneration strategy, are not complemented by any measure that acknowledges the special interest of the airfield as the core component of an historic airport. The lack of any form of designation that registers this special quality, and which recognises the buildings and flying field as one historic landscape, leaves us now with persuasion as a means of negotiating what we consider to be a more sympathetic outcome for the airfield within the context of the development proposals.

I am not suggesting any of this as an implied criticism of the Speke-Garston Development Company, which throughout the planning stages of its project has taken proper account of the listed status of the buildings at Speke, and which clearly values the contribution they will make, in their refurbished form, to the overall strategy. The company has also responded positively in negotiations with the National Trust, whose Speke Hall site rests in a wedge of historic landscape between the old and new airports, directly south of the proposed Estuary Commerce Park. The Trust's interest in establishing a wildlife conservation zone between the estuary and the proposed development areas has been accommodated, without apparent detriment to development proposals. Another of the company's regeneration projects is centred on what is

acknowledged as 'one of Merseyside's best-known industrial landmarks', the former Bryant & May match factory, one of the earliest examples of flat slab construction in Britain and now a listed building. With major historic buildings located on or near to four of its key sites, the Speke-Garston Company may well feel, and with considerable justification, that it has taken full account of all the identified built heritage issues in developing its overall area strategy.

To have a realistic chance of influencing the development and implementation of this strategy, and of placing our perceptions of the special interest of the airfield as an historic landscape on the agenda, we need good answers to two important questions: is such an intervention justifiable and, if we believe it is, by what means do we intervene? I believe the intervention is fully justified by what we now know about Speke airport and other first-generation survivals in Europe. They are landmark sites in the development of transport and communication by air, representing benign and life-enhancing application of a technology that, within one century, has made both travel to the moon and inter-continental aerial warfare possible. We are uncomfortably close both to their creation and their demise as we try to assess their contribution to our culture, but we cannot ignore the need to do so when, as at Speke and at Tempelhof, perceived development opportunities threaten the integrity of what we consider to be of international significance.

But at this stage, at Speke, I believe the only defensible means of intervention is by initiating and informing a new debate as to the most appropriated ways of remodelling the historic airfield landscape. If the development process were to begin today, knowing what we believe to be the significance of Speke, the opportunity would exist to develop a conservation plan for the airfield that identified built conservation issues and constraints on development that might flow from them, as well as adaptive reuses and landscape enhancement opportunities that could form components of a reuse strategy which recognised both development potential and conservation sensitivities. This plan would have been used to help shape and inform the development strategy for the site from the outset and would have given due weight to conservation issues at the earliest opportunity.

What we might attempt now is the creation of a conservation plan for this moment

in the development process, where a full range of conservation objectives could be identified in the context of current perceptions of heritage significance. Development decisions that either coincided with conservation objectives or had a neutral impact upon them could be noted, together with those, benign or not in conservation terms, which had already been implemented. Proposals yet to be carried out, or phases of development yet to be planned that might threaten conservation assets, could be identified, and the nature and likely extent of the threats assessed. Proposals that seem likely to imply high levels of loss or damage could be re-examined to see if alternative means of achieving the same development objectives were feasible. Such alternatives might include the re-alignment of lines of development and access roads rather than any reduction in density or quantity, different shapes for areas of open pace and different forms of landscape definition and enhancement, so as to take account more consciously of former runway dimensions and alignments and the evolution of the open airfield landscape, the airport's essential physical characteristic. If it might be possible to modify existing proposals without significant loss of development potential, surely the opportunity should at least be considered. And it should be considered in the interests not only of Speke, but also those of the many other aviation sites, both civil and military, where the same debate will run and where new perceptions of significance will be used to challenge previously unquestioned development expectations.

The Raphael project has provided the opportunity to define and express this viewpoint outside of the procedures through which English Heritage, local authorities and development companies normally interact. The suggested intervention, however theoretical and optimistic in nature, is nevertheless intended to be a positive one, intended to enhance rather than stifle the creative forces at work at Speke, and to create a new opportunity rather than merely to bemoan a missed one. Since the time of the Liverpool workshop, at which the above paper was delivered, the terminal complex at the former Liverpool Speke airport has been completely transformed. The terminal building has been repaired, refurbished and extended, and developed into a four-star hotel, the number one hangar is now a highly successful sports centre, and the number two hangar awaits confirmation of a new use, its historic fabric, including the 'Lamella' roof structure, now carefully repaired. Far from being a missed opportunity, the site is now widely regarded as the flagship project of the Speke-Garston regeneration programme, and the epitome of a spectacular revival of the area's economic rebirth, with industrial and commercial development centred around the former airfield, the new John Lennon airport and the Jaguar car plant.

The refurbishment of the terminal complex brought a new partner to the Raphael Project – the Speke-Garston Development Company – and a new perspective on the range of options available to those seeking viable new uses for historic airport sites. On one level, Liverpool's Speke Airport can be seen as an outstanding example of creative adaptive reuse, transforming abandoned and neglected historic aviation buildings into 21st-century commercial assets. However, it is now clear that this success will not include the retention of the airport's flying field, which will become a redeveloped landscape. No matter how well-designed the new buildings might be, the context and setting of the original terminal building – the vast expanse of open ground extending down to the waters of the Mersey Estuary – will be completely lost. Perhaps we will have to rely on the sights and sounds of the nearby John Lennon airfield to remind us of why this part of Liverpool's hinterland proved so attractive to the airport planners of the 1930s, and why the terminal complex came to be sited where it was. Though we might avoid the incremental obliteration of an historic airfield landscape such as happened at Croydon, and developments at Speke might be more carefully ordered and rationally planned, the loss may be all the more profound – because we already understood the significance of the airfield landscape we witnessed being destroyed.

Interior of the terminal prior to restoration, showing the base of the control tower (photo Mike Williams © English Heritage)

The Speke-Garston Development Company and the Raphael 'L'Europe de l'Air' project

Bob Lane

When the original plans for Speke airport's facilities were conceived in 1931, they included a hotel. Remarkably, it was seventy years later before these plans came to fruition, albeit in a roundabout way, when Marriott opened their 160-bedroom hotel created within what by then had long been a Merseyside landmark, the Grade II* listed Art Deco former terminal building. This grand event, performed by the Duke of York, heralded the start of another chapter in the amazing story of the site that has been given a new lease of life by the local regeneration agency, Speke-Garston Development Company, and private sector partner, Neptune Developments.

History

The story had begun in 1930 when ground was levelled to create Speke airfield. The first plane to land on the grass runway was a twenty-seater Imperial Airways Armstrong Whitworth Argosy, inaugurating an experimental air service linking Liverpool to several continental cities. Speke airport proper was officially opened in 1933 by The Marquess of Londonderry, the Secretary of State for Air, and in 1937 Lord Derby opened the 90ft (27m)-high control tower and hangar number 1. Hangar number 1, then the largest building of its kind in the country, is now home to a successful David Lloyd Leisure Centre.

In 1939 the airport was requisitioned by the government and various squadrons were based there during the war although its main role was as a base for assembling and testing aircraft, including 11,000 American planes. After the war the airport remained in the hands of the Ministry of Civil Aviation with a visitor noting, in 1949, that although the terminal buildings were the finest in the land, the airport as a whole was semi-derelict. During the next fifty years, there were a number of highlights in the story of Speke airport. In June 1950 the world's first scheduled helicopter passenger service was launched at the airport. In the 1960s it became world famous as a backdrop to the crowds of screaming teenage girls welcoming the Beatles home from their tours. Similarly, in the 1970s and 1980s, the airport was besieged by fans greeting Liverpool Football Club home from their European soccer successes. Concorde landed at Speke for the first time in August 1979 and became a regular visitor, especially during Grand National racing meetings at nearby Aintree. And in 1982 thousands of people gathered to see the Pope arrive and kiss the tarmac before his historic visit to Liverpool.

Overall, however, the airport had been in decline for many years, frequently losing out to near neighbour Manchester in the drive for investment and services. Ironically, the fate of the old terminal complex had finally been sealed in 1966 when the airport's new runway, capable of handling jet aircraft, was opened by the Duke of Edinburgh on land closer to the River Mersey. For many years flights leaving the airport were preceded by a long taxi around the old runways, through a link and on to the new runway. But inevitably it made sense for any new developments to be sited next to this runway. In 1986, with a new terminal building and control tower up and running at the new site, the 1930s complex had been abandoned with the former airfield taking on an increasingly neglected and derelict look. Except for a few private aircraft which continued to be based in old wartime hangars, the airport lay derelict for ten years with only its listed status preventing demolition.

The problems at the airport were mirrored elsewhere in Speke-Garston. The area once known as 'the engine room of Merseyside' had been badly hit by the decline of manufacturing industry and port-related business linked to the nearby Garston Docks. Consequently, Speke-Garston was suffering from very high unemployment. The rate in 1996 was 21.5 per cent, significantly above the Merseyside rate at the time of 18.5 per cent and the national average of 9.5 per cent. Of those out of work in Speke-Garston, 48.7 per cent were long-term unemployed.

It was against this background that Speke-Garston Development Company was formed in late 1996 as a joint venture between the Northwest Development Agency and Liverpool City Council, backed by significant funding from Europe. The company's key objective was to develop new sites and premises in Speke-Garston and to attract investment and much-needed jobs to the area to fill them. Naturally, the former Speke airport site was integral to the Development Company's plans and proposals were sought both for the redevelopment of the airfield and the terminal complex.

Speke-Garston Development Company faced many problems when it inherited the airport site in 1996. The disused flying field presented the company's best opportunity for an early impact and a masterplan was quickly drawn up for the development of a business park. While the possibility of utilising the existing runway pattern for the key infrastructure was considered, it was not a workable solution in terms of the need to create a viable high-quality development capable of attracting much-needed new jobs to the area. The biggest potential problem was the trio of listed buildings, hangar number 1, hangar number 2 and the original terminal building. These were in a very poor state of repair and were a physical blight on the area. Initially, consideration was given to the possibility of demolishing the buildings and specialist consultants were engaged to look into this issue. The conclusion of the study was that there was little prospect of securing consent for demolition, and that the core buildings presented a very real opportunity to create a significant landmark focal point for the regeneration of the Speke-Garston area.

The emphasis then changed to identifying a suitable range of potential uses for these very specialised buildings. These needed to be economically viable, after public-sector subsidy for capital works, and to create local employment opportunities. Potential uses included a hotel – very important in any successful commercial area and also for the nearby Liverpool Airport – leisure, a museum and an event or conference-type venue. The interest of the European Raphael Project in the buildings was beneficial in ensuring that the developers produced proposals of sufficient quality, particularly in terms of the need to secure significant levels of public-sector support funding to enable the works to proceed.

Estuary Commerce Park

The Development Company's first priority was to redevelop the former northern airfield into a high-quality business park. The Estuary Commerce Park, launched in 1997, was the first aerodrome-related project to get under way. The Estuary has been the Development Company's flagship project since day one and is now regarded as Merseyside's premier business park. The first phase of the scheme, developed by MEPC and Intercity, offers a 40-hectare, superbly landscaped, park-style, business environment with striking water features designed to attract the highest calibre of investor. A broad, dual-lane entry boulevard with separate pedestrian ways, cycle paths and landscaped parking areas enhance the 'quality' feel of the development which has attracted interest from national and international business names. Occupiers include Capital Bank whose £15 million call centre and operations unit on the site has brought upwards of 800 jobs to Speke-Garston. Other developments at The Estuary include a new distribution centre for international couriers DHL and new headquarters

Top: The David Lloyd Leisure Centre in hangar number 1, with its outdoor swimming pool (photo Mike Williams © English Heritage)

Hangar number 1 with its new glass curtain wall behind the hangar doors, left open (photo Mike Williams © English Heritage)

The Marriott Hotel, installed in the terminal building, with its new extensions on the landside (photo Mike Williams © English Heritage)

buildings for two local companies, chocolate manufacturer Classic Couverture and pharmaceutical supplies firm PSL. A major speculative office development is also due to get under way at the site. The Development Company has also linked up with Liverpool Airport owners Peel Holdings on a major expansion of The Estuary, opening up a further 97 hectares of land for development and ensuring that Speke-Garston has an ongoing supply of quality sites to offer potential inward investors in the future.

'The Aerodrome' scheme

As work began on the Estuary Commerce Park the attention of the Development Company turned to the former terminal complex. After assessing a number of submissions in a competition designed to find realistic future uses for the site, approval was given to Neptune Developments' proposal for a £22 million scheme to convert the terminal building and hangar number 1 into a hotel and leisure complex. Neptune are a well-known Merseyside-based company who have been a major player in the renaissance of Liverpool. During the past three years they have developed more than 1.5 million sq ft (139,350 sq m) of office, leisure and retail space creating more than 1,300 jobs including the £90 million Queen Square development in Liverpool city centre. Investment for the redevelopment of the terminal building and hangar number 1 came from Neptune, hotel and leisure giant Whitbread, the Northwest Development Agency and the European Union.

Hangar number 1

The first project to open at the site was a David Lloyd Leisure Centre in hangar number 1. The facility opened its doors in early 2000 and has proved to be one of David Lloyd's most successful outlets. The centre houses six indoor and six outdoor tennis

courts, indoor and outdoor swimming pools, squash and badminton courts, a fitness suite and an aerobics studio as well as bar and restaurant areas. It also offers conference facilities, a Sanctuary health and beauty spa, a hairdressers, sports shop and a crèche. The redevelopment of hangar number 1 has been widely praised for the way it has created a high-tech leisure facility while retaining and restoring the architecturally important Art Deco features of the building.

Marriott Hotel, Liverpool South

Fifteen months later, the second part of Neptune's scheme came to fruition with the opening of the 160-bedroom Marriott Hotel. The original terminal building was refurbished to create the hotel's reception, restaurant, conference and banqueting facilities with the accommodation being housed in two newly built bedroom blocks. A remarkable twin-level executive suite is housed at the base of the former control tower. Once again, the building's original features have been carefully preserved and restored with the new areas and internal decoration reflecting its rich Art Deco heritage.

Together, the hotel and leisure centre have brought all the benefits associated with these major national and international chains to Speke-Garston and both facilities are being well used by local residents and people working in or visiting businesses in the area. The importance of the hotel development was reflected in the fact that it was granted a royal official opening in the summer of 2001 when the Duke of York visited Merseyside to perform the ceremony. In the autumn of that year the distinguished history of the site was recalled when a replica of a vintage de Havilland Dragon Rapide aircraft, assembled in nearby hangar number 2, was installed in a prominent position in front of the new hotel.

There are two other key elements of The Aerodrome scheme.

Hangar number 2

The second large hangar has been refurbished by Speke-Garston Development Company offering potential inward investors one of the most unusual accommodation opportunities anywhere in the North West. Hangar number 2 offers up to 13,000 sq m of accommodation suitable for a wide variety of companies including call centre or ICT use. It could serve equally well, however, as an exhibition or leisure facility or

*The hotel restaurant (photo
Mike Williams © English
Heritage)*

even a film studio. In fact, several arts events have been held already in the building, including a major touring production of the Birmingham Opera Company staging of *Votzek* by Viennese composer Alban Berg. The Development Company's £3 million facelift of the building has also involved the provision of new services, landscaping and the creation of 500 car parking spaces.

Damons

A new £2 million family restaurant will also open at The Aerodrome in August 2002. The 120-cover diner is part of the US-based Damons chain. The first Damons restaurant opened in America in Columbus Ohio in 1979 and there are now more than a hundred outlets throughout the USA as well as in Panama and Puerto Rico. Once again, the Speke-Garston outlet has been designed in a way that will complement the other Art Deco buildings on the site.

Restoring other historic buildings

Speke-Garston Development Company has also been responsible for the regeneration of another Merseyside industrial landmark, the former Bryant and May match factory on Speke Road which closed in 1994 after seventy years of match manufacture. Working in partnership with award-winning Manchester-based developers Urban Splash, a new business village has been created where more people will eventually work than in the heyday of the factory. The jewel in the crown of The Match Works scheme is the magnificent Grade II listed frontage building, with its famous water tower and

stunning interior, which dates from 1918. This has been restored to create six two-storey pavilions with ground and mezzanine floor office space and open plan accommodation at first-floor level for call-centre use. New occupiers at the development include call centre operator 7C, Shaw Maintenance and motor claims company The Accident Group. Other features of the extensively landscaped site include the refurbished Mersey House, the former Bryant and May administration building, which houses the headquarters of Speke-Garston Development Company and Speke-Garston Partnership. Warehouse accommodation at the rear of the site, dating from the 1970s, has been converted into thirteen industrial units and the former factory sports grounds have become Hamilton Park, a very successful Wimpey Homes housing development. Urban Splash are now looking to start work on a second phase of the scheme which will see a further 40,000 sq ft (3,716 sq m) of accommodation created for office and commercial use.

Other Development Company projects

Other Development Company projects include the Boulevard Industry Park, next to the Halewood Jaguar plant, which has been the North West's most successful industrial development of recent years, attracting investment from the automotive and biotechnology sectors. Again, MEPC and Intercity are the developers for this scheme where just one plot remains unlet. Evans Vaccines, part of Powderject, has completed a £26 million expansion of its existing

The interior of hangar number 2 after restoration (photo Mike Williams © English Heritage)

human vaccine manufacturing plant that created 170 new jobs, and Aviron are investing in a major research and development facility. The Boulevard scheme has also attracted five automotive developments including a £20 million manufacturing facility for bumper manufacturer Merplas which has created 95 jobs and a 6,600-square-metre factory for seat maker Lear, which will has generate a further 230 jobs. The other projects involve instrument panel maker Visteon, car assemblies and pressings firm Stadco and car fastenings firm Infast. These three developments involve a total investment of £9 million and will create 160 new jobs. In addition to these car component companies, the Boulevard Industry Park is the site of a new local base for US firm Coughlin Logistics where a further 50 new jobs are being created. Elsewhere in the area the Development Company is creating a range of serviced development plots at the successful Speke Industrial Estate.

As these new sites and premises have been created across Speke-Garston, the Development Company has also been working to improve the appearance of the area as a whole for both existing and relocating companies. Three kilometres of the main southern gateway to south Liverpool, the A561 Speke Boulevard dual carriageway, have been transformed with more than a quarter of a million new trees, shrubs and plants. Now the scheme has been extended towards Liverpool along Speke Road.

Award honour

Projects such as these have helped Speke-Garston Development Company to create 2,700 new jobs and 124,000 square metres of new industrial and commercial floorspace during the last five years. This success, and that of its partner organisations Speke-Garston Partnership and South Liverpool Housing, resulted in Speke-Garston being honoured with a prestigious BURA (British Urban Regeneration Award) in 2001. The unique three-part regeneration programme in the area was recognised by the BURA judges for its emphasis on long-term planning and on laying the foundations for continued, sustainable regeneration in the future. They say that it has clearly made a significant difference to south Liverpool and had a real impact on the quality of life of local residents. Overall, the judges said that Speke-Garston had been honoured for its impressive track record of achievements and for the many topical lessons it offers to other major regeneration initiatives. The Development Company's success is just part of the wider regeneration of Speke-Garston. Elsewhere in the area Jaguar has invested £400 million in its new X-type production plant at Halewood which could produce up to 100,000 of the critically acclaimed 'baby Jags' a year. And a £32 million project is in progress to redevelop the terminal building at nearby Liverpool John Lennon Airport, Europe's fastest growing regional airport.

To ensure that local people have the best chance of taking advantage of the new jobs that are being created in the area several major education and training initiatives have been unveiled. These include the £5 million Partnership for Learning centre that provides high-quality training for the private sector and for local unemployed people and Oncall, an innovative call centre training academy. All these measures have made a big difference to people in the area who were out of work. Unemployment has more than halved from 24 per cent to 10.2 per cent and long-term unemployment, which was well above the Merseyside average, is now below it.

According to Development Company Chairman Ray O'Brien, CBE, the Speke aerodrome site has played a critical role in the regeneration of the area:

> The transformation of the terminal complex and the former northern airfield is a wonderful example of regeneration in action. The projects on these sites have created sites and premises that have helped to attract substantial amounts of investment and new jobs to the area. In addition they have found new uses for neglected listed buildings and provided exciting new facilities for people who live and work in the area. The restored buildings now act as a focal point for wider regeneration of Speke-Garston. We are delighted to have been associated with the 'L'Europe de l'Air' programme on this project; this partnership has undoubtedly been of great importance in helping us to achieve these impressive results.

Croydon and Shoreham, a tale of two airports

Bob Hawkins and Jeremy Lake

In the early days of the 'L'Europe de l'Air' project, we quickly focused on the significance of the flying field – the large expanse of uninterrupted level ground that made the whole business of coming and going in aeroplanes possible – as the essential element of the airport, the part of the overall landscape that gave meaning to the ensemble of buildings around its perimeter. When discussing the development proposals for the flying field at Liverpool-Speke, there were some forthright exchanges of view on this point with our colleagues at the Speke-Garston Development Company, arguments that were repeated during the discussion of the options facing those responsible for the future of Tempelhof. To anyone who doubts that the core asset of the historic airport is the flying field, this present contribution has a short and simple message: 'Come to Croydon!'

Croydon is one of a number of extant or former civil aviation sites in England on which significant buildings survive, many of them listed as being of special architectural or historic interest. Our intention is to present the current situation at two of these sites: Shoreham, a municipal airport on the south coast, and Croydon, London's first international airport. Jeremy Lake, who deals here with Shoreham, has undoubtedly had the happier experience, for the two sites could not present greater contrasts in terms of scale, significance and fate.

Located 11 miles (18km) south of London, Croydon was first established as a military aerodrome in 1915, part of the air defence of London against Zeppelin raids. Using former military hangars and huts, it became the capital's official 'air port' in March 1920, with regular services, first and foremost, to Paris-Le Bourget. From 1924, it was the base of the state-owned Imperial Airways. The terminal building, constructed from 1926 to 1928, was designed by the Air Ministry's Directorate of Works and Buildings,

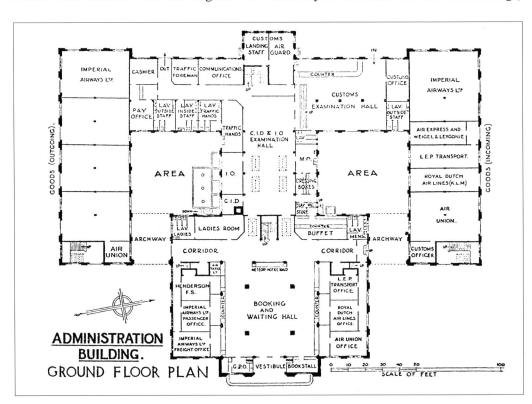

London-Croydon, 1928 ground plan of the airport's administration building (Cluett et al 1980)

and was the first purpose-built air passenger terminal in Britain, at the time the largest in Europe. For the first time in Europe, too, the building incorporated a central, four-storey control tower. Near the terminal, the Aerodrome Hotel, also opened in 1928 and intended for travellers, pilots and aerodrome staff, had a terraced roof and garden enclosure open to the general viewing public.

The Air Ministry was widely criticised for the terminal's conservative architecture, in no way expressive of flight. Clad in grey artificial stone, the building looks rather like a pseudo-classical railway station on the land side and not unlike a city wall, with a fortified tower, on the air side. Nonetheless, this terminal building remained fully in use until 1959, with an interruption during the war when, as a fighter satellite station, Croydon played an important role in the Battle of Britain. After its closure, the terminal building was refurbished as office accommodation (Airport House International Business Centre). Along with the 1928 entrance lodge, it was listed Grade II in 1978. Inside, the Café Rayon d'Or is replete with aviation and airport imagery and more recently, at the instigation of Croydon Council and in association with the Croydon Airport Society, formed in 1978, a visitor centre has been opened on two floors of the former control tower. Children are invited to dress up as passengers in costumes of the 1930s and can view Amy Johnson's flight bag. The top floor houses the radio room, recreated using original equipment.

Despite this commendable initiative, the airport buildings that survive have been almost entirely robbed of their context, setting and functional significance by the incremental development of an extensive industrial estate on the former flying field. The surviving airport buildings – terminal, hotel and ancillary buildings – make up an impressive ensemble when seen from Purley Way, the boulevard which passes along the front of the airport and which is now synonymous with the industrial estate which is spread around the terminal. Hemmed in by characterless sheds and offices of varied form and scale, the former control tower (the location of pioneering developments in air traffic control) now peers anxiously over the engulfing shedscape as if not quite able to believe what has happened. A visitor ignorant of the place's former function would be hard pressed to recognise it as one

of Europe's most important early civil aviation sites. The aircraft – a 1950s Heron – now mounted in front of the terminal building is a massive prompt, although it appears to be taking off from the wrong side of the building range. Other references to flight are very few: a nearby pub named The Propeller, now closed, and, most sadly, within a stone's throw of the terminal, a road sign directing traffic to the airport, not Croydon but Gatwick, adding insult to historical injury.

It is now an almost surreal experience to gaze out from the control tower display area over a vast industrial estate, and then to look at photographs showing the field packed with 100,000 people, there to welcome Charles Lindbergh, the road crammed with cars bringing visitors to welcome the hero flying in from Le Bourget after his transatlantic flight of May 1927. The careful refurbishment of the buildings at Croydon and the imaginative display in the new visitor centre, excellent though they are, cannot disguise the fact that the historic site has suffered a massive cultural loss, sustained at a time before perceptions of the value of a

Top: An industrial estate now occupies the site of Croydon Airport's flying field, here seen from the control tower

The landside view of Croydon Airport's terminal complex. Adaptive reuse here maintains some sense of the site's former context, and includes interpretative displays in a small site museum

Shoreham airport in about 1936, taken from an old postcard.

shared aviation heritage for Europe had begun to develop. We have, at Croydon, a very clear and sad picture of one version of the future for Speke, Tempelhof and many other historic airport landscapes.

Shoreham Airport, in West Sussex, presents a very different picture. The aviation history of the site dates back to 1910 when a local artist, Harold Piffard, began testing a single-seater biplane on a former marsh next to the River Arun at Shoreham, which was officially recognised as an aerodrome early in the following year. Lee Richards' 'Annular Monoplane', one of the more interesting experimental designs of this formative period, flew from this site, as did also, purportedly, the world's very first cargo flight, a box of light bulbs flown to London in July 1911. The same year saw Shoreham participate in the 'Circuit of Europe' air race that involved sites in Britain, France and Belgium. It was used as a training airfield in the First World War, the first fighter squadron of the Royal Canadian Air Force being formed here, after which club flying resumed.

After two years of deliberation, a joint committee was formed in 1930 for the purpose of establishing a municipal airport for Brighton, Hove and Worthing. The airport was officially opened on Saturday 13 June 1936, Brighton, Hove and Worthing municipal authorities sharing the expense of its building. A service between Deauville,

Shoreham and Croydon had been launched in the previous year, the terminal building soon processing internal flights to Bournemouth, Bristol, Cardiff, Liverpool and Portsmouth as well as to Jersey and Le Touquet, further afield.

The architect, Stavers Hessell Tiltman, had settled in Brighton from 1909 and, as architect to Southern Aircraft Limited, had an interest in airport design. M H Volk, a director of the company and an aeronautical consultant, provided technical expertise and advice, and went on with Tiltman to design two more municipal airports – Leeds-Bradford and Belfast – in 1938. The spirited manner of this design provides a contrast with the competent but relatively dull private house commissions, shop developments (for example at Haywards Heath) and pubs (designed for Brighton's Rock Brewery) that characterised the bulk of Tiltman's work.

Shoreham is one of a series of terminals that displayed awareness of European and American progress in terminal design, the exterior being typically evocative of the spirit of flight and speed in its streamlined design. As such, it reflects the modernistic forms advocated by the Royal Institution of British Architects' Building Committee in reaction to the conservative handling of Croydon's terminal. Unlike the earlier combined clubhouse-terminals at Heston (1929, demolished), or Graham Dawbarn's

Brooklands Clubhouse in Surrey (1932, listed Grade II), Tiltman combined terminal facilities with both control tower and offices. He used the control tower as the pivot of his design, around which he placed facilities such as a restaurant, customs and baggage handling. It was all decked out in the International Modern style, and much of the original streamlined interior decoration survives, including a saucer dome in the centre, decorated in a darker hue than the cream-coloured walls around. The axial plan served to separate the various functions of the building, which was designed to accommodate both the requirements of passenger flights, with its booking hall and customs area, and the flying club which, as in other small municipal airports of the period, provided an additional source of income. Thus the double-height booking hall to the centre is flanked by an east wing containing a customs department, emigration hall and offices, and a west wing containing a public restaurant overlooking the airfield; the floor above is given over to bedrooms for pilots and recreational facilities for the flying club. The building was also designed with a rooftop terrace to accommodate strong public interest in flying. The steel-framed structure, clad in rendered 14-in (356-mm) Belgium brick, was provided with cantilevered canopies on the north and south sides. The south elevation is dominated by its entrance block, the main doors (careful reproductions, installed in 1999) being flanked by ridged pilasters. The tall window above the canopy is topped by a variation on the familiar Art Deco sunburst motif. The north elevation on the airfield side is simpler, the marked horizontality of the two wings crashing into the tall central control tower with its ground-floor canopied entrance. Staircases at the end of each wing lead to the public observation terraces on the roof.

In the early stages of the Second World War, prior to the fall of France, Shoreham functioned as the terminal for flights to Britain from France, Belgium, Holland and Denmark, as well as Tunis and Alexandria. It then became a satellite fighter base, reverting after 1945 to its present role as a municipal airport. Remarkably, the building and its associated airfield landscape has been little altered after nearly seventy years of continuous commercial use. Shoreham is, indeed, Britain's only listed terminal building that still serves its original function. It was listed at Grade II in 1984, and it is now clear, by virtue of the 'L'Europe de l'Air' project, that its significance in a wider European context merits its consideration for upgrading to II*. Although the terminal building was not constructed on the principles of flexibility and adaptability that characterised the Hening and Chitty Partnership's terminals at Exeter and Ipswich, designed for the Straight Corporation,[1] it is nonetheless admirably suited to the airport's present-day requirements. The terminal was built close to the railway line, on a site that constricted further development of the airfield but which made linear industrial development possible at its edge, leaving the airfield undeveloped and giving the visitor uninterrupted views across the site to Lancing College. It is this intact relationship between the terminal building and the airfield landscape (which is bounded by a dome trainer for aircraft training, now a Scheduled Ancient Monument, two hydraulically-operated Picket Hamilton forts and other airfield defences installed in 1940 and which also merit consideration for protection) that gives Shoreham its special significance in conservation terms. Although plans at present under consideration might involve the demolition of the steel-framed hangar buildings, the future of the terminal itself is assured through its continuing and profitable use as the hub of a general aviation airport, with its own air traffic control centre, training club and commercial air-taxi flights. The visitor approaching the site from the north gains an interrupted view across the flat airfield landscape adjacent to the River Adur – since 1984 given a hard runway and perimeter taxiway – to Stiltman's jewel-like terminal, still the most prominent building among the industrial units that together comprise a total of 45 companies employing 650 people. To anyone who doubts that the core asset of the historic airport is the flying field, this present contribution has a second simple message: 'Come to Shoreham!'

Shoreham, view of the booking hall in the 1930s (Worthing Borough Council)

Shoreham airport today
(photo Jeremy Lake)

Note

1   This architectural practice pioneered the standardisation of terminal buildings which were thus capable of being extended to meet the future needs of a growing airport. The steel frame was based on a standard 15-foot (4.6-metre) square with easy extendibility in mind, and in fact the Ipswich building was extended soon after its original construction in 1938. Hening and Chitty formed their partnership in 1936, and Chitty's close involvement with the Tecton partnership ensured that he was in the forefront of the functionalist tradition in modern architecture. The system of modular construction used here was developed after the war by local authorities in their school-building programmes. The Secretary of State for Air, Harold Balfour, pronounced on his opening speech at Ipswich in July 1938 that 'This is one of the finest air terminals anywhere in the world.' It functioned as a bomber and later fighter satellite station during the Second World War. The terminal building at Ipswich was listed at Grade II in 1996. (Hening, R and Chitty, A M, 'Notes on the planning of an airport'. Architectural Record of Design and Construction November (1937); Hening, R and Chitty, A M, 'Design for expansion'. Flight February 1939)

Select bibliography

'Brighton airport'. The Builder 4 (January 1935), 14–16, 24

'Brighton, Hove and Worthing airport, Stavers H Tiltman, architect'. Architecture Illustrated 11 (November 1935), 135–40

Cluett, D, Nash, J and Learmonth, B 1980 Croydon Airport, The Great Days. London: London Borough of Sutton Libraries and Arts Services

Hooks, M 1997 Croydon Airport, The Archive Photographs Series. Stroud, Gloucestershire: Tempus Publishing Limited

'Shoreham Airport, designed by Stavers H Tiltman'. Architects Journal 31 (October 1935), 629–30, 633–8

'Shoreham Airport, Stavers H Tiltman, architect'. Architectural Design and Construction 8/13 (November 1939), 511

Thornhill, J M 1981 'Shoreham airport terminal building: An architectural study'. Unpublished typescript at Shoreham Airport Archive

Worthing Borough Council, plans, elevations and sections of 1934. Plan references: 22/4/10/2–22/4/10/8.

Copenhagen airport 1939, Modern Movement 1999

Ola Wedebrunn

New 20th-century experiences such as the cinema, broadcasting and flying changed our notions of space, time and architecture. Movies such as *Der Blaue Engel* with Marlene Dietrich could be shown simultaneously on the silver screens of Berlin, Paris or Liverpool; radio signals could transmit her voice world-wide, while the next aeroplane might bring her across the ocean. The modernist vision of the future was one of a free, open world. As media such as film, radio and airborne transportation spread more ethereal values, new construction technologies and materials provided novel possibilities for physical appearances. Concrete, steel and glass structures, developed in the 19th century, affected not only building technology, but also, to a large extent, the landscape-forming phenomena of industrial production and transportation infrastructures.

The situation in the early 20th century proved that there was no single expression of how something ought to look or how it ought to be. This new outlook obliged man to face realities that he did not yet understand and forced him to explore new values and expressions. The demand for architectural forms based on new conditions that were little understood led to the search for appropriate expressions of new or renewed functions. Traditional as well as modern paths were followed, resulting in shapes of mimetic representation and organic disposition.

Two air terminals serve as examples of this. First of all, the TWA terminal at John F Kennedy airport in New York, built to the designs of the Finnish-born architect Eero Saarinen between 1956 and 1962 and a masterpiece of modern, mimetic construction. Resembling an enormous abstract eagle, it is of great artistic as well as constructional ingenuity. The airport in Lviv in the Ukraine, on the other hand, is a palatial monument of the Stalinist era. Looking like a Corinthian temple, it follows a classic, mimetic tradition: there are spires on the control tower and other motives inspired by folklore, along with the hammer and sickle and red flags flying in the wind. But these signals, of course, do not necessarily make it

into a 'worse' airport terminal, either functionally or from an artistic point of view. Other airports, such as Gatwick near London or Bromma in Stockholm, invite an understanding of the building as part of a process of flow and transition. Even if these structures are of rather geometric and diagrammatic form, they are closer to an organic appreciation of changing needs than to monumental determinism.

Copenhagen airport, 1939

Built in 1924, the first airport terminal at Copenhagen-Kastrup was a two-storey structure clad in red-painted wooden panelling. By 1936, this 'wooden castle' had become too small and an architectural competition for a new terminal was organised. There was no debate about the fact that the new terminal should be an expression of modern architecture. Since the emergence of the Modern Movement – or Functionalism as it was known in Scandinavia – at the Stockholm exhibition in the summer of 1930, there was more-or-less consensual understanding of contemporary architecture.

In 1936, the new terminal of Bromma airport in Stockholm was opened. This was a horizontally emphasised, two-storey, lightweight, white-clad construction, trimmed for function, a diagrammatic machine of communication. Almost naturally, it served as an inspiration for the competitors at Copenhagen. Among the participants for the new Copenhagen terminal were the architects Arne Jacobsen and Flemming Larsen, who won second prize. But it was Vilhelm Lauritzen (1894–1984), another young Danish architect, who won the first prize and who was awarded the final design commission.

Lauritzen was trained at the architectural school of the Royal Danish Academy in Copenhagen. He was interested in the natural sciences as well as in the arts, and he probably saw no need to make distinctions between the disciplines. Just as Poul Henningsen, the Danish lamp designer, calculated the best electric lighting devices, so

Top: Aerial view of Copen-hagen airport in 1939 (collection Ola Wedebrunn)

Interior view of Lauritzen's terminal building in 1939 (collection Ola Wedebrunn)

also Lauritzen calculated buildings as rational organisms intended to perform correctly in terms of light, acoustics and much more. This broad approach was reflected everywhere in his design of the air terminal, as well as in his new Danish Broadcasting House at Copenhagen, dating from the same period.

Lauritzen worked closely with artists as well as with engineers. The resulting terminal building was a two-storey, column and slab construction, allowing for future alterations and extensions. It resembled the so-called 'do-mi-no' system presented by Le Corbusier and Max du Bois in 1915. Le Corbusier's architecture was a major influence and the Copenhagen terminal indeed shows the inspiration of Le Corbusier's five points for new architecture: column and slab construction, terraced roof, free plan, free façade and strip windows. But Lauritzen's architecture for the terminal is not merely an unthinking, formal copy of international recipes. There is a free interpretation of functional necessities, organic sensitivity in the material composition of different colours (wood, stone, metal),

attention to texture as well as to the coherence of detail and overall design. Lauritzen's environmental sensitivity could be traced back to the work of other Scandinavian architects such as E G Asplund and Alvar Aalto. From this point of view, the 1939 air terminal can be seen as an expression of experienced modern reality, taking a critical position with regards to a more simple-minded geometrical version of the Modern Movement.

The terminal was situated close to the Sound (Øresund), so that aircraft landing on the flying field and seaplanes docking at a bridge nearby could come close to the building. Its horizontal forms were faced in 'Eternit', a recently invented, 8-mm-thick concrete cladding material, reinforced with asbestos fibre. This material had been much used on the façades of the temporary buildings of Stockholm's 1930 exhibition. Lauritzen was bold enough to use this new material for the permanent structure of the airport terminal, a major public building, alternating it with details in more traditional materials such as copper and marble.

On the south, landside façade, with its long rows of windows facing the parking area, a large, steel, cantilevered canopy welcomed the visitor. Entering through one of the two revolving doors at the waist of the plan (shaped like an hourglass), the visitor immediately faced a 150-sq-m panoramic window on the other side the central hall, characterised by the divergent perspectives of its axes. This central hall measured 12 x 50m on the ground and was of two-storey height. The roof was a corrugated concrete slab, cast on site, and only 120m thick. Due to its ingenious shape, it covered the whole hall with eighteen shallow sinuous curves, 600mm in depth, repeated every 2.5m.

This structure was achieved by means of the close co-operation between the architect and the civil engineer Christian Nøkken-tved, also responsible for opening up the central perspective of the cross axis by placing an arch over the exit area. This carried the curved roof in a free passage over a triple-spanned suspension of the main hall, supported on double columns. This accommodated the streams of arriving or departing passengers flowing through the revolving doors.

The structure embodied both technical and poetic dimensions. Similar to the corrugated aluminium of Junkers aeroplanes, it was based on lightweight, minimal structural technology, bringing together many different associations: the curves of quantum mechanics (the physician Niels Bohr was, of course, a well-known Danish scientist), the everyday, cloud-grey carpet or Aladdin's carpet. The ceiling was clad with a new acoustic material called 'phonotex', a modular, cellulose product, the design of which combined aesthetic, structural and acoustic qualities. A curved roof had been shown to have a pleasing aesthetic effect, for example in the ingenious curve of the ceiling in the reading room of the Viborg Library (now in Russia), designed by Alvar Aalto in 1930. This also became a principle followed by Lauritzen both at the airport terminal and in his concert hall at the Danish Broadcasting House. It might even be seen as one of the influences in the construction of the concrete 'sky' in the Bagsværd Church (Copenhagen), designed by Jørn Utzon.

Good architecture itself combines many related elements of technical, social and aesthetic value: sculptural forms of stairs, balconies, shapes of light, walls. The furniture was specially conceived by Lauritzen and his companions, and even the advertising signs were colourful works of art, designed with the help of the sculptor, Otto Staehr Nielsen.

Another remarkable space was the restaurant, with its guitar-shaped glass wall growing out of the south-west corner of the building. Light walls, transparency and the shadows of parasols made the building an instrument on which changing light was invited to play. Light and shadow contributed to the building's formal design in a way that could make it resemble the collages of cubist avant-garde art. Finally – and less abstractly – the flow of people on the move completed the composition.

Shortly after its opening, however, with the advent of the Second World War, the terminal was closed down and camouflaged. With the return of peace and freedom in May 1945, it became a turbulent hourglass once again. It began to accommodate charter flights that were making air travel accessible to larger numbers of people, leaving for distant, exotic places.

Famous visitors to Denmark, such as Louis Armstrong and the Beatles landed at Copenhagen, and the heir to the Swedish throne, Crown Prince Gustav Adolf, was one of the passengers who died here in a crash after take-off in 1947. In the last decades of the 20th century, the terminal building was occasionally used as a reception centre for refugees and as temporary

office space for the airport's administration.

In 1939, the terminal of Copenhagen airport was planned to accommodate approximately 35,000 passengers a year. When the airport reopened in 1945, it was already too small, and Lauritzen projected an extension. This project was not followed up, however, and instead the terminal was extended up to 1960 by the construction of barracks. The new terminal of 1960, still in use today, was also built to designs by Vilhelm Lauritzen.

Today Lauritzen Architects A/S, direct successors of Vilhelm Lauritzen, are still active as one of the architectural firms working for Copenhagen airport. In 1999, the new terminal three and the new railway station were opened, designed by the same company. Air transportation has undergone radical and unforeseeable changes during the last sixty years: the annual number of passengers anticipated in 1939 now corresponds with the number of travellers passing through Copenhagen airport in a single day.

The terminal building in about 1990, with its post-war additions (photo Ola Wedebrunn)

Top: *September 1999: the building, mounted on steel girders supported by 744 individually controlled hydraulic wheels, prepares to move to its new location (photo Ola Wedebrunn)*

The great lift: raised half a metre above the ground, the terminal taxies out from its original site, controlled by the man walking in front with a yellow box and a single joystick (photo Ola Wedebrunn)

Modern Movement, 1999

In 1939 the terminal was built not only at the centre of Copenhagen airport but also at the meeting point of intersecting roads and railways close to the Danish bridgehead of the Öresundbridge (the bridge across the Sound). Since July 2000, this bridge has formed a 16-kilometre connection between Denmark and Sweden, and the complex of the terminal building now lies at the heart of the whole airport zone.

During the 1970s, planners and politicians decided that the new Copenhagen airport would be developed at its existing site, leaving little hope for the preservation of the old terminal building. Several propositions for statutory protection were put forward during the 1980s, but they were all turned down. By this time, the heritage values of what used to be a beautiful piece of architecture, now obscured by derelict, poorly designed extensions, were almost impossible to appreciate. All that seemed to be left were nostalgic old photographs.

A project developed in 1991, by Professor Erik Reitzel, a civil engineer, in collaboration

with Lauritzen Architects, was a turning point. This project concluded that it was possible to move the terminal, immediately setting off a debate with many differing opinions. The Ministry of the Environment finally decided that the building had to be protected. But there was a problem with granting it historic monument protection; it was decided that a measure of protection would be enacted only after the building had been moved to its new site.

The art of moving buildings is not without its own history and precedents. Traditional timber constructions have often been dismantled and moved to new places. At the beginning of the 20th century, the Danish architect Anton Rosen proposed to move a 17th-century brick structure, the Round Tower in central Copenhagen, in order to make way for increasing road traffic. In 1996 the Kaisersaal in Berlin was put on rails and moved to the new Sony Centre at the Potzdamerplatz.

The ethics of monument protection were, of course, at issue, if the principles of *genius loci* are taken into consideration. That is why the building will be protected only after having settled at its new address. But the nomadic nature of much modern architecture, functioning as a machine, could also be used as an argument. At a time when old ships are readily listed in Denmark why should architecture not be protected in the same way, even if the building has moved to another port?

During the summer of 1999 the building was prepared for transportation to its new site. Erik Reitzel and the engineering contractors Monberg and Thorsen were in charge of the project – a virtual modern movement – and the Dutch company, Van Seumeren, with considerable experience in moving off-shore constructions, was contracted to carry out the project.

The building was supported by steel girders and trucks, with 744 individually controlled hydraulic wheels beneath the girders. The columns had been cut off flush with the ground and the building was lifted from its original site during the afternoon of Friday 17 September 1999. Buildings of 4,000 sq m do not often move, but this one did, provoking a surreal experience of disorientation among the observers. But this was for real: 2,600 tons in one piece, on the move.

The great lift took place the following night. The terminal, raised half a metre above the ground, taxied out from its original site and set off for its new destination

1.6km across the runways. All this was controlled by one person walking in front of the building with a yellow box and a single joystick. Starting an hour before midnight, the terminal was set down on its new site at six o'clock on Sunday morning.

To reproduce a situation similar to the original plan, with the building at the edge of the field facing the runways, it had to be turned nearly 180 degrees en route. What used to be morning light on the entrance is now the light of sunset. This change set off a debate among curators, architects and authorities about changes to the colour scheme inside the building. But the question of the building's colour scheme and its equivalence in time does not seem to affect the general impression of the building.

The terminal is now restored, performing again as an extremely elegant modern construction of matter and space. Lauritzen Architects, in collaboration with the architect Charlotte Iversen, have been in charge of the restoration of the terminal, now used as an administrative building. The aim, however, is to use it as a small VIP terminal, possibly opening the restaurant for public access when official security controls permit this.

Modern airports are turning into heritage, rich with myth, history and rational technologies hard to grasp but too valuable to loose. Like Hans Christian Andersen's *Ugly Duckling*, the fate of Copenhagen's 1939 airport terminal tells us the almost surreal story of a virtual Modern Movement.

The building crossing the airfield during the night of Saturday 18 to Sunday 19 September (photo Ola Wedebrunn)

The rehabilitation of Orly, Paris

Jacques Repiquet

The exemplary renovation of the Orly-Sud terminal, south of Paris, is nearing completion.[1] One by one, since 1995, the different public spaces have been recovering their sparkle and freshness while gaining in efficiency and comfort. The terminal's original character seems to be surfacing again, but at the same time, there is something different. Various changes have been made which do not detract from the recognised qualities of the 1960s architecture, but serve rather to enhance them. For example, in order to meet the functional requirement of separating flows of passengers in ever increasing numbers, long, glazed circulation corridors have been added on top of the terminal's original piers, offering open views of the runways and the spectacle of aircraft in movement, a principle that inspired the project at the outset.

'*Ils sont plus de deux mille et je ne vois qu'eux deux* … (There are over two thousand of them, and I only see those two)', sang Jacques Brel in 1962, in a song entitled *Orly*. Describing the separation of two sweethearts, the singer-poet was addressing the paradox of the individual's solitude in the crowd, a paradox to be observed in any busy railway station or airport, where personal destinies are being played out and where the crowds are collections of many individual histories. In these bustling places devoted to travel, the individual's recollections are an active component of the collective memory. This helps explain why in places such as Orly, architectural heritage can elicit high levels of public sympathy, inspired more often than not by reasons that have little to do with art or history.

Restoration or renovation?

Most of the major public buildings erected in Paris during the 1960s and 1970s are badly in need of rehabilitation today. The budgets set aside for their upkeep have rarely proved adequate for their satisfactory maintenance. Those buildings that have not undergone drastic alterations have seen their original architecture progressively dis-figured by changing uses and by short-term solutions to urgent problems. But unlike other buildings that should be preserved in their 'historic' state, to be passed on intact to future generations, Orly's terminal is a living monument, a public amenity that has to evolve to keep up with changes in society and with technical developments.

Nonetheless, it is easy to accept that some of these modern public amenities are also valuable witnesses of the past. In the case of Orly, the building was the result of an ambitious project that had few parallels in 20th-century France. Between 1960 and the present day, Orly's history is that of the democratisation of air travel. Setting sentiment aside, it is the exceptional interest of its architecture that gives the building particular value. But how do you go about rehabilitating a building that has no official recognition as a historic monument, under the terms of the French law of 1913? The question of the renovation of the Orly-Sud terminal is more a question of architectural coherence. Since it is not a 'monument' to be 'restored', the initiative of Aéroports de Paris (ADP) is decisive and, as the airport's owner, ADP has complete freedom to proceed as it sees fit. But, in keeping with the two criteria that French law stipulates for the protection of historic buildings – their interest from the point of view of history or art – the aim at Orly is both to preserve the building's architectural qualities and to respect its significance for the collective memory. This recognition of Orly as a part of the national heritage offers the best perspective for the renovation project and is the key to the understanding of the building which offers the best guarantee for its continued architectural integrity.

The rehabilitation project also aims at revamping the building's image, one that had become somewhat tarnished by the impact of changing patterns of use and partial and often badly co-ordinated repair work. Yet, at the same time, air transport is necessarily synonymous with technical change and formal modernity. After forty years in use, many of the 1961 fittings were

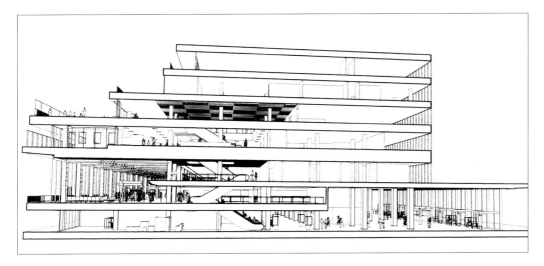

*Cross-section of Orly
terminal showing the main
stairwell with its escalators
(ADP)*

decidedly outdated and difficult to maintain. There has never been any suggestion that the whole building should be carefully restored to some pristine 1961 state, but rather that it should undergo a 'sensitive and intelligent' renovation operation, underpinned by a clear programme setting out a hierarchy of the interventions proposed. The overall aim then was to restore the utility, the beauty and the solidity of a great public building, restating the coherence of its original architecture by identifying its truths and hidden meanings. Alternative solutions to replacement or excessively zealous renovation had to be identified, enabling technical, functional and economic modernisation that would go hand in hand with new safety requirements.

The example of Orly is a good illustration of the recent interest in heritage, still in daily use, which enjoys no form of statutory protection. The question of finding an entirely new use as a condition for conservation does not arise here. Although they have evolved, the uses are still there and the question is one of reciprocal adaptation between these uses and the original architecture.

A 1960s success story

It was in September 1945 that the French press first unveiled the model of the new airport for Paris, which the government had decided to build at Orly, a military airfield originally created by the Americans in 1917. The studies took about ten years, with actual building work, concentrated between February 1957 and February 1961, mobilising up to 1,200 workers on the site. On 24 February 1961, when the new terminal was officially opened by the President of the Republic, the building had already become the heart of the largest airport in continental Europe. Capable of processing 200 planes and 9,000 passengers per day, it was the fourth largest airport in the world, after New York, Chicago and London. The stirring speech given that day by General de Gaulle

hailed the building as a symbol of a modern France that had recovered its dignity, turning the page on the difficult post-war period. After the speeches, 10,000 guests were invited to a dazzling reception that ended with a grand ball under the gilded chandeliers of the first floor hall, a latter-day hall of mirrors.[2] This was the last reception of its kind in Orly's history, however, and marks the end of the site's resemblance to the monuments of the *Ancien Régime*, 'places where authority is on show, inseparable from the staged ceremonies of the spectacle of power'.[3] Henceforth, at Orly, the official ceremonies, the arrivals of heads of state and important dignitaries, took place more discreetly, in a specially built VIP pavilion. Orly's terminal was handed over to the people.

A symbolic structure

The press compared the new building to a cathedral for the modern age and the critics were eager to stress its sheer scale: 'no building as vast as the new Orly terminal has been seen in Paris since the Hôtel des Invalides'.[4] The urban developments that accompanied the building were also praised. The airport was not a mere airfield, simply a place for travellers in transit: it had become a new urban complex with a broad range of functions. Today, the terminal has entered the history of modern architecture in France. Architectural historians speak of it as one of the most representative buildings of the 'French international style'.[5] The man behind the terminal, the architect Henri Vicariot at the head of ADP's design team, worked from 1954 with engineers, technicians and decorators all collaborating in the same spirit to make a success of this prestigious project.

Popular success

For the general public, Orly remains, above all, the place where families used to come and enjoy a day out, watching the endlessly fascinating sight of aeroplanes taking off and landing. Without any obstruction to passenger flows, a system of external staircases and automatic ticket barriers led to 35,000 square metres of terraces that were accessible for one New Franc. In the manner of grandstands at a racecourse, these terraces ran parallel to the runways, enabling the public to follow the movements of the planes, accompanied by a commentary broadcast on loudspeakers. Ice cream vendors added a festive note to the on-going air show. In the terminal's different restaurants and bars, or in its cinema or chapel, day-trippers could come even closer to the reality of air travel, mingling with air-hostesses, passengers heading for faraway destinations or foreigners arriving at Paris. In 1965, with four million visitors, Orly was the most visited monument in France. Open buses even provided a guided tour of the entire complex.

Thirty years later, according to an opinion poll, the French continued to show considerable affection for this, their favourite airport. Even though the quality of services was much diminished and the original architecture almost unrecognisable, with the departure halls at saturation point and the luxury of the original materials much tarnished, the myth of Orly survived. Passengers preferred this terminal to others, still viewing it as characteristic of contemporary France and as a place of escape. The luminous atmosphere of the halls with their panoramic windows still struck a sentimental chord. The airport's accessibility, its human scale and the clarity of its plan also meant that it was still considered to be an efficient terminal. At Orly, this balance between functionality and prestige maintained the terminal's popularity.

An innovative project

At the beginning of the democratisation of air transport, Orly set out to combine efficiency and user-friendliness. The designers sought to attain the highest degree of operational simplicity, concentrating the terminal into a single, linear building which limited the distances to be covered on foot to a maximum of 400m and offered spaces that were as clear and understandable as possible. But the terminal also offered the services of a real community. Never before had so much attention been paid to the way passengers or visitors were dealt with. The efficiency of the boarding and disembarking operations went hand in hand with a concern to provide users with facilities that could make their stay in the terminal as agreeable as possible. The original project led one advertising agency to refer to Orly as 'Europe's first Air City'. The building included a cinema, a hotel, various retail outlets and duty-free shops, bars, restaurants and lounges, as well as a nursery, a clinic and a chapel. Other services and shops at the basement level – a bank, hairdressers, a post office, tobacconists and a supermarket – were reserved for the staff of the airport itself and airline personnel, together giving an estimated total of 14,000.

In order to keep up with the rapid changes in air transport, the project evolved considerably during the design phase and even during building work itself. But the economic, technical and human effort put into the operation ensured that user needs were met and that the terminal gave satisfaction for many years to come, not least in its capacity for adaptation and extension.

Orly and town planning

France at the end of the 1950s was marked by the creation of major new public amenities and the Paris region, with its ever-growing population, was particularly affected by this phenomenon. The creation of Orly airport was undertaken at the same time as development plans for the Paris region, dating from 1936, were being redefined. Integrating the future airport site, the new development plan of 1956 marked a transition towards modern planning solutions that gave greater consideration to road and rail connections, to the development of new towns and to the extension of existing satellite towns.

At Orly, designed to replace a near-saturated Le Bourget, the land surface available made it possible to create an infrastructure of exceptional dimensions, but still sited close to the heart of Paris. A slip road leaving the southbound motorway was specially built to serve the new terminal and the old Route nationale 7 was rerouted. The architecture of the terminal itself was influenced by these infrastructural changes. Facing Paris, the terminal building spans the nationale 7 and integrates the new motorway in an urban composition of monumental scale. Built at the periphery of the city 'the airport's architecture has the good fortune not to be detracted from by older, anachronistic buildings', stated an observer in 1961.[6]

Inventiveness in passenger-handling

Orly's terminal faces onto the runways in the form of a long bar more than 700m in length. The central main building, 200m long, is flanked by two low side piers. The eastern pier, which occupies the site of the first terminal, was completed in 1962. This layout limited the distances to be covered on foot by departing passengers to an average of 300m, less than the length of a railway platform. In order to rationalise the processing of passengers – no longer luxury travellers, but businessmen in a hurry whose time was valuable – the airport's arrangements were made more efficient. Check-in formalities were carried out inside the terminal itself and no longer in Paris, at the old Invalides terminal, a converted railway station. A system of 'continuous passenger flow', baptised the 'Orly-system', was invented, making it possible to avoid the unnecessary grouping of passengers bound for the same flight before they went through customs. Passengers now proceeded in their own time from the check-in counters to the boarding areas close to the planes. It took less time to pass through the frontier filters as customs controls of luggage took place at the check-in counter or, for incoming passengers, at the luggage delivery level. The design of the building itself, with one level on the city side and two on the runway side, enabled the separation of baggage-handling and passenger care. The luggage remained on the ground floor while the passengers took the escalators to reach the planes at first floor level on the airside.

Architecture

Both in its overall design and in minor architectural details, the terminal is marked by the contrast between the city side and the runway side, coinciding with its north and south elevations. The north façade of the administration building is characterised by the entrance porch projecting beneath the curtain wall with its yellow blinds. The south façade is comprised of stepped terraces laid out in the manner of a grandstand looking out over the runways. If large halls in public buildings often lend themselves to ornate architectural expression, at Orly the provision of broad terraces for spectators oriented the project towards simpler volumes with large open platforms and flat roofs. This layout contributes towards a certain

formal 'dryness' in the building, but also made it possible to simplify design and building work. Standard modules meant that it was possible continually to adapt the project until work began on the interior fittings. On the north façade, the canopy over the entrance to the main hall of the terminal clearly indicates the building's function as a public amenity. On the runway side, the central administration block is hidden behind the horizontal lines of the protruding balconies.

The façade of the administration block, a curtain wall in stainless steel, glass and turquoise blue enamelled glass ('murcolor'), was designed with the help of Jean Prouvé. The design of this wall, with its regular rectangular pattern devoid of any hierarchical ordering, is inspired by the Seagram Building built in New York by Ludwig Mies van der Rohe and Philip Johnson between 1954 and 1958. Vicariot, Orly's architect, had met Mies van der Rohe, and Jean Letondeur emphasises how 'Vicariot was fascinated by American façade constructions known as "curtain walls" [...]. He went on to become the precursor of the curtain wall in France'.[7]

1960s architecture

In the 1950s and 1960s, the so-called 'international style' dominated the design of large office blocks, hotels and public buildings throughout the western world. The expression can be overused today, but 'international

Night-time view of the landside of the terminal in 1961, with the decorative water feature in the foreground (ADP)

Airside view of the terminal building in 1961 (ADP)

style' applies perfectly to Orly, at least if we accept the definition offered by Henry Russell Hitchcock and Philip Johnson in the catalogue of the exhibition they organised at the Museum of Modern Art in New York in 1932. This presented the recent work of the architectural avant-garde in Europe and the United States: composition in terms of spaces rather than masses; modular regularity but without axial symmetry; a rejection of ornamentation. Orly can be classified then as a latter-day manifestation of the type of formal expression initiated by Ludwig Mies van der Rohe, Walter Gropius and Richard Neutra.

Between modernity and classicism

Seen from a distance, the terminal has the 'simple' and 'severe' appearance of a large office building. An article published by Vicariot in *Techniques et Architecture* in September 1961 summarises his team's architectural objectives: to provide a modern and efficient amenity that would also be a prestigious showcase for France, an expression of its age with a monumental spirit. Thus, despite its modern appearance and the use of innovating techniques, the influence of classic composition is still perceptible, particularly in the symmetrical layout of the approach roads and the decorative water

feature flanked by lawns aligned on the main axis leading to Paris. 'The north façade acts as a backdrop to the vast open view in the direction of Paris.' The duality between modernity and classicism is also found in the composition of the building itself: a steel and concrete structure faced inside with materials that not only gave a luxurious finish but also provided useful spaces for cables and fluids.

A modular metallic structure

According to the chief engineer E Becker: 'The architectural principles adopted for the terminal did not foresee any exceptionally large volumes; consequently, the general design of the building's frame did not require any exceptional feats of imagination by the engineers.' The use of a metallic frame, however, did make certain technical performances possible. The designers compared the advantages of a metallic structure to those of pre-stressed concrete. For equivalent qualities of performance, concrete turned out more expensive. Concrete was used, however, for the building's foundations and for its flooring. The floors are between 60 and 70mm thick according to their location and help distribute horizontal loads between the numerous outer braced structures. The cheaper solution of using vertical bracing panels was ruled out in order to maximise flexibility of use on the

The main entrance hall in 1961 (ADP)

horizontal platforms. This meant that interior layouts could be modified up to the last minute and also facilitated subsequent changes in use.

Indeed, from the earliest design phases, Vicariot envisaged extensions to the building in order to accommodate the airport's future development. A hypothetical maximum volume was fixed for the building and this served as the basis for calculating the dimensions of the load-bearing structure and the foundations. Thus, with the exception of the central part of the building spanning the Route nationale 7, it would be possible to raise the building to a total of seven floors. This forward thinking led to a systematic over-sizing of most of the load-bearing elements. The adoption of a modular constructive system also made it possible to limit the number of structural components and to facilitate their prefabrication and erection on site.

The choice of an easily divisible square structural module of 8.28 x 8.28m made it possible to fix the precise dimensions of the building from the outset. The dimensions of all the façade components and of many

interior features – check-in counters, luggage conveyor belts, offices of various sizes, doors, corridors – could therefore be decided at an early phase of the detailed planning. Standardised elements ruled at Orly, manifesting both the modernity and the economy of the terminal's construction.

The contribution of Jean Prouvé

Jean Prouvé's contribution to the terminal is an important and visible one. The façades and superstructures, furnished by the Compagnie Industrielle de Matériel de Transport, benefited from the talent and experience of this man who modestly described himself as a 'constructor'. Working at the building department of the CIMT from 1957, he was particularly preoccupied by the design of lightweight façade elements. At Orly, he succeeded in the apparently impossible task of providing a robust but transparent façade in thick glass that was also soundproof. His other contributions were always technically reliable and also introduced some interesting plastic forms into an otherwise rather rigid universe. Thanks to Prouvé and his mastery of working in moulded aluminium, rounded forms were introduced to soften the hard, rectilinear lines of the building, for example, in the curved reinforcement columns for the south façade of the first-floor hall or the ellipsoidal handrails of the staircase. Prouvé also received a direct commission for the layout of the viewing terraces.[8] The sixth-floor terrace was equipped with a long shelter, running from one of the stair exits to a ventilation tower and unifying the whole under a common awning. Against the sky, the building is thus given a clean finish with a long horizontal shadow marking its silhouette like a classic attic. The roof is made of thin aluminium panels attached to articulated frames in steel tubing.

Aluminium and glass

Orly was a precursor of the considerable development in the use of lightweight alloys in the building industry at the beginning of the 1970s. The use of anodised aluminium is one of the characteristics of the built environment of this period. Light yet robust and capable of resisting atmospheric pollution, aluminium was also favoured for its decorative qualities, making it a modern material par excellence. At Orly, the curtain wall of the south façade is a combination of aluminium profiles with large panes of glass. The possibilities of the material were also widely exploited in the interior fittings and partition walls. Aluminium sheets were used in a variety of decorative forms, particularly for the false ceilings.

The architectural appearance of the Orly terminal plays on lightness and transparency, qualities to be found not only in the glass façades of the administration building but also in the public entrance hall on the ground floor. For day-trippers and passengers alike, the terminal is treated as a commercial showcase for an economic sector in full development. Illuminated advertising panels, installed along the façade, soon added the final touches to the ground-floor hall, contributing to this architectural imperative of transparency. From the inside, it is the aeroplanes that are showcased, so to speak. The priority here was an apparently contradictory one: the planes had to be seen without being heard. The huge sheets of glass on the airside of the first-floor hall provide efficient soundproofing. Designed

by Jean Prouvé, the panes of glass measure 2.07m wide by 6.85m high and 18mm thick. They are held in place between 76 aluminium mullions using anti-vibration neoprene joints. They are fixed below but can dilate vertically to absorb the movement of the floor above. 'Each pane of glass weighs as much as a Simca (650 kilograms)' noted Michel Ragon.[9] The curtain wall on the north side of the administration building consists of 1,000 window-panes, each 2m high and 10mm thick, with two pivots enabling the window to be opened, the handle fixed directly to the glass.

Daylight and nightlight

Natural light filters throughout the whole terminal. The long north façade of the ground-floor hall suspended from the canopy is totally glazed. The apparent absence of distinction between inside and outside and the impression of an open space is accentuated by the continuity between the suspended ceiling inside and the lighting panels outside, under the canopy.

From the land into the sky, from the city to the planes, the air-traveller follows a path which can be likened to an initiation. The public halls are all places of transition and their architecture, their natural lighting and the materials and colours all help conduct the passenger in a regular progression from the city to the plane. The main vertical communication well is a good example of this: from the ground floor up to the fourth-floor terrace, the escalators rise towards brighter daylight, the colours becoming lighter and lighter.

Glass, stainless steel and aluminium; if Orly shimmers in the sunshine, Orly by night is even more luminescent. Echoing the constellation of marker lights on the runways and the apron, the terminal positively sparkles. The large glass façades not only let daylight enter the building, they also let light shine out at night, like a beacon. On the city side, inside the ground-floor hall, the continuous red band above the check-in desks acts as a bright signal and the gold-coloured aluminium (specially invented for Orly) shines in all its glory.

The decorators were particularly challenged by how to light the terminal's spaces and the lighting is designed to accompany the architecture and set it off. Of course, it also fulfils its functional purposes with high luminosity for areas such as the ground-floor custom barriers, lit with spotlights in

the ceiling. The lighting also helps to guide the passengers, emphasising the points of transition. For example, above the main stairwell, the ceiling is decorated 'like a star-lit sky', acting as a luminous attraction above the route of vertical communication. With the exception of the monumental chandeliers that give the first-floor hall its ballroom atmosphere, the lighting fixtures are mostly integrated into the architecture and usually hidden, diffusing their light indirectly. The lighting also contributes to the characterisation of the spaces and their particular atmosphere. In the 'Espace' lounge, for example, it is an integral part of the decor, incorporated into the material of the suspended ceiling.

The lighting of the ground-floor hall comes from the suspended ceiling in the form of a sheet of light diffused by translucent altuglas panels. Other strips of light serve to underline the building's architectural profiles, such as the edge of the mezzanine floor in the south hall. Similarly, the building's overall exterior contours are emphasised by lines of light: the sides of the entrance canopy are outlined in light, like the edges of balconies, marked by lines of spotlights. The 'slim-line' lamps and projectors along the edges of the fourth-floor terrace are comprised of a line of aluminium boxes placed 200mm above the floor which reflect the light so that it seems to float above the edge of the terrace.

Interior design

The terminal's exterior of glass and steel, is modern, light and ethereal. It contrasts with the more classical character inside, achieved through the use of more traditional and sober materials – marble, stone and wood. In many ways, the interior design of the terminal is independent of the exterior forms of the building. The metallic structure is totally hidden by a double skin of quality materials, selected according to criteria of durability, expense and modernity, and contributing to a monumental and solid appearance. 'The flooring, wall coverings, walls, suspended ceilings and various facings carried by the frame or attached to it make for an interior design that was elaborated with as much attention as the curtain walls and façade elements that make up the exterior architecture'.[10]

Modern materials characteristic of the 1960s, such as Formica, altuglas, Bufflon, aluminium and stainless steel, introduced

touches of bright colour, alongside more traditional materials: stone, travertine, marble, wood, earthenware, ceramics and glass. This dialogue between tradition and modernity set the tone in even the most functional spaces. The floors in Comblanchien, a marble-like stone, were given a grid of Bakelite bars. The 'Roman blond' walls in travertine stone have a reassuring, solid and tasteful appearance. The rows of columns are sheathed in marble slabs and aluminium sheets with joints that suggest bonding. With their bronze bases, these columns also contribute to the monumental effect.

Within the design team, certain well-known decorators such as Van Hout and Motte were given responsibility for entire areas. Van Hout was entrusted with the interior design of the two major public spaces of the terminal, the large halls on the ground floor and the first floor. The register of colours contributes to the contrast between the two. On the ground floor, harmony is obtained between the dark green of the columns and the bright red of the long band made of panels covered in Bufflon (a textile coated in PVC) and the gold-coloured aluminium strips suspended from the ceiling. The check-in counters, with their simple horizontal lines (a lower shelf for cases, an upper one for hand luggage), follow the line of columns to meet the information desk. All these desks are coated in a wood-coloured Formica veneer, resistant, easy to maintain and reassuring in its tone. Simple

The first-floor departures hall on the airfield side in 1961 (ADP)

199

illuminated panels present the signs of the airline companies.

Towards the main staircase that leads the passengers up to the first floor, a low transitional space, treated in white plaster, is marked by the corner of the red band on the travertine wall. At the level above, closer to the light, the atmosphere is deliberately brighter, with light-coloured flooring, a sky-blue ceiling, white marble and the pale 'Orly blond' aluminium. The light coming in through the vast transparent façade bathes seating carefully set out at right angles to the glass wall. The benches are covered in grey-blue moleskin, alternately light and dark, reminiscent of the colour of the ceiling. Their structure of black steel tubes lets the brilliant surface of the floor disappear beneath them.

Joseph-André Motte[11] was commissioned to design several major spaces inside the terminal. For the 'Espace' lounge, set aside for passengers in transit, he designed comfortable groups of modulated armchairs with original structures of square steel tubing. The atmosphere in this lounge is intimate, warm and relaxing. The suspended ceiling in white plaster is sculpted with broad luminous bands, the walls are covered in rosewood and the orange and white armchairs are set off by the green carpet. A glass partition makes it possible to see the planes and, in the foreground, the visitors passing by on the mezzanine floor above the main hall. On the north side, the view from this lounge opens out towards Paris.

The main stairwell, with its escalators rising from the ground floor, are lined in stainless steel, a material also used at Orly for the lifts. The landings vary in size: on the third floor, the landing widens out onto a fountain designed by Motte. Apart from Van Hout and Motte, two other artists also worked on the terminal: Jean Lurçat signed the large tapestry of the 'Trois Soleils' restaurant while Henri Plisson designed a ceramic wall.

During the 1960s, the aviation industry made a significant contribution to industrial aesthetics and the new Orly terminal was part of this movement. The materials and the way they were used, the details of the interior design, the decoration and fittings of the building, the furniture, the graphics and the signage were all the result of detailed studies and, during the next few years, had a tangible influence on the standard production of other everyday environments. Motte's so-called 'Airborne' furniture and stainless steel furnishings were to be found in many public buildings and offices. The Orly escalators, lift-doors, automatic doors and even litter-bins as well as the Deberny-Peignot/Frutiger graphics and direction signs on their yellow background, were widely adopted elsewhere, particularly in the transport sector, as symbols of modernity.

The Orly sound

It was at Orly too that the special sound environment of the modern airport was invented. In order to avoid the congested noise of railway stations, the airport employees were all equipped with individual radio-controlled buzzers. Free of the endless announcements concerning only the staff, the public-address system, a 'murmuring' system using 3,000 speakers, was now reserved for visitors and passengers. Only the suave voice of hostesses announcing far-away destinations now filled the halls. Similar to Orly's animated 'Solari' information boards, this novel sound atmosphere soon became part of the global airport terminal image.

The rehabilitation project

Despite regular but piecemeal maintenance work, the public spaces of the terminal building of Orly-Sud were in bad repair. In view of this situation, the heads of ADP adopted an original approach, undertaking a renovation programme in keeping with the history of the building and its original character. As owner, responsible for running all the airport installations, ADP is also the project manager and has an integrated structure including architects and engineers that enables it to carry out all the construction and renovation projects on its facilities. At Orly, however, the special conditions justified the exceptional intervention of external consultants[12] entrusted with a historical study that was to underpin the specifications for the rehabilitation of the terminal's interior spaces. For ADP, the head architect for the Orly-Sud renovation programme was Pierre-Michel Delpeuch, assisted by Jean-Claude Flouvat.[13]

The main challenge was how to recover the original coherence of Orly's architecture while carrying out a major project of renovation, adaptation and up-dating to modern security standards. What 'ideal reference state' could be identified to give form to this renovation project? An overall approach made it possible to make specifications for the work to come and to establish a hierarchy in the interventions.

Forty years of minor modifications had left their mark. The original transparency offered by the large panes of glass had been lost with the accumulation of retail outlets. The lines carefully drawn by the check-in counters had become illegible. The carefully planned lighting scheme had become redundant or was dominated by the sheer number of signs. The colours had become tarnished and what were originally bright patches of colour had disappeared behind the glare of even brighter brand names. Use and wear and tear had got the better of Henri Vicariot's work. Setting nostalgia aside, it was necessary to restate the 'memory' of Orly while taking account of today's realities. Individual measures could be taken as long as they were underpinned by an overall logic.

Analysis

The history of the construction of the terminal, its evolution and successive extensions and alterations was thoroughly researched, based on the systematic examination of the periodical literature of the time and on the examination of private and public archives, those held by ADP in particular. Based on this research, and along with investigations *in situ*, it was possible to define an initial state as a point of reference. Understanding the original architectural choices was essential for the understanding of the building as a whole. Architectural drawings, samples of materials and the identification of techniques used then provided more detailed information about the initial state. An inventory of the major alterations and an analysis of the essential features still in place made it possible to evaluate levels of alteration and the conservation of permanent features. The diagnosis then led to selection, the grading of the changes and the examination of the principal dysfunctions.

Intervention principles, specifications, reference guide

Following the conclusions of the analysis, the initial state was used to underpin the proposals for certain zones and certain structures. For other spaces, however, this initial state is considered more as a basis for reflection. All the public halls of the terminal have been divided up into 24 areas and identifiable spatial units, divided into four categories that call for different approaches: 'major' spaces to be restored, 'functional' spaces to be adapted, 'neglected' spaces to be revitalised and spaces 'in mutation', to be rehabilitated. The different spatial units are the object of documentary files that include descriptions of the original architecture, the conditions at the time of the study and the corrections and interventions proposed, with regard to the overall spatial layout as well as the materials and furniture.

A synthesis set out the architectural priorities and the principles of spatial reorganisation. Graphic documents make it possible to pinpoint various interventions and to visualise typologies of forms, and standards for the dimensions of fittings and furniture. A palette of colours is determined for each space while a materials file identified the original materials and the recommendations for restoration.

The hierarchy of spaces and the graduated approach to renovation

For the four categories of space identified, the different renovation approaches vary from rigorous restoration to complete renovation. The main volumes of the terminal in terms of their sheer size and the importance of the public they accommodate have been categorised as 'major' spaces. They include the two large halls as well as the main communications that connect them. These spaces obviously correspond with different functional requirements of the terminal but they are also the most prestigious areas and concentrate much of the building's historic interest. The interventions must therefore preserve this historical interest while resolving the contradictions between the spirit of restoration – the only way of recovering the coherence of the original architecture – and the necessary adaptation to new patterns of use.

The constant evolution of the constraints associated with air travel and its commercial exploitation makes it necessary to define a type of growth and adaptation that is in keeping with the objectives generated by historical and architectural interest. Thus the terminal's furniture and interior fittings which are clearly dissociated from the built exterior, can often bear the brunt of the necessary adaptation. The restoration of

floors, ceilings, vertical facings, the claddings of the columns and the lighting fixtures, must be accompanied by corrective measures, however. Without affecting their form, it is necessary to take into account the practical problems raised by their everyday maintenance.

A series of rooms adjoining the major spaces, and often located at their limits, are heavily determined by the precise functions that they fulfil in the processing of passengers. These 'functional' spaces are the check-in areas, the luggage retrieval zone on the ground floor and underground levels, the gallery beyond the customs barriers with its duty-free shops, and first floors of the piers. Following changes in use, all these spaces have been profoundly modified since 1961. Here, however, historic interest does not dominate the makeover operation. Most of these spaces call for new design programmes as a result of their successive adaptations throughout the years. Interventions aim, in particular, to improve their relations with the adjoining 'major' space. The proposed corrections to volumes and atmospheres seek to re-establish a continuity that has been lost, particularly by means of materials, the colours of the claddings, the lighting and the forms of the furniture.

The 'neglected' spaces are the public spaces at the underground level of the terminal – a public gallery and a shopping centre – as well as the fourth-floor terrace and the former cinema, still occasionally used as a conference room. These parts of the terminal have gradually lost their attractive qualities, although, in the original project, they were never dealt with as prestigious spaces

with luxurious materials. They were not dominated either by changing functional requirements and since they were not obligatory points of passage for visitors, they tended to fall into disrepair. Today, these 'neglected' areas are waiting to be reinvented and revitalised.

The last category of spaces 'in mutation' are those situated near the major spaces, but on the fringes of the functional ones: the second floor 'promenade gallery' and the mezzanines that extend from it to the east and the west, the prestigious 'Espace' transit lounge, the stairwell on this floor and on the third and fourth levels with their restaurants and terraces. The original qualities of these spaces, created by talented interior designers, have made it possible to avoid total neglect but they are, to a lesser extent, architecturally impoverished and ignored by the public. They all offer interesting possibilities for architectural redevelopment and represent one of the key issues for the future of the terminal. It would be possible to give them new significance and new uses without radical alterations.

This type of project, still only too rare in France, highlights the importance of pilot studies and of the need for architectural and archaeological understanding where the rehabilitation of the heritage of the second half of the 20th century is concerned. Compiling information, creating specific tools and drawing up guidelines makes it possible to resist loss of meaning, to inform renovation work and, last but not least, to encourage creativity and innovation within identified constraints. Whether it is during the architectural survey phase, limited to the

definition of the objectives, or the phase of implementation, modesty and humility are two essential qualities necessary for those involved in this type of project. It is not so much a question of conventional architectural design but rather a mission that requires the patient teaching of all the participants and technicians in charge of the facility: in short, a collective heritage project.

Notes

1 This text is inspired in part by my contribution entitled 'Archéologie d'Orly-Sud', published in Pierre-Michel Delpeuch (ed), *Orly, La Métamorphose*. Paris: ADP, 1997.

2 The original hall of mirrors (*galerie des glaces*) is the one at the Palace of Versailles. The events of 24 February 1961 were widely covered by the press, and several articles followed in architectural reviews: see *Architecture d'Aujourd'hui* 17 (September 1961); *Travaux* (December 1961); and, above all, the special edition of *Techniques et Architecture* 6 (September 1961). These texts are precious documents today, bearing witness to the original state of the terminal and giving much background information on the project.

3 Gérard Monnier, 'Pour le néo-monument', and J Rykwert, 'Keynes et le Pharaon'. *Le Débat* 10 (May–August 1992). Paris: Gallimard.

4 Michel Ragon, *Journal des Arts,* June (1961).

5 See, for example, Jean-Pierre Epron (ed) *Architecture, une anthologie*, Vol 1. *La culture*

architecturale. Liège: IFA/Mardaga, 1992.

6 Michel Ragon, *Journal des Arts*.

7 Jean Letondeur, *Hommage à Henri Vicariot, 1910–1986*. Letondeur was chief engineer at ADP's architectural and engineering department.

8 See *Bulletin de l'association des amis de Jean Prouvé* 8 (February 1999), Nancy.

9 Michel Ragon, *Journal des Arts*.

10 Henri Vicariot, *Travaux*, December (1961), or *Techniques et Architecture*, September (1961).

11 Born in 1925, in the course of thirty years of a brilliant career, J A Motte was entrusted with large-scale projects by the government (maritime station and administrative centre of Le Havre, participation in the renovation of the large gallery of the Louvre). In the 1960s, which he described as an era that was overflowing in ideas, he chaired the Société des Artistes Décorateurs (SAD). Various seats and tables were created by Steiner; in 1967 he created a series of desks for top civil servants in stainless steel for the *Atelier de Recherche et de Création du Mobilier National*. Exhibited at the Centre Georges Pompidou in 1984, his Airborne unit chairs and his office chairs are still part of the collections of the *Mobilier National*.

12 Cécile Briolle, Claude Marro, Jacques Repiquet, architects, with Jean Percet colourist, Paul Smith, historian and Lightec, consultant lighting engineers.

13 See Pierre-Michel Delpeuch (ed), *Orly, La Métamorphose*. Paris: ADP, 1997.

The main entrance hall in 1997, with the new check-in counters designed by Briolle, Marro and Repiquet (ADP)

The Future of the Historic Airport

Air transport in the Berlin-Brandenburg region

Michael Cramer

The debate surrounding the future of the region's air transport infrastructures has flared up again, the Christian Democrat party (CDU) distancing itself from an earlier agreement and now demanding that the airports at Tegel and Tempelhof be kept open. The Social Democrat party (SPD) is standing by the 'joint decision', signed in May 1996, by the then Federal Minister of Transport Matthias Wissmann (CDU), the Minister-President of the Land of Brandenburg Manfred Stolpe (SPD) and the Mayor of Berlin, Eberhard Diepgen (CDU). According to this decision, the airport at Schönefeld is to be converted into Berlin's 'single airport' (Berlin Brandenburg International); Tempelhof is to be closed as soon as official planning permission is granted (in 2002 or 2003) and Tegel will be shut down as soon as the work on expanding Schönefeld has been completed. The real issue, however, is whether the region really needs a major, hub-status platform at all, although this question does not seem to worry Berlin's Senate, for whom size is everything.

The joint decision was taken in 1996 after a debate held in the euphoric context surrounding the reunification of Germany, at a time when the dream was of a large airport, capable of handling 60 million air passengers a year, a sheer 'fairytale castle' as the then CDU Minister Wissmann observed at the time.

The real problem is whether the expected numbers of passengers, on which the large airport is counting, can actually be achieved. After all, the whole Brandenburg region, with a catchment area of 5 million people, is simply too sparsely populated to justify a large airport. The countless attempts to set up direct transatlantic air links were never profitable and were all quickly abandoned. No one can say for sure how long the latest transatlantic route will survive.

Berlin likes to point to the example of London's five airports. In doing so, however, it tends to forget that these handle 104 million airline passengers every year, compared with Berlin's 13 million. The CDU's vision of three Berlin airports is flawed in economic and ecological terms.

Nor can Berlin hope to compete with Frankfurt on Main. Its catchment area of 20 million inhabitants is four times larger than that of Berlin. While empty flight slots are gold in Frankfurt, Berlin can't give them away. Six hundred direct intercontinental flights leave Frankfurt every week; Berlin only offers thirty. Connecting flights make up 60 per cent of Frankfurt's business, compared with only 3 per cent in Berlin. Even its new status as Germany's capital has failed to change matters. After all, despite being close to the seat of government, Cologne/Bonn airport never became an aviation hub and the banking district in Frankfurt generates more air traffic than the seat of parliament and government. What's more, 60 per cent of Berlin's destinations are short-haul flights of fewer than 600 km, which are facing increasing competition from trains since the completion of high-speed railway links.

The journey time between Berlin and Hamburg has already been shortened to two hours; Berlin to Hanover takes one and a half hours; Berlin to Frankfurt, by the ICE Sprinter, only three and a half hours; Leipzig is now only 59 minutes from Berlin. As the train can takes passengers directly from city centre to city centre, it is the preferred means of transport when the overall door-to-door journey time does not exceed a flight by more than an hour. With few exceptions, domestic air transport in Germany will soon by replaced by the train.

Berlin certainly needs to be integrated into the international air transport network. This has already been achieved, however, by the existing southern runway at Schönefeld. This runway has sufficient capacity to triple its intercontinental and long-haul traffic. In reality, what makes an airport productive is not so much the capacity of its runways but that of its terminal check-in facilities. Whereas the runway has a capacity for 15 to 18 million passengers, the terminal capacities at Schönefeld can currently handle only 4 million passengers a year. This means that

Tegel can only be closed when the necessary check-in facilities have been made available at the 'Single Airport' at Schönefeld.

Tempelhof Airport is currently operating with a deficit of 25 million DM per year. It could be closed down immediately. The 80,000 passengers that pass through it every year could easily be transferred to Schönefeld, as this airport is working at only half its capacity.

In the 1994 land use plan, drawn up by parliament for the whole of the Berlin conurbation, Tempelhof was already eliminated as a functioning airport. All the political parties, except the CDU, are still calling for its closure. The Senate has come up with a concept for the reconversion of the site that gives due consideration to its decades of use as an airport. The 'Airlift Park' (Park der Luftbrücke) retains the expanse and openness of the Tempelhofer Feld, thus preserving its ecological function as an area of formation of cold air and as an important climatic mechanism for the city. Traces of the runways are to be kept with their current layout, underlined by landscaping and by their slight elevation above the surrounding field. This new park is also designed to become a spatial continuation of the neighbouring Hasenheide Park. The airport's building complex is one of the largest in Europe with a surface area of about 300,000 sq m. It is protected as a historic monument and offers countless possibilities for conversion to new uses.

Tempelhof could be closed immediately, Tegel only with the completion of Berlin Brandenburg International. Until the opening of this new airport at Schönefeld, air traffic could be divided up for international flights to be handled at Schönefeld and domestic ones at Tegel. As domestic flights are becoming few and far between, as a result of the improvement of the rail network, this solution is a way of preparing Tegel's closure.

The generous subsidies granted to air transport today will no longer be justified in the future. It is important to note here that the Federal Land of Berlin, with its enormous debts (on which it has to pay 100 million DM every day in interest), granted the Berlin airport holding company (Berlin Brandenburg Flughafen Holding) an interest-free loan of 164 million DM, from 1993 to 1996, subsequently writing off this debt. Furthermore, air transport, unlike the railways, is exempt from oil taxes, and international air tickets are also exempt from VAT. Doing away with such fiscal advantages would mean an increase in the costs of flights and the consequent use of larger aircraft.

That is why it will not be possible to offer profit-making direct transatlantic flights leaving several locations in this sparsely populated part of Germany. Today, there is no common, national, let alone European organisation of air transport. Only two alternatives remain: co-operation between the airports or fierce competition between them, fought out at the expense of the taxpayer and the security of air passengers.

Berlin's airports are already in competition with other nearby airports in north-east Germany. It will be impossible for Berlin, Hanover, Hamburg, Halle/Leipzig and Dresden all to offer daily, non-stop transatlantic flights if each one is only 20 per cent full. So why don't these air passengers travel together in one large plane, for example on Monday from Berlin, Tuesday from Halle/Leipzig, Wednesday from Hanover, Thursday from Hamburg and Friday from Dresden? Today's connecting traffic at Frankfurt would no longer be necessary because people living in the regions to the north-east would have their own, daily, direct flight to the United States. Planes would be full to capacity with trains fulfilling a feeder function.

Hence the importance of creating links between the airports and other transport networks. As far as railways are concerned, instead of building a terminus at Schönefeld, a future airport railway station could be integrated into the existing network so that the airport could be reached by rail from all directions. Where road links are concerned, the logics of the 1950s and 1960s still dominate: despite shortages of public money, the Teltowkanal motorway is to be built as a new access road to the airport. It will run parallel to a six-lane expressway (Adlergestell) and the four-track Görlitzer railway, which already has a shuttle service to the airport every thirty minutes, as well as the metropolitan railway, offering connections every ten minutes.

The shuttle takes only twenty minutes from the city centre to the airport. The journey by car will take twice as long, even by the planned motorway which the CDU and SPD consider indispensable. London has found a more intelligent solution to this problem of access. Paddington Station, in the city centre, offers full check-in facilities for twenty-seven airlines operating from

Heathrow, through which 60 million air passengers pass every year. These passengers travel to the airport without their luggage, their air journey beginning at Paddington. So who still needs to go to Heathrow by car? If Berlin adopted this system, the air journey would commence at Lehrter Bahnhof and not at the airport, 25 km away. Railway boss Mehdorn has therefore also authorised full check-in facilities to be installed at Lehrter Bahnhof for all airlines.

An oversized new airport in the Brandenburg region would mean that every effort would be made to seduce as many travellers as possible in as many planes as possible to make it at least reasonably profitable. This, however, would be in flagrant contradiction with the ecological commitments of the Federal Government and Federal Länder in terms of carbon dioxide reduction.

When an Airbus 310, with a maximum of 200 passengers on board, takes off from Frankfurt for New York, almost 160 tonnes have to be heaved up into the sky. After about ten hours' flying time, covering just less than 7,000 km, 50,000 litres of kerosene have been burnt. The noxious substances emitted by the burning of huge quantities of fuel – 80 per cent during take off and landing – end up directly in the air above the conurbations to which the airports belong. As a result of air traffic, about 5,000 tonnes of carbon monoxide and 2,000 tonnes of hydrocarbons rain down every year on the Frankfurt area; the resulting carbon dioxide leads to the warming of the planet (the greenhouse effect). The Climate Select Committee of the Bundestag has calculated that 15 per cent of all traffic-related carbon dioxide emissions in Germany are generated by aircraft engines. Furthermore, during high-altitude flights, harmful substances are emitted into the stratosphere, directly reaching the ozone layer at a height of 20 to 30 km. There is little doubt that this represents a considerable contribution to the destruction of the earth's protective ozone layer.

Alongside these harmful effects for the environment, safety issues are also neglected in the public debate. The rapid growth in narrowly missed catastrophes is kept quiet, as is the enormous development of stacking above the airports: 50,000 flying hours a year over Frankfurt are not unusual.

Advocates of the vast expansion programme at Schönefeld always stress its function as a 'job-creating machine'. There is no guarantee, however, that more jobs will be created than before this concentration of air traffic at Schönefeld: the airport wheel will not be reinvented in Berlin. The jobs and the people who hold them exist already. Job losses are a more likely scenario and we will probably count our blessings if no one loses their job as a result of the restructuring. One thing is clear, even the new Schönefeld airport will not bring the promised levels of prosperity.

In view of its negative side effects, air transport must be cut down to size. A giant airport in the Brandenburg region will frustrate all the efforts that are being made to reduce carbon dioxide emissions. The idea contradicts any environmental and climate policy. It is not even compatible with market principles.

Historic transport landscapes in Berlin

Almut Jirku

Before looking at a few examples of the way in which Berlin has approached its historic transport landscapes, some observations might be useful on the relationships between landscape and perception, and on the relationships between parks and man's domination of nature. These remarks are of a general nature, with no systematic theoretical underpinning, but they can help us here to understand some of the projects underway in the Berlin region, and the particular phenomenon of the conversion of derelict transport landscapes into urban parks and gardens.

Landscape and perception

Many students of landscape planning and design are astonished to discover that the 'landscape' can be considered as an abstract notion, in the manner of space and time, a concept that has not always existed as something tangible. It comes into being only when a subject 'turns nature into a landscape in a constitutive act of seeing'.[1] In many European languages, 'landscape' initially referred more or less to the active population of a given area. It was only indirectly, via the art of painting, from the 15th century onwards, that the word became a specialist term meaning the depiction of a piece of nature; the concept entered literary language where it acquired its current general acceptance during the 18th century. As an aesthetic construction, 'landscape' is therefore relatively recent.

The landscape can only be perceived when the natural sciences are no longer viewed in their entirety but in their modern form, in which nature is broken down into individual and increasingly differentiated component parts. Following the emergence of modern natural sciences, the global vision of the world that was possible during antiquity and the Middle Ages as a 'contemplation of the cosmos', could henceforth only take place aesthetically, in the landscape. In order to see a part of reality as a 'landscape', it is necessary to be able to consider it without any feeling of urgency, outside the context of work and with no immediate fear for survival. A view can only become aesthetic when it is contemplated with Kant's 'disinterested pleasure'. Farmers, for example, do not see landscapes. They see more or less fertile pastures, land that is more or less easy to cultivate. They find it difficult to see fallow land as something beautiful.

When applied to railway stations and airports, this perhaps means that we can only see them as landscapes when they have lost their usefulness. As long as they remain in use, attention is focused on other points of reference, on tasks that need to be done, on the business of travelling. When you are in a hurry, it is difficult to distance yourself enough internally to gain an aesthetic view.

Another aspect of this question that influences our perception is the extent to which we have succeeded in dominating nature. The gardens of the Renaissance and baroque periods were still proud to demonstrate newly discovered means of controlling nature, for example with their fountains, which required knowledge of hydraulics. With the dawn of the Industrial Age, and with increasing technical progress, the notion of the landscaped garden emerged, where nature was tamed using more subtle techniques. The *genius loci* was respected and emphasis put on 'natural' features. This meant that landscape paintings, such as those of Claude Lorrain and Nicolas Poussin, could become three-dimensional. This is particularly evident with the example of the landscaped garden at Stourhead, which, in some places, gives the impression of being a copy of Lorrain's picture.

Today, we have dominated nature to such an extent that we are happy when it reasserts itself for once. The secret thrill provoked by harmless 'natural catastrophes', when the whole of the country is under snow, for example, and public life grinds to a halt, is proof of this. Today, it is much more of a feat simply to leave things as they are, to abandon a piece of nature to its own, natural devices: the 'wild' is more exceptional than the tamed. It is interesting here to look at the analysis of the symbolic contents of ruins, following Georg Simmel in his essay *Die Ruine*. The destruction by natural forces of the intellectual form – in the case of railway stations and airports, of the engineering and technical structures – is perceived as a 'return to nature'. For Simmel, the attraction of the ruin lies in the fact that here 'the work of man is finally experienced as nature'.[2]

The types of landscape that are considered to be beautiful are also subject to change. Classical landscape paintings first of all depicted pastoral landscapes, Arcadia. The Alps were not thought to be beautiful at this time. Similarly, the seaside was a conquest of the late 18th and early 19th centuries with the emergence of the first resorts. The history of tourism, amongst other things, is the history of the changes in our perceptions of landscape. Much as adventure holidays today – although these are also connected with sacrificial effort and mortal danger – wastelands can also be experienced as attractive.

As Pierre Bourdieu observes, however, it is the fate of the new in art to be judged first of all according to the criteria of the old. 'The inertia that is inherent in the understanding of art means that in periods of "change", the works that have been created using new tools of artistic production are destined to be perceived for some time with the conventional ways of seeing, in opposition to which they were created in the first place.'[3] The first landscaping experiments conducted more than twenty years ago approached new types of surface, mostly consisting of long-abandoned transport infrastructures, and were often misunderstood. Since then, however, our perceptions have changed and the charms of invasive nature are increasingly appreciated. This change has perhaps been influenced also by the increasing aestheticisation of all things, possibly also by 'trash culture'. Our perceptions will continue to change in the future.

The whole phenomenon of changing consciousness and perception is demonstrated by the process that the Ruhrgebiet underwent during the planning and conversion projects of the IBA-Emscher Park, as observed in a report of 1999. After the closure of the mines, a succession of different environments developed in the Ruhrgebiet, including new young forests. These were often extensive zones, mainly in private ownership. They were fenced off and often represented vast obstacles that had to be driven around. For the people of the Ruhrgebiet, these areas and their appearance at first were negatively perceived. They represented economic decline, dereliction and unemployment, but thanks to the planning and regeneration processes, it was possible to alter these mental associations. By 'staging' technical relics, using floodlighting for example, by accentuating particular features and by creating new amenities, these areas gradually came to symbolise a new beginning, while still bearing witness to the technical and cultural legacy of the steel and coal era.

This project has been particularly successful in linking up the individual parks and areas of housing. Thanks to an elaborate network of well-designed bridges, traffic arteries and other obstacles have been overcome and the former 'exclaves' integrated into a now familiar environment.

Transport landscapes in Berlin

In Berlin, abandoned railway sites were left for years to develop undisturbed into natural areas of scientific and aesthetic interest. These sites also bear witness to Berlin's modern history. The historic centre of the city was surrounded by main-line stations from the middle of the 19th century, the metropolitan lines coming later. After the Second World War these main-line stations lost their function and the metropolitan railways took up the remaining traffic. These old railway infrastructures are all situated today in densely populated neighbourhoods of the city, ideally placed to make up for the lack of other open spaces in the city centre. Another advantage of turning them into parks is that the basic layout of the sites can be maintained, along with their character.

Without the special status of West Berlin as an autonomous political entity, and the management by trusts of the former properties of the Reichsbahn (the German State Railways up to the end of the war), nature would never have been able to thrive undisturbed and for so long in these areas. Without any doubt, they would have fallen victim to development pressures. This fact emerged clearly during discussions about land use in the Gleisdreieck area, a disused railway site close to the Potsdamer Platz. The area earmarked as a park has been whittled away with each planning phase since the fall of the Berlin Wall.

Mauerpark: the old Schwedter Straße was dug up and restored; granite blocks and trees structure the open space of the former railway site without detracting from it (design, Gustav Lange, Hamburg; photo Almut Jirku)

There are clear differences between airports and railway wastelands in terms of the vegetation that can flourish there. The grass of the airfield is permanently mown, preventing any trees from growing. These conditions are therefore propitious for valuable dry grassland. The broad expanse also attracts many bird species that need extensive open areas, such as larks. Railway installations, on the other hand, after years of dereliction, are marked by sequences of plant growth with very specific characteristics. Kowarik calls this vegetation 'nature of the fourth kind'.[4] It can only develop in the city centre with its particular climatic conditions. Annual averages are 10 degrees Celsius warmer in the city centre than in the surrounding countryside. The climatic conditions of Berlin are to be found south of the Alps in the Milan region. The nature of the soil, frequently 'meddled with', is another factor. Thus the vegetation is specifically urban, largely made up of 'immigrant' species that arrived by rail to find favourable conditions on these sites. Last but not least, railway stations and airports are also special features within the city, large, cumbersome 'outcrops' that interrupt the usual fabric of the city. If their form, at least, is maintained by their reconversion, then a layer of the city's history is also preserved.

Railway station sites

Görlitzer Bahnhof

The first railway station to be transformed into a park in Berlin was the Görlitzer Bahnhof in the Kreuzberg district. As a park, its layout was characteristic of the visions of the 1970s and early 1980s. The local citizens who had fought for the creation of a park on this site had considerable influence on its plans and on the choice of the winner of the design competition. This team, the Freie Planungsgruppe Berlin, took into consideration all the wishes expressed by the local

population. Historic relics such as the boundary wall and some small railway buildings have been kept. The expanse and openness typical of railway sites, however, were lost by the stringing together of various functional areas, leading to the parcelling out of the whole area into small units. Since the fall of the Berlin Wall, it is possible to follow the old railway track via a bridge over the Landwehrkanal, giving access to other parks in the Treptow district.

Mauerpark

The site of the former Stettiner goods station has been transformed by Gustav Lange into the Mauerpark, the 'Wall Park'. Here, not only have the physical traces of history been preserved but also the character of the place. The railway station's history was not the only one to be taken into account, however. Even more significant were the traces of German post-war history: the construction of the Berlin Wall, its repositioning and final fall.

The emptiness that characterised this space, both as a railway yard and as a frontier zone, has been preserved and reinterpreted as a clearing within the city. The large central lawn creates a feeling of expanse in the middle of a densely built-up area. It ends with a slope on the eastern side. When the last phase of the project has been completed, the western side of this lawn will be bordered by a chestnut grove. This zone still comprises a small industrial estate, which, naturally, does not offer a suitable boundary for this lawn.

Clear structures characterise the design. The Schwedter Straße, rediscovered during construction work, was the site of the advanced part of the Berlin Wall: the holes of the border posts can still be made out, running along the foot of the slope. Parallel to this is the future central path that will be laid out northwards, flanked by trees and statues. It marks the later trace of the wall, after a territorial exchange in 1988. This path currently borders the first project phase. Between these two lines, a flight of steps, followed by a grove, forms the prelude to the Mauerpark. Another flight of steps leads up the slope, accompanied by a zigzagging path for bicycles. Small benches have been provided at each turn to allow visitors to take a rest. The rear wall, covered with graffiti, still stands as a border between the neighbouring stadium and the park. Here, granite blocks offer seats, from which a panoramic view over the city can be enjoyed.

The slope itself, inspired by the landscape of Tuscany, turns into an ocean of blossom in the spring and early summer, when apple trees, surrounded by flowering herbs, take centre stage. Throughout the year, oak trees mark the open spaces that are so many invitations to sunbathers. The modelling of this slope was continually corrected by Gustav Lange during the development phase until its profile corresponded exactly with his ideas.

To the west of the Schwedter Straße, rectangular areas framed in granite encroach onto the lawn, alternating with geometrically shaped evergreen conifers. The visitor comes across a collection of roughly cut granite stones, shaded by ash trees. This is followed by a basin (unfortunately still not completed, for financial reasons), and, opposite, an amphitheatre, nestling in the slope. A square of shaped conifers, surrounding various deciduous trees, borders the park to the north.

While Gustav Lange's fascination with high quality stones is clearly visible in this park, the gardening tradition in which it expresses itself is more discreet. The combination of plants characterises the different sites within the park, although habitats and robustness also govern the choices. On the gravel surface over the Gleimtunnel, birch trees constitute a sparsely wooded grove, while ivy and hornbeams cover the retaining wall. In springtime, a blanket of blue scilla under the birch trees offers a charming sight with herbs and grasses developing untamed. The flower-covered slope mentioned above also reflects a wealth of gardening experience.

Trees in particular, but other plants as well, need time to grow. When judging the Mauerpark, this fact is sometimes forgotten. The underlying structures are clearly visible, but they still strike some as too strict because the vegetation has not yet clothed them. Those familiar with garden shows, where time is often saved by planting large, but expensive trees, tend to find the park bleak. But it also makes a break with aesthetic traditions in other ways, in particular the tradition of the scenic, un-geometrical layout, which prevailed longer in the eastern part of the city than in the west. Not all residents see the open expanse as something positive. They would like to see more undergrowth and smaller spaces. Thus the park not only has a unifying force but also highlights our differences. Art history shows that new aesthetic forms need time before they are accepted. We can but agree with Gustav Lange when he writes: 'A park needs its own time ... Park time means tree-times, plant-times, earth-times, water-times, stone-times. Man is only a visitor and has other times for himself. The main problem with this kind of park is that the demands made on its use and the aesthetic demands change more rapidly than tree times'.[5]

In order to allow the poetry that resides in this park truly to develop, in order to appreciate it as a breath of fresh air, it needs not only to be completed (only half of the project has been realised so far), it also needs time and care, often in short supply today. But if time and care are given to the Mauerpark, one day, visitors there will appreciate Rilke's lines, which could have been penned for it: 'And you feel as if you are under stones/That hear, and you do not move'.

Other planned railway parks

New parks at the railway sites of Nordbahnhof, Potsdamer Personenbahnhof and Anhalter Bahnhof are also underway. Nordbahnhof, part of which is still used by the metropolitan system, rises on a man-made mound to the north of the city centre. At its highest point, it offers a magnificent view over the historic centre of Berlin. The design, by Fugmann/Janotta, has integrated this viewpoint into the new space of the park. A structural design concept is currently being developed for the Anhalter Bahnhof, part of the façade of which survived the demolition of the old station. The design for the future Tilla-Durieux Park near the Potsdamer Platz is by DS Landschapsarchitekten of Amsterdam. This long, narrow site is occupied almost entirely by one single impressive earth sculpture that dialogues harmoniously with the architecture around, holding its own but without any overstatement.

A bridge links this park to the Gleisdreieck. Here again, most of the old railway site has been abandoned. The urban wasteland that existed here for several decades has partly given way to new logistics and storage uses, but some railway remains are still to be found in the outdoor area of the Museum for Transport and Technology and in the neighbourhood close by. No decision has yet been taken as to the future layout and use of the whole site, to what extent it will be developed and whether this

Südgelände: metallic grids placed over the old railway tracks lead through the exceptional vegetation of the site (design concept Ingo Kowarik and Planland, Berlin; grids Künstlergruppe odious, Berlin; photo Dr Rainer Raderschall)

self-contained, elevated and recalcitrant urban outcrop will retain its character or be broken up by new streets.

Südgelände

Elsewhere, at the Schöneberger Südgelände site, nature 'of the fourth kind' has been successfully preserved and carefully developed, following the design concept of Kowarik and Planland. Railway vestiges have been preserved and, where necessary, repaired and made safe. Metallic grids mounted over the old railway tracks allow for the protection of zones of natural vegetation worth keeping. Several observation towers have been erected to allow visitors to gain panoramic views. Thanks to this arrangement, the 'wasteland', instead of being treated as such, is put into a new setting; weeds are reinterpreted and the way is opened for new perceptions that revise older patterns, helping us value the hitherto unappreciated beauty of natural forms. The arrangement does not alter the 'work' but the way it is considered.

Airports

In addition to the reflections on the Tempelhof site, presented elsewhere,[6] two other former Berlin airfields, at Adlershof and at Gatow, have already witnessed concrete transformation programmes.

Adlershof

Johannisthal-Adlershof airfield was of considerable significance for aviation history in Germany, but has been closed since the end of the Second World War. The airfield itself has grown into a valuable nature resource, the preservation of which was a condition of the competition for the major urban development organised in 1994. The concept of the architects Jourdan and Müller and the landscape designer von Reuß, made provision for

three green corridors to link the central open space with other green spaces in the surrounding area. The octagonal form of the old airfield was marked out anew either by vegetation at the edges or newly laid roads.

A specific landscape competition for the open spaces was won by the Kiefer bureau. It comprises three basic components: the green landscaped corridors, the peripheral bands for various sports and recreational activities, along the roads, and the central, open space of the airfield, crossed by two footbridges. Isolated by vegetation, the spaces reserved for various activities are aligned along the bands at the edge and slightly raised above the level of the 'nature reserve'. This allows for its vegetation to be protected from damage caused by people walking on the site. The corridors, especially the one to the east following the former gantry way, open up views from a distance towards the inner space. This layout gives the open expanse of the airfield a new frame, which helps preserve its character. The park is under construction in 2001.

Gatow

In Gatow, air traffic only ceased in 1994 after the British handed over the area to the German Federal Army. Built from 1934 to 1935 as a training airport, it was occupied by the British in 1945 and played an important role in the airlift during the Berlin Blockade of 1948. Several of the buildings on the airfield are protected historic monuments, while the former airfield is a designated heritage zone.

In 1997, a concept was sought as part of an urban development project to create 1,200 homes for civil servants moving from Bonn to Berlin, while safeguarding and developing a valuable natural resource. A design competition was organised but which excluded the part of the former airfield now occupied by the Luftwaffe museum.

Along with other advantages, the winning design by the Linie 5 architectural team and the landscape designer Ariane Röntz offered the best concept from a heritage point of view. A 'common', around which public buildings are to be constructed (schools in this case), is connected to the abandoned runways, which remain as a visible trace. The axis thus formed is continued as a view line to faraway Teufelsberg. In the airfield area, the surface is kept open, with only a few paths, highlighted by individual groups of trees. The vegetation thickens around the

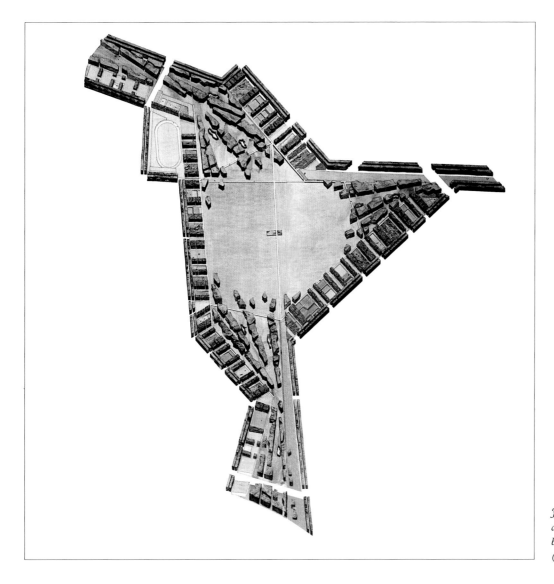

*Johannisthal-Adlershof:
design for the former airfield
by Büro Kiefer, Berlin
(graphics Büro Kiefer)*

periphery, framing the whole area. After the competition, however, it was decided to enlarge an area devoted to the museum so that most of the runway is now an exhibition area for historic aircraft. As for the park, its definitive layout will be decided by a second competition. The legibility of the runways and the preservation of the airfield's open character, however, will have to be respected by all future design propositions.

What these successful examples have in common is a respect for the specific history of each place. Where open expanses dominate, they have been (or will be) highlighted, as at the Mauerpark. Such open areas do not necessarily mean barrenness, as conventional views would have us believe. At the heart of a built-up metropolis, they are more like a gift. The gift needs to be carefully wrapped, however, so that its value can be more readily recognised. In three or four years, in addition to the two completed parks, Berlin will hopefully succeed in preparing other gift packs and paying tribute to places that is in keeping with their historic and contemporary significance.

Notes

1 Rainer Piepmeier, 'Das Ende der ästhetischen Kategorie "Landschaft"', in Westfälische Forschungen, Mitt. d. Provinzialinstitutes für westf. Landes- und Volksforschung des Landschaftsverbandes Westfalen-Lippe, Vol 30. Münster: Aschendorffsche Verlagsbuchhandlung, 1980.
2 Georg Simmel, 'Die Ruine', in Philosophische Kultur. Leipzig, 1911, 137–46.
3 Pierre Bourdieu, 'Elemente zu einer soziologischen Theorie der Kunstwahrnehmung', in Zur Soziologie der symbolischen Formen. Frankfurt am Main: Suhrkamp, 1970, 159–201.
4 Antonia Dinnebier and Ingo Kowarik, 'Natur der vierten Art', in Architektenkammer Berlin (eds), Architektur in Berlin – Jahrbuch 1992. Hamburg: Junius, 1992.
5 Gustav Lange, 'Erläuterungsbericht zur Überarbeitung'. Unpublished manuscript, 1992.
6 See the paper by Vogt Landschaftsarchitekten in this volume, pp 216–18.

Berlin-Tempelhof: the 'Airlift Park' project

Vogt Landschaftsarchitekten

The possible reconversion of Tempelhof airport's extensive flying field has given rise to several planning projects. The plan for transforming the site into an 'Airlift Park' – Park der Luftbrücke – and thereby preserving the expanse and openness of the airfield, along with traces of the site's history, was commissioned by the Berlin Senate in 1998.

Identity in context

Gardens and parks have always been at the heart our vision of paradise. They are a founding myth and an expression of the deep-seated yearnings of our society. Even in the classical modern age – the age of the machine – the garden often continued to represent an attribute of the bourgeois identity. Beyond formal platitudes, the artistic production of the avant-garde, marked by immediacy, left few lasting traces in landscaped gardens. Natural processes in the garden – growth and decay – call for longer time spans.

Today, in our age of spectacular effects, we are confronted with an ever-increasing flow of digital images without references. The Internet opens up a public arena that is unrelated to any particular place, even though protocols are still required for accessing it.

In this context, in their day-to-day work, landscape designers are faced with the challenge of formulating questions and approaches. If their work is to be credible, it must be based on the respect shown for the site in question and for the way it relates to its surroundings. Vegetation and materials, with their formal expression, can thus be interpreted within the urban context as geological stratifications, to be read as a historical narrative. The continuation of this narrative can contribute to the preservation of the meaning of a place. The endless transformation of cities is not always easy for the individual to grasp. As part of the process of memory and recognition, parks, squares and gardens play a key role by providing an unchanging feature in the evolving urban scene, helping to nurture a sustainable identity. In contrast to virtual experiences, familiar pictures from our physical reality provide real points of reference. Through their interplay, both realities acquire new meanings and contribute to an urban culture that is in keeping with the time.

Nature in the city encompasses nature in all its forms, whether natural or cultural in origin. Although all of us have internalised, if idealised, visions of nature, its individual perception has become more superficial. The opposition of artificial worlds is today much more present than an understanding of simple natural contexts. Only those who understand nature can appreciate it fully; to those who are unfamiliar with them, plants are often believed to be poisonous or exotic. Even our own profession of landscape gardeners has neglected the special sensory qualities of plants, and their potential for giving exteriors a precise, physical and atmospheric character. Careful use of vegetation, in keeping with the thematic context of a particular place, enables various readings and interpretations. These lead to the individual generation of meaning, desires and associations, revealing the essence of urban nature in a multicultural society.

Tempelhof: the name evokes an airport and the airlift, the famous *Luftbrücke*, of 1948. Today, large parts of the airport are closed to the public. The aim of our project is to open up the Tempelhofer Feld to the city as a park for the 21st century, transforming it into a new attraction at the heart of Berlin. The design project takes its inspiration from the context of the site itself and from the demands that will be made on its use; it defines a programme for the structure and contents of a central outdoor space in the city.

Along with the Volkspark Hasenheide, the vast expanse of the Tempelhofer Feld plays an important role in regulating Berlin's climate, and must be preserved as a special site with its wide-open spaces. Studies show that the air cools down over green areas similar to air in the countryside outside the city. Islands of cold air are thus formed in the middle of densely built-up

districts. Ecological functions, as a producer of oxygen and an important mechanism for the city's climate, will be preserved for years to come. At the same time, a large new inner-city recreational area will be developed for the city's population.

The ring road forms the boundary of a clearly defined inner park. Its open, green space sets off the various urban and park features in a stimulating contrast between density and emptiness. True, the ring road fences off the airfield, but at the same time it constitutes the link with the neighbouring districts.

The differentiated structure of the park with its various neighbourhoods around the ring road give the central park area its unifying force. The various demands made of it

call for a flexible, long-term development of the individual park sections that do not detract from the integrity of the whole.

The airport complex remains as an important architectural and historical entity within this unique historic site. By its conversion to new cultural and commercial uses, along with the creation of a theme park devoted to flight, the original monument can be saved and new life breathed into it.

Main features of the park

Tempelhof-Boulevard

The ring road that encircles Tempelhof gives the park its basic structure. Bordering the neighbouring city districts, it serves as a

Plan for the 'Airlift Park'. The airfield is to remain a wide-open space, a 'sea of green'. Along its periphery, zones are set aside for building development (Vogt Landschaftsarchitekten, Zurich, Prof Bernd Albers, Dipl-Ing Architect, Berlin)

217

recreational and play area. Along with its important role as a transport artery, the boulevard offers room for sports and games such as roller-skating, street ball games, children's play areas, etc.

The 'sea of green'

The park's central feature is its vast lawn, a 'sea of green' (Wiesenmeer). This levelled meadow is unique in terms of its dimensions and conveys an immediate impression of openness. A new park with wooded alleys will be laid out on the southern part of the airfield, following the runway. Surrounding a topographical landmark, the 'flight hill' (Fliegerberg), this will offer more possibilities for recreational activities and games.

The island

An island already exists in the middle of this sea of green, standing out from the rest of the field in terms of its topography and vegetation. This island is to be preserved as a trace of the first Templehof airport of the 1920s and turned into a children's play area with tall trees. The grove thus created will emerge from the former airfield as an autonomous feature.

The flight hill and garden in the sky

A 50-metre-high mound of earth is proposed as a spatial contrast to the open airfield. This 'flight hill' provides an aviation link with the history of the site: the gliding pioneer Otto Lilienthal took off on his first experimental flights from a similar hill in Berlin-Lichtenfelde. Steep paths and steps of varying gradients lead up to the top of this mound. The plateau on top will be set aside for a landscaped 'garden in the sky' (Himmelsgarten). From here, the view will extend out over the roofs of Berlin and the cityscape on the horizon.

Runways

The original layout of the post-war runways will be respected. Individual sections will be broken out of the hard surface and sown with grass. A slight increase in level will emphasise the difference in height with the surrounding lawn.

Parks along the ring road

The part of the park to the north of the ring road will create a functional and spatial link to the Volkspark Hasenheide. The area to the south of the airport site is earmarked as a new type of commercial and recreational facility, associated with the flight theme park. Existing playing fields will be integrated into the 'Sports park on the Boulevard'. These new sports facilities will be partly covered and will offer scope for commercial use and for fashionable new sports.

Paris-Le Bourget: a luxury airport?

Didier Hamon[1]

Le Bourget is a splendid 1930s airport, renowned throughout the world for its historic associations. This is the airport where Charles Lindbergh landed in May 1927 after the first Atlantic crossing from New York to Paris. It is associated too with other, less glorious events, such as Hitler's arrival in France in June 1940. The airport is currently occupied by the French National Air and Space Museum, installed in the former terminal building and in a succession of rather disgraceful hangars (except for the 1922 Lossier hangars that are still in use and which deserve better protection). Other small installations on the airport site are used for private business flying. These uses, in my opinion, do not do real justice to the indisputable historic value of the place.

Moreover, capacity limits have been imposed on Paris's other airports. Roissy-Charles-de-Gaulle, for example, is not allowed to exceed a ceiling of 55 million passengers per year. During the next fifteen years, prior to the entry into service of the third airport planned for the Paris region, it will therefore be necessary to better exploit the potential offered by the capital's existing airports.

An ill-fitting museum

The installation of the Air and Space Museum at Le Bourget is far from ideal. The historic site is inconvenient and difficult to reach by public transport. Without a doubt this museum would be better located elsewhere in the Ile-de-France region where the visitors come today, that is to say close to Disneyland-Paris, which is still expanding. The concentration of theme parks is a logical development today in the leisure industry, as suggested by the American example at Orlando in Florida, which boasts not only a Disney park but also several other theme parks. The idea of creating an aviation theme park in France is more than justified: France, as a nation, can lay as much claim as the United States to being the cradle of aviation. But to attract the hundreds of thousands of visitors that this museum-cum-theme park would deserve, another site is necessary, one that is more easily accessible and more in keeping with the museum's remarkable collections. These are not displayed to advantage at Le Bourget today. A new museum interpretation could well take its inspiration from the magnificent air and space museum at the Smithsonian Institute in Washington, where the aircraft are presented in a dynamic fashion, rather than as static exhibits. True, at Le Bourget, the museum is located directly on an airport that is still in use, though, in my opinion, this is not necessarily an advantage. The Washington museum is located in the city centre but is nonetheless a cutting-edge air and space complex of considerable educational interest and with its own Imax cinema. With all the films that are available today on aviation and space, it is inconceivable, in marketing terms, for an aeronautical museum not to have this kind of cinema.

The museum therefore deserves a better site than its present one, relatively isolated from its potential clientele. In the same way, the airport deserves better uses than that of a museum, at least in its present-day configuration. The first step is therefore to move the museum so it can show its collections in a more dynamic manner and attract the larger numbers of visitors that it merits.

Market segmentation

Freed of its museum, the next step would be to breathe new life into Le Bourget with a precise marketing and heritage strategy. The airport could meet the needs of a specific segment within the air-travel market, that of city-to-city routes for passengers travelling between city centres. This segment, mainly comprised of business flights, will certainly develop in the coming years. It is no longer possible to consider the air transport market as an un-segmented one: segmentation is a feature of all markets today. A real niche market can be created then for passengers who want to travel from the centre of Paris – and Le Bourget is very close to the centre of Paris – to the centre of London or Berlin, for example. It is necessary to put small, urban airports, such as London's City Airport or Tempelhof in Berlin, back on the map. They can be used by 80- to 100-seat aircraft with a short landing range, such as British Aerospace's BAe-146, a four-engined jet that is also remarkably silent.

A luxury airport

At Le Bourget, the terminal would be reopened as a passenger building. Its refurbishment could revive the spirit of the 1930s. This period is in fashion today, and its refined, well-tempered style has recently attracted much attention. Labro's 1930s terminal building has not been profoundly altered, at least not on the outside, and all the original drawings and photos have survived, making possible a faithful restoration of the interior. This restoration would be real regeneration, the aim being a reinterpretation rather than a carbon-copy of the original. Furniture and objects from the French School of the 1930s – real collectors' pieces today (Le Corbusier's chairs, for example, or furniture designed by Ruhlmann) – could feature inside the terminal.

Le Bourget airport will meet a specific need. Once the terminal is restored, the quality of its installations would make it a 'luxury' destination, an up-market airport that would attract up-market clients. A really exceptional monument could be created, one which would certainly attract sponsorship from Vuitton, the famous French firm that has made its name in the world of travel. Le Bourget could become the Louis Vuitton airport. Other prestigious brand names also come to mind, such as Cartier, or Bréguet (which belongs to Cartier). This is the concept of brand-mixing. The airport would thus become a showcase of the best that France has to offer, as well as an admirable exercise in heritage conservation. True, this up-market airport will not cater to tens of millions of passengers; the specific market I'm thinking of represents only a few million at most. But at the same time this exercise that would bring about a better distribution of air traffic and meet the specific demands of clients and companies who are ready to pay large sums of money for direct, city-to-city connections. Of course, this would also involve moving the private aviation activities that are currently based at Le Bourget, or, at least, managing their coexistence. Although these present-day users pay dearly for the luxury of arriving at Le Bourget, the current facilities are sparse and, on the whole, rather shabby. It is more than likely that they would be attracted by the opportunity to share in the facilities offered by a smarter airport. Could this kind of project win the support of the public authorities? Probably not: today's decision-makers are technicians and technocrats who do not really think in these terms. Marketing and heritage are notions that are foreign to them.

The public transport links between Le Bourget and Paris are clearly far from satisfactory today. They could be improved by building a tramway or a new dedicated metro system. The luxury airport that I have in mind, however, would hardly be compatible with a public transport system that is too 'public'. Passengers would use their personal vehicles or some form of 'quality' collective transport; neither is unfeasible nor unthinkable.

Airports with themes

In general, I believe that airports with specific themes represent a long-term marketing trend. In France, at Orly we have a remarkable 'sixties' airport. I was instrumental in the preservation and rehabilitation of this terminal in its original, 1961 style, though, in my view, the concept was perhaps not taken far enough: its atmosphere as a 'pop' airport was not sufficiently underlined. Orly-Ouest is the most characteristic airport of the 1970s. As for Roissy-1 at Charles-de-Gaulle, which is currently being rehabilitated, it should be restored to a style characteristic of the mid-1970s. To simplify, Roissy is a very 'Courrèges' terminal. We should try to introduce this kind of reference, but it is difficult. How do you convince the engineers that are in control of the aviation industries throughout the world, and in France in particular, that it is necessary to join forces with heritage, culture and fashion? The only person who can bring about this alliance is the marketing man, but he is not yet in command. His only influence is to talk, to think, to launch ideas. But he is not the decision-maker and even if he were, the state of mind of the techno-structure has not yet evolved sufficiently. These people think technology, capacity, safety, and so on, rather than in terms of marketing positions, or thematic, cultural and heritage references. We are faced with two totally different mental frameworks.

I believe in airports with themes, just as I believe in thematic hotels, which are becoming increasingly widespread. At Las Vegas, for example, the Americans have recreated a copy of a Venetian hotel. To our European sensitivities, this might seem extremely kitsch. In Europe, we are lucky enough to have real, authentic places and buildings. But we also want to buy into a lifestyle, embark on journeys into new worlds. They must be coherent however. At Le Bourget, we could create a very coherent universe. The latest marketing trends are perfectly compatible with our concerns for heritage and a thematic approach.

Airports as spectacle

We must not limit ourselves to purely technical, technological or logistic visions of the airport. The airport is a place that needs to be imbued with greater humanism, even with philosophy; the airport is also a philosophical place. The French philosopher Vladimir Jankélévitch developed the concepts of *déjà-plus* and *pas-encore*, the 'already-no-more' and the 'not-quite-yet', which apply to airports, in-between places, already no longer the earth but not yet quite the sky. The airport is an extremely contemporary place, corresponding with a world in which individuals are never exactly where they should be. They are always in a situation of in-betweenness: between two jobs, two women, two countries, and so on. It is a kind of schizophrenia and the airport is a schizophrenic, frenetic, dynamic object.

At the same time, the airport has always been a place of spectacle, of entertainment.

And isn't the modern world itself one big spectacle, more concerned by the image than by reality? Up to the 1960s, many people used to visit airports without ever taking a plane. This function has disappeared from airports today for so-called security reasons. The viewing platforms at Le Bourget and Orly-Sud are no longer in use. That is a marketing mistake. The airport should be a place to visit, a showcase. Orly-Sud and Versailles have something in common: they are two places designed for the staging of a spectacle: the spectacle of the king at Versailles and that of the aeroplane at the airport. But this function had already been abandoned at Orly-Ouest, opened in 1970, and is even less visible at Roissy-1, opened in 1974, which can best be seen in terms of a womb, an inward-looking cocoon. With the necessary security precautions, this function could be reinstated at Le Bourget by making the viewing platforms accessible to visitors and thus helping to put some of the magic back into air travel. The renovation of the airport would also be a rehabilitation of air travel itself, recreating its dream and its poetry.

Note

1   These remarks on a potential future for Le Bourget airport do not represent an institutional project but are intended as a contribution to the debate by an executive at Aéroports de Paris, responsible for public relations. They do not reflect current thinking or policies either of this institution or of the French transport ministry.

The future of the historic airport

Paris international workshop round table, Friday 22 June 2001
Chaired by Corinne Bélier, *Curator at the
Cité de l'Architecture et du Patrimoine, Paris*

Participants:

Didier Hamon, *Director of Public Relations, Aéroports de Paris (ADP)*
Jean-Luc Lesage, *General Inspector, Direction générale de l'Aviation civile*
Paul Andreu, *Architect, Aéroports de Paris (ADP)*
Yves Abbas, *Head of Airport Development, Air France*
Wolfgang Voigt, *Deputy Director, Deutsches Architektur Museum, Frankfurt am Main*

Corinne Bélier: Over the past three years of studies and conferences, the Raphael 'L'Europe de l'Air' project has helped us appreciate the significance and the fragility of our common airport heritage. We have been able to define the contours of this heritage and to scrutinise some of its major sites, from the early age of the grass airfield to that of today's complex runway systems. The need to set the whole debate in an international or, at least, European context was immediately apparent to us, and has been confirmed by what we have seen of the issues involved in preserving the rare historic airports that have been handed down to us more or less intact.

In many cases, the future of these historic airports is still in the air. Something worth keeping? Certainly, but what for and in what economic environment? Is it reasonable for us to argue for their continued aeronautical use or should we encourage the quest for new, non-aeronautical functions? In order to find viable solutions, we thought it was important, at the conclusion of our cycle of workshops, to focus attention on the present-day organisation of the sector. Today, in the summer of 2001, what are the forecasts for the evolution of air traffic? How do the main players in this sector – the airport operators and airline companies – see the future? What, in their view, will its repercussions be on the organisation and architectural design of new terminals? And what is the current context of our historic airports? These questions take on particular importance when large sites such as Orly-Sud and Roissy-1 in France, or the late 1950s terminal at Brussels, already considered as

'historic', need to be modernised if they are to remain competitive.

This round table therefore brings together some of the key players within the sector: France's air traffic control organisation (Direction générale de l'Aviation civile), an airport owner (Aéroports de Paris), an airport architect (Paul Andreu), an airline company (Air France), as well as a historian specialised in buildings for air travel, Wolfgang Voigt.

Didier Hamon, as director of public relations at ADP, what do you expect from an airport and what kind of position can a historic airport hope to occupy today?

Didier Hamon: I would like to open the discussion with a question of my own. What is an airport? First and foremost it is a logistical and technical structure that serves the commercial policies of the airline companies, particularly the ones based on the site. But it is also a political object. The strategic problem now faced by all the major European airports is their 'acceptability'. Can the environment accept their continuing development? As things currently stand, the answer is no. But 'airport' has other meanings as well, of a sociological or even philosophical nature. It is an eminently contemporary object that belongs to the modern world in ways both positive and negative.

Positive, in the sense that it represents an 'in-between', as Vladimir Jankélévitch might have put it, a 'not-only', a 'not-quite-yet' and an 'already-no-more'. It is no longer quite the earth, a country or a city, but it is not yet the sky, the plane or the journey.

Negative in the loss of orientation that is inherent to this situation of in-betweenness, a situation that can be seen as particularly characteristic of the modern condition, in its dream-like, poetic and even erotic dimensions. Who are we? Where are we going? Who with? The passenger at an airport is no longer quite his usual self. To a certain extent he can shrug off something of his social and economic status. He thinks he has acquired a certain freedom. If gate 32 leads to his plane, gate 34 means flying off to another destination, another destiny. This imagined margin of liberty is a false one, of course, an illusion, and, as such, quintessentially modern too. On a more mundane level, the airport is also a place of confusion because the signage is nearly always complicated, problematic. The difficulty of finding one's orientation in a place where usual bearings and meanings are suspended is no coincidence, particularly in French, where 'sense' can mean 'direction'. Architecture can bring both meaning and direction to these places, giving them symbolic or even metaphorical contents. Paul Andreu will explain this better than I can.

But this leads to another question. Who does the architecture of an airport belong to, particularly when it becomes architectural heritage? The architect, the 'great architect', naturally imagines that it is his creation, and up to a point, this is true. But as soon as the airport is recognised as a success, it ceases to belong to him.

Another issue today is the conflict of interests between the airport's owner and the architect, between client and builder, or, to put it more simply, the equilibrium between functionality and aesthetics. In France, conferences and seminars on this topic always conclude that the two are by no means incompatible and that it is just a question of balance. This happy medium, the typically French *juste milieu*, seems to me to be inoperative however. The owner – the airport authority or, in certain countries, the Ministry for Transport or Civil Aviation (ie the State) or independent companies such as the British Airport Authority or the Frankfurt Airport Authority, privatised this year – is the entity that pays for the airport. Behind the owner are the airline companies such as Air France, which Yves Abbas represents here. Their requirements mean that they are never entirely satisfied with the airport. An airline company operates according to imperatives which are not those governing the owner or the architect. The president

of an airline company does not really know what his company will be up to in two years' time. The owner, on the contrary, has to plan on a far longer timescale, the life of the building, which might be thirty, forty or fifty years, including modernisation and renovation phases. Finally, beyond the airport owner and the airline company, there is the most important player of all, who is rarely mentioned, even if he has the last word: the client. The market does not express itself clearly. We put our questions to some of its ambassadors, a few spokespeople, a few directors of communication, but the market itself is impossible to fathom.

What part can heritage play in this context? It is a modest one, even if, here and there, a handful of talented people are doing their best to give airport heritage better recognition. The splendid 'L'Europe de l'Air' programme, which is supported by ADP, has highlighted the threats hanging over some of our exceptional 1930s airports in Europe. In Liverpool, the airport has witnessed a superb programme of reuse, but its airfield is no longer in activity. For Berlin, we can still be optimistic, even if we should remain wary of the energy for reconstruction shown by the decision-makers of the 'new Berlin'. As for Paris, I am constantly dismayed that the terminal at Le Bourget is no longer used for air travel, but I expressed my views on this subject at the workshop in Berlin.[1]

In France, the whole debate about the creation of a third airport in the Paris region is organised in a simplistic, state-dominated and technocratic manner, and technocratic is the term that should put us on our guard. But is the concept of a third airport a judicious and pertinent one? In the future, the market for airport provision, similar to the air transport market itself, will have to segment itself to a far greater extent than is currently the case. There is no reason why the rules of marketing should not apply to airports, which, after all, are also commercial objects. Around Paris, we could imagine not three airports but five or six, each with a specific function and catering to a specific section of the market. Here, in keeping with these marketing developments, a splendid building such as the terminal at Le Bourget, once rehabilitated, could be reopened as an airport, with a magnificent future ahead of it.

Corinne Bélier: Jean-Luc Lesage, is the growth in air traffic really inexorable? And if the answer is yes, is there no other viable form for airports of the future than as major hubs, or are there other niche markets to be explored?

Jean-Luc Lesage: I suppose I am one of the technocrats mentioned by Didier Hamon, working on the project for Paris's third airport in the light of market considerations, while forgetting that an airport has a soul. But put this way, the question seems to me to be too simple. Before I started working for the Direction générale de l'Aviation civile, I was involved for four years with the renovation of the Louvre. I am perhaps well placed then to provide a few elements of response to the question of the concept of the airport as both air terminal and museum.

Thirty-five years ago, at the Ecole nationale d'Aviation civile, I had a teacher who worked for an airline company. He described to us the ideal airport from the company's perspective: a simple post at the edge of the tarmac, equipped with a telephone (today this would be a computer screen) indicating the time of arrival of the next plane. Since then, airports have developed into gigantic complexes.

What are the future prospects for air transport? Is there a place for the 'interstitial' airports imagined by Didier Hamon? In France today, the market is governed by mass demand for increasingly frequent flights to distant destinations. But talk about the market should not lead us to forget the passenger. Everyone talks about the passenger, but this passenger rarely expresses himself personally. The situation is a classic one: the market is examined from a marketing point of view by the airlines and the airport operators, who do the talking on behalf of the passenger. In actual fact, the data, and qualitative data in particular, fails to take his expectations into consideration, his reaction, for example, to the time spent waiting for a connection, more often than not delayed.

Today's main marketing tendency then is to concentrate air traffic at hubs. These are the major platforms that process so-called local passengers – the ones at the point of departure of their journey – but also a large proportion of passengers in transit. In Paris, 35 per cent of the passengers at Roissy and 13 per cent at Orly are in transit. At Frankfurt and Amsterdam, this proportion rises to 42 per cent. During a recent tour of Europe to meet the managers of these large platforms

and the representatives of the main European airlines, it became clear to me that these players who dominate the market today now reason exclusively in terms of hubs, where traffic is therefore expected to develop. This trend will be reinforced with the appearance of huge airliners such as the A-380, concentrating passengers even more in what we might call the 'large pipelines' between Paris and New York, for example, or Paris and Montreal, Paris and Tokyo.

We currently estimate that this traffic will increase in France at a rate of about 3.5 per cent per annum during the next twenty years. This rate might appear low and our colleagues at Air France consider this estimate to be too modest. During the past decade, and in particular the past five years, France has witnessed a considerable increase in traffic, about 10 per cent per annum, most of it concentrated at Roissy. But this growth rate has recently fallen slightly. For example, throughout the first four months of the year 2001, it stood at 3.5 per cent. The future of Paris's airports clearly depends on international flights from France, with long-haul flights on the one hand and medium-haul flights, mainly to European destinations, on the other. Domestic traffic in France is declining, as a result of the progressive disappearance of Air France's competitors, and the competition from high-speed trains, the TGVs.

This phenomenon should not lead us to neglect the emergence on the European scene of low-cost companies such as RyanAir or EasyJet, with their strategy of avoiding the large hubs. These carriers certainly have a bright future in Europe, particularly for flights coming into France, one of the world's principal tourist destinations: Paris and its region, the South of France and the Alps during the winter. For the time being, France is less affected than northern Europe by these low-cost companies, but a huge development in low-cost flying is undoubtedly on the way. Such companies, on the lookout for operational bases, would probably be happy to use Le Bourget, where traffic is not as busy as at the large airports of Roissy or Orly and where passenger processing costs would be lower.

Two competing networks are therefore likely to develop: the large companies with their operating partners, their transit hubs and their scheduled flights to the large platforms, and the charter and low-cost companies providing direct flights without connections. Airports will segment themselves according to these functions: the large and extremely busy hubs such as Roissy, with about 100 flights an hour (in the United States, there are up to 200) and the cheap, outlying airports. In the Paris region, the example is Beauvais, 74 km from Paris in Picardy. Every year, this airport handles about 100,000 extra passengers; RyanAir alone, with only two destinations, attracts 500,000 extra passengers per annum.

Business airports represent another category, with activities generally described as non-commercial. Their evaluation is complicated. For an airport such as Le Bourget, for example, no statistics are available. There is clearly a future for Le Bourget here, just as there is for other airports of its type. The major airports integrated into the international network have considerable difficulty in managing large numbers of non-commercial flights, transporting small numbers of passengers, often as few as ten per flight. In the shorter or longer term, between five and fifteen years from now according to the sites, the large airports will become clogged by this problem of coexistence. Thus, any airport that offers room for non-commercial aviation will be highly sought after.

So, is it necessary to maintain commercial aviation activities in these historic airports, while at the same time keeping them open as museums, such as the one at Le Bourget, considered 'dormant' by some?

Corinne Bélier: Paul Andreu, as an architect, could you give us your views about how these predictions for the evolution of air traffic are changing the expectations of owners and users where airports and their architecture are concerned?

Paul Andreu: I have to admit that I am somewhat confused. Today, I was expecting to talk about the future of historic airports and, next week, at another conference, I am supposed to speak about the airports of the future. I have the feeling that I have got my dates wrong. Where to start?

Air traffic is changing: we see that every day. As Didier Hamon explained, a requirement of a very short-term nature leads to some extraordinary demands. The tendency, highly characteristic of today's situation, is to interpret an immediate economic demand as an absolute good. Obviously, I appreciate all the advantages offered by the hub, and I'm perfectly able to make a distinction between long point-to-point flights

and flights that transit via a central hub. But if the passenger appreciates the economy that the hub can offer, he only accepts it if there is no direct, point-to-point connection. If my discussions with passengers are anything to go by, what they really want is to board a plane and be flown directly to their destination without getting off, without the risk of finding themselves on the wrong flight, on a flight other than the one they expected or with an airline company whose name is not the one on their ticket. We need to take a step back from the 'inescapable economic necessity' for the hub. The hub is a present-day requirement that we should try to satisfy as best we can. But there are thousands of scenarios in which a short-term need is transformed into an overriding good. It is not healthy to think in these terms, with such a short-term view.

As far as the architecture of airport passenger terminals is concerned, uncertainty still prevails. The history of their design comprises several periods, and some of them can be seen as heroic. The buildings of the 1930s, clearly inspired by maritime architecture, bear witness to the ambitions of the age. Le Bourget or Chicago's first terminal are buildings conceived as gateways that proclaim the importance of the city, while dealing at the same time with the problems posed in technical and organisational terms. The 1960s was another period of research. At Tampa, Houston, Los Angeles and so on, new models were invented, aircraft holding positions and movements on the ground were rethought and, above all, the distances covered by passengers were reduced, controls made more efficient with magnetic passports and so forth. Facility was the key word.

For the time being, however, this intensive typological research left architecture aside. When I began my career, some people told me that putting architecture into airports was pointless. When I advised the Japanese to commission Kenzo Tange to design their terminal, they replied that his buildings were complicated and that they leaked! In the United States, people at Tampa told me: No, no architect! Just the engineer and the decorator! The guy who writes the brief and the guy who chooses the carpets are quite enough. At Aéroports de Paris, when I praised the beauty of Saarinen's TWA terminal at New York, people said it was an 'absolute horror', a concrete construction you couldn't do anything with. These were the same kinds of people who wanted to cut down all the trees along the roads of France because they could be inconvenient for car drivers.

And then architecture made a comeback. After having designed museums, architects started to look at the airport passenger terminal as a fantastic and prestigious type of building. Every 'great architect', as Didier Hamon calls them, was impatient to design an airport terminal. The owners, for their part, suddenly realised that the airport terminal was as visible 'as a nose in the middle of the face', that it represented the point of passage everyone went through. Developed countries as well as developing ones witnessed ambitious projects which all wanted to express something special. But, just as every silver lining has a cloud, typologically speaking, the airport became a desert. A single, ultra-simple terminal model imposed itself, with its satellites and the little trains leading to them. This model could be found throughout the world. I remember the disappointment of certain people at Air France who deplored the fact that this wonderful model, capable of ensuring their well-being for centuries to come (or at least a couple of years), was still not available in France. In the end, it was decided that it would be a good idea to let the architect wrap this model up in 'quality packaging', in 'good taste', forgetting that architecture is not about good taste, on the contrary....

Because of constant change, even the most carefully tailored buildings are obsolete within ten years, whence the return to basic concepts, that is to say large hangars designed above all to facilitate movements of people. But today, in airports, fluidity is practically non-existent. Controls have increased but are slower than in the past, insufficiently staffed for the volume of traffic. You need only to take look around Roissy at midday to see this: most of the gates and check-in points are closed and an arrow instructs the traveller to move along another 100m. Walking is no longer a problem, however. The passenger is taken care of by various technical devices, people-movers that facilitate this endless displacement. On this score, the latest developments beat all records: a distance of 700m used to be considered as a maximum, whereas today, 1,500m is no problem.

In this new, rather uncertain phase, architecture has a part to play. Like the psychoanalyst explaining to parents that they will never be good parents, it can explain 'You will never have the terminal you really want. But a more or less convenient terminal, that is possible, a terminal with beautiful architecture if possible, and which offers passengers the chance to think about something else'.

As for historic airports and the question of their future, I would simply like to draw attention here to our amazing propensity to honour and save only what is dead. Whereas in some countries, people are building new terminals and spending fortunes on them, others, elsewhere, are destroying what they already have. The airport operator has endless imperious and immediate needs – a new machine for shining shoes, another for handling luggage, another to sell Coca Cola – that gradually clutter up and degrade the space. The question has been raised in terms of who these buildings actually belong to, whom they are for. Usually, they only become a part of heritage, of the national estate, when they are worn out and damaged beyond repair. But why not consider them straight away as common property that should be used carefully and responsibly? The economy of an airport terminal is a complex one and the heritage questions will not be settled at a stroke.

Corinne Bélier: Yves Abbas, for today's public, largely made up of heritage specialists and architecture fans, you promised some provocative comments. What does an airline company expect of a terminal, and can its architectural qualities help you with your customers?

Yves Abbas: As spokesman, here, for the airline companies, I shall look mainly towards the future and only briefly at the past. If there are historic airport buildings, there are also historic companies. Founded in 1933, Air France is one of the world's oldest airline companies. It has had several lives and been based at several different addresses. When it was created, it was located at the Invalides terminal, in the heart of Paris, a building that still exists today, where the passengers checked in before leaving for Le Bourget. It is soon to move into the wonderful E terminal at Roissy, designed by Paul Andreu. So the company moves at fairly regular intervals, trying, as far as possible, to be housed in the most recent building, best suited to meet its needs.

How does it function? Air France is a commercial company that sells transport in a competitive environment. It has two types of customers. The first is the businessman. Global exchanges are developing regularly and, contrary to what could be heard a few years ago, travelling and face-to-face meetings remain indispensable, despite progress in communication technologies. These businessmen need to travel all over the world and within their own country as well. Satisfying their demand is not simple, since they also want to arrive quickly. These two demands lead to the concept of the hub airport, although some apparently think this is not a lasting solution.

The principle of the hub is a simple one. From Montpellier, Stuttgart or Venice, for example, there will never be a direct flight to Tokyo. Hub platforms are therefore unavoidable, as only they make it possible to assemble the passengers who want to travel to this destination. The essential issue arising from this situation is the question of comfort. The airport and its passenger terminal building have an important function where the passengers' comfort is concerned, especially when they are in transit, a stage most would be happy to avoid altogether.

Our second type of customer is the private individual. In rich countries, increasing numbers of people can afford to fly. In real terms, the price of an airline ticket has come down considerably during the past thirty or forty years, even if recent increases in oil prices have led to slight price rises. But a huge demand still exists, and needs to be met.

Our first stimulus is therefore the customer. Contrary to what has been said here, we are constantly trying to find out what his opinions are, by means of frequent surveys. You could have been asked to complete a questionnaire on board one of our flights already. In fact, each flight is an opportunity to ask our passengers about their expectations, their satisfaction and their experience. This sort of procedure is one common to all commercial companies. We try to represent the views of our passengers, to act as their spokesperson.

The second stimulus is competition. We will never be alone in this market, despite the difficulties currently suffered by some of out competitors. Competition covers various areas and is played out between the airline companies who all share the same coherence, based on their presence in large airports. The emergence of airport hubs has given rise to a new form of competition, that between the airports themselves. Until recently, airports led a quiet existence based on their natural catchment areas. Paris had its reservoir of clients, obliged to use the existing airports regardless of whether they were beautiful, functional and easy to reach. Today, with the growth in transit passengers, the situation is changing. A commercial war is being waged for the passenger who wants to go from Venice to Tokyo. In this case, the competition is played out not only between Air France and Lufthansa but also between the airports of Paris-Roissy and Frankfurt am Main. Finally, in France, there is another form of competition between different modes of transport. This has come to the fore since the inauguration of the new high-speed TGV line between Paris and Marseilles. The TGV is a serious competitor and its competition is not wholly fair. A large part of the TGV infrastructure is paid for by the tax payer (I need only remind you here of the huge debt of Réseau Ferré de France, France's railtrack operator). Transport by high-speed train can therefore be cheaper than air transport, which has to cover all its infrastructural costs. At the same time, however, the TGV is a valuable partner, bringing passengers from Poitiers, for example, to catch their connection to Tokyo at Roissy.

There is no single answer to the problems of passenger transport. Airports cannot all fulfil the same function. This function depends on their geographical location and their possibilities for development. Four main categories of airports can be identified. The first is the airport of a capital city that generally functions as a hub, since, for an airline company, the capital is the best place to concentrate passengers for international flights. In the United States, the situation is slightly different, because the airports are particularly large and their domestic platforms operate as hubs. The second category includes the airports of major cities, which can constitute secondary hubs, such as Saint-Exupéry airport at Lyons, or simply offer point-to-point flights. Whatever the future evolution of these airports, they will offer few or no international flights. The third category includes the airports with low operating costs, such as Beauvais or Luton, that correspond with the specific demands of low-cost carriers. The fourth category is comprised of small airports such as Le Bourget, used for business aviation today and uncertain about their future. To date, this last category presents little interest for the international airline companies such as Air France. A few companies, however, are becoming interested in business flying today but it is not yet clear how this will materialise.

The demands we make on airports are varied. The installations must meet the companies' needs that are not necessarily what the designers believe to be satisfactory for the passengers. For us, there are basically two types of infrastructure: the new and the old. The first is still in the process of definition and development. The latest construction is terminal E, with its future satellites, at Roissy-2. Here, ADP and Air France, the tenant company for this terminal, worked together to design a building corresponding with the required functions. For Air France, the main consideration is the efficiency that the new infrastructures will offer. We also know, however, that in our own interest the system needs to be able to evolve. When we drew up the specifications for these future terminals in 1997, we were looking forward to the year 2010, which is more than the two years of which some have spoken. It is undeniable that demand evolves. The organisation of the first phase of Roissy-2 no longer suits us completely today, but it has to be accepted. The greatest difficulty is the evolution of old terminals such as Orly-Ouest, dating from the 1970s and which currently is being extended.

Among the functional features that are important in an airport, and in a hub airport particularly, clearly marked directions are absolutely essential. A passenger, more often than not in a state of stress, has to be able to find his way around easily. Dedicated channels for each category of passenger, in transit or not, can be organised. Another essential feature is the link between the aircraft on the ground and the terminal building: the 'little trains', the 'fingers' or the 'piers'. You have perhaps lived through those annoying moments when your plane is parked out on the tarmac but you have to wait for a bus, leave it in the rain ... only to miss your connection. Finally, the luggage handling systems are fundamental; they must be robust which means that they can evolve only with difficulty. Here again, it is necessary to be wary of fashions and not to underestimate the aggravation of the passenger whose luggage gets mislaid.

The financial aspect has been mentioned several times here. In France, the airport is not paid for by the State but by the passengers and the airline companies: Air France, for example, will be financing a considerable part of the new terminal E at Roissy. It is important that we participate in this work and that our partner, ADP, gives due consideration to our economic requirements. If, together, we are less expensive than our competitors at Frankfurt, London or Amsterdam, then the customer will benefit, as the savings will be reflected in the price of his ticket.

The architecture of the airport is therefore only one aspect of the question. As I have already mentioned, we frequently consult our customers, especially about repurchase criteria: why does a customer choose our company a second time? Why doesn't he fly with another company or leave from another airport? For Air France, it is essential to know what is important for the passenger. Here, the airport's architecture is never given as a repurchase factor, at least not explicitly. Above all, the user wants a simple structure that enables him to find his way around easily. When the architecture does present aesthetic qualities, however, these are recognised, even if they have no real influence in terms of repurchase. Terminal F at Roissy is undeniably a success and it is often mentioned by our customers.

To sum up, for airline companies, economic considerations rule. This economic reasoning can lead to terminals like shoe boxes, as simple as possible, meeting all the functional requirements but perfectly devoid of aesthetic qualities. If a terminal can be aesthetic as well, without costing any more, the companies will be even happier.

Corinne Bélier: In this economic context, what becomes of the historic airport terminals? Wolfgang Voigt has drawn up a catalogue of the solutions found, some of them successful, some of them less so.

Wolfgang Voigt: At this round table, my task then is to speak for architectural historians and heritage specialists. In a quick overview, let's take a look at some different places where the question of what to do with the existing historic buildings, mainly the passenger terminals, has found answers, and some other sites where decisions have yet to be taken.

We can begin with the three sites of the 'L'Europe de l'Air' project. At Le Bourget, there have been some very positive developments since the 1970s, when the younger Paris airports at Orly and Roissy took over the increasing traffic of the jet age and jumbo dimensions. It has been possible to keep a whole typology of airport buildings, including some very early reinforced concrete hangars and two generations of terminal buildings. The first airport terminal ever built, at the beginning of the 1920s, was conceived as a series of small pavilions for different functions. At least one building of this very first generation still survives at Le Bourget. The second terminal was constructed in 1937 and housed all the airport's functions – traffic control, weather services, radio, customs, airline check-in counters, baggage handling, restaurants, and so on – in one building, which was the largest of its kind in the world, until Berlin-Tempelhof was completed shortly after. In my view, since air traffic is maintained at Le Bourget, albeit on a small scale, the commemorated past is linked with the present in an ideal way. This seems to have predestined Le Bourget not only to become the home of France's national Air and Space Museum, but also to show us an architectural ensemble of the highest quality, representing the evolution of commercial air travel between the two wars. As there is now a fairly good chance of restoring Labro's terminal building to its original appearance of the 1930s, this is really a good example.

At Speke airport, near Liverpool, there is a typical 1930s ensemble formed by two hangars placed either side of the terminal building on a symmetrical axis marked by the control tower, in the shape of a lighthouse. With their rich, Art Deco brick modernism, the terminal and hangars are among the finest of the age. These three buildings at Liverpool are listed monuments today, owned by a publicly funded development company which is adapting them to new functions at the moment: the terminal into a luxury hotel with conference centre, and the first hangar into a leisure centre, with tennis courts, fitness spaces, a swimming pool, etc.[2] In 1999, during our Liverpool conference, we saw how this hangar was being adapted to its new functions. Since traffic has moved to the new airport opened nearby in 1986 (John Lennon airport today), the direct context of aviation is no longer present, but clearly commemorated by this ensemble of outstanding quality. And, what is very important, the airfield, or rather, what is now the empty space in front of the buildings, has been preserved, so far at least. Without that, such an ensemble cannot have the same quality. We heard yesterday that the Marriott hotel at Speke opened a short time ago and is already proving highly successful. Speke's reuse could be an example for other places.

Built at the end of the 1930s to the designs of the architect Ernst Sagebiel, Tempelhof, the historic airport of Berlin, is still in use for small aircraft. Planned for five million passengers a year, this ambitious project of the Third Reich is still a surprise for visitors today, mainly for the dramatic dimensions of its curved cantilevered canopy on the airfield side. Under this 1,100-metres-long steel construction, passengers could board without getting wet. The largest aeroplanes of the day could be accommodated under the roof. This roof was also designed as a raised stand for 65,000 spectators at air shows, which never took place however, as the building was not completed before the outbreak of the Second World War. This largest terminal of its age was closed in 1975, replaced by the new Berlin airport at Tegel. But, since 1990, Tempelhof is again in operation for small aircraft, until the new airport at Schönefeld will group all Berlin's air traffic on a site at a considerable distance from the city. The buildings at Tempelhof are owned by the city since the US Air Force left the site, and were protected as historic monuments in 1994. Their maintenance is ensured by the value of the large spaces inside, used today by public administrations or rented out to private firms. We need to be worried, however, about the 160-acre (65-ha) oval airfield which, according to current landscape projects, will be developed as a public park.[3] Only its small circular centre will be left free of buildings, half of the surface being developed for housing and business. Since the city of Berlin is more or less bankrupt today, and does not have the means to develop Schönefeld rapidly, however, the status quo, which is by no means the worst situation, will doubtless last longer than foreseen.

Now some less brilliant cases from my country: Rhein-Main airport near Frankfurt. Today this is the largest airport in Germany, and number three worldwide, behind Chicago and London's Heathrow. Frankfurt was founded in the 1930s as a combined airport and airship terminal for the Zeppelin routes to North and South America. It was sited next to the first German autobahn to facilitate communication between the most modern means of travel of the time. The airship hangars did not survive the war, but the 1936 terminal, designed in a modest modernist style – very different from Tempelhof – remained in operation until 1972. It was demolished in 1991 to make way for terminal two. This new terminal could easily have been built some hundred or so metres away if the value of the earlier building had been properly recognised.

Another sad story is told by the vestiges of another airport designed by Ernst Sagebiel at Munich-Riem and opened in 1939. As at Tempelhof, the buildings were aligned at the curved edge of an oval airfield. On a photo of a model, we see the clear functional division between the hangars, with the workshops in front, the terminal, with its control tower at the centre, and the large open stands for the spectators at air shows. When Munich's air traffic was moved to the new Franz-Joseph-Strauß airport in 1992, the whole site was earmarked to become the city's new fairground. When I visited them in 1995, the buildings were of course much altered, but 90 per cent of the original substance still survived. Critics were appeased with two fragmentary monuments, spared by demolition: the departure hall and the control tower that were separately integrated into new constructions. In my opinion, this is a very poor example, an alibi solution, completely separated from its context and showing nothing but ignorance.

Even less will remain of one of the earliest terminals in Europe, opened in 1929 and out of use since 1983. The curved building at Fuhlsbüttel airport in Hamburg was in a way the typological ancestor of all the terminals that followed. Inside this modernist brick construction, the functions were strictly separated into different zones and floors, a feature without which every present-day air terminal would immediately seize up. The building's sophisticated arrangement of ramps and stairways inside and out made it possible for travellers to be kept separate from spectators and restaurant customers, and from the flows of luggage and freight. The view from the airfield was unusual. The façade was stepped in a series of terraces, reminiscent of an amphitheatre. No other terminal showed so clearly the typological legacy of the hippodrome and of the early air shows, before the First World War. In the 1930s, several other terminals in Europe were directly inspired by this example, notably Liverpool-Speke and Barajas, near Madrid. The building was enlarged and altered in 1961, but still retains much of its original architecture, and a reconstruction of missing parts and details would be possible. When the future of the airport became the object of an architectural competition in 1986, the local architects von Gerkan, Marg und Partner, who are now quite well known

in Germany, won the first prize with the concept of new terminal buildings aligned on a pier, making it possible for the preservation of the older building, shoulder to shoulder with the new ones. But this solution was not adopted: in 1994, the political authorities of the city of Hamburg, which owns the airport, decided for a tabula rasa, without keeping any old structure, and with no opposition on the part of the municipal historic monuments office. Demolition is scheduled for next year.

Another forward-looking construction was the terminal completed in 1936 at Gatwick airport near London.[4] With its circular form, this unpretentious modern building, known as 'The Beehive', allowed six aeroplanes to approach it at the same time. With its six telescoping passageways that emerged from the building, this terminal remained in use until 1956, and with the exception of the passageways, is still standing. It was listed in 1996 and has recently been refurbished. Gatwick was a milestone in the typological evolution of the airport terminal, the ancestor of the insular types and satellite systems of the 1960s and 1970s, such as Los Angeles, San Francisco, Cologne and many others. I don't know whether Paul Andreu, architect of the magnificent terminal buildings at Roissy, knew about Gatwick when he designed Roissy-1 in the late 1960s, but that terminal undoubtedly follows the scheme that was first conceived at Gatwick.

A rich field for the preservation of aviation buildings, but a difficult one as well, appeared in Germany and in the countries of Eastern Europe in the 1990s, when airfields occupied by the Red Army since 1945 returned to state ownership. *Terra incognita* came back into the public mind. In Jüterbog, near Berlin, the organic forms of the hangars of the German Luftwaffe were discovered, built in a kind of pre-stressed concrete, which in the mid-1930s, was ahead of its time. A hangar nearby shows another modern technique of the period with wide concrete buttresses designed to achieve a maximum span. Another example is Rangsdorf, also near Berlin, where the Soviets had occupied the airfield of a former aircraft factory. Hangars, a control tower and test beds for aero-engines are still there, as well as production halls and the administrative buildings. As so many of the Soviet sites, they are in a miserable state today. In Germany, these places are now owned by state-run development agencies, which have begun to search

Paul Andreu's preliminary sketch for the Roissy-1 terminal, March 1967 (reproduced with the kind permission of Paul Andreu)

for new functions, a difficult task, as the quantity of buildings is enormous and most of these airfields are situated in populated areas, often with stagnant or depressed economies.

The Western Allies also left airfields in Germany. Tempelhof is one example, the civil airport being part of an American air base. On one US military base, at Böblingen, near Stuttgart, a forgotten jewel of modernist terminal architecture still survives. In the 1920s, this site was the first airport for the city of Stuttgart. An inconspicuous wooden pavilion was built in 1925, when air traffic meant five small planes per day, with four passengers each. This building is apparently the oldest terminal at a German airport. When air travel increased in 1928, a much larger building was constructed, a terminal of white modernism and clear lines, with a control tower crowned by a glass box at its summit. The airfield was later taken over by the Luftwaffe, then used, after 1945, by an American tank repair unit. As on the Russian side, the buildings remained in use, although apparently better maintained. The future of this site was uncertain for a long time, the city of Böblingen hoping to develop it as a business park. The building is now a protected monument, even if no decision about a suitable function for it has been taken yet. But here also, the future of the airfield is a matter of concern.

At Kastrup airport, near Copenhagen, in 1939, a remarkable terminal was opened, a building of functionalistic design by the architect Vilhelm Lauritzen.[5] In 1999, the whole building was put on wheels and moved across the airfield to a new site, where it would not interfere with necessary extensions. Today, this building has no specific function, but, most importantly, its historic and architectural significance is recognised.

In Seattle, in the United States, Boeing's earliest production building has also been relocated to another Boeing site in the same city. Associated with a new construction, it today houses the Boeing museum of flight. Once again, the value of the building has been recognised. Such moves are perhaps not the best solution, since the buildings are taken out of their original context, but they are certainly better than demolition.

Let me conclude with Helsinki airport, where two buildings of significant quality are under threat today. The former terminal, designed in a functionalist modernism by the architects D Englund and V Rosendal, and opened in 1938, is apparently to be demolished. The building was constructed on a spectacular circular ground plan, situated at the apex of a wedge-shape building zone that projected forward from the edge of the airfield towards its centre. This scheme had been put forward by the French engineer A B Duval in 1929, with the idea of preventing building on most of the periphery of the airfield, building that might prevent later extensions. Not only Helsinki, but also Lyons in France and Birmingham in England were laid out according to this plan.

We are all familiar with the famous TWA terminal building at John F Kennedy airport in New York, opened in 1962 to the designs of the Finnish-born architect Eero Saarinen.[6] In this building, the idea of giving a futurist signal for the competition between airlines led to the expressive roof construction, which makes not only for the best-known airport terminal building in the world, but also a classic to be found in every history of 20th-century architecture. As we heard yesterday, this building is under threat today, not so much in its nucleus, the hall, but as an ensemble in a specific context.

Corinne Bélier: Following on from this overview of some surviving pre-war terminals, I would like to come back to those dating from the 1960s and 1970s. Various examples have been mentioned. Orly-Sud and Roissy-1 are today relatively well preserved whereas at Zurich the original terminal is totally hidden, buried under gangways, satellites and other extensions.

I would like to ask Paul Andreu a question about Roissy-1. This terminal is almost thirty years old today, an age at which renovation is usually necessary. You are in the exceptional situation of being the architect of the most recent buildings on this site and also the person responsible for the renovation of its first building, which you also designed. Can you tell us how this terminal, now a historic one, will be adapted to the current context of air travel?

Paul Andreu: Roissy-1 was designed from 1967 to 1968 and entered service in 1974. This terminal is indeed reaching a respectable age. Externally, it has changed very little, except for a few additions that I find regrettable but that most people probably don't notice, such as a lift shaft that is larger than the two others. Inside, however, the terminal has witnessed a gradual but constant degradation. With current security norms, the whole check-in area has turned into an indescribable labyrinth that is impossible to cross and is marked by permanent and often unnecessary additions. The numerous working 'positions' in the terminal, for example, are only manned at a rate of 10 per cent at certain times, but everyone wants to 'mark his territory', so to speak.

This degradation finally led to the conclusion that it was time to refurbish the terminal, this decision being taken, interestingly enough, at the same time as it was decided to renovate the Centre Georges-Pompidou in Paris. These are two very different buildings, but they were designed and put into service at the same time; both have aged at more or less the same rhythm, raising similar problems. The difference is that the Centre Pompidou could close down and then reopen after its refurbishment, thus avoiding a period of extremely complicated use. For the Roissy terminal, ADP, in order to avoid extra

investment and for several other reasons, has decided otherwise, Today, a far-reaching renovation programme is planned for a terminal that will remain in service, causing difficulties for passengers and companies alike for about four or five years. But it was that or nothing.

Personally, I find myself in the rather delicate situation of being the architect of the building now entrusted with its renovation. My first reaction was to refuse, considering the request to be unacceptable; commissioning another architect for the task seemed to be preferable. But after several discussions and much personal reflection, I finally decided to accept this mission, in association with a young architect, Nathalie Roseau, who represents the future. She is at the beginning of her career, just as I was when I started work on the Roissy terminal.

We decided not to 'restore' the terminal but to carry out certain modifications in keeping with the spirit of the building, a spirit that we would like to rediscover. This building does not necessarily require all the alterations we are planning, and could make do with something less. We are trying to create what would have been done at the time, but with today's techniques, and without turning our backs on reinforced concrete, which remains the terminal's dominant material. We are even trying to show it off to better advantage by creating transparent elements that will underline its strong structural presence.

Discussions about the economic value of the building, however, prove to be impossible. In my opinion, this building was an appropriate response to the requirements for which it was built in the early 1970s. Throughout its history, its use has been twice as heavy as that initially planned for. Economically speaking, then, it has clearly given satisfaction. People tell us today, however, that new commercial spaces are necessary inside the terminal in order to make even more money, even more return on the initial investment. But a simple financial calculation would prove that it is sufficient to restore the terminal in a 'reasonable' way, without endlessly trying to make the existing space more dense and more profitable. I hope that this debate, which still has to be settled, will come to the right conclusions.

I view space, and built space in particular, as common property, a heritage that is perhaps unrecognised, difficult to recognise in certain cases, and not always officially labelled as heritage. But in reply to Didier Hamon's question 'who do airports belong to?', I would answer that they belong to all of us. And I also believe that we should know when to refuse the 'hysterically economical' that, in reality, the economy does not demand.

Corinne Bélier: Over our past three years of work on historic airports, it has become clear to us that an airport terminal is always of its age. At the time of its construction, it manifests the technical progress and the modernity of its owner, whether this is the State, a chamber of commerce or a local authority. But nothing is more ephemeral than an image of modernity, constantly replaced by something even more modern. Without any doubt, Roissy-1 bears the mark of the 1970s, and has even come to symbolise those years. Is this image an asset or a handicap?

Paul Andreu: Yves Abbas' comments are highly pertinent here. Clearly, architecture is not a vital requirement for air passengers. It is more of a gift, something extra, a small enhancement of life, but not a factor taken into account by market surveys, although marketing does not deny its existence. Architecture belongs to another realm, but a realm we need. Despite the image of modernity that a terminal projects at a given moment, it is not only the image that counts: it is what it is. We should also think about what things are, not only what people say about them.

The Roissy-1 terminal exists, then, with its faults, its qualities and its place in time, clearly, now, a historical time, considering the materials used, the aesthetic approach, etc. People find themselves in it as they find themselves inside the Louvre or the Chartres Cathedral. It would be useful to adopt the notion, a sublime one, of such large buildings as permanent building sites, as work always in progress. The curators at Chartres put it this way: 'We have never stopped building the cathedral.' Thinking about the building in this way is thinking with a mixture of respect and disrespect, which takes into account what the people have created but with an attitude that can remain free. It is the attitude that declares: 'I am not someone who is dead, celebrating the dead, but someone who is alive, speaking to the living.' It is in this way that objects from another age can meet another generation, simply and without drama.

Corinne Bélier: You once wrote that the most important feature at an airport site was the network established between the various terminals. A network enables the multiplication of passenger terminals and their gradual specialisation. This specialisation would make it possible to preserve older buildings. A question then for Yves Abbas and Jean-Luc Lesage. Must every airport take on freight, passengers, short-haul flights and international ones? What differences will there be, for example, between Orly, Roissy and the planned third Paris airport?

Yves Abbas: We reason in economic terms. An airline company will always say one airport for one city is quite enough. Various operators, thinking about the creation of a second airport, regularly consult us, just as they go and see ADP and the British airport authority for London. They ask us how we work with more than one airport for one city, as this is counter-productive for an airline company. With Orly and Roissy, we do not presently need a third airport. For the time being, our aim is to use the existing structures to the best of their capacity. But one day, inevitably, this third airport for Paris will become necessary.

We are having discussions today with the Direction générale de l'Aviation Civile and ADP about how to link Roissy to the third airport in such a way as to create an ensemble that will function as efficiently as a single airport. We do not plan to abandon Orly, as it has an excellent catchment area but one of our directors thinks it might be better, more efficient, to concentrate everything at Roissy. This is not on the cards for the moment, but....

Jean-Luc Lesage: We have talked here mainly about terminals and in particular about the role that old terminals can play in a modern airport system. I would like to draw on my experience at the Louvre. When we rehabilitated it, the question of the future functioning of the existing buildings was raised. In the same way, it is necessary to question how the terminal works and draw up a preliminary programme for any development or renovation project. The programme designer intervenes before the architect. He lists the functions of the buildings, draws up specifications in terms of space, volumes, movements, etc. The circulation movements are particularly important at the Louvre where Pei's pyramid takes care of their distribution.

Certain terminals are still clearly based in the marketplace. Roissy and Orly-Sud, even if they have aged, can be adapted. Others, however, have fallen out of the market. But they can offer fantastic views over the activity of an airport site. I have seen this in certain meeting rooms at airports such as Geneva's. The 'natural' animation makes these rooms much more pleasant than premises without an outside view. Whether a terminal stays in the market or not, conclusions have to be drawn. It might be necessary to transform it, but getting rid of it is to be avoided. Either the building can keep some form of aeronautical activity or it can be converted, for example, into business premises or a conference centre. Here, I put my trust in contemporary architects who are capable of creating remarkable functional spaces inside old buildings. Where buildings are concerned, decadence is by no means inevitable. So, if some airport buildings are no longer economically viable, let us consider them as heritage. As was the case for the Louvre, the State or the local authorities might have to bear the extra cost that is generally incurred in keeping old buildings in use and renovating them.

Marieke Kuipers (Rijkdienst voor de Monumentenzorg, Netherlands): The airport has been viewed today as a combination of modernism and functionalism. It has been noted that most passengers feel that the architecture itself is not important, that what they are concerned about is the efficiency of the building as a machine. At the same time, however, as we have seen, the airport also becomes a symbol of the city it belongs to. This sense of place is a key factor, both in terms of design and from a preservationist point of view. And it seems that there is a certain paradox here: air travel has made globalisation possible and increased our sense of denationalisation, while at the same time this sense of place is nowhere more powerfully felt than in the airport itself. I wonder if anyone would like to comment on this, particularly Paul Andreu in terms of designing airports and Wolfgang Voigt in terms of preserving them.

Wolfgang Voigt: I think that historic buildings have a place in existing airports, even the largest ones, and I'm convinced that coexistence is possible in most cases. As a passenger of course, my concern too is for efficiency, for avoiding stress. Being able to

look at fine spaces is an extra. But the passenger's view is not necessarily the most important one for us, nor for the airport owners. Airports should be concerned about their public image, their corporate identity. I live in Frankfurt, home of one of the hub airports we talked about. And this airport has enormous political problems at the moment. Vast extensions are necessary and these extensions are the main issue of local elections. If an airport can demonstrate that it is concerned about something more than the economy and increasing traffic, this could be important, making debates easier about how to handle the future of such an airport. But at Frankfurt, today, there is a total absence of any sensitivity to history.

Paul Andreu: What characterises an airport is its in-between situation. The airport can be defined as the meeting place between the air and the earth, the distant and the nearby. It is also a place frequented by the most cosmopolitan of machines. Aeroplanes have no culture, their design is the same almost everywhere and they are one of the vehicles of globalisation.

Architects, preservationists after them perhaps, and operators before, all have to meet a demand, to fulfil a programme. But an important part of their work consists in seeing to what is not demanded, deeper needs, more far-reaching ones, needs that exist in the same way as we need dreams. No one has ever drawn up a brief for a dream. But dreaming is indispensable; you go mad if you no longer dream. And the architect also has to take care of what is not asked of him, of what cannot be expressed in a building programme, but something which is nonetheless indispensable for life. He does this without knowing exactly how, that is clear, because there are no recipes for this mission.

Jean-Luc Lesage: Today we function with essentially quantitative and productivist attitudes. A terminal must be functional, the user must be able to get around it rapidly, etc. It is possible, however, that one day we will give greater consideration to its qualitative aspects. The passenger is spending more and more time in the terminal and has to arrive earlier and earlier. In many airports, for a long-haul flight, the passenger now has to be there two hours before take-off, two hours that will be spent inside the terminal. But what is actually done for the passenger? When you arrive at terminal T9 in Roissy, for example, do you really have the impression that you are commencing a journey, that there, in the terminal, you are at the beginning of a dream? Change rather than novelty is in fashion and maybe one day a fun dimension will infiltrate the terminals, leaving some scope for the imagination. And the historic terminals, by offering another setting, will be ideally suited for this change, for this evolution towards quality.

Bernard Toulier (Inventaire général, France): This marketing approach already exists and can be seen in the railways. During the 1980s, all the Pullman railway carriages were scrapped. Nobody wanted to invest any longer in these old machines. It was the era of high speed and new notions of comfort. But today, this old railway sector is not totally without its openings. And it is not only the old aeroplane or the old train that are interesting here. Some travellers enjoy using old railway stations and voyaging in a different way, not in charters with thousands of other people, but in small groups. They want different sorts of journeys, to experience, for example, the Trans-Siberian express. Offering this type of travel experience could be profitable and transport companies are already studying the question. Today, people want tours that are not mass tourism, and they want different types of transport. Of course, mass tourism will always constitute 95 per cent of the market, but it is important to cater to the remaining 5 per cent, capable of preserving not only the dream, but also the heritage that can be part of it.

Yves Abbas: I gree that there are several niche markets in air transport that are still to be explored. But the large companies are concerned first and foremost with the efficient transport of the 95 per cent. But the commercial exploitation of the niches is a possibility, even if companies the size of Air France are not best suited for it. It is up to other companies to take up this challenge.

Bernard Toulier: A specifically heritage-oriented marketing approach could give Air France considerable popularity. A heritage subsidiary for quality travel would make it possible to increase the volume of passengers for this type of journey. Quality always pays, even at quantitative levels.

Jean-Luc Lesage: In point of fact, it is not the 95 per cent that represent the economy of the company. According to a survey of seventy European and Asian airlines, the so-called business class comprises about one-third of passengers, but these passengers account for 99 per cent of the profits. They subsidise the tourists and the first-class passengers.

Paul Andreu: At this point, I would like to draw attention to the admirable work now being carried out by the SNCF (French rail). After having disfigured their railway buildings for years, they have recently understood that they were assets, to be taken advantage of. They have succeeded in finding the right balance between existing and renovated buildings and the construction of modern, ambitious stations that are extremely interesting. But if these richer experiences can take place in the railway sector, it is above all because the station is part of the city, unlike the airport, outside it.

For twenty years, the idea prevailed that the railway stations should copy airports, with their jingles, and that the only solution for survival was to imitate the airport. But the other day, on television, I heard a journalist talking about a survey carried out for the opening of the new Paris-Marseilles TGV. One of the questions asked was whether passengers preferred railway stations with an airport atmosphere or a museum. The replies were massively hostile to the airport atmosphere. This worried me. The airport terminal has ceased to be a model.

Bob Hawkins (English Heritage): I was very interested by Paul Andreu's remarks and by what he termed (if the translation is correct) the 'hysterically economical'. One of the concepts we might develop is being 'historically economical'. What we are doing in a sense is dealing with the detritus of the air traffic industry. As things grow, things are thrown away. We have a whole series of sites that are now deemed to be disposable. We've got bigger, we need more this, we need more that, we move on.... The places aren't big enough, aren't sophisticated enough, there is not enough comfort, and so we look at expansion and the abandonment of things which some of us nonetheless think are worth keeping. And I think Paul Andreu was saying the same thing, that you don't have to throw it all away. When we use our railway systems, for example, we're using bridges, stations and infrastructure that were built in the 19th century, and we have to make do. When you build an airport, you construct it at great social, economic and environmental cost. It seems to me once you've created a huge ensemble such as Tempelhof, on the edge of one of our great capital cities you can't then say: 'Sorry! We can't use this anymore for air traffic. It doesn't fit what we want now.' Instead we should perhaps be saying 'We've got an environmental and airfield asset which we've got to try and keep going, keep in use. It's too valuable in everybody's perceptions to just abandon to redevelopment.'

The architects of great airports created something that they probably didn't imagine would ever be perceived in the value terms that we are now expressing. We are adding a layer of appreciation on top of all the other systems of evaluation, and which might begin to alter the way we perceive these sites and the way we use them. If you come to Liverpool today and look at what's happened to the buildings at Speke, and then you go to the shed put up as the terminal building for the new Liverpool airport – and you can't call it anything else but a shed – it might be an efficient point of departure for cheap flights all over the place, but this new building is a dog's dinner by anybody's standards, without a single architectural feature that could be appreciated now nor, I imagine, in the future. We've lost an airfield. We've lost an airport. We've saved the buildings and we've provided something else which actually contributes nothing to the travelling experience other than a shed for transit, a shed with no ambience, and nothing apart from a place to leave.

Wolfgang Voigt: I hope we're now reaching a stage which can integrate the old buildings, with their cultural values and their atmosphere, into the process of developing new airport buildings or rehabilitating existing ones. I would like to recall the 1970s, when the mainline railway stations were rediscovered, largely thanks to an exhibition held at the Centre Pompidou in 1978, *Le Temps des Gares*. This created a movement in favour of these stations, without which many would probably have been pulled down. I think that discovering airports as heritage and developing aviation can go together, and the one can profit from the other.

Corinne Bélier: I would like to thank all the participants at this round table. After our work of a more historical nature on airports that are no longer in use, the confrontation with today's economic and commercial issues is fundamental for our conclusions. The current and future contexts of air travel do not necessarily condemn the historic airport. On the contrary, specific niche sectors seem to be emerging, corresponding with a demand that the larger structures and airlines will probably be unable to satisfy. But the profitability of these niches remains to be proved. There is no doubt that there is a future for historic airports, but this future still has to be invented, its activities defined and its actors identified.

Notes

1 See the contribution by Didier Hamon in this publication, pp 219–21.
2 See the contribution by Bob Lane in this publication, pp 176–81.
3 See the contribution by Vogt Landschaftsarchitekten in this publication, pp 216–18.
4 See the contribution by John King in this publication, pp 136–42.
5 See the contribution by Ola Wedebrunn in this publication, pp 187–91.
6 See the contribution by Thomas Mellins in this publication, pp 127–35.

Conclusion

Aviation architecture: a European heritage

Gabi Dolff-Bonekämper, Bob Hawkins and Bernard Toulier

Based on the three pilot sites of Berlin-Tempelhof, Liverpool-Speke and Paris-Le Bourget, the 'L'Europe de l'Air' project has laid the foundations of an international network of specialists on aviation architecture. The project has enhanced understanding of the world's earliest airports, and its three workshops, in 1999, 2000 and 2001, provided valuable opportunities for assessing the historic and architectural interest of these places in both national and European contexts. Case studies of the restoration of different examples of this heritage – certainly one of the most emblematic of the 20th century – will help in its preservation for future generations. The project's publications and exhibitions on this 'new' European heritage offer some innovative perspectives on conservation and interpretation practices within broader strategies of sustainable development.

A European observatory on aviation architecture

The project was focused primarily on airport architecture, a field of investigation lying somewhere between the industrial heritage and military heritage. An airport can be defined as a flying field chosen and laid out for the landing, taking-off and ground manoeuvres of aircraft and comprising the infrastructures and buildings necessary for these operations and for the requirements of air passengers and visitors. Airports constitute highly specialised landscapes that today can spread across several thousand hectares. They are hubs of communication, linked together in networks variously governed by commercial, industrial or military considerations.

The component parts of the airport complex include the ground installations and the flying fields directly associated with civil or military aviation uses: hangars, workshops, control towers, passenger terminals and, often, hotels and overnight accommodation for pilots. But in more general terms, the architecture generated by aviation also encompasses flying clubs, flying schools, aircraft factories, research facilities such as test beds and wind tunnels, dwellings or apartment buildings, administration, control and defence centres, storage spaces, commercial premises and temporary living quarters.

In the three countries associated in the 'L'Europe de l'Air' programme, systematic inventories of aviation's built heritage have been undertaken in collaboration with various associative and institutional partners. Similar inventories must be set up or pursued in other European countries in order to identify, locate, date and study these ensembles, establishing the basis for a comparative architectural history covering the whole of Europe. These inventory projects are particularly suited to presentation in the form of electronic files integrated into geographical information systems. The knowledge they provide is a prerequisite for heritage management policies at local, national and international levels. This knowledge should be made freely available to all citizens and to their elected representatives, providing them with a decision-making tool necessary for heritage conservation strategies and spatial planning.

A European observatory of the aviation heritage, working in co-operation with each member state of the Union, should be set up to validate the methodology of this inventory work, to control and evaluate the information gathered and to draw attention to the historic, architectural and technical interest of what survives as heritage. If aviation sites are threatened, either by destruction or by alteration, this observatory could also undertake emergency assessments of the sites.

A coherent European conservation policy

Inventory work, surveys and monographic studies generate broader understanding at national and international levels that can help identify:

- the oldest aviation sites and buildings, and the innovations to be found in different building types
- the technical systems and specific construction methods used in buildings and infrastructural elements
- the features that document a specific series, family or period, and individual examples that are characteristic of political, cultural, economic or social developments
- values of homogeneity and coherence, to enable an accessible and 'pedagogical' reading of the surviving complexes, along with their surviving interior decoration and the historic layers of their use
- the memories and symbolic values associated with civil or military uses or with specific aeronautical or historic events.

Protective measures for these airport installations must seek, first and foremost, to preserve the unbuilt space of the flying field and its runways, the heart of the airport facility without which flight is inconceivable. These selection criteria, which are partly inspired by the recommendations of the Council of Europe for the 20th-century heritage and the industrial heritage, should also be approved by the Ministers for Culture within the European Union member states, in order to be integrated into a European charter for aviation heritage. Such recommendations are indispensable for coherent conservation policies, to be implemented in each country according to its own specific customs and legislation on historic monuments and sites or designated conservation areas.

It is important for such measures of statutory protection to be preceded or accompanied by studies evaluating in detail the importance of the structure to be conserved, determining appropriate new uses for it and analysing investment and running costs so as to ensure the survival of the site's historic fabric according to its perceived historic interest. This preliminary evaluation should help planning authorities and member states to decide on the nature, extent and constraints of the proposed protective measure, as well as the opportunities created by them.

Policies for reuse and restoration

Whether they enjoy statutory protection or not, airport installations are in a state of permanent obsolescence. The oldest sites have been subjected to the hazards and air raids of the Second World War. Those not abandoned since the war have been extensively altered and enlarged in order to keep up with the evolution in air traffic and with the technical development of aircraft. Keeping these sites alive in order to pass them on as heritage requires:

- their continued use for flying, as close as possible to their original use (the example of Berlin-Tempelhof)
- their integration into a larger aviation complex with a change of use (the example of Paris-Le Bourget)
- their adaptation to entirely new uses, not linked to aviation (the example of Liverpool-Speke).

If airport buildings are to be reused, alterations, needed to adapt them to new uses, are inevitable. This work must refer to full historical information acquired by preliminary studies. Such studies, carried out on two of our pilot sites (Tempelhof and Le Bourget), include general contextual research, archaeological analysis, description of the site in town-planning and landscape terms, and the understanding of the successive layers of use and change that the site has witnessed, both in general and for each of its component parts.

Drawn up in co-operation with the site's owners, its managers and the heritage departments concerned, restoration programmes should seek to reconcile the demands made by new uses with the physical preservation of the site and its buildings. They should also seek to safeguard the intangible, memorial values associated with the complex. The adaptive reuse of buildings and infrastructures should involve the endorsement of these values by all the players concerned, and the subsequent integration of the site into economic life as a new cultural 'product'.

Heritage values and economic values

The development and interpretation of this type of heritage can help meet new demands for cultural and tourist products. Keeping an airport in use can help stimulate new forms of aeronautical tourism – airship cruises, flights on prestigious air routes in historic aircraft (or replicas of them) – following the examples set by historic trains or boats. Tourist products of this nature would obviously be aimed at clients seeking the nostalgic thrills of aviation's golden age between the wars. They are particularly compatible with museum activities on the ground; several European museums hold collections of civil and military flying machines, but, as yet no museum located on the site of a former airport is specifically devoted to the architecture generated by flight.

In addition to this potential for new cultural uses, airport installations offer other intrinsic advantages for new economic uses:

- they are isolated and protected sites with few buildings but strong landscape features, generally well connected to road, rail and air networks
- as industrial sites, they are relatively close to urban centres and present a rational and flexible use of space, with installations, such as hangars, of vast dimensions.

Successful adaptations of airport sites towards other sectors of activity have sometimes made it possible to conserve some sense of the significance of its past alongside new commercial, service, industrial or recreational uses. Demands for this kind of adaptation by local authorities are booming, calling for specialist economic skills at national and international levels. But these 'private' projects must respect heritage interests, ensuring that the original values and uses of the site and its buildings remain understandable.

Communication and awareness-raising

Within the framework of the Council of Europe's observatory of cultural policies, the network of specialists brought together by the Raphael programme should continue taking inventory, protecting, interpreting and restoring Europe's heritage of aviation architecture – ambitions that are set out at www.culture.fr/europe-air/. This site, currently hosted by the French Ministry for Culture and Communication, should be managed in the long term by a European team under the aegis of the Council of Europe, ICOMOS and UNESCO. Updates and supplements to the site will enable the exchange of information.

This appropriation of a shared aviation history is essential for understanding the 20th-century phenomena that revolutionised traditional notions of space and time, drastically changing the nature of our exchanges and our perceptions. An international exhibition on 'The Airport Age' – *Le Temps des Aérogares* – is planned for the 2005 opening of the *Cité de l'Architecture et du Patrimoine* in Paris. Benefiting from the 'L'Europe de l'Air' network, this exhibition will evoke both this joint heritage and the creation of contemporary airport buildings: two aspects of a new architectural culture in Europe.